The Genius and the Goddess

Jeffrey Meyers is a Fellow of the Royal Society of Literature, and has recently been given an Award in Literature by the American Academy of Arts and Letters. He has written extensively on literature, film and art; his books have been published on all six continents, and twenty-five of them have been translated into twelve languages. His biography of Samuel Johnson was published in 2008. He lives in Berkeley, California.

Books by Jeffrey Meyers

BIOGRAPHY
A Fever at the Core: The Idealist in Politics
Married to Genius
Katherine Mansfield
The Enemy: A Biography of Wyndham Lewis
Hemingway
Manic Power: Robert Lowell and His Circle
D.H. Lawrence
Joseph Conrad
Edgar Allan Poe: His Life and Legacy
Scott Fitzgerald
Edmund Wilson
Robert Frost
Bogart: A Life in Hollywood
Gary Cooper: American Hero
Privileged Moments: Encounters with Writers
Wintry Conscience: A Biography of George Orwell
Inherited Risk: Errol and Sean Flynn in Hollywood and Vietnam
Somerset Maugham
Impressionist Quartet: The Intimate Genius of Manet and Morisot, Degas and Cassatt
Modigliani
Samuel Johnson: The Struggle

CRITICISM
Fiction and the Colonial Experience
The Wounded Spirit: T.E. Lawrence's Seven Pillars of Wisdom
A Reader's Guide to George Orwell
Painting and the Novel
Homosexuality and Literature
D.H. Lawrence and the Experience of Italy
Disease and the Novel
The Spirit of Biography
Hemingway: Life into Art

The Genius and the Goddess

ARTHUR MILLER AND

MARILYN MONROE

Jeffrey Meyers

arrow books

Published by Arrow Books 2010

2 4 6 8 10 9 7 5 3 1

First published in Great Britain in 2009 by
Hutchinson
Random House, 20 Vauxhall Bridge Road,
London SW1V 2SA

www.rbooks.co.uk

Addresses for companies within The Random House Group Limited can be
found at: www.randomhouse.co.uk/offices.htm

The Random House Group Limited Reg. No. 954009

A CIP catalogue record for this book
is available from the British Library

ISBN 9780099524892

The Random House Group Limited supports The Forest Stewardship
Council (FSC), the leading international forest certification organisation.
All our titles that are printed on Greenpeace approved FSC certified paper
carry the FSC logo. Our paper procurement policy can be found at
www.rbooks.co.uk/environment

Mixed Sources
Product group from well-managed
forests and other controlled sources
www.fsc.org Cert no. TT-COC-2139
© 1996 Forest Stewardship Council
FSC

Typeset by Palimpsest Book Production Limited, Grangemouth, Stirlingshire

Printed and bound in Great Britain by
CPI Bookmarque, Croydon CR0 4TD

Contents

Illustrations

Acknowledgements

This book is based on a substantial amount of new information. Between 1981 and 1998 I had nine long talks with Arthur Miller and took thorough notes immediately afterwards. He also sent me many letters. I've studied his papers in the Harry Ransom Humanities Research Center in the University of Texas at Austin; his letters to Saul Bellow in the University of Chicago Library; his unpublished screenplay, *The Hook*, in the Lilly Library, Indiana University; his unpublished last play, *Finishing the Picture*, in the Goodman Theatre in Chicago (courtesy of Julie Massey); and a copy of his will in the Roxbury, Connecticut, Probate Court.

I've read the papers of Charles Feldman in the American Film Institute in Los Angeles; of John Huston and George Cukor in the Margaret Herrick Library, American Academy of Motion Picture Arts and Sciences, Beverly Hills, California; of Ben Hecht in the Newberry Library, Chicago; of Spyros Skouras, the president of Twentieth Century-Fox, in Stanford University (courtesy of Polly Armstrong); and the unpublished memoir of Natasha Lytess in Texas. I've studied the papers of Joseph Rauh, and the letters of Dr. Ralph Greenson to Anna Freud, in the Library of Congress, Washington, D.C.; the extensive FBI files on both Miller and Monroe; material from the American Academy of Arts and Letters in New York (courtesy of Kathy Kienholz); and the files about Marilyn's tour in Korea in the National Archives, College Park, Maryland (courtesy of Paul Brown). The library of the University of California, Berkeley, a major source for all my work since the 1960s, has been enormously helpful.

These unpublished papers illuminate Marilyn's relations with her acting teacher, her agent and her psychiatrist; her roles in *The Asphalt Jungle*, *The Misfits* and *Something's Got to Give*; her quarrels with the studio; her ghostwritten autobiography; her trip to Korea; and her appearance when Miller received a Gold Medal for Drama in 1959. There's also new material in this book about Miller's testimony before the House Un-American Activities Committee and the FBI's reports on his political engagement.

I interviewed Angela Allen, John Huston's script supervisor on *The Misfits*; Walter Bernstein, one of the screenwriters of *Something's Got to Give*; the actress Joan Copeland, Miller's sister; Brian Dennehy, who starred in *Death of a Salesman*; Patricia Rosten Filan, the daughter of Miller's close friends; Lydia Kaim and the poet William Jay Smith, of the American Academy in New York; Walter Mirisch, the producer of *Some Like It Hot*; Don Murray, the co-star of *Bus Stop*; and Curtice Taylor, son of the producer of *The Misfits*, who gave me a vivid account of Marilyn in Connecticut. I had conversations about Miller and Monroe, before I began work on this book, with their old friends, most of them now gone: Jack Cardiff, Dorris Johnson, Gloria Mosolino Jones, Evelyn Keyes, Joseph Mankiewicz, Arthur Schlesinger, Jr., Budd Schulberg, Robert Stack, Richard Widmark and Billy Wilder. Other actors and friends refused to be interviewed: Lauren Bacall, Jeanne Carmen, Cyd Charisse, Tony Curtis, Faye Dunaway, Celeste Holm, Kevin McCarthy, Patricia Newcomb, Mickey Rooney, Jane Russell, Stefanie Skolsky and Audrey Wilder.

I had phone talks with Severio DiMaggio, Joshua Greene, Daniel Greenson and Mary Slattery Miller; and letters from Michael Adler (for Anna Strasberg), Edward Albee, Agnes Barley, Adam Bellow, Sondra Bellow (who described Miller's residence in Nevada while waiting for his divorce), Martin Cribbs, Jane Miller Doyle, Tony Huston, Gail Levin, Richard Meryman, Robert Miller, Edward Parone, Elizabeth Paterson, Lawrence Schiller, Eli Wallach and Gareth Wigan; as well as from the John F. Kennedy Library, Mills College, UCLA Library and Wesleyan University Library. Stacy Kit was helpful during my visit to Hollygrove, formerly the Los Angeles Orphans Home Society.

Dr. Ellen Alkon, Dr. Michael Aminoff, Dr. Joel Fort, Dr. Henry Lee, Dr. Mario Papagni and Dr. Alan Skolnikoff advised me about Marilyn's medical problems. I'm grateful to other friends who provided addresses, books, photographs, information and unpublished material:

Rudy Behlmer, Mary Berg, Enoch Brater, Leo Braudy, Barnaby Conrad, Frederick Crews, LeAnn Fields, Laurence Goldstein, Ronald Hayman, Valerie Hemingway, Charlene Hess, Sylvia Howe, Francis King, Michael Korda, Neal Kozodoy, Ellen Nims, Susan Rabens, Carl Rollyson, Michael Scammell, Philip and Ellen Siegelman, James Spohrer, Gail Steinbeck, Stephen Tabachnick and Victoria Wilson.

As always, my wife, Valerie Meyers, assisted with the archival research, read and improved each chapter, and compiled the index.

For
Paul and Ellen Alkon

For everything that's lovely is
But a brief, dreamy, kind delight.
O never give the heart outright.

W.B. Yeats,
"Never Give All the Heart"

One
First Encounter
(1951)

I

In January 1951 Arthur Miller and his close friend, the director Elia Kazan, took a train from New York to Los Angeles. They wanted to sell his first screenplay, *The Hook*, to Harry Cohn at Columbia Pictures. The tall, handsome, thirty-five-year old Miller was a serious young man, married with two young children, and the author of two enormously successful plays. In Hollywood he would face two moral crises: negotiating with Cohn over the content of his screenplay and falling in love with Marilyn Monroe. When they met she was an insecure and little-known model and actress; by the time they married five years later she had become a glamorous star whose image was known all over the world. They wrote to each other during those years, as she pursued her career in Hollywood and he struggled to maintain his marriage in New York. She was briefly married to Joe DiMaggio in 1954, yet told a friend, just as she was marrying DiMaggio, that one day she would marry Miller. They were a most unlikely couple, yet on their first meeting they formed an emotional bond that survived their long separation.

Kazan played a key role in Miller's relations with both Cohn and Marilyn. The two friends, both passionate about politics and the theater, were temperamentally very different. Miller was a shy intellectual from a solid Jewish family in New York. Kazan, a few years older – short, energetic and intense, with dark curly hair, rough-hewn features and a Levantine look – had been born into a poor Greek family in Constantinople. Brought to America when he was four years old, he had made his way in the world through his talent and ambition. He'd graduated from Williams College, and in the 1930s had been an actor and director in the left-wing Group Theater, joined the Communist Party and helped found the influential Actors Studio. In 1951 Kazan was the coming man in Hollywood and New York. He'd directed the films *A Tree Grows in Brooklyn*, *Gentleman's Agreement* and *Boomerang* (in which Miller appeared in a line-up of criminal suspects). He'd also achieved spectacular success on Broadway, directing Tennessee Williams' *A Streetcar Named Desire* as well as the plays that established Miller's reputation: *All My Sons* (1947) and *Death of a Salesman* (1949).

The FBI took a keen interest in Miller and Kazan, as they had in many leading writers and intellectuals since the 1930s. They particularly monitored the political content of Hollywood films, which exerted tremendous influence on public opinion. According to Miller's typically pedantic and inaccurate FBI file, compiled because of his left-wing political views, "In early 1951, according to — [name blanked out], Harry Cohn, President of Columbia Pictures, Inc. Hollywood, California, obtained a story entitled, 'The Hook,' from Arthur Miller, for $50,000." Miller and Kazan knew that the script, about a doomed attempt by New York longshoremen to overthrow the gangsters who controlled their union, would be controversial. But Kazan, who had many contacts in Hollywood, also knew that Cohn had grown up on the waterfront and had the reputation of a maverick. Kazan thought that if Miller went with him to Hollywood to pitch the idea, they might convince him to make the film.

But Cohn, after consulting Roy Brewer, the leader of the Hollywood unions and personal friend of the head of the longshoremen's union, demanded radical changes. He said that Miller's script was anti-American, even treasonable, and that the gangsters had to be portrayed as communists. Kazan, who'd left the Party and become a staunch anti-communist, saw nothing wrong with this response. But Miller flatly refused to falsify his script and turn it into propaganda. After Miller had finally left Hollywood in disgust, he received an insulting telegram from Cohn: "IT'S INTERESTING HOW THE MINUTE WE TRY TO MAKE THE SCRIPT PRO-AMERICAN YOU

PULL OUT." This was the first (but not the last) time that he would get into trouble about the political content of his work. It was also the first crisis in his friendship with Kazan.

The studios had turned out anti-Axis propaganda during World War II and during the Cold War felt obliged to make anti-communist movies. Paranoid about the Russian threat, the United States government pressured the studio heads to make films that expressed the prevailing political views, and eventually supported Senator Joseph McCarthy's persecution and purges of left-wing writers and actors. In turn the movie industry exerted pressure on writers and directors. Miller and Kazan were prominent players in the 1950s conflict between artists and the government forces that tried to control them.

II

Marilyn Monroe had recently advanced her career with small but significant roles in two first-rate films: *The Asphalt Jungle* and *All About Eve* (both 1950), but she was still playing bit parts in trivial movies. Miller first saw her on the Twentieth Century-Fox set of a fatuous comedy, *As Young as You Feel*. She had a small stereotyped part as a sexy but inept secretary, with pencil poised above her pad. (Anyone could type, but no one looked liked Marilyn.) Miller recalled that she was talking to Kazan (always on the lookout for a pretty and obliging girl) and weeping about the recent death of her lover, agent and protector Johnny Hyde. She was "telling Kazan that Hyde had died while calling her name in a hospital room she had been forbidden by his family to enter." In fact, Marilyn was shopping in Tijuana when Hyde passed away in Palm Springs on December 18, 1950. Though excluded from the funeral, not the hospital, she managed to bluff her way into the service at Forest Lawn Cemetery.

Marilyn's clichéd account of the dying Hyde calling for her in the forbidden hospital, like a scene in a B-movie, suggests that she was still publicly grieving about Hyde a month after his death. It's more likely that she was crying about her own career, now more uncertain than ever without Hyde's crucial help, or about her poor performance in her current film. She complained that the director had ignored and insulted her. She may also have been weeping to attract the attention and arouse the sympathy of Kazan and Miller, and to make herself even more appealing to them. If so, she was more convincing in this role than the one in the movie. Miller poignantly recalled that "she was so striking and so terribly sad that the combination struck me"[1] – as it was meant to.

Miller and Kazan had been invited to stay in the lavish home of the attractive, suave Charles Feldman, who'd produced the film version of *A Streetcar Named Desire*. Feldman told them, following Hyde's demise, that Marilyn was up for grabs and both men were keenly interested. Miller invited her to a party at Feldman's house and, behaving like a real gentleman, insisted on picking her up instead of letting her come on her own by taxi. He was a good dancer and she was clearly delighted as he whirled her around the room. When they sat down to talk, he gently squeezed her toe – a kind of seductive acupressure – and she took his timid approach as a sign of respect. He told her that his marriage was collapsing, that he'd been terribly unhappy for several years and that he was now completely alienated from his wife. But a man on the make always claims his marriage is unhappy, and he'd gallantly picked her up so he could also take her home. An uninhibited hedonist, always willing, even eager, to sleep with men she liked or she thought could help her, Marilyn probably tried to seduce him that night.

In his self-serving autobiography, Kazan was more frank and perceptive than Miller himself about his friend's relations with Marilyn. Though Kazan didn't mention that he too was eager to seduce her, he called her "a decent-hearted kid whom Hollywood had brought down, legs parted. She had a thin skin and a soul that hungered for acceptance by people she might look up to." Marilyn's sexual humiliations made her especially responsive to Miller's dignified restraint. She confided to Kazan that "Art was shy and this pleased her after all the mauling she'd taken. She said that Art was terribly unhappy in his home life. She'd certainly opened him up." Deeply moved by their first meeting, she gushed poetically to her acting teacher, Natasha Lytess: "It was like running into a tree! You know – like a cool drink when you've got a fever. You see my toe – this toe? Well, he sat and held my toe and we just looked into each other's eyes almost all evening."[2] Their gestures and expressions were more meaningful than words.

Miller was a leading playwright – intelligent, moral and respected; Marilyn (no doubt, unfairly) was considered just another stupid, vulgar and sluttish starlet. Though his father had lost everything in the

Depression, Miller grew up in a secure family. Marilyn's broken family had almost nothing to lose, and during the thirties she'd led a miserable life in an orphanage and with a series of harsh foster families. Miller's mother had been forced to sell her lamps, tables and carpets, but had refused to part with her piano – her last connection to the middle class. Marilyn's mother had lost her precious white piano, which her daughter later managed to recover, and placed in the luxurious white décor of a flashy New York apartment. But, like Marilyn, Miller had worked in a humble factory job during the war. He instinctively sympathized with her impoverished background and her desire to escape to a better life.

Miller's feelings for Marilyn – romantic infatuation compounded with adulterous guilt – were conflicted from the start. He believed that with no place to go and no one to go to she needed his protection. He noted her childish voracity (which would one day destroy him) and desperately wanted to help and possess her, but felt he had to leave Hollywood immediately or "lose himself" and his old life for ever. Thus began a long inner struggle between his fierce attraction to Marilyn, made up of lust and pity, and his need to maintain his moral stature and role as a faithful husband. Like the dignified Emil Jannings, bewitched by Marlene Dietrich in *The Blue Angel*, he eventually found her sexuality irresistible.

Miller later described Marilyn's traumatic background, which would make her difficult, and finally impossible, to live with: "she had a crazy mother. That is not a good start; her mother was quite mad. She was a paranoid schizophrenic who ended up spending half her life in an institution. The mother tried to kill her three times and [Marilyn] was convinced that she was a worthless creature because she was illegitimate." Marilyn constantly sought sympathy by exaggerating her miserable childhood. In fact, her grandmother (not her mother) may have tried to kill her once (not three times). But Miller was moved by her sad account. As the cowboy Bo tells Cherie (played by Marilyn) in *Bus Stop*: "I like ya like ya are, Cherie, so I don't care how you got that way."

Kazan – himself blissfully free of bourgeois scruples – carefully observed Miller struggling between Marilyn's liberating sexuality and his own intolerable remorse. He was subject, Kazan wrote, to that "domestic peril which results when certain ties of restraint that a middle-class man has always lived with are snapped. . . . He respected the moral law, but he must also have found it constricting to a suddenly reawakened side of his nature: the life of the senses." Miller had sought relief from his problems in psychoanalysis, but his sessions with the analyst intensified rather than relieved his repression, and made him distraught and ill. His life, he told Kazan, "seemed to be all conflict and tension, thwarted desires, stymied impulses, bewildering but unexpressed conflicts. 'What a waste!' he cried. . . . He had sex on his mind, constantly. He was starved for sexual release." After ten years of marriage, "Art was on the verge of something disruptive, and [his wife] Mary could only wait and prepare to apply moral sanctions when the inevitable happened."[3]

Though married and with children himself, Kazan – a charismatic seducer – was consistently unfaithful to his wife. While Miller gently held Marilyn's toe, the lusty Greek boldly took her to bed and grabbed all the rest. At Feldman's house she spent her nights with Kazan while Miller, tortured by jealousy, writhed alone in a nearby room and faced the contented couple over breakfast the next morning. Kazan later revealed that during their liaison, early in 1951, Marilyn became pregnant by him and had a miscarriage. Toward the end of her life, Marilyn had fond memories of her old lover and recalled, "Kazan said I was the gayest girl he ever knew and believe me, he has known many. But he *loved* me for one year and once rocked me to sleep one night when I was in great anguish. He also suggested that I go into analysis and later wanted me to work with Lee Strasberg." Ironically, Marilyn's sexual relations with Kazan intensified Miller's bond with his friend, made her seem more desirable than ever, and stimulated Miller to take her from him.

In the midst of all this sexual rivalry, Marilyn took a cameo part in the protracted but futile negotiations with Cohn over *The Hook*. Kazan thought it would be amusing for her to reprise her movie role as secretary, equipped with heavy spectacles and stenographer's pad, and accompany Kazan and Miller to Cohn's office. In 1948, as a young starlet under contract to Columbia, she had to have sex with Cohn. As all three men lusted after her, with Miller the odd man out, the sexual tension was palpable.

A few of the love letters that Miller wrote to Marilyn, after he returned to New York and she remained in Hollywood, have survived. Sensing her vulnerability and her essential innocence (despite her sordid past), he sent paternal advice about how to protect herself while advancing her career: "Bewitch them (the public) with this image they ask for, and I hope and almost pray you won't be hurt in this game, nor ever change." Kazan recalled a rapturous letter of 1951 in which Miller confessed that before he left Hollywood Marilyn had given him his long-sought sexual fulfillment:

> He felt extra fine and had been thinking joyous thoughts. . . .
> He was a young man again, in the grip of a first love, which
> was – happily – carrying him out of control. He didn't read like
> the constricted man I'd known. I remembered the lovely light
> of lechery in his eyes as he was dancing with Marilyn in Charlie
> Feldman's softly lit living room. I hadn't known he had it in
> him, that light in his eyes. I'd really done something for my
> friend, something he could not have done for himself.[4]

Egocentric and self-satisfied as ever, Kazan was proud of his role as go-between and felt as if he, not Marilyn, had fired up and liberated Miller.

TWO

Marilyn's Traumatic Childhood
(1926–1946)

I

"Family breakdown," a social historian observed, "is truly a feature of Los Angeles . . . a city of loneliness." Marilyn grew up in the lower depths of Hollywood during the Depression, in the world of unattainable hopes and shattered illusions that Nathanael West satirized in *Miss Lonelyhearts*. Born into an impoverished family, who went in for bigamous marriages and petty crime, she was subjected to a fatal mixture of fundamentalist religion and sexual molestation. Both made her feel sinful and guilty, polluted and ashamed.

Marilyn's maternal grandfather, Otis Monroe, worked for the Mexican National Railway and lived just across the Texas border, in Piedras Negras, about 150 miles southwest of San Antonio. Otis died of tertiary syphilis in an insane asylum. His wife Della (according to Marilyn's autobiography, ghostwritten by Ben Hecht), "had also been taken off to the mental hospital in Norwalk [part of Los Angeles] to die there screaming and crazy. And her brother had killed himself." Marilyn's mother, Gladys Monroe, was born in Mexico in 1902. It's not clear why Della didn't cross the border to give birth in the United States.

Extremely good-looking and eager to escape from her ghastly family, Gladys married a businessman, John Baker, when she was only fourteen, in 1917. She had a son, Jack, that year, and a daughter,

Berniece, in 1919. The following year, Jackie fell out of a car and became permanently crippled. (He died at the age of fourteen.) The couple were divorced in 1921, Baker took the children to be brought up by relatives in his native Kentucky, and Gladys soon lost touch with them. She married her second husband, Martin Mortensen – a handsome, religious man, with a steady job – in October 1924, but left him, after only four months, in February 1925. In September she became pregnant with Marilyn, who did not find out that her two siblings existed until the end of her life.

These stark facts reveal Gladys' troubled background: broken families, unwanted pregnancies, lost children and a history of insanity, all of which would recur in Marilyn's life. But Gladys was a good-time girl – fond of dancing and drinking (during the Prohibition era), attractive to men and sexually promiscuous. By the time she was twenty-three, she'd been divorced twice, had two children and been abandoned by the father of her third child.

Gladys had a low-level, mechanical job in the movie business, where she gossiped about the stars and longed for their glamorous way of life. She worked as a film cutter at Consolidated Film Industries, a lab that developed and printed the daily scenes, or rushes. They were viewed in the studio the next morning and showed the progress of the movie. Another lab where she worked, the RKO film-cutting room, was housed in a small, one-story, low-roofed cottage with thick cement walls. Editors perched on high stools, wearing white cotton gloves, running strips of film from one spool to another, winding and unwinding them, snipping away frames and gluing them to other pieces of film. There were no windows or air-conditioning, and the room was uncomfortably warm. A large red no smoking sign warned that the celluloid film was inflammable.

Marilyn's father was the handsome, mustachioed, philandering lab supervisor, Stanley Gifford. He jilted Gladys on Christmas Eve, when she told him she was pregnant, and did not acknowledge the child nor offer to help. Marilyn said that "he walked off and left her . . . without ever seeing me,"[1] and never recovered from the stigma of illegitimacy and the wound of rejection. She was born Norma Jeane Baker, in Los Angeles on June 1, 1926, and named for the popular actress Norma Talmadge. In 1926, in the era of silent films, Ramon Novarro appeared in *Ben Hur* and John Barrymore in *Don Juan*. Hemingway published *The Sun Also Rises*, which portrayed the wounded spirit of the Lost Generation who'd fought in the Great War. The German poet Rainer Maria Rilke, whose work Marilyn admired, died; and Queen Elizabeth II, whom Marilyn would meet, was born.

In her twenties, when Marilyn was a promising movie star, she hired a private detective to track down her mysterious, elusive and long-sought father. Her friend and confidante, Natasha Lytess, recalled that "he owned a dairy farm near Palm Springs and she wanted me to drive there with her. . . . She wanted him to love her immediately, and she tried to look her prettiest." When they arrived and Natasha phoned the house for her, Gifford "was incredibly rude and horrible. His voice was common, pinched, with a mid-western nasal quality. He said he was married and had a family and didn't want to know anything about this girl Marilyn Monroe. And when I turned the receiver over to Marilyn, she said she wanted nothing from him, but only to see him for the first time, to talk to him. He refused. He was filthy in his conversation with her."

In another version of this story, Marilyn drove out to Palm Springs with the gossip columnist Sidney Skolsky. On this occasion her father, more reasonable in his refusal, spoke to her and acknowledged his paternity, but he did not want to get involved with her, admit he'd behaved badly or make any emotional reparations. He said, "Marilyn, I'm married. I have children. I don't want you to start any trouble for me now, like your mother did years ago." After finding her father, Marilyn hoped that he would accept her and love her, but instead of achieving a healing reconciliation, her visit reopened old wounds and made her embittered. Abandonment and then rejection by her father taught her early on that men were selfish and irresponsible. But she was compelled to repeat her mother's mistakes. Like Gladys, she married in her mid-teens, and later became pregnant and was jilted.

Marilyn always believed, with good reason, that her birth disgraced Gladys and her mother didn't want her, that she got in Gladys' way and interfered with the carefree life she wished to lead. Marilyn also claimed that her grandmother, Della Monroe, tried to smother her in her crib when she was a year old. It's difficult to believe that a helpless infant could resist an adult who tried to smother her, or remember an incident, however traumatic, that occurred at such an early age. But Della *was* insane and the baby *was* unwanted, and shortly afterward Norma Jeane's grandmother was confined in an insane asylum. Marilyn may have been told about the episode later on, or this memory, real or imagined, may have emerged during her extensive psychoanalysis.

Gladys could not take care of her baby when she was working. She therefore paid foster parents, Albert and Ida Bolender, five dollars a day for Norma Jeane's board and lodging, from her birth until the fall of 1933. Albert had a secure job and steady income as a postman, and never lost a day's work during the Depression. The Bolenders lived in Hawthorne, on the same street as Norma Jeane's crazy grand-mother, a working-class district near what is now Los Angeles International Airport. The modest bungalows had front porches, weed-filled vacant lots stood between the houses and the graveled streets turned to mud after a rainstorm. In *Farewell, My Lovely* (1940), Raymond Chandler described a similar place, reeking of poverty and decay. A character lives in "a dried-out brown house with a dried-out brown lawn in front of it. There was a large bare patch around a tough-looking palm tree. On the porch stood one lonely wooden rocker, and the afternoon breeze made the unpruned shoots of last year's poinsettias tap-tap against the stucco wall. A line of stiff yellowish half-washed clothes jittered on a rusty wire in the side yard."

The Bolenders, fundamentalists who loved Jesus, were devout members of the United Pentecostal Church, and loyal followers of the flamboyant, fraudulent but extremely popular evangelist Aimée Semple McPherson. When off duty Albert turned out little tracts on salvation from his own printing press. The Bolenders were resolutely opposed to smoking, drinking, card-playing and frivolous entertain-ments. Ida taught Norma Jeane to vow, in a little jingle during her nightly prayers, "I promise, God helping me, not to buy, drink, sell, or give alcohol while I live. From all tobacco I'll abstain, and never take God's name in vain." Ida also warned her, with threats of fire and brimstone, that even minor transgressions would send her straight to Hell: "If the world came to an end with you sitting in the movies, do you know what would happen? You'd burn along with all the bad people. We are churchgoers, not moviegoers."[2]

Norma Jeane spent her first seven years with the strict but decent Bolenders. Better parents, by far, than Della and Gladys, they provided a proper home and did not mistreat her. Yet these respectable people were quite fanatical, imposed severe and inflexible discipline, and considered Norma Jeane a bastard, an outcast and a sinner. They constantly ordered her to stop doing anything that gave her pleasure, stifling her natural feelings and making her feel she was dirty. She learned to avoid conflict by being passive and docile, and as a child she retreated into a fantasy life. She said she had a powerful impulse to take off all her clothes, before all the pious worshippers in church, and stand up naked so God and everyone else could see her. (Obsessed with her own sensuous figure, Marilyn was never ashamed of nudity. She loved to show off her naked body at home and in public, in photographs and in films.)

In 1933 Gladys qualified for a government-sponsored, low-cost mortgage. In the fall she reclaimed her daughter and moved into a modest, three-bedroom house just next to the Hollywood Bowl. To help meet expenses, Gladys took in tenants, a couple of English actors, George Atkinson and his wife. George played bit parts; his wife was an extra in crowd scenes and a stand-in for Madeleine Carroll. Like so many camp followers in Hollywood, the Atkinsons were infatuated with its glamor and fantasized endlessly about the big break that would make them great stars.

Gladys' hedonistic regime, the complete antithesis of the Bolenders', transformed Norma Jeane's daily life and moral values. Gladys loved to indulge in cigarettes and alcohol, candy and perfume, frequent trips to dance halls and long nights at the movies. Norma Jeane, with her strict religious background, was shocked by her mother's wild life. She thought Gladys would be sent to hell and spent a lot of time praying for her. For the first seven years of her life she had never known a mother's tender voice or affectionate touch. She now lived with her mother, but did not feel close to her. Always self-absorbed, Gladys never gave her the love and care she sought. Her mother never smiled at her, never kissed or caressed her. She was so nervous, Marilyn recalled, that she'd become upset when she heard someone turning the page of a magazine.

Gladys had attempted suicide several times, swung perilously between depression and mania, and had her first mental breakdown in January 1935. She suddenly started to laugh, scream and curse hysterically and, with a sudden outburst of violence, to shatter dishes against the wall. She would lie on the floor, stare up the staircase and yell that someone was coming down the steps to kill her. One night, after accusing her co-worker and best friend, Grace Goddard, of trying to poison her, she grabbed a kitchen knife and stabbed her. The tenants called the police, and two officers finally overpowered her. She was taken to Norwalk state hospital, where in 1927 her mother had died in a straitjacket. The sight of Gladys' nervous collapse terrified the eight-year-old Norma Jeane and remained, for the rest of her life, a warning that the same thing might also happen to her. The memories of her promiscuous and unstable mother were disturbing and shameful.

Norma Jeane's half-sister, Berniece, later explained the reasons for Gladys' breakdown: "divorce, desertion, the death of her mother, separation from two of her children, the frustration of dead-end dating, the toll of working overtime, and now a strike at her company just when she had taken on the huge financial obligation of a home." Apart from brief intervals when she seemed to improve and was temporarily released from confinement, Gladys spent the rest of her long life in insane asylums. Norma Jeane occasionally saw her, but since Gladys became a fanatical Christian Scientist and retreated into herself, they could never establish meaningful contact. Norma Jeane's first husband, who met Gladys during World War II, found her affectless, remote and withdrawn: "Gladys seemed to be reaching for something but there was nothing there to grasp. She couldn't find it. I never saw her angry and I never saw her laugh. She was very pious and apparently content."

The Hungarian photographer André de Dienes, who drove up the coast to the Northwest with Norma Jeane in 1945, described another dutiful but dreary encounter. On that occasion, the forty-three-year-old Gladys failed to respond either to her daughter or to the presents she'd brought: "Norma Jeane's mother lived in an old hotel in the center of Portland, in a depressing bedroom on the top floor. The reunion between mother and daughter lacked warmth. They had nothing to say to each other. Mrs. Baker was a woman of uncertain age, emaciated and apathetic, making no effort to put us at our ease. . . . A silence ensued. Then Mrs. Baker buried her face in her hands and seemed to forget all about us. It was distressing. She had obviously been released from the hospital too soon." The visitors escaped as quickly as they could.

Despite her history of mental illness and apparent estrangement from the world, Gladys recovered sufficiently to find another husband. In April 1949, without bothering to get divorced, she contracted a third marriage to an electrician, John Eley. After his death three years later, she sent a sad and rather paranoid letter from a state mental hospital, which made Norma Jeane feel both guilty and distressed, as she always did whenever they had any contact: "Please dear child Id like to receive a letter from you. Things are very annoying around here & Id like to move away soon as possible. Id like to have my childs love instead of hatred. Love, Mother."[3]

II

After Gladys' violent crack up and sudden disappearance, Grace Goddard became Norma Jeane's legal guardian. From January to August 1935 she made temporary and increasingly desperate arrangements for the child. At first Norma Jeane lived with Gladys' lodgers, the Atkinsons, but when the house was sold they gave up their hopes of stardom and returned to England. She then moved in with new foster parents, the Harvey Giffens, and then with Grace's mother, Emma Atchinson. This proved equally unsatisfactory, and the little refugee must have been very troubled during these frequent displacements. In September 1935 Grace took the drastic step of putting her into a children's home, where she remained for the next two years. Her father, mother and sister were alive, but she had no one to care for her. Technically, she still had a family; practically, she did not. Condemned to be an orphan, she felt fear, loneliness and utter despair.

Orphanages were then notorious for their poor food, onerous chores and harsh discipline, and seemed to punish children for their parents' disappearance or death. One authority, emphasizing the physical and mental deprivation, stated that orphanages

> were, quite literally, a last resort for almost all who turned to them. . . . [They] were often highly regimented institutions where children had relatively little positive interaction with adults and limited opportunity to develop emotionally or psychologically. . . .
>
> When disaster struck their families, such children were provided with food, clothing, shelter, companionship, and at least some education. . . . Such children probably lacked emotional warmth from a parental figure and the opportunity to act independently in society.

During the Depression, as orphanages became increasingly over-crowded (as prisons are today), the food, facilities and adult supervision deteriorated, while neglect, punishment and abuse increased. The reputation of orphanages was so forbidding that many of them took names with pleasant connotations. The Jewish Orphan Asylum became Bellefaire, St. Mary's Female Asylum became Parmadale, the Protestant Orphan Asylum became Beech Brook. The orphans were eager to be adopted or taken into foster homes, where they would at least have the semblance of family life. When pro-mising parents appeared, the children were exhibited like slaves on an auction block. In 1925, pedestrians looked up to see an institution with "barred windows, tiny hands clutching the bars, against which were placed listless white faces." One girl, lamenting the lack of affec-tion, "felt so lonely and forlorn." Many children, not surprisingly, had chronic physical illnesses and severe psychological problems.

But foster parents, especially during hard times, could be quite mercenary; and officials, desperate to place the children, often ignored the minimal standards required for proper care. Another authority noted that "in 1933 an estimated 120,000 children stretched the foster care system to its limits." The journalist Art Buchwald, who spent most of his youth in foster homes, observed that "the foster parents were more interested in the money they received than in the chil-dren." In Tennessee, two-year-old twins were placed "in the care of a seventy-nine-year-old blind woman who was losing her mind. . . . Sixteen children were living in the attic of a home that failed to pass a fire inspection."[4]

In Oscar Wilde's *The Importance of Being Earnest* Lady Bracknell's memorably witty remark shows the absurdity of blaming the victim: "To lose one parent . . . may be regarded as a misfortune; to lose both looks like carelessness." Yet children usually react to their loss by blaming themselves. Both Charles Dickens and Rudyard Kipling described traumatic experiences of abandonment in childhood that left them, like Norma Jeane, permanently angry and hurt. Dickens wrote that "my whole nature was so penetrated with grief and humil-iation . . . that even now, famous and caressed and happy, I . . . wander desolately back to that time of my life." Kipling agreed that "when young lips have drunk deep of the bitter waters of Hate, Suspicion, and Despair, all the Love in the world will not wholly take away that knowledge."[5] Norma Jeane had been suddenly separated from her mother, her guardian and several foster families. Grace now told her they were going for a pleasant car ride, but she soon arrived at a strange, hostile and frightening place.

The Los Angeles Orphans Home Society – now called Hollygrove and still standing at 815 North El Centro in Hollywood – was not as forbidding as it first seemed to a small child. The privately endowed, nonsectarian home was founded in 1880, and its colonial-style, two-story red-brick building was set back on a wide lawn. The dormitories, dining room and play areas were clean and neat. Inside, there was a large recreation room with toys and games, radio and phonograph, auditorium and stage. Outside, on five acres, were swings, seesaws, exercise bars, sandboxes and even a swimming pool. The Home housed fifty to sixty children, a third of them street urchins or runaways, the rest actual orphans. Norma Jeane lived with twenty-five other girls, aged six to fourteen, in a high-ceilinged dorm, with large windows, behind the main building. The boys slept in a separate dorm, but all the meals, sports, games, activities and schooling were coeducational.

According to her over-optimistic file, which reads as if she were on holiday and trying to please her keepers, Norma Jeane seems to have adjusted remarkably well. Her dossier states that her "behavior is normal. . . . She is bright and sun-shiny. . . . The school reports on her are good. . . . She is quiet. . . . She sleeps and eats well. . . . She is well behaved. . . . Her grades are good. . . . She participates in all activities willingly. . . . She is co-operative." But – like Jay Gatsby watching the alluring lights across the sound – she dreamed of escaping to a glamorous life in the movies. "When I was nine," she recalled, "I used to look out of the orphan asylum window at night and see a big lighted-up sign that read 'R.K.O. Radio Pictures.'"

Some notable orphans have left poignant accounts of their life in institutions. Charlie Chaplin's experiences in London were remarkably similar to Norma Jeane's in Los Angeles. His father abandoned the family soon after Charlie was born; his mother retreated into her own world of silence and indifference. She sent Charlie and his brother to a school for "Orphans and Destitute Children." While they were in the orphanage, she had a mental breakdown and was committed to an insane asylum. Like Norma Jeane, Charlie was not actually an orphan, since both his parents were alive, but psychologically he felt he *was* one. In his autobiography, he observed that though "we were

well looked after, it was a forlorn existence. Sadness was in the air."[6]
His head was shaved and stained with iodine for ringworm; he was
mocked by the village boys as an inmate of a "booby hatch"; and,
too terrified to protest, he was severely beaten for a crime he didn't
commit.

The American poet Elizabeth Bishop, born in 1911, was also a
damaged orphan. Her father died when she was eight months old;
her mother was committed to an insane asylum when Elizabeth was
five, and she never saw her mother again. Brought up by her paternal
grandparents, she suffered from severe eczema, asthma and numerous
childhood diseases. As an adult, she became an alcoholic and experienced suicidal depressions.

Eileen Simpson – a psychotherapist, once married to the poet and
suicide John Berryman – has written perceptively about her experiences with the "drab surroundings, ill-fitting clothing, and inadequate
diets" of an orphanage, with the children who "cried incessantly,
refused to eat, slept poorly, were alternately clinging and detached."
As with Norma Jeane, "there had always been a broad vein of sadness"
in her character and very little talent for happiness. She "knew what
it was like . . . to cry out for reassurance that she was not alone, and
to hear only the opaque, tomblike silence that, in the middle of the
night, isolated me from the living."

Simpson explained why "foster care was as problematical as institu-
tional care had been. A successful match between child and surrogate
parents was not easy to arrange, especially since many foster families
were more interested in augmenting their income than in looking
after someone else's child. Few of the children were adopted by their
families, and far too many were shunted from one household to
another, with predictable results."[7] Chaplin and Simpson had the
comfort of a sibling, Bishop lived with sympathetic relatives; but
Norma Jeane, rejected by everyone, was absolutely alone. Like Chaplin
and Simpson, she was severely damaged by her years in the orphanage.

Marilyn emphasized that she was brought up very differently from
the normal American child and never believed she would have a
happy life. Natasha Lytess criticized Marilyn's habit of frequently referring to her miserable childhood, excusing her bad behavior and
appealing for sympathy. But she had suffered terribly, and felt justified in embellishing her story to advance her career. A publicist at
Twentieth Century-Fox, writing a brief account of her early life,

noted that the first money she ever earned was five cents a month for setting tables at the orphanage; and that she later spent at the local drugstore the ten cents a month she got for washing dishes. She began to stutter in the orphanage and continued to stutter as an adult whenever she was nervous. Her happiest childhood memory, an image of freedom, was "running through high grass in a vacant lot in Hawthorne." Her saddest memory was "disappointment in people when she was a little girl."

Norma Jeane was released from the orphanage in June 1937 and lived for the next year with a series of foster parents: first with Grace's sister and brother-in-law, Enid and Sam Knebelcamp; then with her own elderly great-aunt, Ida Martin; next with her guardian, Grace Goddard; finally with Grace's aunt, Ana Lower; and with other foster families when Ana's health was poor. Ana, divorced and living on rental property, was fifty-eight when the twelve-year-old Norma Jeane came to live with her in 1938. She looked plump, white-haired and grandmotherly, but her manner was stern and severe. A devout Christian Scientist (like Gladys), she went to church several times a week. Norma Jeane's grandmother, her mother, her guardian, her great-aunt, and even the sensible and compassionate Ana, all had had – and warned Norma Jeane to beware of – untrustworthy husbands and disastrous marriages.

Norma Jeane had to adjust not only to many different families, moods, rules, beliefs and ways of life, but also to nine different schools, for her first ten grades, between 1932 and 1942. Hardened to being the least important person in her foster family, she nevertheless remembered the disgusting humiliation on her weekly bath night: "I never minded coming 'last' in these families except on Saturday nights when everybody took a bath. Water cost money, and changing the water in the tub was an unheard of extravagance. The whole family used the same tub of water. And I was always the last one in." No wonder that she later luxuriated in long, perfumed and purifying baths.

Norma Jeane, a pretty and obedient girl, was never beaten. But she had to endure something far worse than repulsive bath water. When she was a child, most psychiatrists believed that "sexual abuse was rare and that children often lied about it. In 1937 two prominent American psychiatrists not only denied that sexual assault traumatized most children but argued that 'the child may have been the actual seducer rather than the one innocently seduced.'"[8] By the time she was twelve years old, Norma Jeane – with no one to protect her – had been sexually assaulted at least three times. At the age of eight, she was molested by a boarder in a foster home. When she tried to explain what had happened to her, the foster parent became very angry and – following the current belief – blamed *her*. "Don't you dare say anything against Mr. Kimmel. Mr. Kimmel's a fine man. He's my star boarder! . . . Shame on you, complaining about people!" After she left the orphanage and entered puberty, she was again molested by adult predators: by a cousin when living with Ida Martin and by Grace's husband, "Doc" Goddard, a six-foot five-inch drunkard.

Though Marilyn claimed she'd been raped as a child, her first husband stated she was a virgin when they married. She later gave a more accurate, though equally repulsive account of what actually happened: "I wasn't really raped, but he forced me to do something, and I had a shock. . . . He forced me to take him in my mouth." Virginia Woolf was also sexually molested, at six years old, when her adult half-brother, George Duckworth, lifted her onto a table and fingered her private parts. As an adult, Woolf always associated sex with degradation and contempt. She became sexually frigid, had several mental breakdowns and finally committed suicide.

But at the age of twelve, showing no outward signs of her emotional scars, Norma Jeane looked in the mirror at her smooth, shapely body and was pleased by what she saw. She first aroused the attention of young boys by wearing a tight sweater to show off her breasts, and soon realized that her well-developed body was the key to popularity and success. Though sexy, she repressed her sexual feelings, and recalled "that with all my lipstick and mascara and precocious curves, I was as unsensual as a fossil."[9]

III

Norma Jeane was always threatened with confinement in the orphanage if she failed to behave. That threat became real in 1942 when she was sixteen. She could no longer stay with the increasingly ill Ana Lower, and "Doc" Goddard was transferred with his family to West Virginia. Grace then told her that she'd either have to get married or return to the dreaded institution. Grace had dominated her early life, and had been Norma Jeane's legal guardian for

eight years. In between spells of caring for her, she'd placed her in
the orphanage and found various foster homes. She now arranged
to marry her off. On June 19, 1942, six months after America entered
World War II and three weeks after her sixteenth birthday, Norma
Jeane dropped out of the tenth grade and married a neighbor's son:
the attractive, athletic and popular twenty-one-year-old James
Dougherty.

In 1941 Robert Mitchum, not yet a movie star, worked with
Dougherty in the sheet metal department of Lockheed Aircraft in
Burbank. He said that his co-worker "looked like a large brick, red-
haired, square-shouldered and [like Mitchum himself] solid all the
way down." Norma Jeane liked the man Grace had chosen, but had
to adjust to yet another radical change in her life. She later told her
New York maid, with becoming modesty, that "Jim was handsome,
well-mannered, and had a good job – and a car. What I couldn't
figure out was what a guy like Jim would want with me." Dougherty
– who later remarried, became a Los Angeles policeman and wrote
a memoir of Norma Jeane – admitted that she was sometimes a little
naïve, a little dumb.

Dougherty gave a positive, even idealized account of their conventional and essentially happy marriage. He stated, for example, that
Norma Jeane liked to prepare meals and was a good cook, though
she favored peas and carrots because she liked their color combination. But Shelley Winters, who roomed with her in 1950, revealed
(perhaps with some comic exaggeration) that Marilyn was absolutely
hopeless in the kitchen: "Not only could Marilyn not cook, if you
handed her a leg of lamb, she just stared at it. Once I asked her to
wash the salad while I went to the store. When I came back an hour
later, she was still scrubbing each leaf. Her idea of making a salad was
to scrub each lettuce leaf with a Brillo pad."[10]

Norma Jeane was certainly naïve, at least in the beginning, about
sex. The first time she used a diaphragm, Jim had to get down on his
knees to help her extract it. But he insisted that their sexual life was
passionate and satisfying: "Norma Jeane loved sex. It was as natural
to her as breakfast in the morning. There were never any problems
with it. . . . Never had I encountered a girl who so thoroughly enjoyed
sexual union. It made our lovemaking pure joy." Sometimes, overcome by desire, she'd even insist they pull off the road and make love
in the car.

Norma Jeane loved children but, nearly a child herself, never wanted to have them with Dougherty. When she thought she was pregnant, she became frightened by the pain of childbirth. The screenwriter Nunnally Johnson recalled that when Marilyn played a young mother in *We're Not Married* (1952), she held a baby on camera, but – remaining strangely remote – paid absolutely no attention to it when it cried. She suffered severe menstrual pains, which would plague her throughout her life. But, according to Dougherty, she had no other physical or psychological problems: "There were no pills needed to put Norma Jeane to sleep at night. Mom never heard her complain about her nerves or even about being depressed." Her sexual problems came when years of psychoanalysis dredged up painful memories and made her acutely conscious of her childhood traumas. Later on, when Marilyn became famous, she wanted to obliterate her marriage to a pleasant but commonplace husband. Rewriting her past, she unconvincingly claimed that she'd been emotionally and sexually estranged from Dougherty: "We hardly spoke to each other. . . . We had nothing to say. . . . The first effect marriage had on me was to increase my lack of interest in sex."

One source of contention, which became a major theme in Miller's *The Misfits*, concerned Norma Jeane's outrage at Dougherty's cruelty to animals. She hated to go on hunting trips and had to close her eyes when he killed rabbits. Once, when he'd shot a deer and put it in the back seat of the car, it suddenly "came to life and lifted its head. Jim stopped the car and began strangling the deer. She tried to stop him," but couldn't do so. Nevertheless, he said, she was affectionate and never held a grudge: "When we had an argument – and there were plenty – I'd often say, 'Just shut up!' and go out to sleep on the couch. An hour later, I woke up to find her sleeping alongside me, or sitting nearby on the floor. She was very forgiving."[11]

Dougherty, with an essential wartime job at Lockheed, would not have been drafted, but for patriotic reasons chose to enlist in the merchant marine. His first, pleasantly soft job, late in 1943, was on Santa Catalina Island, off the coast of Los Angeles, where he trained Marine recruits. On that nearly all-male post, he became upset when his sexy wife attracted enthusiastic attention on the beach and at dances by wearing tight-fitting, provocative clothes. He knew the men were swarming around Norma Jeane, but six months later, in the spring of 1944, he sailed to Asia. Norma Jeane, yet again, felt abandoned and deeply hurt.

Yet Norma Jeane's letters of June 15 and December 3, 1944, to Grace Goddard in West Virginia, express her admiration and affection for Dougherty, and confirm his belief that they were happily married:

> I love Jimmie just more than anyone (in a different way I suppose than anyone) and I know I shall never be happy with anyone else as long as I live, and I know he feels the same towards me. So you see we are really very happy together. That is, of course, when we can be together. We both miss each other terribly. We will be married two years June 19th. And we really have had quite a happy life together. . . . I love him so very much. Honestly. I don't think there is another man alive like him. He really is awfully sweet.

With Dougherty gone and nothing to do at home, Norma Jeane looked for wartime work. His mother, who worked as a nurse at the Radio Plane plant in Burbank, got her a job there. She started by packing the parachutes which were attached to miniature target-practice planes, operated by remote control. The chutes brought the planes down safely so that they could be used again. She was then "promoted" to the dope room, where she sprayed foul-smelling liquid varnish, made of banana oil and glue, onto the fabric of the fuselage. In this extremely unpleasant job, she earned the minimum wage of twenty dollars a week for sixty hours of work. The varnish was pretty strong stuff, and there was constant danger from sniffing glue. But the noxious fumes also provided her first high and introduced her to the attraction of drugs. After a year of this taxing work, the exhausted Norma Jeane complained to Grace that she had to be on her feet for ten hours a day. On June 4, 1945, she wrote that she'd finally found a way to escape from this dead-end job in a noxious factory: "I haven't worked at Radio Plane Company since January. They keep asking me to come back but I don't really want to do that kind of work any more because it makes me so darn tired."

Norma Jeane escaped from this drudgery when the photographer David Conover "discovered" her. He was working for the Army's Motion Picture Unit, commanded by the actor Ronald Reagan. To boost the morale of soldiers in combat, he'd been sent to the factory to get still photos of beautiful girls toiling on the home front. On June 4 she enthusiastically told Grace about the promising new life that had suddenly beckoned:

> The first I know the photographers had me out there, taking pictures of me. . . . They all asked where in the H— I had been hiding. . . . They took a lot of moving pictures of me, and some of them asked for dates, etc. (Naturally I refused). . . . After they finished with some of the pictures, an army corporal by the name of David Conover told me he would be interested in getting some color still shots of me. He used to have a studio on the Strip on Sunset. He said he would make arrangements with the plant superintendent if I would agree, so I said okay. He told me what to wear and what shade of lipstick, etc., so the next couple of weeks I posed for him at different times. . . . He said that all the pictures came out perfect. Also, he said that I should by all means go into the modeling profession . . . that I photographed very well and that he wants to take a lot more. Also he said he had a lot of contacts he wanted me to look into.
>
> I told him I would rather not work when Jimmie was here, so he said he would wait, so I'm expecting to hear from him most any time again.
>
> He is awfully nice and is married and is strictly business, which is the way I like it. Jimmie seems to like the idea of me modeling, so I'm glad about that.[12]

But Jimmie, fearing the worst, did *not* like the idea of his wife modeling, and Conover became her first lover. She later confessed that the anguish of solitude rather than the desire for sex made her succumb to other men: "I didn't sleep around when I was married until [after one year] my husband went into the service, and then it was just that I was so damn lonesome, and I had to have some kind of company, so once in a while I'd give in, mainly because I didn't want to be alone."

Like Dougherty, Conover found sex with Norma Jeane more than satisfactory. In fact, he recalled that she exhausted him and that "her sexual appetite far exceeded my capacity to give her pleasure." But the photographic sessions, rather than their affair, changed her attitude to life and to her husband. When Dougherty returned from the war, she greeted him coolly, seemed completely self-absorbed and informed him that their marriage was over. Dougherty, still in love with her, was surprised to discover that "Norma Jeane wasn't talking about our future anymore. It was her career nearly all of the time. In the year and a half I had been at sea, she had changed into almost another human being."[13]

Three

A Star Is Born
(1947–1954)

I

In her autobiography Marilyn said, with some exaggeration, that during her childhood and early adult life, "the Hollywood I knew was the Hollywood of failure. Nearly everybody I met suffered from malnutrition or suicidal impulses." Thinking of the English actors who'd lived in her mother's house, she contrasted their unreal hopes with the grim reality of their lives: "Among the phonies and failures were also a set of has-beens. These were mostly actors and actresses who had been dropped by the movies – nobody knew why, least of all themselves." By the end of the war Norma Jeane was ready to pursue the same difficult goal, and aspired to be a model, singer, dancer and actress. She had learned to live without her husband, had no desire to go back to housework and was sick of the factory. Photogenic, with blue eyes and fine skin, she was five feet five inches tall, weighed 117 pounds, and had a voluptuous 36-24-34 figure. She'd earned twenty dollars a week at the plane factory; her first job as a model paid ten dollars a *day*.

In 1945 David Conover introduced her to Emmeline Snively, owner of the Blue Book Modeling Agency. A formal woman in her late forties, she ran a successful business that supplied young models for scores of popular photo magazines. She made the most of her respectable image, always wore a hat and spoke with an English accent, which had considerable snob value in Hollywood. She signed up Norma Jeane for one of her courses and advanced her the money to pay for it. Her initial assessment emphasized her new client's eagerness to learn, willingness to work and tremendous ambition:

> She was a clean-cut, American, wholesome girl – too plump, but beautiful in a way. We tried to teach her how to pose, how to handle her body. She always tried to lower her smile because she smiled too high, and it made her nose look a little too long. At first she knew nothing about carriage, posture, walking, sitting or posing. She started out with less than any girl I ever knew, but she worked the hardest. . . . She wanted to learn, wanted to be somebody, more than anybody I ever saw before in my life.

In May 1946 Norma Jeane went to Las Vegas for several weeks to get her divorce. While there she wrote a girlish, star-struck letter to Miss Snively about her first contact with a movie crew:

> I'm having lots of rest and I'm getting a tan. It's very warm and honestly the sun shines all the time.
>
> Las Vegas is really a colorful town with the Helldorado celebration and all. It lasted for five days, they had rodeos and parades every day.
>
> Roy Rogers was in town making a picture. I met him and rode his horse "Trigger" (cross my heart I did!). What a horse!
>
> I was walking down the street one day last week and noticed they were shooting a movie so like everyone else I stood and watched. In between shootings a couple of fellows from Republic Studio walked over to me and asked me if I would please come over and meet some actor (I don't remember his name. I think his last name was Cristy or something like that). Anyway he wanted to meet me so I did and I met most of the studio people including Roy Rogers and I rode his horse, gee he is nice.
>
> They asked me to have dinner with them at the Last Frontier and then we went to the rodeo. What a day! Ever since I've been signing autograph books and cowboy hats. When I try to tell these kids I'm not in pictures they think I'm just trying to avoid signing their books, so I sign them.

They're gone now. It's quite lonely here in Las Vegas. This is certainly a wild town.[1]

She loved being young, pretty and desirable, and enjoyed her brief moment of behaving like a film star.

In her years as a model Norma Jeane learned how to use make-up skillfully, including a special foundation to disguise the fuzz on her fair skin. She had plastic surgery to lift her nose slightly, which gave her more upper lip and improved her smile, and had some cartilage put into her jaw to improve the line of her chin. The results were splendid and she became a popular pin-up. The war was over, but many young Americans, the major market for these magazines, were still in the armed services. "Soldiers in the Aleutians voted her the girl most likely to thaw Alaska, and the Seventh Division Medical Corps elected her the girl they would most like to examine." Despite her success and financial independence, she felt as conflicted about modeling for girlie magazines as she would, later on, about playing dumb parts in third-rate movies. She craved respectability. "When I was a model," she said, "I wanted more than anything in the world for my picture to be on the cover of the *Ladies' Home Journal*. Instead, I was always on magazines with names like *Peek* and *See* and *Whiz Bang*. Those were the kind of movies I made, too."

Though she had steady work and a decent income, Norma Jeane remained as transient as an adult as she'd been as a child. In this respect, she was a typically rootless resident of Los Angeles. "This lack of a sense of permanency," wrote two social historians, "accounts for the unreal appearance of the region and the restless character of its population. . . . The houses have no earthly relation to the environment. They are unreal, as unreal as motion-picture sets." She had very few possessions, and lived at more than sixty addresses in her thirty-six years.

She owned a car, essential for seeking work in Los Angeles, getting to her agents and to auditions at the studios. Early on, the photographer Philippe Halsman was surprised to find his glamorous model living in a cheap one-room apartment on the edge of the city and driving about in a beat-up old sedan. She cemented her friendship with the neurotic columnist Sidney Skolsky, who was afraid to drive, by chauffeuring him through the city. Her professional progress can be measured from the decrepit Pontiac she drove at the beginning of her career to the brand-new Cadillac she was given in September 1953 for appearing on the Jack Benny show. In America the car had always had social and (as Jim Dougherty noted) sexual implications. As the California historians nicely observed, "to have a car meant being some-body; to have to borrow a car meant knowing somebody; to have no car at all, owned or borrowed, was to be left out – way out."[2]

In 1946 Norma Jeane signed on with her first agent, Harry Lipton, who for the next two years helped her secure several short-term contracts with Hollywood studios. She signed a six-month contract with Fox in July 1946, renewed it in January 1947 and was termi-nated by Fox – who didn't know what to do with her – in August of that year. She changed her name in 1947. She signed a six-month contract with Harry Cohn's Columbia Pictures, then a minor studio, in March 1948, and was crushed when they dropped her in September. Finally, she signed another six-month contract with Fox, which was converted to a seven-year contract with incremental pay raises, in May 1951.

In these early years Marilyn had tiny parts in five forgotten movies. She was almost entirely cut out of her first two pictures. Just before Fox dropped her in 1947, she appeared in *The Dangerous Years* as a waitress in a teenage hangout. She warned a relative not to blink or she might miss her fleeting appearance. This was a common career path for young film actresses like Marilyn: she worked as a model, became a starlet under contract to a studio, posed for publicity photo-graphs and got small parts in movies, often by performing sexual favors for influential men. Such tiny parts were barely a step away from modeling: she was just a blank, pretty face in a sexy body. Very few young women got the breakout part that made them stars.

As a starlet in the studio system, Marilyn was often treated with contempt. Orson Welles recalled that she was even humiliated in public: "At a Hollywood party which Marilyn attended (circa 1946 or '47) while she was still a lowly starlet, he saw someone actually pull down the top of her dress in front of people and fondle her. She had laughed. 'Just about everyone in town had slept with her.'" Being sexually available, Marilyn felt, was an essential if unpleasant part of her job. It focused attention on her greatest asset and allowed her to show off her body. Laughter in this situation was her only defense; moral indignation would have been pointless. She was certainly sexu-ally exploited, but in her casual and carefree way she was also complicit.

Marilyn had many brief affairs, but quickly learned the difference between one-night stands that assuaged her loneliness but achieved nothing, and liaisons with powerful but unattractive men that advanced her career. Her first "protector," the influential producer Joseph Schenck, whom she met in 1948, was fifty years older than Marilyn. Like many Hollywood moguls, he was a self-made man with a colorful past, born in eastern Europe and from a Jewish background. He came from a Russian village on the Volga, where his father was a wood-fuel merchant, emigrated to America in his teens and worked his way up from errand boy to owner of several New York drugstores. In 1912 he acquired the Palisades Amusement Park, across the Hudson River from Manhattan, then built a chain of nickelodeons and movie theaters with Marcus Loew. In 1933, with Darryl Zanuck and William Goetz he founded Twentieth Century Pictures, which two years later merged with Fox. Schenck made movies with the director D.W. Griffith, the comedians Fatty Arbuckle and Buster Keaton, and the popular silent film actress Norma Talmadge, Norma Jeane's namesake. Schenck had been married to Talmadge from 1917 (when she was twenty years old) to 1934. In 1941 he was convicted for bribing union officials to prevent strikes, and spent four months in a federal prison in Danbury, Connecticut.

Marilyn refused to marry the wealthy Schenck, but agreed to move into his guest cottage. According to a Hollywood columnist, Schenck needed medical assistance to get an erection, which did not last very long. Marilyn was amusing about her role in their urgent arrangement: "It's all very complicated. Sometimes when the doctor comes, I have to synchronize my watch. That's why I'm living in the guest house. This stuff can't wait for a studio limousine to drive me across town." During these years she also spent a lot of time on her knees, servicing movie executives like Harry Cohn in their offices, but this phase of her life came to an end in 1951. After signing her first long-term contract with Fox, she triumphantly declared: "I have sucked my last cock."[3]

II

In 1948, during her six-month contract with Columbia Pictures, Marilyn was sent to their drama coach Natasha Lytess, and began the acting lessons with a series of teachers that would continue until the end of her life. A natural comedienne with a sexy face and figure, Marilyn yearned to be a dramatic actress. She was utterly devoted to all her mentors, most of them of them heavily influenced by Konstantin Stanislavsky's school of "Method" acting, which emphasized the inner truth of the actor's feelings, moods and expressions. Born into a Jewish family in Austria and a former actress in Max Reinhardt's company in Germany, Lytess claimed Franco-Russian descent to dissociate herself from the wartime enemy and connect herself with the Russian acting tradition. Tall, angular, even emaciated, with flashing eyes, short-cropped gray hair, a strong accent and forbidding appearance, Lytess was energetic, volatile and intense. Several biographers have suggested (though there's no evidence for this) that Lytess was the mistress of the German-Jewish émigré novelist Bruno Frank and that he was the father of her young daughter, Barbara.

Like most of her teachers, Lytess influenced Marilyn's personal as well as her professional life. A devout and submissive disciple, Marilyn became a close friend. When Lytess was desperate for money to pay the mortgage, or risk losing her house, Marilyn sold the mink stole that one of her admirers had given her – the only valuable thing she owned – and gave Lytess $1,000. Marilyn had known real poverty in her youth and was always generous with money. Emphasizing her characteristic openhandedness, Lytess said the self-absorbed actress frequently gave material gifts because "she was unable to give of herself." Marilyn admired her as a teacher, but complained that Lytess was jealous of her boyfriends and behaved as if she were Marilyn's husband. When Lytess wanted to have sex with her, Marilyn passively agreed. "I'd let any guy, or girl," she insouciantly explained, "do what they wanted if I thought they were my friend."

Like Snively, Lytess had to start from scratch. She recalled, Marilyn's "voice, a piping sort of whimper, got on my nerves" – though Marilyn developed this breathy whisper as her trademark. Lytess encouraged her inhibited pupil "to let go, to say things freely, to walk freely, to feel expansion, to know what it is like to speak with authority." Then, using a sub-aqueous metaphor that would recur in descriptions of Marilyn, she said she wanted her pupil to know "the difference between existing under water and coming alive." She taught Marilyn how to express character and reveal the meaning of a scene, and to under-stand that acting was best when "the emotion shows, not the words."[4] Like Lee Strasberg later on, she urged her pupil to concentrate on herself instead of on the writer's words, on the interpretation of her own role instead of on relating to the other actors.

Lytess, like Strasberg, also exacerbated Marilyn's self-consciousness, intensified her anxiety and increased her childlike dependence on her teacher. In stressing the actor as an individual, rather than part of an ensemble, she encouraged Marilyn's intense self-concentration, which seemed to her co-workers like narcissism and selfishness. At the same time, Lytess, like many others, was content to enjoy sex with Marilyn without considering Marilyn's feelings. Despite her intense obsession with herself, Marilyn curiously dissociated her body from her emotions and allowed others to have their way with her in exchange for emotional support.

In the fall of 1951 Marilyn began lessons with Michael Chekhov at the same time as, but secret from, Lytess. The sixty-year-old Chekhov had impeccable credentials. Nephew of the great Russian playwright Anton Chekhov, he had worked with Stanislavsky at the Moscow Art Theater. He was also writing the widely used book, *To the Actor: On the Technique of Acting* (1953), which became Marilyn's bible. Chekhov "devoted himself to the fulfillment of the actor's personality – not only in the profession but also in their personal lives." Like all her teachers, he practiced a kind of amateur psychotherapy. He spoke *ex cathedra* and confused her, since she was obsessed by her own body, by declaring that "our bodies can be either our best friends or worst enemies. You must try to consider your body as an instrument for expressing your creative ideas. You must strive for complete harmony between body and psychology" – though few actors ever managed to achieve this ideal.

Annoyed by Marilyn's habitual lateness and absence – which was caused by nervousness and fear of failure, and would later destroy her career – Chekhov felt she was not serious and advised her to leave his classes. Marilyn, suitably chastised, begged for understanding. "Please don't give up on me yet," she pleaded. "I know (painfully so) that I try your patience. I need the work [with you] and your friendship desperately. I shall call you soon."[5] After this abject apology, she was forgiven and continued her classes. Marilyn had also taken lessons, before she met Lytess, from Morris Carnovsky and his wife Phoebe Brand at the Actors Lab in Los Angeles. She continued to take instruction in movement and body language, after she left Chekhov, with the mime artist Lotte Goslar at the Turnabout Theater in L.A. All these teachers – as well as Lee Strasberg and Joshua Logan later on – were strongly influenced by the ideas of Stanislavsky.

Marilyn's principal teachers were supplemented by a cadre of minor instructors. Lytess had tried to build up Marilyn's bruised ego and make her believe she could some day become a star. At the same time, Fred Karger was giving her voice lessons and doing his best to undermine her self-confidence. He too became an influential mentor, teaching her about clothing and manners, books and music. He also sent her to an orthodontist who improved her bite and bleached her teeth. Separated from his wife, Karger was living with his young son in his mother's house. Marilyn fell deeply in love with him, and moved in with the family for several months.

Marilyn said that Karger, preying on her vulnerability and trying to dominate her, savagely condemned her intellectual and moral weaknesses: "He criticized my mind. He kept pointing out how little I knew and how unaware of life I was. . . . 'Your mind isn't developed. Compared to your breasts it's embryonic.'" He refused to marry her because, as he insultingly told her, if he died he wouldn't want his son "to be brought up by a woman like you." Elia Kazan attributed Karger's hold over Marilyn to his sexual prowess: "Fred was a musician, scrawny but able in love. She came as many as three times with him in one go. He was vulgar and coarse and scornful with her. He said she was no good for anything but fucking. He found her dress 'cheap.' He told her her breasts were too big. He didn't like to sleep in the same bed with her. He thought her beneath conversation, said she was stupid and only good for one thing." Marilyn meekly accepted this treatment, and when Karger finally rejected her, she may have aborted his child. In 1952 Karger married the actress Jane Wyman, recently divorced from Ronald Reagan. Karger and Wyman were also divorced, but married again in 1961 and four years later divorced again.

In 1949, despite extensive tuition and several contracts, Marilyn's career was going nowhere. Her first break came through her new agent, advocate, protector and lover, Johnny Hyde. As in a Shakespearean comedy, she loved Karger, but he didn't love her; Hyde loved her, but she didn't love him. Like Schenck, Hyde was a short, homely man, much older than Marilyn, who came from a Russian-Jewish family, had emigrated to America as a boy and worked his way up to the top. He began as Ivan Haidebura, a child juggler and acrobat in Loew's vaudeville circuit, and eventually moved to Hollywood. After his legendary discovery of Lana Turner in Schwab's drugstore, he became an important executive in the influential William Morris agency.

Kazan, who succeeded Hyde as Marilyn's lover, observed that she gave Hyde "that dazed starlet look of unqualified adoration and utter dependence. Clearly she lived by his protection and was sure of his devotion." Marilyn, then making the difficult transition from orphan and factory worker to model and actress, explained that Hyde "not only knew me, he knew Norma Jeane, too. He knew all the pain and all the desperate things in me. When he put his arms around me and said he loved me, I knew it was true. Nobody had ever loved me like that. I wished with all my heart that I could love him back." But Marilyn was not mercenary. She refused to marry the thrice-divorced Hyde, as she'd refused to marry Schenck, though both elderly wealthy men promised to leave all their money to her. Hyde even asked for a list of friends she trusted and begged them to plead his case with her. Marilyn's sexual demands and Hyde's weak heart were almost certain to finish him off in a short time, but she feared that if Hyde failed to die on cue, she'd be trapped with him. Incurably romantic, despite her promiscuous past, she told Hyde that "if I married you I might meet some other man and fall in love with him. I don't want that ever to happen. If I marry a man I want to feel I'll always be faithful to him – and never love anyone else." Unfortunately, it never worked out this way.

In December 1950, when Hyde died on schedule, Marilyn suddenly lost his power and protection. Fearing her career would come to an end, she wept for herself as well as for him. Though he left a substantial estate of $600,000, she got nothing. Joseph Mankiewicz, who directed her in *All About Eve*, described Hyde's relations with Marilyn and how he restored the self-confidence that Fred Karger had nearly destroyed:

That major force [in her career] was a very important agent named Johnny Hyde – at the time certainly no less than the #2 or #3 power at William Morris. Like most great agents, he was a tiny man. . . . Hyde was a very honest and a very gentle man. He was deeply in love with Marilyn. And more than anyone in her life, I think, provided for her something akin to an honest *ego* of her own; he respected her. Permitting her, in turn, to acquire a certain amount of self-respect.[6]

III

Shortly before his death, Hyde got Marilyn a small but significant part in her first serious film, *The Asphalt Jungle*, the first of two excellent pictures she made in 1950. Marilyn was still cast for her sexy looks – in one she plays a criminal's mistress, the other a starlet on the make – but she worked with first-rate material, fine actors and superb directors. John Huston knew how to get the best out of scripts and actors. An incorrigible risk-taker, he was born in 1906 in Nevada, Missouri, south of Kansas City, a town his grandfather had supposedly won in a poker game. The son of the famous stage and screen actor Walter Huston, John had a weak heart and had been an invalid in childhood. But he was a man of wide interests, restless energy and fierce appetites. He had been a teenage boxing champion, had served in the Mexican cavalry, become an actor and playwright on Broadway, and studied painting in Paris. He was an expert fisherman, big game hunter and art collector, and a fine writer and director. He'd made first-rate documentaries under fire in World War II, as well as three brilliant films: *The Maltese Falcon* (1941), *The Treasure of the Sierra Madre* (1948) and *Key Largo* (1949). A persuasive and charismatic charmer, he impressed studio executives with his intelligence and won the loyalty of actors by giving them a free hand. Tall and rugged, courtly and eloquent, gambler and raconteur, he had a passion for horses, would marry five times and leave a long trail of mistresses.

Marilyn was perfectly cast as Angela Phinlay, the blond mistress of a polished but corrupt lawyer, played with waxed mustache and suave manners by Louis Calhern. He's an accomplice of a group of criminals, who plan to pull off a perfect crime, and is supposed to buy the jewels they steal. W.R. Burnett's novel, published only a year before the film was produced, describes Angela as "voluptuously made; and there was something about her walk – something lazy, careless, and insolently assured – that was impossible to ignore." As in many of her best roles, Marilyn's glowing skin and soft, dreamy sensuality contrasts sharply with the hard, striving male characters around her, and she remains rather vague about what's really going on.

Marilyn makes a powerful impact in three short scenes. In one she kisses Calhern goodnight and waits for him in the bedroom. Then she plans a romantic holiday with Calhern, who intends to steal the jewels and escape with her to Cuba. Finally, bullied and threatened by the police after Calhern has been arrested, she breaks down and admits that she'd provided him with a false alibi. She then apologizes to him as he continues to read a stool-pigeon's confession with apparent nonchalance. He suggests that he'd always expected her to betray him, cynically tells her that she'll take many exotic trips with other men and ironically exclaims, "Some sweet kid."

Huston achieved a strikingly original film despite the censorship in force at the time. The moralistic movie Production Code drained a lot of originality and interest from the eccentric cast of characters. The lubricious mastermind of the robbery, Dr. Riedenschneider, expertly played by Sam Jaffe, is caught by the police while watching young girls dance at a roadside café. In a letter of October 6, 1949 to the studio head Louis Mayer, the censor Joseph Breen insisted that Riedenschneider had to be one-dimensional and must "be played as a pitiful character trying to recapture his youth, not at all as a lecherous man." As the studio made concessions on these issues, Breen did all he could to cramp Marilyn's physical assets and sexy style. "It is mandatory," he wrote, "that the intimate parts of the body – specifically the breasts of women – be fully covered at all times." There must be no "indication that [Calhern] follows her into the bedroom, or any more definite suggestion of intimacy."[7] So, after saying goodnight to her sugar-daddy, Marilyn sways down the hallway to the alluring bedroom, leaving her nocturnal adventures to the spectators' imagination.

The star of the film, the hard-drinking Sterling Hayden, an ex-Marine and highly decorated war hero who'd fought the Nazis as a special commando alongside Tito's partisans in Yugoslavia, is another tough man in the story. *The Asphalt Jungle*, as its title suggests, is an urban crime film, but Huston loved horses and often brought them into climactic moments. Hayden's character comes from a Kentucky horse farm, which his family has lost after his father's death, and he hopes to get enough money from the robbery to buy it back. Badly wounded in a shootout with Calhern's henchman and accompanied by his gun moll, Hayden drives all the way back to the family farm and dies in the paddock as the horses gather mournfully around him.

When the film was completed Hayden gratefully told Huston that working with him had been "a pleasure, a privilege and an education all in one."

Two other professionals, praising the film, noted Marilyn's fine performance. The director Howard Hawks wrote that "*Jungle* is beautifully done and I envy you for it. The girl is a real find." The writer Budd Schulberg told Huston that the performances reflected "a hard-eyed and hardly ever sentimental conception of what your people were. . . . Calhern was really on the spot, trying to hide naked nerves with charm; and with Hayden you went farther into an understanding of violence than I have seen on the screen before. . . . The thought-processes of the little kept blonde were for once accurate."[8]

In 1950 Marilyn also played Miss Caswell, the mistress of another wicked smoothie, George Sanders, in *All About Eve*. It was written and directed by the intelligent, sophisticated Joseph Mankiewicz. Deliberately using Marilyn's sexpot image, Mankiewicz gave a cynical but accurate history of her couch-casting and two-bit roles: "For the most part she auditioned a great deal, afternoons, in executive offices. She also functioned agreeably as a companion for corporate elder statesmen visiting from the east, and on hostess committees for sales conventions. Occasionally, she was squeezed into old Betty Grable costumes and used as a dress extra for unimportant bits in some films." As a useful antidote to all the bewildering Russian theories she'd half-absorbed from Lytess, Chekhov and Carnovsky, Mankiewicz advised Marilyn to "put on some more clothes and stop moving your ass so much." (She ignored this advice and attracted considerable attention by moving her ass more than ever in *Niagara*.) In *All About Eve* she was, for once, given a few good lines. Commenting on a producer she's been advised to cultivate at an elegant party, Marilyn disdainfully asks, "Why do they always look like unhappy rabbits?" But most of all she is a naïve and stunning blonde, a moral and visual contrast to the dark-haired, cunning and ruthless actresses at the center of the film.

George Sanders – like Chekhov, Schenck and Hyde – was born in Russia. He was attracted to Marilyn and falsely accused by his current wife, Zsa Zsa Gabor, of having an affair with her. But he admired her character, and emphasized her insecurity, her professional standards and her intellectual curiosity: "She was very beautiful and very inquiring and very unsure – [as if] she was somebody in a play not yet written, uncertain of her part in the overall plot. . . . She was humble, punctual and untemperamental. She wanted people to like her. . . . I found her conversation had unexpected depths. She showed an interest in intellectual subjects which was, to say the least, disconcerting. In her presence it was hard to concentrate."

In contrast to Sanders, Celeste Holm – who was seven years older than Marilyn and played Bette Davis' friend – failed to see Marilyn's brightness and assumed she'd slept her way into the part: "I saw nothing special about her. I thought she was quite sweet and terribly dumb, and my natural reaction was, 'Whose girl is that?' It was the performance of a chorus girl [she's described in the film as 'a graduate of the Copacabana School of Dramatic Arts']. She was terribly shy. In fact, she was scared to death, because she was playing in a pretty big league, you know, but Joe relaxed her into it."

Mankiewicz himself saw yet another side of Marilyn's character, and understood her insecurity and self-imposed isolation both on and off the set: "I thought of her, then, as the loneliest person I had ever known. Throughout our location period in San Francisco, perhaps two or three weeks, Marilyn would be spotted at one restaurant or another dining alone. We'd always ask her to join us, and she would, and seemed pleased, but somehow she never understood or accepted our unspoken assumption that she was one of us. She was not a loner. She was just plain *alone*." It's hardly surprising that Marilyn lacked the confidence to socialize with the fiercely intelligent Bette Davis and the older actors who had experience on the stage. But close contact with these stars made her long to be a serious and respected actress.

Mankiewicz had an unexpected encounter with Marilyn that revealed that her endless striving for self-improvement, though apparently pretentious and absurd, was actually quite serious and sincere. When he saw her reading Rilke's *Letters to a Young Poet* as she waited to rehearse her dumb blonde role in *All About Eve*, he thought, "I'd have been less taken aback to come upon Herr Rilke studying a Marilyn Monroe nude calendar."[9] He asked how she happened to choose that highbrow book, and she naïvely but sweetly explained that "every now and then I go into the Pickwick [Bookshop on Hollywood Boulevard] . . . and just look around. I leaf through some books, and when I read something that interests me – I buy the book.

So last night I bought this one. Is that wrong?" Realizing that Herr Rilke's advice to an aspiring artist was an instinctively good choice, Mankiewicz assured her that it was not wrong at all.

Rilke's book, in fact, clearly expresses several themes that were especially meaningful to Marilyn. He emphasized the close connection between art and sex, mind and body, which she'd been trying to understand in her lessons and express in her roles: "artistic experience lies so incredibly close to that of sex, to its pain and its ecstasy, that the two manifestations are indeed but different forms of one and the same yearning and delight." Usually treated as a beddable body rather than as a woman with real feelings, she responded to Rilke's hope that sexual differences could be transcended, that "man and maid, freed of all false feelings and reluctances, will seek each other not as opposites, but as brother and sister, as neighbors, and will come together *as human beings*, in order simply, seriously and patiently to bear in common the difficult sex that has been laid upon them."

Marilyn, who saw the world as hostile and (as Holm noted) was "scared to death" on the set, found solace in Rilke's belief that "we have no reason to mistrust our world, for it is not against us. Has it terrors, they are *our* terrors; has it abysses, those abysses belong to us; are dangers at hand, we must try to love them." Two poetic passages were also charged with personal meaning for her. The "Sonnet" by the young poet, quoted in the *Letters*, echoed her own sadness: "Through my life there trembles without plaint, / without a sigh a deep dark melancholy." And, constantly in the process of transformation from Norma Jeane to the persona of Marilyn Monroe, she would have been struck by the famous last line of Rilke's "Archaic Torso of Apollo": "You must change your life."

The nude calendar that Mankiewicz mentioned originated in May 1949 when Marilyn was an obscure and occasionally impoverished model. Tom Kelley photographed her perfect body, a modern Venus, in several poses and paid her a modest $50. He sold the pictures for $500 to a company that put them on calendars, sold them throughout America and made a huge profit of $750,000. In the best photo Marilyn is shot sideways (to hide her pubic hair) and from a ladder ten feet above her. Her long wavy blond hair flows from her back-tilted head and mingles with the blood-red waterfall of drapery beneath her. This velvet suggests not only the softness of her skin and voice, but also the folds and texture of the most intimate parts of her body.

The outstretched fingers of her left hand seem to claw up to the right corner while her right foot points balletically down to the left. Her legs form a sexually suggestive triangle, and her back arches above her narrow waist and descends to the gentle mound of her buttocks. Her alluring breasts promise pneumatic bliss, and her pink nipples merge with the red velvet. Her body surges and flows in languorous undulations and, with all its sensual weight, is offered, in pure isolation, as an ecstatic end in itself. Marilyn seems to have slipped out of her clothes as easily as she'd slipped into men's beds. She seems ready to respond with erotic compliance and represents, in William Blake's words, the "lineaments of gratified desire." Her friend Nan Taylor, who once saw her get out of the bath, recalled that Marilyn's body was beautiful all over, as perfect in life as it was in the photos.[10]

The pose in Kelley's photo seems to have been inspired by François Boucher's portrait of Miss O'Murphy (c.1751), the daughter of an Irish soldier and mistress of King Louis XV of France. This lovely girl, with hands supporting her chin, is sprawled belly down on the ruffled drapery and ample cushions of a velvet sofa. Her legs are spread, her naked bottom is center stage and, with a shamelessly engaging expression, she gazes upwards as if seeking some sort of royal command or divine absolution.

Always casual about nudity, Marilyn forgot all about the photo. But in March 1952, when she was making *Clash by Night* and being courted by Joe DiMaggio, someone recognized her as the girl in the calendar and threatened to blackmail Twentieth Century-Fox. The Hollywood studios, in matters ranging from film scripts to actors' private lives, constantly trod the minefield of public opinion. America in the 1950s was (and in many ways still is) a puritanical and rather hypocritical society. Films regularly maintained the sugary fiction that young girls were always innocent and demure, and studios spent heavily on public relations to persuade the public that movie stars had a moral and dignified private life. Actors' contracts contained morals clauses that threatened instant dismissal for scandalous or disgraceful behavior. In 1950, for example, Ingrid Bergman had been publicly condemned and professionally exiled for having an illegitimate child with the Italian director Roberto Rossellini.

The discovery of the calendar sent the Fox executives into a panic, and they urged Marilyn to deny that she was the naked model. But Marilyn, intuiting the public's response and acting more wisely, admitted that she'd posed in the nude and gained valuable publicity from the potentially scandalous incident. She defended modeling as honest work, bravely said she was not ashamed of her body and claimed she had needed the cash to avoid repossession of her car (a sacred object in Los Angeles). The public was convinced that she'd had no other means of earning the money, and that economic necessity should prevail over moral values. Often silent and tongue-tied in private, Marilyn won over her audience by answering reporters' questions, like Mae West, with a series of witty ripostes. She defiantly declared, "I've been on calendars, but never on time." Playing on words when asked what she had on, she suggestively replied, "I had the radio on." In a variant of this question, "What do you wear to bed?," she answered, "Chanel No. 5." Marilyn's nude photo achieved even greater fame when, in December 1953, it became the centerfold of the first issue of *Playboy*.

Before the nude calendar scandal, and while she was making *Love Happy* with the Marx Brothers in 1949, Marilyn posed for a second series of less successful nude photos, this time for Earl Moran. Leaning backwards, resting on her extended arms, she tucks her right leg underneath her and stretches her left leg toward the floor. Wearing the bottom of a bathing suit, with her long blond hair flowing sensuously down her back, she sits sideways on a wooden case, smiling innocently and baring her breasts.

IV

Marilyn played an important part in the transformation and revival of Hollywood in the 1950s. Two historians described the major reasons for the sudden decline of the studios at that time:

> While as late as 1951 Hollywood made nearly 400 feature films, by 1960 only 154 were produced. 'B' films, shorts, and newsreels all disappeared during the fifties. . . . By 1960, when Americans possessed some 50 million TV sets, a fifth of the nation's theaters had closed for lack of business. . . .
>
> From a record weekly attendance of 82 million in 1946, film audiences alarmingly plummeted to about 36 million by 1950. Labor troubles, higher production costs, adverse court rulings [forbidding studio ownership of theaters], highly publicized anti-communist

hearings all hurt the movie industry. . . . [The fifties witnessed] the demise of the old film-making system – the Hollywood of big studios, glamorous stars, formalized plots, packaged dreams, predictable profits.[11]

Marilyn's rise to stardom and box-office magnetism helped to halt the radical decline of the studios.

Marilyn has often been compared to the platinum-blond actress Jean Harlow. But in her colorful public life she was more like Clara Bow, the "It girl" of the 1920s. Bow also came from a desperately impoverished background. Her father was an alcoholic, her mother insane. Sexy, feverishly animated and intensely emotional, she won a beauty contest in her teens and came to Hollywood when she was seventeen. After she became a star, she lived quietly in her Beverly Hills and Malibu houses, and amused herself by playing poker with her servants. But she was flamboyant in public, driving a bright red car filled with seven chow dogs whose coats were dyed to match her flaming red hair.

In the early 1950s, after those two small roles in first-rate films – *All About Eve* won Academy Awards for best picture, director, screenplay and supporting actor – Marilyn had more prominent parts in a series of mediocre movies, which, rather surprisingly, vaulted her to stardom. Her performances were more significant than the pictures themselves, and paved the way for her best roles later on.

Clash by Night (1952) was based on a Broadway play by Clifford Odets that starred Tallulah Bankhead. A left-wing melodrama set in the 1930s, the play showed how poverty and unemployment drive a deceived husband to murder his wife's lover. The film, by contrast, centered on the classic eternal triangle. Barbara Stanwyck betrays her crude but devoted husband, Paul Douglas, in an adulterous liaison with Robert Ryan, but repents and returns home. Stanwyck's disillusioned remark, "Home is where you come to when you run out of places," echoes Robert Frost's lines in "The Death of the Hired Man": "Home is the place where, when you have to go there, / They have to take you in." Marilyn plays a tough, independent but essentially sweet girl, who works in a Monterey sardine-canning factory. Fresh, blond and young, in contrast to Stanwyck's dark-haired, bitter and disillusioned character, she looks good in her simple jeans (as she would in *The Misfits*) and seems engagingly natural. In contrast to the overwrought, tempestuous triangle of the three main characters, she achieves love and happiness with her young husband at the end of the film.

Robert Ryan, like George Sanders and Joseph Mankiewicz, recalled Marilyn's fear and isolation: "I got the feeling she was a frightened lonely little girl who was trying awfully hard. She always seemed to be so mournful-looking around the set, and I'd always try to cheer her up. She never went out with the rest of us socially after work." The movie's Austrian director, Fritz Lang, who'd made the great German Expressionist film *M*, analyzed Marilyn's character and was the first to note her inability to memorize her part: "She was a very peculiar mixture of shyness and uncertainty – I wouldn't say 'star allure' – but, let me say, she knew exactly her impact on men. . . . I don't know why she couldn't remember her lines, but I can very well understand all the directors who worked with her getting angry, because she was certainly responsible for slowing down the work. But she was very responsive." She was a minor if promising actress, but the publicity generated by the nude calendar forced the studio to tolerate her costly and unprofessional behavior. A newsman on the set, concentrating on the hottest story, exclaimed, "We don't want to speak with Stanwyck. We know everything about her. We want to talk to the girl with big tits."[12]

Marilyn seemed more at ease on screen in the comedy *Monkey Business*, her third movie of 1952, but did not get on with the director, Howard Hawks. Physically impressive (like Huston) Hawks was "six-feet-three, broad shouldered, slim-hipped, soft-spoken, confident in manner, conservative in dress, and utterly distinguished overall." Born in Indiana, the son of a wealthy paper manufacturer, Hawks was educated at Exeter and graduated from Cornell in 1917 with a degree in mechanical engineering. He was a lieutenant in the Army Air Corps in World War I, and after the war built airplanes and a racing car that won the Indianapolis 500. In 1922 he came to Hollywood, where screenwriter Niven Busch found him impressively distant and formidably frigid: "He gave me his reptilian glare. The man had ice-cold blue eyes and the coldest of manners. He was like that with everyone – women, men, whatever. He was remote; he came from outer space. He wore beautiful clothes. He spoke slowly in a deep voice. He looked at you with these frozen eyes."

This haughty patrician directed the absurd and labored *Monkey Business*, in which a chimpanzee in a research lab accidentally concocts an elixir of youth that makes Cary Grant and Ginger Rogers behave like children. Marilyn has the decorative but unrewarding role of Charles Coburn's secretary. In one scene the seventy-five-year-old Coburn "had to chase and squirt Marilyn with a siphon of soda, a moment he approached with glee. Any seeming reluctance, he later explained, was only his indecision about *where* on Marilyn's . . . um . . . *ample* proportions to *squirt* the soda." Despite her small part, Marilyn also caused trouble on this picture and forced Hawks to shoot around her when she failed to show up. The problem, as everyone later discovered, was her infected appendix, which she had removed, in late April 1952, as soon as her work was completed.

No doctor performing an appendectomy would excise her reproductive organs. But Marilyn, who hoped to have children, taped a pleading note to her abdomen before the operation:

> Dr. Rabwin − most important to Read Before operation. Cut as little as possible. I know it seems vain but that doesn't really enter into it. The fact that I'm a woman is important and means much to me.
>
> Save please (I can't ask enough) what you can − I'm in your hands. You have children and must know what it means − please Dr. Rabwin − I know somehow you will!
>
> Thank you − thank you − thank you. For God's sake Dear Doctor No ovaries removed − please again do whatever you can to prevent large scars.
>
> Thanking you with all my heart.
>
> Marilyn Monroe.

The formidable Hawks, mistaking her pain and fear for stupidity, was even more critical than Fritz Lang. Hawks considered Marilyn "'so goddamn dumb' that she was wary and afraid of him. Still, Hawks admitted that she did a fine job in the film and that 'the camera liked her.'" Cary Grant, like Celeste Holm and many other colleagues, was surprised by her meteoric rise to fame the following year: "I had no idea she would become a big star. If she had something different from any other actress, it wasn't apparent at the time. She seemed very shy and quiet. There was something sad about her."[13] To the other actors

Marilyn could seem ordinary, unresponsive and apparently "dumb," but on camera she seemed to glow.

In *Don't Bother to Knock* (1952) Marilyn had a spectacularly unsuitable role that revealed her inability to play a dramatic part. She gave an unconvincingly hysterical performance as a drab, unglamorous, psychopathic babysitter who almost murders the child in her care. In *Niagara* (1953) she played a beer-hall waitress, a good-time girl married to a psychopath, Joseph Cotton. Oscar Wilde had called Niagara Falls "the second great disappointment of the American bride," but Marilyn managed to complement the orgasmic *fortissimo* of the cataract. The film was advertised with a poster of a gigantic Marilyn, reclining across the entire width of the Falls, which equated her powerful sexuality with its immense volume, everlasting duration and uncontrollable force. When she sees some young couples dancing outside her motel room, she puts a record on the phonograph and sings, "Kiss me . . . take me in your arms and make my life perfection. . . . *Perfection.*" The gloomy Cotton, who seems impotent when confronted with Marilyn's seductive sensuality and mocked by the romantic theme of her song, rushes out of their room and smashes the record.

Marilyn is naked in bed as well as in the shower, and wears a tight, red-hot dress (one man observes) "cut so low you can see her kneecaps." In one scene, as she lies in a hospital bed, a fringe of down shows up on her cheek. Adorned with heavy make-up, she has characteristically pouting lips, half-open mouth and girlish giggle. The camera then follows her and captures, from behind and in a long-shot, her patented sensuous walk. Always fueled by an erotic flame, she stirs the men around her as she moves. But her acting in this melodrama is mannered, uncertain and unconvincing.

When a Hollywood columnist noted that "her derrière looked like two puppies fighting under a silk sheet," Marilyn, stretching the truth in an amusing remark, defended her natural gait: "I learned to walk when I was ten months old, and I've been walking this way ever since." In a rather stilted statement, almost certainly written by a studio publicist and designed to separate her sleazy character on screen from the respectable Miss Monroe, she tried to dissociate herself from her role: "The girl I played was an amoral type whose plot to kill her husband was attempted with no apparent cost to her conscience. She had been picked out of a beer parlour, she entirely lacked the social graces and she was overdressed, over made-up, and completely wanton.

The uninhibited deportment in the motel room and the walk seemed normal facets of such a character's portrayal. I honestly believe such a girl would behave in that manner."[14]

In Marilyn's last two films of 1953 she played her typical and most popular incarnation: the gold-digger with a heart of gold. In *Gentlemen Prefer Blondes* – based on the book and musical comedy by Anita Loos and directed by Howard Hawks – a dumb blonde and a showgirl, both well endowed, sail to Paris to find rich husbands. In one scene of *Gentlemen* Marilyn wears a top hat, long black gloves, transparent black stockings, high heels and a gaudy sequined costume cut like a bathing suit. In another, wearing a strapless, floor-length, pink satin gown, with long-sleeved gloves, she steals the show by singing "Diamonds Are a Girl's Best Friend." The best lines in the film – "Those girls couldn't drown. Something about them tells me they couldn't sink" – were cut by the censor.

In *Gentlemen* Marilyn has pouting lips, whispery speech and a kittenish way of saying, "don't wowwy" and "get mawwied." She arrives at the ship bound for Cherbourg dressed in a leopard skin cape and muff, and asks, "Is this the way to Europe France?" When introduced to people on the ship, she says, "A pleasure to meet you I'm ever so sure." She's comically obsessed by jewels and money, and there's a long shot of her wiggling her behind while dancing in order to attract rich men. A little boy on the ship, who has a deep voice and uses uncommonly long words, provides an amusing contrast to her character. In a French court, the black-haired Jane Russell, wearing a blond wig, pretends to be Marilyn and imitates her peculiar mannerisms. Her rich but nerdy fiancé, Tommy Noonan, ironically praises her "wonderful willingness to learn." At the end of the movie, in a spirited exchange with Noonan's disapproving father, she seems serious but is not afraid to make fun of herself and allow him to mock her:

FATHER: They told me you were stupid. You don't seem stupid to me.

MARILYN: I can be smart when it's important. But most men don't like it. Except Gus. He's always been interested in my brains.

FATHER: He's not such a fool as all that.

While making *Gentlemen* Marilyn formed a rare friendship with her co-star. "Jane Russell, a down-home gal with no pretences or complexes despite her status, welcomed Marilyn at once and gained her confidence personally and professionally. She stuck with her endlessly through rehearsals and privately confided to her about life as the wife of a professional athlete, as Russell's husband, Bob Waterfield, was the Los Angeles Rams' quarterback" – and Marilyn was planning to marry Joe DiMaggio. She needed Russell's crucial support in this demanding role. Under the hot lights and with millions of dollars riding on her performance, she had to dance without losing her breath and, at the same time, hit her musical notes, her camera marks and her key light. Though *Gentlemen* was one of the most popular musicals of the 1950s, Marilyn felt justly aggrieved that Russell earned $200,000 for the picture and she – the blonde whom the gentlemen preferred – got only $18,000.

In the comedy *How to Marry a Millionaire*, three attractive women rent a New York penthouse and plan to trap three millionaires. The script of *Millionaire* alludes to Betty Grable's husband, the bandleader Harry James, and to Lauren Bacall's husband, "the man in *The African Queen*," but Marilyn had no husband to enhance her fame. The women's apartment is on Sutton Place, where Marilyn actually lived at the time. She arrives in her first scene wearing a fur muff, drinks her favorite champagne, and is breathy, naïve and excited. Too vain to wear glasses, especially when hunting for a husband, she has only one bit of business, constantly crashing into doors and furniture. The near-sighted joke is not funny. At the end of the movie, she gets on the wrong plane and sits next to David Wayne, who's on his way to unromantic Kansas City. The bespectacled Wayne has been beaten up by the crooked colleague who's stolen his check instead of sending it to the IRS, and Marilyn, for no apparent reason, marries her battered beau.

All three gold-diggers, including the "brainy" and sophisticated Bacall (who has the best part, but with third billing), are incredibly dumb. This movie suggests that pretty, empty-headed women are irresistibly attractive and desirable. Bacall mistakes the millionaire Cameron Mitchell for a gas-pump attendant merely because he's not wearing a tie. She deceives the elderly William Powell by declaring that she loves him, but cruelly jilts him at the altar to marry the younger Mitchell. The plot is hopelessly contrived, the male characters equally stereotyped, and all the women get married suddenly and unexpectedly. The picture could have been called "How *Not* to Marry a Millionaire." The forest ranger, Grable's husband, is poor; Wayne's money must be used to pay his huge tax debt; Mitchell is the only rich man.

In a scene cut from *Millionaire*, Marilyn is supposed to answer a phone call while having breakfast in bed. For some reason, she became hopelessly confused about the sequence, drank the coffee before it had been poured and answered the phone before it rang. Bacall, though sympathetic to Marilyn, was brutally frank about her faults: "She was really very selfish but she was so sad you couldn't dislike her. You just had to feel sorry for her, her whole life was a fuck-up." Bacall also recorded an incident in which Marilyn was either ironic-ally witty or hopelessly dim. When Bacall brought her little son, Stevie, onto the set, Marilyn asked, "'How old are you?' He said, 'I'm four.' She: 'But you're so *big* for four. I would have thought you were two or three.'"

Employing a metaphor that colleagues often used to describe the frequently remote, self-absorbed and almost somnambulistic Marilyn, the screenwriter and producer of the movie, Nunnally Johnson, said Marilyn "is generally something of a zombie. Talking to her is like talking to somebody *underwater*. She's very honest and ambitious and is either studying her lines or her face during all of her working hours, and there is nothing whatever to be said against her, but she's not material for warm friendship." Johnson also felt she was as unre-sponsive as "a sloth. You stick a pin in her and eight days later she says 'Ouch.'"[15] Despite Marilyn's difficulties, this first Cinemascope picture was a great success and grossed five times its lavish budget of $2.5 million.

Fox rewarded Marilyn's lucrative success in *Gentlemen* and *Millionaire* with a wretched part in *River of No Return* (1954), a cliché-ridden Western shot in the Canadian Rockies. Marilyn plays a saloon-singer, rigged out in tacky costumes, and sings four songs. She also falls in love with the hero, Robert Mitchum, who'd once worked in a wartime airplane factory with her ex-husband. In a reprise of the dangerous raft scene in *Niagara* – in which an innocent young woman escapes and the killer, Joseph Cotton, plunges over the falls to his death – Marilyn, Mitchum and his young son, played by Tommy Rettig, fight off outlaws and Indians while negotiating the perils of a treacherous river. While shooting the dangerous raft scene, Marilyn tripped over a rock in the river and tore a ligament. Her ankle swelled up badly, she was put into a cast and hobbled around on crutches for ten days.

Marilyn had even more trouble with the director Otto Preminger, another authoritarian Viennese, than she'd had with Fritz Lang. Preminger had recently played the brutal commandant of a prisoner-of-war camp in Billy Wilder's *Stalag 17*, which provoked Wilder's remark that he had to be very nice to Preminger because Wilder still had relatives in Germany. A strict disciplinarian, in absolute control of every aspect of the picture, Preminger quickly lost patience with Marilyn. Though she responded best when treated gently, he launched a frontal assault, yelled at her in front of everybody and reduced her to tears. He also insulted her by alluding to her shady past and declaring "she was so untalented that she should stick to her original 'profession.'"

Another major problem, which persisted throughout Marilyn's career, was her contentious practice of bringing her drama teacher onto the set, relying on her to decide whether a scene was successful or should be reshot, and obeying her instructions instead of the director's. After Preminger had ordered Lytess off the set, he was astonished to find that Marilyn had the power to bring her back. The final showdown came when Lytess tried to extend her authority over another actor. Preminger recalled that the thirteen-year-old Tommy Rettig, who'd always spoken his lines perfectly through many takes with Marilyn, suddenly forgot the words and began to cry. When Preminger asked what was troubling him,

> his mother said that Miss Lytess talked to Tommy and told him that at the age of fourteen all child actors lose their talent unless they take lessons and learn to use their instrument.
>
> "Just disappear," I told Miss Lytess. "You will never be on the set again and you are never to talk to this boy." Then I received a wire from Zanuck and he told me how many favors he had done me, giving me extra time on vacation, etc. "And now you must do me one favor. As a personal favor to me, you must let Miss Lytess on the set. She promises she will just watch and not talk to anyone." And so I did, and she was silent, just watched.

Marilyn was so unhappy about her injured ankle, her *mano a mano* with Preminger and the poor quality of the movie that she refused to do retakes in the Hollywood studio and simply disappeared. She was not afraid to defy the tyrannical Zanuck, who became apoplectic and complained to her agent Charles Feldman: "This is a crime for someone to hold up the completion of a picture. It's never happened before."[16]

By the time she became a major star, Marilyn had developed her full suite of typical mannerisms: her undulating walk, whispery voice, hesitant speech, half-open mouth and quivering upper lip. Her gestures are strikingly similar to those of Faye Greener, the heroine of Nathanael West's Hollywood novel *The Day of the Locust* (1939), who'd also modeled herself on silent movie stars:

Faye's affectations were so completely artificial that [Tod] found them charming. . . .

She lay stretched out on the divan with her arms and legs spread, as though welcoming a lover, and her lips were parted in a heavy, sullen smile. . . .

[She was] smiling in a peculiar, secret way and running her tongue over her lips. It was one of her most characteristic gestures and very effective. It seemed to promise all sorts of undefined intimacies. . . .

[All the men watched her] laugh, shiver, whisper, grow indignant, cross and uncross her legs, stick out her tongue, widen and narrow her eyes, toss her head so that her platinum hair splashed against the red plush of the chair back. The strange thing about her gestures and expressions was that they didn't really illustrate what she was saying. They were almost pure. It was as though her body recognized how foolish her words were and tried to excite her hearers into being uncritical.[17]

Marilyn's own day of the locust was fast approaching. She continued to suffer from physical illness as well as extreme insecurity and fear. She was habitually late and kept people waiting even after she arrived on the set, failed to learn or remember her lines and required an excessive number of takes for every scene. All this caused expensive delays in the shooting schedule and overruns in the budget. Her sudden disappearances, dissatisfaction with mediocre roles, fights with directors, interference by her drama teachers and battles over salary enraged the studio executives. All her difficulties in these early movies intensified when she became a star.

Four

Image and Identity
(1950s)

I

By 1953, against almost impossible odds, Marilyn had achieved the stardom she longed for. Yet her celebrity intensified her insecurity and unhappiness. The novelist Daphne Merkin wrote that Marilyn's "desperation was implacable in the face of fame, fortune and the love of celebrated men. . . . There is never sufficient explanation for the commotion of her soul" – though the reasons can, in fact, be found. Her wretched background, together with the pressures of life as a movie star, created her mental and emotional chaos. The psychiatrist Arnold Ludwig identified Marilyn's self-destructive personality traits (now all too familiar from the early deaths of so many young actors and singers): fear of rejection, abandonment and betrayal, confusion about her image and identity, emotional chaos, inability to control anger, damaging impulsiveness, lack of self-awareness, feelings of emptiness and suicidal behavior. All these problems made her difficult to deal with. She became impossible when everyone told her she was perfect, an idol who could do no wrong. Ambitious, driven by self-love and narcissism, she was also filled with self-loathing, with "smothering feelings of inferiority"[1] that made her feel she did not deserve the success she'd striven to achieve.

Accustomed to secrecy, she'd learned early on to distrust people: they had rebuffed and abandoned her as a child, seduced and discarded her as an adult. She loved animals, children and old people, who didn't threaten her. When married to Dougherty, she once tried to drag a cow out of the rain and into the house. To Marilyn, the young and the old, as Miller wrote, "were altogether vulnerable and could not wreak harm. But the rest of humanity was fundamentally dangerous and had to be confounded, disarmed by a giving sexuality."

This deep distrust made her unable to maintain friendships and establish normal contact with her colleagues. Marilyn had a way of protectively withdrawing into herself and cutting herself off from anyone who tried to get close to her. The cinematographer Jack Cardiff described it as "an aura of blank remoteness, of being in another world." Hildi Greenson, her psychiatrist's wife, sometimes "had a feeling she wasn't there because she wasn't paying much attention to you. She'd be very preoccupied with herself." And Miller's sister, Joan Copeland, observed that "she blocked you out if she didn't want you around. She just looked right at you without seeing you."[2]

Marilyn hid her toughness and iron ambition beneath a remote and kittenish demeanor, and knew how to use the people who used her. She had an uncanny ability to make people feel sorry for her and, as Sidney Skolsky observed, "everybody wanted to help her. Marilyn's supposed helplessness was her greatest strength." But she also remained trapped in the past. During emotional crises (and there were many) Marilyn would assume the role of helpless orphan and demand sympathetic compensation for childhood injuries. This sense of entitlement ruined her professional and personal relationships, and her role as victim became an excuse for her bad behavior.

Following the pattern of her rootless childhood, when she lived with the Bolenders, the Goddards and many others, she would move into new foster families – the homes of husbands, teachers, lovers and even doctors. She lived with the families of Jim Dougherty, Natasha Lytess, Fred Karger and (later on) of Joe DiMaggio, her manager Milton Greene, her teacher Lee Strasberg, Arthur Miller and her psychiatrist Ralph Greenson, and remained close to the families of her ex-husbands. Fearful of rejection, Marilyn was the victim of her own poor judgment. Many so-called friends convinced her that they were indispensable, and she allowed photographers, agents and movie executives, psychiatrists, publicists and parasites to exploit her and control her life.

Marilyn cut herself off from her childhood and early adult life by constantly severing relations with family, friends, teachers, lovers, husbands, managers, business partners and studio chiefs.[3] The Hollywood journalist Ezra Goodman, who wrote a *Time* cover story about Marilyn that was too critical to be published, observed that she "has a neat habit of latching onto people, of having them mother and father her, and then dumping them unceremoniously by the wayside when she has done with them. This goes for agents, drama coaches, columnists, lawyers, foster parents and just plain folk. She acquires them – and gets rid of them – in shifts. She likes to change people like other women change hats." But Goodman does not explain the reasons for her behavior. She distrusted people, wanted to reject the exploiters before they rejected her and thought she needed a new entourage for each new phase of her life. "Everybody is always tugging at you," she complained. "They'd all like a chunk of you." She moved from Lytess, Karger and Hyde to Greene, Miller and Strasberg, but had no close friends and was all alone when she most needed help.

Norman Mailer, confirming Goodman's point, detected another significant pattern in her life:

> For years she had obviously been capable of cutting people off. She had dropped Dougherty and Grace Goddard as well as her first agent Harry Lipton; she would speak poorly of DiMaggio in the Miller years, and would soon cut off Greene, and then eventually Miller. . . .
>
> It is characteristic of her to play leapfrog in love and work. She will start with Miller, then go to DiMaggio, come back to Miller, and pick up again with DiMaggio, just as she will alternate from Lytess to Chekhov back to Lytess and then on to the Strasbergs and the Method again, just as she leaves Hollywood to live in New York to return to Hollywood to leave again and return to die.

Once Marilyn turned against people, and it didn't take much to trigger her anger, she remained adamantly hostile and cut them out of her life. But (later on) she remained tragically loyal to the doctors who facilitated her drug addiction and the psychiatrists who failed to help her.

Miller explained why the ever-fearful Marilyn shifted impulsively from naïve optimism to bitter disillusionment with friends:

She was so extremely sensitive. She had this fear of any involvement which would endanger her personally. People in her
situation are either the victim or they're the aggressor, which
they can't bear the thought of. As time went on, the process of
her relationship with others quickened. A person would appear,
a stranger, some new person in her life, and he or she would
be a source of hope and confidence. But as she saw it, they were
deceitful because they wouldn't admit the selfishness of their
motives. It was a closed circle. If they were honest about their
intentions and told her that they *had* some ulterior motive, why
they were dead anyway. Neutralized persons, people like Rupert
Allan [her homosexual publicist], who made no demands upon
her, were okay. She loved [her make-up man] Whitey Snyder.
He was a simple, uncomplicated human being. She knew where
she stood with Whitey. She could turn to him with complete
confidence, always knowing he was predictable. She would always
know what he was going to say about anything.[4]

The always protean Marilyn wanted to be loved for her real self,
but didn't know who her real self actually was. She altered her names
from Baker and Mortensen to Dougherty, Monroe, DiMaggio and
Miller. She also adopted and abandoned several religions at each new
stage of her life. Though a non-believer, she was evangelical with the
Bolenders, a Christian Scientist with her mother, Catholic with
DiMaggio and Jewish with Miller.

Marilyn had spent her early life playing a series of submissive roles
and adapting herself to please other people. She was a dutiful daughter
to her mother, an obedient foster child to Grace Goddard, an enthusiastic wife to Jim Dougherty, an eager pupil to Natasha Lytess and
Michael Chekhov, a humble disciple to Fred Karger, a devoted mistress
to Joseph Schenck and Johnny Hyde. But after she became a great
star she was no longer the same person. She obliterated her past and
created a new identity, but found it strangely unfamiliar and became
alienated from the face and body that had made her famous. As the
publicity and pressure increased, it became more difficult and more
frightening to live up to her newly created image.

Shelley Winters noted that Norma Jeane didn't look at all like
Marilyn Monroe: "she was invisible when she wasn't wearing her
make-up and glamor outfits. No one, but no one, ever recognized

her." "Marilyn" was created by a cadre of Hollywood people – drama teachers, voice coaches, make-up artists, costume designers, publicity men, photographers, screenwriters and directors – who put her together. In addition to her dental improvements and plastic surgery, she had her hairline changed and other "work" done to her body. Her make-up man explained that, paradoxically, her "natural hair coloring and skin tone were actually improved by making them more artificial. The more make-up she wore, the more artificial her hair color, the softer and more natural she looked." As Howard Hawks remarked, "there wasn't a real thing about her. Everything was completely unreal." When a model, made up to look like a faithful replica of Marilyn, arrived in a studio where she was being photographed, "the copy was more convincing than the real thing: the Marilyn without make-up, with pale lips, dark-circled eyes, silent and tense, shrank back at the sight of her mirror image."[5]

The dream factory stole her real self – that profoundly insecure little girl, with a hunger for love that could never be appeased – and replaced it with an artificial goddess, with breathless voice and platinum hair, voluptuous body and alluring walk. No wonder she found it strange and disorienting. The more glamorous her public persona became, the more she searched for her inner being. Recognizing the fissure in her character, she'd look in the mirror and encourage her alter-ego to match the ideal by pleading, "Come on, face, give me a break." She never got used to her new self and wondered, if she couldn't be herself, who else *could* she be?

The transformation forced her to adopt a new identity. "I always felt I was a nobody," she said, "and the only way for me to be some-body was to be – well, somebody else. Which is probably why I wanted to act." Her two identities and her profession as an actress allowed the shy exhibitionist to play many different roles. But she also claimed to be aware of the dangers: "I can be anything they want. If they expect me to be innocent, I'm innocent. . . . Of course, you gotta watch out not to get confused."[6] Marilyn was in character and behavior remarkably like another flamboyant performer: Oscar Wilde. Both were artificial, witty and amusing, and loved performing in private life. Both were hedonistic, promiscuous and defiantly immoral, addicted to drugs, recklessly self-destructive and finally devoured by their public persona.

II

Marilyn's lifelong quest for self-improvement, her constant attempts to better her acting and her mind, were her most persistent and most admirable qualities. In this respect, she was like the young Ben Franklin and the ambitious young heroes in pursuit of the American Dream: Horatio Alger's Ragged Dick and Scott Fitzgerald's Jay Gatsby. Hollywood people in general were educated and sophisticated. In 1941, a few years before she broke into films, 57 percent of the movie colony had gone to college. She was not educated, cultured or intellectual, but she was clever, witty and bright, and wanted to be socially at ease.

Marilyn sometimes had difficulty absorbing, or even finding, the information she was so eager to acquire. After taking an evening course in art appreciation and literature at UCLA extension school in 1951, she naïvely said "there was a new genius to hear about every day. At night I lay in bed wishing I could have lived in the Renaissance. . . . Of course, if I had lived in the Renaissance I would be dead by now." When she wanted to find out more about her body, she bought a reprint of Vesalius' gorgeous, grisly woodcuts, originally published in 1543, which tore off the human envelope and revealed the bones and the nervous system. She treated the book as if it were a popular exercise manual rather than a complex and often incomprehensible anatomical study that had no practical use.

Marilyn owned 400 books by serious American, English and European writers, and she must have lost or abandoned many others during her frequent moves.[7] She'd flip through magazines and read film scripts, but her last secretary, May Reis, never saw her read anything but pulp novels by Harold Robbins. Miller confirmed that "with the possible exception of Colette's *Chéri* and a few short stories, I had not known her to read anything all the way through." Photos of her holding *The Brothers Karamazov* and *Ulysses* seemed absurd, but Christopher Isherwood saw her studying Molly Bloom's monologue in the last chapter of Joyce's novel. Her reading was haphazard, and she probably tried to read at least part of the books she acquired by impulse or intuition. She was entirely serious about improving her mind, was encouraged and taught by Miller, and wanted to be able to understand conversations about books.

Marilyn not only read poetry, but also wrote it to express her feelings when she was depressed. She often sent her poems, which resembled the musings of a sentimental teenager, to Miller's college friend Norman Rosten, who preserved and later published them. In one poem she identified with a weeping willow tree in a storm:

> I stood beneath your limbs
> and you flowered and finally clung to me
> and when the wind struck with . . . the earth
> and sand – you clung to me.

In an untitled poem Marilyn, like a mother, tries to give to a doll the love she never had as a child. The orphan wants to have her own baby, but also has to fight off her suicidal impulses:

> Don't cry my doll
> Don't cry
> I hold you and rock you to sleep.
> Hush hush I'm pretending now
> I'm not your mother who died.
>
> Help help
> Help I feel life coming closer
> When all I want is to die.

"A Sorry Song" describes her struggle to emerge from depression and pain after trying to kill herself:

> I've got a tear hanging over
> my beer that I can't let go.
> it's too bad
> I feel sad
> When I got all my life behind me.
>
> If I had a little relief
> From this grief
> Then
> I could find a drowning
> straw to hold on to.

it's great to be alive
They say I'm lucky to be alive
it's hard to figure out
when everything I feel – hurts![8]

If Marilyn's great strength was a desire to learn, her great personal and professional fault was chronic lateness. One of her make-up men, who had to put up with her whims, complained that "if I was two minutes late she was furious, though she thought nothing of keeping others waiting for hours and days." Billy Wilder, who suffered terribly from her lateness on the set, made many bitter cracks about it. "If she wanted to go to school," he said, "she should go to railroad engineering school and learn to run on time." But she didn't have the normal sense of time, didn't distinguish early from late, and was often puzzled (or pretended to be) when colleagues became irritated or enraged by her behavior.

The reasons for her lateness were practical and psychological, self-indulgent and egoistic. She began to suffer from insomnia, took sleeping pills and had a hard time getting up in the morning. Early calls at the studio were for her almost impossible. It took her an inordinately long time to prepare her face to meet the faces that she'd meet: to bathe, dress, put on her make-up and create a glamorous look. Despite all her coaching, she always felt she was never properly prepared. She was afraid that she might not know her lines (*the* unforgivable sin of acting), might give a poor performance or might not look her best. When she was chided for keeping everyone waiting, she justified her behavior by saying, "I've been waiting all my life."[9]

Her lateness became an assertion of power that confirmed her status as a star. Her behavior as an operatic diva tested the patience of the director and endurance of the studio executives, yet proved that they would put up with anything to have her in their film. The more difficult she was, the more indecisive and dilatory, the more desirable she seemed. She became the center of attention when she was *not* there as well as when she *was*. She made everybody wonder – as if they were an audience waiting for her appearance on stage – where she was and when she would arrive. She wanted people to be keen to see her, to make her feel that she was desperately wanted. She could always play the orphan card, and felt a strange satisfaction in punishing the people who'd once rejected her. Unaware of or ignoring the intense hostility she aroused by her selfish and costly behavior, she confessed that "It makes something in me happy to be late. People are waiting for me. People are eager to see me. I remember all the years I was unwanted, all the hundreds of times nobody wanted to see the little servant girl, Norma Jeane – not even her mother." Her lateness was a display of power and form of revenge for past humiliations and neglect. It forced the studio to spend millions of extra dollars on the movie that they'd refused to spend on *her*.

Marilyn also enhanced her status and displayed her power by creating (in the absence of any real friends) her own paid courtiers, palace guard and personal support group. The members of her entourage – which included drama coach, publicist and manager, masseur and make-up man, hairdresser and driver, secretary and maid – acted as her babysitter, nanny, governess and minder, as her companion, confidante, comforter and confessor. Oblivious of the impression she made, she claimed that "I feel stronger if the people around me on the set love me. It creates an aura of love, and I believe I can give a better performance." But she created more animosity than affection, expected too much from people and was frequently disappointed.

There are some intriguing similarities between the lives and characters of Marilyn and Evita Perón (1919–52). Both came from poor backgrounds; were illegitimate outcasts, rejected by their fathers. Each began as a model, became a singer, dancer and actress, and made some terrible movies early in her career. They recreated themselves as blondes and became national idols. They slept their way to the top, replacing mistresses and wives, and discarding protectors when they were no longer needed. They were sexually involved with the president of the country, and Evita actually realized Marilyn's dream of becoming First Lady. They fulfilled the fantasies of the masses, who adored them, and inspired crowds to respond with hysterical adoration. They died early, in their mid-thirties, and were mourned by millions.

The life of Diana, Princess of Wales, who was born the year before Marilyn's death and also died at the age of thirty-six, was also remarkably like Marilyn's. Like Marilyn, Diana seemed normal and happy until she was thrown into the cauldron of publicity and overwhelming fame, and had great trouble adjusting to her new image and identity. "Before Diana was famous," Tina Brown observed, "she was an uninteresting schoolgirl – nice, polite, uninquiring, uninspiring. What made her change was being royal, rich, famous, watched, desired." Just as Marilyn became a star in the particular Hollywood environment, a world with its own strange rules and behavior, so Diana was even more abruptly swallowed up into a closed and ritualized family who tormented and ultimately rejected her. Unable to escape unscathed from the obsessive attention of the media, both women became angry and abusive, physically and mentally ill, depressed and suicidal. They exerted tremendous power over other people, but could not control their own lives.

Both women were poorly educated and, in Diana's words, believed they were "thick." Aware of their intellectual limitations, they often wanted a quick conversational fix. Marilyn asked her doctor, "how can I learn something about the most famous philosophers in a few hours? I'm going to a party tonight and I want to be able to hold my own." Diana asked a clever friend, "I'm sitting next to [the French president] Mitterrand at lunch in fifteen minutes. Quick! Give me something to say."[10] Both expected their so-called friends, as well as their elusive lovers, to be constantly available on the phone, and when suffering from insomnia would often wake them in the middle of the night. They never seemed to get enough love from their romantic attachments.

To compensate for her lack of affection, Diana, like Marilyn, employed "a squadron of brisk apparatchiks whose job [was] to answer" her whims and keep her spirits up. Just as Marilyn had her masseurs, drama teachers and psychiatrists, so the New Age Diana, desperately in search of salvation, hired "the celebrity servant class of healing therapists, astrologers, acupuncturists, hairdressers, colonic irrigationists, aromatherapists, shoe designers, and fashion therapists." Both women had a profound sympathy for poor, sick and outcast people, but could alienate and enrage as well as charm and seduce everyone else. Like Marilyn, Diana, "so genuinely compassionate with strangers, was capable of being cruelly dismissive of people closest to her."

Both women summoned up "the best of the nation's image makers to help them create her alternative reality."[11] Marilyn helped revive a declining Hollywood, Diana revived the increasingly unpopular royal family. Both encouraged and cooperated with the media, which then invaded their private lives and made them miserable. Norman Rosten described Marilyn's dilemma:

Individuals who make up the crowd regress, and they can be unpredictable, even violent. They follow her, wait in doorways, shout at her, leap after her into taxis, keep watch on the street below her window. They send letters – imploring, demanding, weeping, threatening – the mad or bewitched seekers. They ask for autographs, money, photos, articles of her clothing. They propose marriage or trysts, find her phone number and use obscenities.

Marilyn noted how intrusive and offensive the crowd could be: "People you run into feel that, well, who is she – who does she think she is, Marilyn Monroe? They feel [your] fame gives them some kind of privilege to walk up to you and say anything to you, you know, of any kind of nature – and it won't hurt your feelings – like it's happening to your clothing." After creating an elaborate public image, both women had to hide and disguise themselves to avoid the threatening mob.

Marilyn and Diana hid their intense distress behind a radiant image and, with a star's natural ability, conveyed a public impression that was quite different from the way they actually felt. Both became weary of their demanding and oppressive public persona. As the princess exclaimed, "Let's face it, even I have had enough of Diana now – and I *am* Diana."[12] Paradoxically, both extraordinarily desirable women were often rejected and frequently alone. The fatal car crash on Marilyn's wedding day, when she was pursued by reporters in a high-speed car chase, seemed to foreshadow the similar accident that killed Diana in 1997.

III

Hollywood movies, governed by the moralistic Production Code, depicted sexual and social life the way it was supposed to be, not as it really was. Criminals were always punished, embraces led to marriage, sex was chaste. On screen, open-mouthed kisses were proscribed and married couples were not allowed to share the same bed. In 1953, the year Marilyn became a star, Alfred Kinsey published *Sexual Behavior in the Human Female*, a book which tore away the puritanical façade to reveal the difference between conventional morality and actual sexual practices. People who took their ideas about sex from movies must have felt their own behavior was somehow wrong. So they were relieved and delighted to discover, as Kinsey showed, that in the early 1950s more than half of American women had lost their virginity before marriage, that a quarter of married women had committed adultery and that most women actually *liked* sex. His scientific study unexpectedly sold 250,000 copies. His enlightening and liberating views were widely discussed in the press and paved the way for the sexual revolution of the 1960s.

Marilyn's rise to prominence coincided with Kinsey's revelations. A free spirit whose personal behavior seemed to match her image on the screen, she reinforced Kinsey's belief that it was all right to do anything (between consenting adults) that provided sexual pleasure. Wittily outrageous in her last interview, she declared, "I think that sexuality is only attractive when it's natural and spontaneous. . . . I never quite understood it – this sex symbol – I always thought symbols were those things you clash together! . . . If I'm going to be a symbol of something I'd rather have it [be] sex than some other things they've got symbols of!"

It's sadly ironic that Marilyn herself did not live to see the sexual revolution and suffered greatly for being its symbol. She'd experienced intense sexual pleasure with Jim Dougherty and with Fred Karger in the mid-1940s; but by the 1950s, under the stress of promiscuous sex and stardom, she'd become frigid. In the late 1940s, when she was modeling and trying to break into movies, she rarely had natural and spontaneous sex. Instead, she was a prostitute, in cars on shady side-streets, in return for small amounts of money to buy food. It's astonishing – after all her acting lessons and her brief appearances in movies – that she would not only sell her body for the price of a meal, but would also risk humiliation and shame, predatory pimps and police, robbery and beating, sadism and sodomy, venereal disease and pregnancy.

When selling herself, or with romantic liaisons and long-time lovers, Marilyn, always eager to please, meekly agreed to men's demands to have sex without contraceptives and got pregnant again and again. She later made the horrifying confession that she'd had as many as twelve abortions. The Hollywood screenwriter Ivan Moffat, who knew about this from personal experience, wrote that "in 1951 there was no question of anyone getting an abortion without extreme difficulty, danger and great cost." In these sleazy surgeries Marilyn repeatedly risked severe pain, hemorrhage, infection, puncture of her womb, permanent injury and even death.

Orson Welles remarked that almost everyone in Hollywood had slept with her. When the photographer Larry Schiller argued with Mailer about their book on Marilyn, Schiller tried to settle the dispute by claiming, "At least I fucked her and you didn't." Apart from the men she bedded while married to Dougherty, street clientele, casual pick-ups, movie moguls and the legions who claimed to or may actually have been her sexual partners, she had two dozen significant lovers (including three husbands) during the last twenty years of her life.[13] Marilyn's apparently superficial and transparent character was actually quite ambiguous. She was naïve and innocent as well as flirtatious and seductive, unaware of conventional morality as well as completely indifferent to it, in love with her companions as well as merely distracted by them. She was at the same time Henry James' disingenuous and daring Daisy Miller and James Joyce's earthy and funny, unfaithful and sexually voracious Molly Bloom.

With no parents, siblings or relatives to guide and protect her, Marilyn was essentially on her own: always vulnerable and frequently hurt. Unable to form a solid union with anyone, she suffered from lifelong depression and a profound sense of loss. Men, sensing her emotional chaos, tried to rescue or exploit her. The photographer Philippe Halsman wrote that "when she faced a man she didn't know, she felt safe and secure only when she knew that the man desired her; so everything in her life was geared to provoke this feeling." But after arousing this desire, she found the men were intimidated – both before and after bedding her – by her overwhelming sexual reputation. As she told Susan Strasberg, "I have to initiate relationships. . . . They don't know what the hell to do with me. . . . I almost have to say 'Do you want to fuck?' to get it out of the way. After they get me, they don't know what to do, either." Awkward and unsatisfactory sex was usually followed by disappointing silence and a hasty departure.

Marlon Brando described Marilyn as a "sensitive, misunderstood person, much more perceptive than was generally assumed. She had been beaten down, but had a strong emotional intelligence – a keen intuition for the feelings of others, the most refined type of intelligence." Despite all her sexual experience, Marilyn also felt insecure about her own technique. The morning after sleeping with Brando, she confessed, "I don't know if I do it the right way." She not only had to be the bold seducer and active performer, but also had to fulfill men's erotic fantasies. "They go to bed with *her*, and they wake up with *me*," she told Susan Strasberg, "and they feel cheated. I feel for these guys. They expected the rockets' red glare, fireworks, and bombs bursting, you know, all that stuff, only I feel sorry for me, too." She could not possibly satisfy their passionate imaginings nor match the sexual newsreels that played in their heads.

After strenuous efforts, she complained that "I'm a failure as a woman. My men expect so much of me because of the image they've made of me and that I've made of myself, as a sex symbol. Men expect so much, and I can't live up to it. They expect bells to ring and whistles to whistle, but my anatomy is the same as any other woman's. I can't live up to it."[14] But her body, beautiful on the outside and ruined within, was not the same as other women's. She liked the companionship of homosexuals, who would escort her without expecting a sexual payoff at the end of the evening.

Marilyn's memories of her childhood abuse made sex seem dirty and repulsive. Yet, lonely and desperate for affection, she hoped to win men's love by trying to please them. Like the beautiful but frigid writer Martha Gellhorn, Hemingway's third wife, she was willing to sleep with almost any man who really wanted her. Serious yet naïve, Marilyn took sex lightly and offered the only commodity she had as a reward. Sex was her way of saying thank you.

Though sexually available, she was emotionally distant and unresponsive. She gave pleasure and asked nothing but approval in return, and admitted that she could not have orgasms. She made a free-flowing tape for her psychiatrist, with "extensive comments about her problems achieving orgasm – in very blunt language." Emphasizing the crucial paradox in her life, she bitterly said, "I just don't get out of sex what I hear other women do. Maybe I'm . . . a sexless . . . sex goddess."

Her lovers and supposed friends confirmed that she became sexually frigid, and that neither her affairs nor her marriages satisfied her. The photographer André de Dienes said that "Marilyn is not sexy at all. She has very little feeling toward sex. She is not sensuous." The make-up man George Masters frankly called her "an ice-cold cookie, as frigid as forty below zero, and about as passionate as a calculating machine."[15] The costume designer Billy Travilla, who knew her in the early 1950s, was more sympathetic and felt the need to protect her, but was also disappointed by her inability to respond: "Her lips would tremble. Those lips! And a man can't fight it. You don't want that baby to cry. . . . I think she wanted to love, but she could only love herself. She was totally narcissistic." Nico Minardos, a young Greek actor who met her in 1952, declared "she could never have a climax, though she would try so hard." And the actress Jeanne Carmen, her neighbor in 1961, stated that "Marilyn got nothing out of sex at all. She'd never had an orgasm – she used to fake it."[16]

Marilyn's frigidity seems to have been caused by searing guilt about her prostitution and abortions, by her inability to meet the unrealistic expectations of her lovers, and by the psychoanalysis that revived painful memories of childhood abuse. She could never regain her girlish innocence, tainted early on by sexual molestation. Apart from countless liaisons, she'd been debased by prostitution as a starlet, couch-casting as an actress and adultery as a wife. Hollywood was filled with people who'd slept with her and who might at any time reappear, with disgusting leers and probing hands, to remind her of her past. No wonder she felt, in her innermost being, polluted and damaged, ashamed and desperate for redemption. She felt she was being punished for her sexual sins in two essential ways: she could not have orgasms and she could not have children.

Five
Joe DiMaggio
(1952–1954)

I

Marilyn met Joe DiMaggio in March 1952, the month of the nude calendar scandal and just before her appendix operation, when she particularly needed emotional support. She became a star, while she was seeing him, the following year; married him, nearly two years after their first meeting, in January 1954; and divorced him, only nine months later, in October. Marilyn and DiMaggio had very different temperaments and expectations, but thought their problems could be overcome, or at least ignored. Though they loved each other, they were essentially incompatible and couldn't live together.

DiMaggio, the eighth of nine children born to a Sicilian fisherman north of San Francisco, was the greatest baseball player of his time. He had a fifty-six-game hitting streak in 1941 that has never been surpassed, and led the New York Yankees to ten American League pennants and eight World Series championships. In Hemingway's *The Old Man and the Sea* (1952), the brave Cuban fisherman frequently mentions "the great DiMaggio" as a touchstone of stoicism and humility. Strong and manly, with an athletic, muscular body, impeccably dressed and manicured, he was a handsome and dignified American hero.

DiMaggio had been married to Dorothy Arnold, a nightclub singer and small-time actress, from 1939 to 1943 and had a son, Joe, Jr., who would become close to Marilyn. Retired from baseball in 1951 at the age of thirty-seven, DiMaggio interviewed guests on television before and after Yankee games and played exhibition baseball. He was a well-paid corporate executive and a wealthy man who owned a house in the Marina district in San Francisco, a boat, a Cadillac and a substantial portfolio of investments. He hung around his restaurant on San Francisco's Fisherman's Wharf, dined with friends, signed autographs, read the sports section of newspapers, went to the racetrack, toured the golf courses, played poker and gin rummy, and was adored by his pals. But he had more energy than occupations.

Marilyn was reluctant to see DiMaggio, who whetted his appetite on the nude calendar, when he first tried to meet her. Imagining him to be more like a Mafioso in movies than a professional athlete, she said, "I don't like men in loud clothes, with checked suits and big muscles and pink ties. I get nervous." She was two hours late for their first date, at an Italian restaurant on Sunset Strip, but DiMaggio, always the gentleman, waited patiently with his friends. Marilyn, who'd never been to a baseball game, was pleasantly surprised by his appearance:

> I had thought I was going to meet a loud, sporty fellow. Instead I found myself smiling at a reserved gentleman in a gray suit, with a gray tie and a sprinkle of gray in his hair. There were a few polka dots in his tie. If I hadn't been told that he was some sort of ball player, I would have guessed he was either a steel magnate or a congressman.
>
> He said, "I'm glad to meet you," and then fell silent for the whole rest of the evening.

Calling the great DiMaggio "some sort of ball player" was like calling Marilyn "some sort of actress." But (as with Miller) words were less important than looks and gestures, physical attraction and intuitive sympathy. After driving around for a while after dinner, they spent their first night together.

They were surprised to discover that they had many things in common. Both came from a working-class background and, completely on their own, had achieved tremendous success. Both had left high school in the tenth grade, and had poor health: DiMaggio suffered from calcium deposits, bone spurs, arthritis and stomach ulcers. Both were loners, shy and uneasy with strangers, and had the well-founded suspicion that everyone tried to exploit them. DiMaggio, immediately wanting to protect her, called her "a warm, bighearted girl . . . that everybody took advantage of." Most important, he seemed to accept her for what she was, despite her promiscuous past, though he never actually forgave her for it.

They saw each other as frequently as possible in Los Angeles and San Francisco. They went fishing on his boat, and she learned to cook his favorite spaghetti sauce (though he liked Mama's better). When Marilyn opened the door of his house for young trick-or-treaters on Halloween, word quickly spread around the neighborhood and grown-up men put on costumes and rang her bell. Their sex life, according to Marilyn, was extremely satisfying. "Joe's biggest bat," she later declared, "is not the one he uses on the field. . . . If that's all it takes, we'd still be married." He was one of those lovers who performed well in bed, but didn't know what to do with her afterwards. Mailer wrote that they'd "lie around in the intervals suffering every boredom of two people who had no cheerful insight into the workings of the other's mind."[1]

DiMaggio had been divorced for a decade; Marilyn had been mostly on her own since Dougherty went overseas in 1944. The adjustment to domestic life, after playing the field for so long, was difficult for both of them. They decided to get married, on very short notice, at San Francisco City Hall. The only guests were his closest friends: the manager of his restaurant, Reno Barsocchini, and his old teammate, Lefty O'Doul, accompanied by his wife. Marilyn, dressed demurely for the occasion, invited neither friends nor Hollywood associates to the ceremony. The Catholic Church did not recognize the marriage of a divorced man, and the Archbishop of San Francisco excommunicated DiMaggio as a wedding present. They drove down the coast to Paso Robles; and DiMaggio – not entirely occupied with his bride – made sure the motel room had a television set on the first night of their honeymoon. She told the press that she hoped to have two, or even six children, but never became pregnant with DiMaggio.

DiMaggio had agreed to play exhibition games in Japan in February 1954 and Marilyn, who'd never been abroad, went with him on their honeymoon. He got his first bitter taste of her fame when they were dangerously mobbed at Honolulu airport and when she completely upstaged him in baseball-crazed Japan. As she stood on the balcony of the Imperial Hotel in Tokyo to greet her fans, she recalled Mussolini addressing the crowd from a balcony in Rome and felt "like I was a dictator or something." While she was in Japan, an American army general asked if she would entertain the soldiers in Korea (the war had ended the previous July, but there was still a big military presence) and she readily agreed. A military newspaper called her "the biggest thing to hit Korea since the Inchon landing."

Performing for the first time before a live, rapturous audience, Marilyn did ten shows in four days and entertained 100,000 troops. The soldiers were muffled up in fur hats with ear flaps, heavy winter jackets and thick combat boots, while she gamely appeared, outdoors and in the extremely cold Korean winter, in high heels and a tight, strapless, low-cut dress. She enlivened the show with some suggestive jokes, and asked, when describing sweater girls, "take away their sweaters and what have you got?"

She sang four songs: "Diamonds Are a Girl's Best Friend," "Bye Bye Baby," "Somebody Loves Me" and "Do It Again." The refrain in the last song – "Come and get it, you won't regret it" – was considered too provocative for the sexually starved troops and had to be dropped from the repertory. She excited the audience, who screamed with delight and craved what she was offering, and brought the shows to a frenzied climax. (The scene in *Apocalypse Now*, when the exotic dancers are flown in to Vietnam, captures the kind of excitement that Marilyn aroused.)

A military photographer who accompanied the tour praised both her exciting performance and her sympathetic attitude:

> This wasn't an obligation she had to fulfill, and it wasn't a self-promotion. Of all the performers who came to us in Korea – and there were a half dozen or so – she was the best. She showed no nervousness and wasn't anything like a dumb blonde. When a few of us photographers were allowed to climb up on the stage after her show, she was very pleasant and cooperative. . . . It was bitter cold, but she was in no hurry to leave. Marilyn was a great entertainer. She made thousands of GIs feel she really cared.

When she came back from the successful trip, she told DiMaggio that 100,000 men had been clapping and cheering for her, and exclaimed, "You've never seen anything like it." To which he replied, "Yes, I have."

DiMaggio's baseball career ended just as Marilyn's fame reached its peak. They never resolved the central conflict, either before or during their brief marriage, about whether she would retire or continue to work in films. Like Jane Russell, she hoped to maintain both her movie career and a stable private life, but discovered that she could not have both. He expected her to give up films and become a wife, mother and housekeeper; she said, "he wanted me to be the beautiful ex-actress, just as he was the great former ballplayer." (Grace Kelly would give up her career in 1956, but – unlike Marilyn – she became Princess of Monaco, had many official duties, and received only the most dignified and respectful publicity.)

DiMaggio didn't think she had talent and discouraged her career as an actress. He disliked the movie business and was unhappy about the time she spent at work. Used to the spotlight himself and jealous as a husband, he resented the publicity that not only focused on Marilyn, but was also an intrusive, prurient and vulgar violation of his wife. Marilyn explained their irreconcilable differences: "He didn't like the women I played. He said they were sluts. He didn't like the actors kissing me. He didn't like my costumes. He didn't like anything about my movies. And he *hated* my clothes. He said they were too tight and attracted the wrong kind of attention. . . . Joe said when he was a baseball star, he got whatever he wanted, but there I was, a movie star, and Hollywood people just pushed me around."[2]

II

In late 1953, Joseph Schenck, still an executive producer at Fox, hired Ben Hecht to generate publicity by ghost-writing Marilyn's autobiography. A leading Hollywood screenwriter, Hecht had written *Wuthering Heights* (1939) and Hitchcock's *Notorious* (1946), and had worked on three of Marilyn's minor pictures: *Love Happy* (1950), *Monkey Business* and *O. Henry's Full House* (both 1952). Hecht signed a contract with Doubleday and, subject to her approval, sold the serial rights to *Collier's* magazine. Shortly before Marilyn's marriage, Hecht went to San Francisco and spent four days with her, talking to her about her life while his secretary took notes. After he began the book, she went over the first twelve pages, and made some intelligent and helpful suggestions.

When Hecht finished the book, he rented a bungalow in the

Beverly Hills Hotel, where Marilyn was living, and spent two more days reading the story to her in the presence of his secretary and his sometime collaborator, Charles Lederer. Hecht had to project a favorable, if false, public image of the star. He had to base his book on Marilyn's unreliable or deliberately distorted memories, and he needed sensational material in order to sell it. She explained how one aspect of her past had been considerably exaggerated: "I never intended to make all that much about being an orphan. It's just that Ben Hecht was hired to write this story about me, and he said, 'Okay, sit down and try to think up something interesting about yourself.' Well, I was boring, and I thought maybe I'd tell him about them putting me in the orphanage, and he said that was great and wrote it, and that became the main thing suddenly."

After Hecht's reading, Marilyn was pleased with his work and said her life had finally been portrayed in "a dignified and exciting manner." Hecht's wife, Rose, later recalled that "Marilyn laughed and cried and expressed herself 'thrilled,' said she 'never imagined so wonderful a story could be written about her' and that Mr. Hecht had 'captured every phase' of her life." When Marilyn had approved the book, Doubleday paid him an advance of $5,000.

Hecht's agent, Jacques Chambrun, then entered the scene and ruined the project. A charlatan and bogus count, Chambrun was an ugly man with "a certain charm and elegance. Everything about him gave off an aura of prosperity and good-natured joie de vivre." Chambrun, who'd been Somerset Maugham's wartime agent, "not only charged exorbitant commissions of 20 to 30 percent, but also kept more than $30,000 of Maugham's royalties." Chambrun, true to form, forged Hecht's signature on a contract, secretly sold Marilyn's story to a London tabloid, the *Empire News*, for £1,000 and kept all the money.

The unauthorized appearance of the story in the scandalous English newspaper upset Marilyn. Advised by DiMaggio, who strongly objected to publication, she withdrew her agreement, began a vitriolic legal dispute with Hecht – and then flew off to Japan. Enraged by the sudden turn of events, Hecht felt that if Marilyn prevented him from publishing the book, the results would be catastrophic. He would have wasted all his time on the project, the writing he'd done and the money he'd spent, and would have to repay Doubleday's advance. But, like the Hollywood directors and studio executives, Hecht found Marilyn extremely stubborn and difficult to deal with.

Rose Hecht, writing or at least signing her husband's letters to Marilyn's lawyer and to his publisher, emphasized Marilyn's vacillating, irresponsible and often impossible behavior. She declared that Marilyn had lied to the Hollywood columnist Louella Parsons by claiming she'd never seen any of the written material. By changing her mind and reneging on their agreement, Rose maintained, Marilyn had acted in bad faith and responded to their pleas with "lies, fantasies and broken promises." Referring to Marilyn's sleazy past, Rose wrote, "far from harming her reputation, or libeling her in any way, Mr. Hecht aggrandized a young woman whose story has appeared in every pulp magazine." As Rose became more and more furious, she called Marilyn schizophrenic, her lawyer offensive, and Chambrun a liar and fraud. Ken McCormick, the editor at Doubleday, said that Hecht had been "dealing with thieves and dolts" and agreed that he'd been "thoroughly and abominably cheated."[3] But if his firm could not publish the book, Hecht would have to – and did – return the advance. The possibility of publication was revived after Marilyn's death, but *My Story*, which did not discuss the last nine years of her life, was not published until Stein and Day brought it out in 1974.

When Marilyn and DiMaggio returned from Japan and tried to live a normal life, they soon became aware of their radical differences in character, temperament and interests. He liked to live in San Francisco, she had to work in Los Angeles; he hated the movies, she had no interest in sports; he disliked her teacher, Lytess, she was devoted to her; he disliked publicity, she thrived on it; he was punctual, she was always late; he was neat and orderly, she was messy and chaotic; he was cautious and outwardly calm, she was impulsive and emotional; he spent his time with family and old friends at home, she liked to go out to movies and restaurants; she'd become interested in books, he read only newspapers. While he was riveted to the television set, which she felt should be removed from the bedroom, she read scripts, learned her lines and spoke to colleagues on the phone. She complained that "he's so boring I could scream. All he knows and talks about is baseball." Only quarrels relieved the boredom.

They soon found they had nothing to say to each other. When they lived in a rented house in Beverly Hills, Marilyn recalled, "Everything went fine for a while, until Joe started complaining about my working all the time. He would even find little things to upset him after a while. It got so we didn't even talk to each other for

days. I began living in one part of the house and Joe in the other."
When they did speak, she deliberately provoked him into arguments,
even violence. A friend said that "Marilyn could be a smartass, and
when she drank champagne she'd goad him. And they weren't intellectuals, they couldn't discuss their pain, so they lashed out at each
other." DiMaggio would sometimes lose his temper and begin to slap
her around. Marilyn told friends that he'd hit her and they saw bruises
on her body. But she did not, as expected, mention this fact in the
divorce court.

DiMaggio had strict ideas about how a wife should behave and a
well-founded Sicilian jealousy. After they'd moved to separate
bedrooms, Marilyn looked elsewhere for affection and "had two or
possibly three affairs, all brief, all casual, late in her marriage to Joe."[4]
But at least one them, with her voice coach Hal Schaefer in July
1954, was not at all casual. Schaefer tried to commit suicide when
DiMaggio forced her to break off the affair, and DiMaggio again
became jealous when Marilyn visited Schaefer in the hospital.

III

The witty and sophisticated Billy Wilder, who made *The Seven Year
Itch* and *Some Like It Hot*, was (along with Huston, Hawks and George
Cukor) one of the few directors with enough courage, patience and
masochism to do two pictures with Marilyn. The resourceful and
enterprising son of a hotelier and small-time businessman in the old
Austro-Hungarian Empire, he had briefly studied law in Vienna and
worked as a newspaper reporter in Berlin, where he supplemented
his income as a dance partner and gigolo. When Hitler came to power
in 1933, Wilder fled to Paris and directed his first feature film. He
reached Hollywood in 1934, and roomed with a fellow exile, Peter
Lorre. A versatile genius, Wilder was both co-author and director of
superb films: *Double Indemnity* (1945), *The Lost Weekend* (1948), *Sunset
Boulevard* (1951) and *Stalag 17* (1954), as well as many witty and
romantic comedies.

In *The Seven Year Itch* (1955), co-produced by Wilder and Marilyn's
agent Charles Feldman, she plays "The Girl," a sexy blonde on the
loose in a summer sublet in Manhattan who gets involved with the
man downstairs. Her co-star Tom Ewell plays the married New York
publisher who's sent his wife and son to Maine for the summer. Ewell

had played the role of the unattractive, ineffectual and permanently frustrated man in the successful Broadway play, and had a much bigger part than Marilyn.

The Girl is the classic dumb blonde character, whose speech is peppered with sexual innuendos and unconscious double entendres. When the trailing cord of her electric appliance gets stuck, she exclaims, "my fan is caught in the door." She gets her big toe (the one Miller had delicately held on their first date) suggestively stuck in the faucet of her bathtub and has to have it extricated by a distracted but discreet plumber. She excites Ewell by declaring, "When it's hot like this, I always keep my undies in the icebox." And she has a touching speech about her preference for the kind of timid, unassuming man (like Ewell himself), rather than for the handsome and conceited hero a pretty girl is supposed to like.

The film was laced with sly allusions and in-jokes that delighted the knowing audience. There's a reference to Charles Lederer, who wrote the script of *Gentlemen Prefer Blondes*, and a parody of the daring scene – passionate kissing in the wet sand as the waves break over their bodies – in *From Here to Eternity* (1953). The film confounds Marilyn's screen character with the real life and habits of the star. The Girl drinks Marilyn's favorite champagne, has posed in the past for sexy photos at twenty-five dollars an hour and, when she fails to turn up, provokes Ewell's question, "It's late. Where is she?" At the end of the film he says, "Maybe The Girl is Marilyn Monroe."

The comic idea of the movie – a beautiful woman offering herself to a frustrated man whose moral scruples force him to refuse – is funnier than the execution. Ewell's long soliloquies, in which he fantasizes about sex instead of acting out his desires, worked better in the play than in the picture. Admitting he "has one child, very little, hardly counts," Ewell makes fumbling attempts to bed Marilyn while imagining that his wife is being seduced by his friend. During his wife's imaginary hayride with his dashing rival, the horses pulling their cart discreetly "wear blinkers." Ewell reads one passage from a book that parodies the lyrical lovemaking scene in Hemingway's "Fathers and Sons" and another that sounds like Kinsey's account of the sexual habits of middle-aged men.[5] Oscar Homolka, an inept and mercenary psychiatrist and one of Ewell's authors, turns up early with his manuscript because his "patient jumped out of the window in the middle of a session." He admits that "at fifty dollars an hour all my cases interest me."

The undies emerge from the icebox and reappear in the most famous scene in the movie, when Marilyn and Ewell leave the air-conditioned Trans-Lux Theater on Lexington Avenue and 52nd Street. They've just seen *The Creature from the Black Lagoon* (1954), a 3-D horror movie in which an Amazonian fish-monster falls in love with and abducts a pretty coed. In a line cut by the censors, the icebox girl asks Ewell, "Don't you wish you could wear skirts? I feel so sorry for you men in your hot pants." She then steps onto a subway grating, with a huge wind machine underneath it, which sends her white pleated skirt fluttering above her waist like a wide-winged bird. The air from the New York summer subway would heat her up rather than cool her off, but that's part of the joke.

Marilyn did not reveal any more of her body than if she were wearing a bathing suit on the beach, but seemed delighted to show what was not supposed to be seen on the street. Publicity agents had leaked the news that the scene would be shot at 2:30 in the morning, and a huge crowd turned up to watch. Happily exposing herself in front of Ewell, the technicians shooting the scene, the underground men working the wind machine and the crowd straining to watch the repeated takes, she suggests her sexual availability in an enticing but charming way. Back in 1943, when Norma Jeane and Dougherty were stationed on Catalina Island, he complained that "every guy on the beach is mentally raping you!" In the windblown skirt scene – which, like the nude calendar, became her iconic image – Marilyn seemed eager to act out and take pleasure in male fantasies as well as her own. It seemed as if the men, speeding underground in the subway, lifted her skirt and, in a penetrating rush, had sex with her.

To enhance her sexy image, Marilyn had often said that she never wore underwear, though she usually did. One of the still photos from *The Seven Year Itch*, illuminated by powerful lights, reinforced her popular image and pleased the crowd by showing the dark patch of hair showing through her white panties. A photo by Eve Arnold captured her in the ladies room of Chicago's airport with her tight dress lifted high up – so she could raise her arms to comb her hair – and her lace panties and pert bottom in full view. Yet another photo, unexpectedly shot between her open legs, confirmed her assertions and revealed her pubic hair.[6]

The gossip columnist Walter Winchell, knowing that DiMaggio would be furious about the display that everyone else adored but wanting a good story for his newspaper, maliciously brought him over from Toots Shor's nearby restaurant to watch the scene being shot. First puzzled and then enraged, DiMaggio asked, "What the hell's going on around here?" Many husbands would be proud to have the woman whom millions of men desired. But DiMaggio, combining Sicilian possessiveness with American puritanism, hated all the publicity and wished to keep her in purdah. He'd wanted Marilyn to be his wife, and did not want her to behave like "Marilyn Monroe." The flagrant exhibition of her body and underwear reminded him once again of her disgraceful past, her numerous lovers and her vulgar image. To DiMaggio, *The Seven Year Itch* was a recurrent: when the scene was shot, when the photograph was blown up into a gigantic fifty-two-foot advertising poster that dominated Times Square and when he – and millions of others – actually saw the movie. That night, after DiMaggio returned with the exhausted Marilyn to the St. Regis Hotel, they had a fight and he hit her. The next day he flew back to California alone; three weeks later they publicly announced their separation. The marriage that began with her exposure on the nude calendar ended with the flying skirt in *The Seven Year Itch*.

Though the movie was a great success, Wilder was also angry with Marilyn, who'd caused many delays by turning up late and forgetting her lines. Emphasizing her artificiality and her dimness, he declared, "The question is whether Marilyn is a person at all, or one of the greatest Du Pont products ever invented. She has breasts like granite, and a brain like Swiss cheese, full of holes." He then added, with surprising animosity, a backhanded compliment: "Marilyn was mean. Terribly mean. The meanest woman I have ever met around this town. I have never met anyone as mean as Marilyn Monroe nor as utterly fabulous on the screen, and that includes Garbo," for whom he'd written *Ninotchka*. Wilder, too severe on himself, described the difficulty inherent in the script: "Unless the husband left alone in New York . . . has an affair with the girl there's nothing. But you couldn't do that in those days, so I was strait-jacketed. It just didn't come off one bit and there's nothing I can say except I wish I hadn't made it."[7]

DiMaggio suffered another public humiliation during their closely watched divorce. On October 4, 1954, he finally left 508 North Palm Drive, "grim-lipped and walking the last mile," and had to face a barrage of photographers and reporters at a miserable moment in his personal life. One of them asked, "Where are you going, Joe?" "I'm going home," Joe said. "We thought this was your home, Joe." "San Francisco has always been my home." Marilyn hired the best lawyer in town, Jerry Giesler, a short, pot-bellied but rather courtly man, who'd successfully defended Charlie Chaplin and Errol Flynn in scandalous sex cases. Coached by Giesler, she stated in court that DiMaggio "didn't talk to me. He was cold. He was indifferent to me as a human being and as an artist. He didn't want me to have friends of my own. He didn't want me to do my work. He watched television instead of talking to me." Oscar Levant, the pianist and wit, wisecracked that their divorce "proved that no man can be a success in two national pastimes."[8]

Like many ex-husbands, DiMaggio remained jealous and possessive. On November 5, a month after their separation, he took part in a scene right out of a Marx Brothers' farce, an episode the tabloids called the "Wrong Door Raid." A private detective had informed him that Marilyn and her lover Hal Schaefer (now recovered from his attempted suicide and back in action) were sequestered in the apartment of Hal's friend on Waring Avenue in Hollywood. DiMaggio's pal Frank Sinatra hired a few mobsters, who broke down the door. The heavies charged in and began taking pictures, but found the fifty-year-old Florence Kotz – asleep and alone in her flat – who clutched the bedclothes to her bosom and let out a terrified scream. "Meanwhile, through a door just a few yards away, Marilyn and Hal Schaefer left the apartment of actress Sheila Stuart (another of Schaefer's clients) – and they got clean away." The cops were paid off and called the break-in an attempted robbery. Kotz sued Sinatra for $200,000 and settled for $7,500. Two years later, after an exposé in *Confidential* magazine, the California State Senate, investigating scandals in the magazine industry, forced Sinatra and his cronies to testify. DiMaggio, who'd wisely remained hidden in a nearby car, was never called.

When journalists asked about the break with DiMaggio, Marilyn used her recently acquired psychoanalytic jargon and declared, "I feel I have to avoid the psychological confinement that marred our relationship when we were married." DiMaggio – who always felt sorry for her, never gave up his urge to protect her and often came to the rescue in later crises – later asked her, "Who in the hell else do you have in the world?"⁹

IV

After she became a star, Marilyn became increasingly difficult to work with. But many outstanding directors were willing, even eager, to benefit from her luminous quality on the screen and her enormously profitable films. Fritz Lang and Otto Preminger were authoritarian, angry and explosive, while Joshua Logan and Laurence Olivier were astonishingly patient, kind and tolerant.

Though Marilyn attracted first-rate directors, she rarely got serious roles. (Fox lent her to RKO for her first dramatic part in *Clash By Night*.) She began as a decorative secretary in three early movies; was a model in two other pictures; and ended up as a singer and dancer in almost all her starring roles from 1953 to her last film in 1961: *Gentlemen Prefer Blondes*, *River of No Return*, *There's No Business Like Show Business*, *Bus Stop*, *The Prince and the Showgirl*, *Some Like It Hot*, *Let's Make Love* and *The Misfits*. In four cliché-ridden, thematically similar pictures – *How to Marry a Millionaire*, *Gentlemen Prefer Blondes*, *The Prince and the Showgirl* and *Let's Make Love* (1953–60) – she plays a poor girl who attracts and snares a millionaire. Her four great films – *The Asphalt Jungle*, *All About Eve*, *Some Like It Hot* and *The Misfits* – all shot in black and white, were infinitely better than the Technicolor and Cinemascope extravaganzas that made her a star.

Apart from her performance in her best film, *The Misfits*, Marilyn was one-dimensional, melodramatic, even hysterical in her serious roles: *Don't Bother to Knock* and *Niagara*. But she had a subtle knack for comedy. She could be both sexy and naïve, blatant and vulnerable, semi-serious and amusing, and created distinctive comic effects by speaking her lines as if she didn't quite comprehend them. Miller noted that "she was both able to feel what she was doing and comment on it at the same time. So that irony made her sexuality funny."

Though Marilyn's success as a comedienne was based on her sexy image, which she carefully cultivated, she bitterly resented being treated as a mere sex goddess. The movie Production Code, which at first inhibited her impact, began to break down after Otto Preminger's liberating sex comedy, *The Moon is Blue* (1953), which was banned (but screened anyway) for using shocking words like "virgin" and "mistress."When interviewed by the press, Marilyn threw out provocative one-liners like "I do not suntan because I like to feel blonde all over" and, when daringly asked if she wore falsies, replied, "Those who know me better know better."[10] She usually wore, and sometimes had to be sewn into, very tight, low-cut, shimmering dresses, and attracted rabid attention by contriving to have a vital dress strap break during a packed press conference.

Contrasting Marilyn to a famous predecessor, a critic observed that Jean Harlow was "tough, wisecracking, even masculine in type. With a slight, lisping voice, a soft curvaceous body, and a seriousness about life, Marilyn Monroe projected an intense femininity and an inner vulnerability." Marilyn puckered and twitched her lips like a fish coming up for air. She swayed her hips as if trying to balance on a tightrope. But she never learned (or never wanted to learn) how to suggest sexiness in a subtle way. She always appeared, all guns firing, with the sensuous appeal of a *Playgirl* bunny: breasts projecting, bottom wiggling, mouth half-open, eyes half-closed.

In March 1953 Marilyn appeared in all her glory to receive the prestigious Gold Medal for the "Fastest Rising Star" at the *Photoplay* awards ceremony. Joan Crawford, inappropriately assuming the role of grande dame, condemned her behavior with an insulting remark: "The publicity has gone too far, and apparently Miss Monroe is making the mistake of believing her publicity. Someone should make her see the light. She should be told that the public likes provocative feminine personalities; but it also likes to know that underneath it all the actresses are ladies." Playing the orphan card and using her insider's knowledge of Hollywood, Marilyn ironically praised Crawford, long before her adopted daughter exposed her sadistic acts in *Mommie Dearest*: "I've always admired her for being such a wonderful mother – for taking four children and giving them a fine home. Who better than I knows what that means to homeless little ones?"

Marilyn's public and professional image as a stupid sexpot clashed with her desire to become a serious actress. She first wanted attention, then demanded respect. In 1950 she'd do anything to get a part; by 1954 she was understandably weary of dumb blonde roles. Ezra Goodman showed how Marilyn had followed the trajectory of a typical Hollywood glamor girl:

—If only I could get a part.
—They like me! I wonder if I'm gonna get another part?
—I should be getting bigger and more important parts.
—How can I get more money?
—[I've] become surrounded by sycophants and suckerfish.
—I have to make lots of money now. How long can I last?
—[I've] reached the first plateau. Everybody wants interviews with me.
—[I've] become a mature star and accept everything.
—[I] break from the friends who disagree with me.
—[I] need help from someone, so change agents and boyfriends. There's a feeling of constant insecurity.
—[Finally, I] get culture.[11]

Marilyn was best when playing a character who was essentially like herself. When demanding serious roles, she rather naïvely asserted that the movie studio was not a "manufacturing establishment" and should be making artistic rather than commercial films. It *was*, however, a huge money-making corporation, knew that high art didn't produce profits and constantly remade successful formulaic films.

Not satisfied with her achievement as a comedienne, Marilyn hoped to gain respect and recognition by playing Grushenka in *The Brothers Karamazov*. Dore Schary, a producer at Metro-Goldwyn-Mayer, had for years planned to film Dostoyevsky's novel with Marilyn and Marlon Brando, and had commissioned a screenplay for these stars. But Marilyn was under exclusive contract with Fox, whose executives did not believe she could be a serious actress and refused to lend her to MGM. Marilyn sounded foolish when she told reporters, "I don't want to play the brothers. I want to play Grushenka. She's a girl." But very few reporters had read the novel. She was familiar with it and may well have stated the obvious because of *their* ignorance, not hers. She understood Grushenka's character and quite properly said that Grushenka is much more than a sexpot, that "she grows and develops because of her love for [Dimitry]." A beautiful and bewitching "fallen woman" who's been seduced by a lecherous Pole, Grushenka is loved by both the crude buffoon, Father Karamazov, and by his son Dimitry. At the end of the book, when the son is wrongly sentenced to Siberia for the murder of his father, she remains loyal to Dimitry and is prepared to accompany him to prison.

Billy Wilder confirmed that "Marilyn knows what she's doing. She could play a good Grushenka. People think this is a long-hair, very thick, very literary book. But there's nothing long-hair about Grushenka. At heart she is a whore." Like Marilyn, she is also in search of redemption and tells the saintly Alyosha: "I've been waiting all my life for someone like you, I knew that someone like you would come and forgive me . . . would really love me, not only with a shameful love!" Marilyn said, "She's very erotic, you know," and Joshua Logan agreed that she was well prepared to play this demanding role: "The only thing she felt herself an authority on was eroticism; therefore, anything that suggested sensuality or sexuality gave her instant, joyful confidence."[12] In the end, the demure Maria Schell got the coveted part.

V

Natasha Lytess observed that Marilyn had "an almost frightening perception of what was right for Marilyn Monroe." The actress now realized that her contract with Fox exploited her and was determined to do something about it. In the first four years of her seven-year contract (1951–54), she began at $500 a week for forty weeks a year, rose to $1,500 a week and earned a total of $160,000, or an average of $40,000 a year, while her movies made a total of $15 million for the studio. By 1954 she was an international celebrity, admired by millions of people, yet (as DiMaggio noted) Fox still treated her shabbily. As the actor Robert Stack wrote, "The prevailing view at Twentieth Century-Fox was that actors were children and the parent (the studio) had to keep the upper hand. Marilyn Monroe was denied a [star's] dressing room on the set because . . . a pocket-sized executive with a peculiar set of priorities didn't want her to develop a big head."[13]

Unlike most actors, Marilyn was not intimidated by the formidable chief of production, Darryl Zanuck, who'd pace up and down during interviews in his vast office, chomping a cigar and whacking his polo mallet against his high polished boots. She wanted not only a fair contract, but also revenge for a long and bitter list of grievances: her suddenly terminated short-term contracts at Fox and Columbia; her predatory couch-casting, sexual exploitation and public humiliations. Producers had shown contempt for her as a woman, disdain for her supposed stupidity and scorn for her as a slut. Tyrannical studio executives had typecast her in mediocre movies and refused to give her serious roles or lend her to other studios for better parts. And her pay was grossly unfair.

Marilyn naturally turned to her new agent, Charles Feldman, of Famous Artists, for help in dealing with Fox. She was surprised to find that his first loyalty was to the studio, where he also produced pictures, and that he did not always work for her benefit when re-negotiating her contract. But she was as tough with Feldman and Fox as she'd been with Ben Hecht, and staunchly defended her own inter-ests. As early as December 1, 1953 – the month before she married DiMaggio, who took an active part in the negotiations – Feldman's colleague at the agency impatiently told him that "she was getting kind of antsy pantsy about not wanting to do any more pictures for 'those coolie wages.'" Feldman was then in Switzerland to make deals with European directors for Kirk Douglas and several other stars. His wife had fallen ill and was in the hospital, and he soon became distracted and exhausted by all the long phone calls and cables about Marilyn's unfair pay and poor screen roles. Feldman was also concerned that Famous Artists had lent her $23,000 and if she left them it would be difficult to recover it. In fact, after she'd left the agency, it took five years to collect the money.

Matters heated up again in June 1954 when Feldman's colleague anxiously reported that Marilyn had learned how to use her newly acquired power and stubbornly confronted the hard-nosed president of the studio about her contract:

> Once again I had a meeting with Miss Monroe and Mr. Skouras this evening to try and find some solution to this problem, but I am afraid we reached an absolute impasse. In a talk I had with Marilyn afterwards, she seemed even more adamant and would only listen to her own point of view. Mr. Skouras at the same time does not feel it is possible for Fox to go any further. . . .
>
> She has made up her mind that unless they give in on the particular point she is requesting she will sit it out for four years.

The following month the colleague was also troubled by Marilyn's intransigence about her choreographers – and distrust of her agents. He tried to persuade her to negotiate, but she was convinced she was right and gave no ground: "She was absolutely rigid and adamant in her position; despite the fact that I told her very firmly that from a practical point of view the two or three points that bothered her in the contract would automatically be overcome. . . . She said she was tired of having to fight the studio and all she was interested in was getting great parts." Marilyn ground them down in a battle of wills, and astonished both the agents and the studio. She maintained that if she didn't get exactly what she wanted, she was willing to break with Fox, give up making movies at the height of her career and wait until her contract expired.

Marilyn continued to distrust Fox and Feldman. In April 1955, after she'd carried out her threat and left Fox, the studio tried to win her back. At one point her lawyer Frank Delany asked the photographer Sam Shaw to intercede on her behalf with Fox. Shaw, who wisely refused to get involved, explained the prickly situation to Feldman (who may also have been *his* agent): "I told Marilyn . . . that you gave her the best deal and lost money by putting her in [*The Seven Year Itch*] – as good as she is. . . . She is sore as hell at me – and personally I don't care, except the publishers want her cooperation for my book. . . . What really pissed me off on this dame is her intense animosity towards you."[14]

In 1954 Marilyn was besieged with offers to star in movies and sing on records, appear on television shows and radio programs, be interviewed for magazine and newspaper articles, make public appearances and contribute to charitable events. As her marriage broke up and she quarreled with her agents and the studio, she couldn't bear the intense pressure. Though spontaneous and intuitive, she had found it difficult to make professional decisions. She had to consider her image, her publicity and her relations with Fox as she weighed the possibility of forming her own production company. Charles Feldman, an astute attorney, agent, producer and powerful Hollywood insider, would have made an excellent business partner, but she associated him with Fox and did not trust him. Norman Mailer, alluding to *River of No Return* and *There's No Business Like Show Business*, described her complicated situation at the end of that year: "on the edge of separating from her husband, she has two atrocious films behind her, is . . . drinking too much, and all the while thinking of breaking her contract and beginning a new life in New York to make movies with a photographer who has never produced a film."

Marilyn refused the wise counsel of her own lawyers, publicists and accountants, who advised her to stick with Fox and improve her contract. Instead she unexpectedly formed Marilyn Monroe Productions with Milton Greene, a handsome New York fashion and celebrity photographer whom she liked and trusted. Born Greenholtz and four years older than Marilyn, he had had a brief affair with her at the Chateau Marmont in Los Angeles in 1953. (When I asked his son Joshua whether, as rumored, they resumed their affair during Greene's second marriage, he did not deny it but merely said "no comment.") Greene's contract with Marilyn stated that he would finance her for a year in New York, and allow her to live in high style and study acting. He would find new films and great parts for her, and she would finally have the power to guide her own career. Her contract with Fox was bad, but she exchanged it for an equally bad one with Greene, who knew almost nothing about film making and wound up owning 49 percent of the company and the most successful star in Hollywood.

Marilyn traded a powerful studio and agent for a family who took her in as other families had. She spent many weekends at the Greenes' house in Connecticut, and they helped smooth the way for her new life in New York. Greene's second wife, Amy, a thin, elegant, high-fashion model with dark hair pulled straight back like a ballerina, had the uncomfortable task of being the new best friend of her husband's partner. The svelte Amy and the voluptuous Marilyn of the bountiful bosoms represented two ideal but contrasting images of American beauty. An indiscreet but unidentified lady-friend of both women said, "I got the feeling that Amy looked down on Marilyn Monroe as a stupid little bitch. Amy was better dressed, more chic, more sophisticated, and much cleverer than Marilyn. She even looked better. In fact, you couldn't believe that this queer little duck you saw sitting around the Greenes' was really Marilyn Monroe."[15]

The striking difference between the two women came into sharp focus when they both appeared on a popular television show, *Person to Person*. Hosted by the distinguished, chain-smoking newsman Edward R. Murrow, who had sent stirring broadcasts from wartime London, it was filmed when Marilyn was living with the Greenes in Weston, Connecticut, and shown in April 1955. Other actors interviewed by Murrow, like Kirk Douglas and Tony Curtis, seemed happily married, confident, at ease and living in luxurious houses with swimming pools, while Marilyn seemed an uneasy guest, taken in by the Greenes as if she were still an orphan. Murrow's biographer noted that his "questions were dreadful. 'I saw some pictures of you the other day at the circus riding an elephant. Did you have fun?' 'Do you like New York?' 'Do you like Connecticut?' And to Mrs. Greene, 'Does she make her own bed?' And puzzlingly, 'Do you play a part to impress directors or please them?'"

Murrow's questions did not allow Marilyn, who seemed nervous, passive and possibly stoned, a chance to respond with her usual wit. Amy, who was much brighter, prettier and self-possessed, sometimes answered for Marilyn and dominated the rather awkward program. Zanuck voiced the pervasive Hollywood response when he angrily wrote Feldman that Marilyn had thrown away a great chance for publicity and "made an idiot of herself on Ed Murrow's show last week with obvious repercussions."

Miller, pretending to speak for Marilyn but actually expressing his own hostility toward the Greenes, condemned Amy's character: "[Marilyn] thought Amy was someone whose values were superficial and a little insubstantial; who married someone who was 'in,' who was successful and could help her meet the *right* people, the famous, the 'in' people. That's her whole life and interest. When Marilyn needed somebody, as she did then, [Marilyn] would seem to be powerfully connected with [the Greenes]." In fact, Marilyn admitted that she was not really close to them at all.

Breaking with Fox and starting her own company was a bold move, and Marilyn was optimistic when she left Hollywood for New York. From then on, she alternated between the East and West coasts, and considered the rest of America a vast, unknown hinterland. Miller, who resumed their relationship when she reached the East coast and replaced DiMaggio in her life, explained why her film company was doomed from the start:

> The concrete reason was that they were both in an impossible position. [Greene] was acting as a manager, so to speak, and was very jealous of his authority, as he would have to be in such a situation, but their standards were different. He really was basically trying to upset her arrangement with Fox. . . .
>
> She had originally thought that his interest was in furthering her career, going about the world seeking the best properties. She had hoped that it would create a situation where she could

pick and choose among the best available. But the way it worked out, Greene thought that he would be this big-shot producer and she would be working for him. . . . It was [supposed to, but didn't] work out that her salary would not be taxable, as it had been. . . . He never did anything about all that. He wasn't capable of that. This was all talk. You have to be a special kind of person to pull this sort of operation together. He just didn't have it.[16]

Six

Miller's Path to Fame
(1915–1949)

I

While Marilyn was making her way as an actress in Hollywood, Miller was working as a playwright in New York and trying to maintain his precarious marriage. In contrast to Marilyn, he was stable, purposeful, educated and confident. He came from an upper-middle-class Jewish family and his life, like his art, was firmly grounded in reality.

Though Miller never knew the poverty and abandonment that Marilyn endured, he suffered the trauma of the Depression when his father lost his business after the stock-market crash of 1929. He expressed his ambivalence about his parents by simultaneously idealizing and denigrating them. He said that his father, Isidore, who came to America from Poland when he was five years old, "grew up to be six feet two inches tall with blue eyes and red hair and everybody thought he was an Irishman." But photographs of Isidore, slightly taller than Marilyn and only as high as Arthur's chin, reveal that he was only of average height. Miller also said that though his father "built one of the two or three largest coat manufacturing businesses in the country," he was completely uneducated and could not "read or write any language." Isidore's "Miltex Coat and Suit Company boasted a factory, showroom, front office and more than 800 employees." The family "lived on the top floor of a handsome six-story building at a very respectable address, 45 West 110th Street, facing the north end of Central Park just off Fifth Avenue." Isidore was driven to work in a chauffeured automobile.

Despite her husband's astonishing immigrant's success, Miller's mother constantly humiliated his father, both before and after he'd lost his money and his business, demeaning his social status and self-esteem: "The children regularly overheard their mother belittling Izzy for his grubby ladies' clothing company, his coarse associates, his educational shortcomings and his inability to appreciate *the finer things*"[1] – which of course he had provided. Though Miller loved his father, he inevitably adopted his mother's condescending and critical attitude. "I couldn't help blushing for him," he recalled, "when she made him her target, since I admired his warm and gentle nature as much as I despaired of his illiterate mind." For Isidore, after the crash, "there would never be a recovery of dignity and self-assurance, only an endless death-in-life down to the end." Arthur, as a teenager and young man, felt pity and contempt for his father and scarcely spoke to him. He said they were isolated "like two searchlights on different islands. I had no animosity toward him. I simply had no great relationship with him." But Marilyn, always in search of a father, would develop a powerful bond with her ignorant but warmly responsive father-in-law.

Miller described his mother Augusta (known as "Gussy") as warm and nice, musical and a lively storyteller – as well as high strung and subject to sudden fits of depression. After Isidore's financial collapse and their descent from the luxurious life of Manhattan to a modest dwelling in Brooklyn, Gussy had to sell her furs and pawn her jewelry. The once glamorous and well-dressed woman turned into a slovenly and lethargic Hausfrau, shuffling around in crushed-back slippers. She only seemed to revive when condemning her husband for ruining her family and destroying her life. Like most modern American writers, from Hemingway and Fitzgerald to Lowell and Berryman, Miller had a strong mother and weak father.

Miller entered manhood in the 1930s, and formed his political and cultural views after witnessing the threatening events of that low, dishonest decade: the rise of fascism, the economic hardships of the Depression, the heartbreaking defeat of the Loyalists in the Spanish Civil War, the spread of Nazism throughout Europe and the plague of anti-Semitism. After graduating from high school in 1933, Miller took a job to earn money for college. He made fifteen dollars a week at Chadick-Delameter, "the largest wholesale auto parts warehouse east of the Mississippi, an old firm that sold to retail parts stores and garages all over the eastern seaboard."[2] The huge warehouse – with a dour, pasty-faced boss and Miller the only Jew in the firm – stood on the corner of Tenth Avenue and West 63rd Street. Thirty years later, Lincoln Center was built on the site and Miller's plays were produced there.

His father wanted Arthur to attend City College in New York, where tuition was free and he could live at home, and to follow him into the coat business. But Arthur held out for the University of Michigan in Ann Arbor, where he studied from 1934 to 1938. He said he chose it because it was the only college in America that offered a playwriting course and gave prize money for the best student plays. In fact, George Pierce Baker had been teaching his famous play-writing courses – to students like Eugene O'Neill, Philip Barry and Sidney Howard – at both Harvard and Yale since 1908. Michigan had twice rejected Miller because he'd repeatedly failed algebra and had a poor academic record. But an enlightened dean of admissions reversed his decision after Miller sent several letters arguing that he'd been working for two years, and was now more mature and serious about academic life.

In the 1930s the university was a radical outpost in the generally conservative Midwest. The energetic Miller washed dishes in a caf-eteria in exchange for meals and supported himself on the fifteen dollars a month (a quarter of his warehouse salary) he earned by feeding mice in a cancer research laboratory. After classes he worked as night editor at the *Michigan Daily*. His main expenses were for room, laundry, tobacco, books and movies. At Michigan Miller met his first wife, the Catholic, idealistic and high-principled Mary Grace Slattery. "The first time I saw him," she recalled, "he came toward me, ducking overhead heating pipes. . . . When he did notice me, he asked for a date. I proposed a movie, but he didn't have any money. I treated to the movies, and afterwards to malted milks."

E.M. Halliday, then a graduate student and later a college professor, described an extraordinary incident that revealed Mary's sexual inno-cence and naïveté as well as her desire to appear sophisticated and free-spirited. On a rainy spring night, Mary and her close friend Hedda Rowinski unexpectedly knocked on the door of Halliday and his roommate Bhain Campbell. The women were invited in and, after considerable awkwardness and hesitation, Hedda shocked Halliday with a bold proposal:

> This is kind of embarrassing, but we couldn't think of what else to do. You know I've been seeing a lot of Norman [Rosten], and Mary has been seeing a lot of Art, and things are getting – well, things are getting kind of serious. The thing is, I'm still a virgin – which is probably no surprise to you – and Mary is, too. And Norman and Art want to go to bed with us; but we think *they* think we're women of the world, and we're afraid they'll be disillusioned if they find out we're so innocent. So we wondered if you and Bhain. . . .
>
> But just as friends! No complications; just as friends! You like me, and I know that Bhain likes Mary; and you both like Norman and Art. We thought if you'd just – well, you know, show us how it's *done*? We don't want to seem stupid about it when the time comes with *them*. We wouldn't *tell* them about it, of course.

Halliday, gallantly refusing their enticing offer, told them, "I was sure their maiden condition would not be scorned by Norman and Art, who undoubtedly loved them." Miller's previous experience seems to have been limited to an encounter with a prostitute when he was sixteen. But both college girls, thinking their boyfriends and potential lovers would be disappointed by virgins and prefer women of the world, sweetly credited the men with more *savoir faire* than they really had.

Miller's first visit to Mary's family in Lakewood, Ohio, a suburb of Cleveland, was like the scene in *Annie Hall* when Woody Allen visits Diane Keaton's hostile and demented Christian family in Wisconsin. Mary's father, a retired boiler inspector for the city of Cleveland, was both stupid and crude. He spat tobacco juice onto the front lawn while his embarrassed wife almost groaned in despair and the dourly humorous Miller tried to pretend nothing had happened. He found Mary's mother absurdly pious and extremely repressed. Though he and Mary – after surmounting the hurdle of virginity – had lived together in Ann Arbor, he had to maintain propriety by sleeping in a rented room.

Mary's first visit, in August 1938, to his more tolerant family was not quite as traumatic: "For a while it did not go down well, but pretty soon they got used to her and she to them. She, in any case, was not a practicing Catholic by then. It was far more difficult for her parents because they were still very devout and I was a heathen. Actually, that is part of the ceremony. There are special ceremonies for Mohammedans, heathens and Jews who marry Catholics. You are not married in the church and you have to get a special dispensation from the church in order to do that."[3]

Mary, a year behind Miller, made one of her many sacrifices by dropping out of the University of Michigan and moving to New York with him when he graduated in 1938. Marilyn's biographer Maurice Zolotow wrote that Mary "was political, literary, intense in the style of the 1930s, and she was . . . the family intellectual. She had been Miller's creative inspiration, his economic support. She had worked as a waitress and later as an editor . . . to support him while he established himself as a writer." But Miller's friends and family found Mary (who remains a shadowy figure in *Timebends*) rather stern and withdrawn. Kazan's daughter called her "a rather joyless creature . . . a skinny, silent, disapproving figure"; and Joan Copeland described her as "upright, a straight arrow, even if a little bit cool, not emotional."[4]

Mary also worked at a magazine for China specialists called *Amerasia*. The magazine argued, during the Chinese civil war, that Mao Tsetung's victory over Chiang Kai-shek was inevitable, even desirable, and that America's support of Chiang was futile and foolish. In 1945 extracts of classified reports written by the OSS (the wartime intelligence agency and forerunner of the CIA) were unaccountably published in the magazine. *Amerasia*'s prediction about Mao turned out to be correct, but Miller was inevitably associated, through Mary, with backing the Communists during the Cold War.

After living together for two more years in Brooklyn, Arthur and Mary finally married on August 5, 1940. Their daughter, Jane, was born in 1944 and their son, Robert, three years later. When a nursemaid moved in with the family after Robert's birth, Miller wryly remarked, "there are so many women in the house, I spend half my time raising the toilet seat." A few years later, as their marriage began to disintegrate, Mary desperately tried to stay youthful. Miller, self-absorbed as always, told the English author James Stern that he was puzzled about her dance-and-exercise class, but never bothered to question her about it: "Mary is taking some kind of lessons in body movement or some damned thing. I always forget to ask her what it's about. But she does it in a class every week and is convinced she is growing younger." Despite their estrangement and eventual divorce, Miller did his best work toward the end of their sixteen-year marriage, and wrote very little during his tempestuous years with Marilyn.

II

The young Miller was inspired to become a dramatist, while a student at the University of Michigan, after seeing a Chicago production of Clifford Odets' play about a troubled Jewish family, *Awake and Sing!* (1935). Miller had tremendous energy, ambition and desire to learn his craft. For a decade after graduating from college, he turned out many failures before suddenly achieving great fame with *All My Sons* (1947) and *Death of a Salesman* (1949). His dozen or more plays, which were never produced, included two that won prestigious Hopwood Awards at Michigan (the first, *No Villain*, was twice revised and also won a Theater Guild Award); a satiric comedy, *Listen My Children*, in collaboration with Norman Rosten; and a historical play, *The Golden Years*, about Montezuma, Cortés and the destruction of Mexico by the Spanish *conquistadores*. When America entered World War II he was rejected for military service because of a knee injury he'd received in a football game, so he tried to justify his existence by writing several radio plays on patriotic themes. His first play on Broadway, *The Man Who Had All the Luck*, portrayed a character who feels guilty about his success and is convinced that he's heading for disaster. It had a terrible reception and closed after only four performances in November 1944.

Miller (like Marilyn) aided the war effort by manual labor. From 1941 to 1943 he worked thirteen out of every fourteen nights, from four in the afternoon to four in the morning, in the ship-fitting department of the Brooklyn Navy Yard. Like many other workers, Miller was unskilled and was surprised when the ships they'd worked on actually stayed afloat:

> Whenever a drydock was finally flooded and a ship instead of sinking floated safely into the harbor and sailed out into the bay, I was not the only one who stared at it thinking it miraculous that out of our chaos and incompetence, our bumbling and

goofing off and our thefts . . . we had managed to repair it. More than one man would turn to another and say, "How the hell'd it happen?" as the ship vanished into the morning mists and the war.[5]

Toward the end of 1943 Miller was offered $750 a week to write a screenplay based on Ernie Pyle's frontline war dispatches during the Italian campaign. His film script was rewritten and made into the successful *Story of GI Joe* (1945) with Burgess Meredith and Robert Mitchum. Miller got no screen credit; but his first book, *Situation Normal* (1944), about the problems that soldiers had when they returned from combat and tried to adjust to civilian life, grew out of his research for the Ernie Pyle film. This book was dedicated to his older brother, Kermit, who was serving as a lieutenant in the American army.

Miller's editor, Frank Taylor, at the highbrow publishers Reynal & Hitchcock, was a tall, handsome, stylish man. He had serious left-wing views and socialized with politically committed artists at his home in Greenwich Village. Taylor became a close friend and, later on, the producer of *The Misfits*. He also published *Focus* (1945), Miller's only novel, with the fashionable postwar theme of alienation. The central character is a gentile whose new glasses make him look Jewish. His appearance provokes anti-Semitic hostility, and he at first tries to maintain his non-Jewish status. Eventually he accepts his new identity and fights against the prejudice he's encountered. The subject of anti-Semitism was especially relevant between the liberation of the Nazi extermination camps in 1945 and the founding of the state of Israel in 1948. Readers were eager for serious fiction after the war and *Focus* (according to Miller) sold a surprising 90,000 copies.

Miller disliked his mother-in-law's flat, unemphatic Ohio speech and her Catholic belief that earthly life was a disaster. But she told him the story that inspired *All My Sons*, his first triumphant success in the theater. A local newspaper reported that during the war the Wright Aeronautics Corporation of Ohio had bribed army inspectors to approve defective airplane engines. The novelist and critic Mary McCarthy pointed out that Miller used Henrik Ibsen's device of the fatal secret, in which crime and guilt enter an ordinary domestic scene and build up to a tragic climax. She observed that "*All My Sons* was a social indictment taken, almost directly, from Ibsen's *Pillars of Society* [1877]. The coffin ships, rotten, unseaworthy vessels caulked over to give the appearance of soundness, become defective airplanes sold to the government by a corner-cutting manufacturer during the Second World War." Other critics noted the influence of Ibsen's *An Enemy of the People* (1882), which Miller adapted for the American stage in 1950. In this play, "an idealistic doctor discovers that the spring waters from which his spa town draws its wealth are dangerously contaminated. As Stockmann's fellow citizens realize the financial implications of his research, he comes under increasing pressure to keep silent."

In Miller's realistic tragedy – brilliantly directed for the stage by Elia Kazan and starring Ed Begley and Arthur Kennedy – Joe Keller sells cracked cylinder heads to the Army Air Force, which cause a number of fatal plane crashes. He also allows his employee and neighbor to take the blame and go to jail. When Keller's son, a pilot, dies in the war, his younger son tells Keller that his brother had discovered the fatal secret and committed suicide out of shame. Appalled by his own greed, and faced with the ruin of his name, business and family, Keller finally accepts his guilt and kills himself. After Miller won the Drama Critics' Circle Award for the best new American play of the season, and several reviewers suggested that the director and actors were more responsible for its success than the author, he ironically remarked, "Everyone's son but mine!" His sudden fame attracted attention in Hollywood and in 1947 he was offered, but turned down, $2,500 to write the screenplay for Alfred Hitchcock's *Rope*, made the following year with James Stewart and Farley Granger.

In a frenzy of inspiration Miller wrote the first act of his best-known play, *Death of a Salesman*, in less than twenty-four hours. The play, again directed by Kazan, starred Lee J. Cobb and Mildred Dunnock as Willy and Linda Loman, Arthur Kennedy and Cameron Mitchell as their sons. Like *All My Sons*, it was a domestic tragedy that portrayed the rivalry of two brothers, a loyal wife and a father who kills himself. Willy's brother Ben, a ruthlessly successful figure who thrives in a cutthroat world, makes a dream-like appearance. No one has noticed that the exotic, authoritarian Ben was inspired by Kurtz in Joseph Conrad's *Heart of Darkness* (1899). Marlow, who's been sent upriver and into the jungle to rescue the pitiless and fanatical Kurtz, says with a mixture of awe and condemnation that Kurtz "had collected, bartered, swindled, or stolen more ivory than all the other agents together." Ben boasts to Willy, a weak failure: "When I was seventeen I walked into the jungle, and when I was twenty-one I walked out. And by God I was rich."[6] Ben, a modern-day Kurtz, is more interested in accumulating fabulous wealth than exerting absolute power. He feels a sense of pure triumph rather than horrified remorse about exploiting the natives and tearing the riches out of the African earth.

Miller earned a fabulous $160,000 a year from the New York production of *Salesman* and an equal amount from several touring companies. Always careful with money, he now lashed out by buying a house in Brooklyn Heights, a farm in Connecticut and a new car. When Frank Taylor sent Miller's script to Dore Schary at MGM and suggested he buy the film rights, Schary called it "the most depressing fucking thing I ever read. Nobody would ever want to see this kind of film." The play won the Pulitzer Prize, and became a film in 1951, with Fredric March playing Willy, Kevin McCarthy his son Biff, and Dunnock and Mitchell reprising their Broadway roles. It is widely taught in schools and colleges, and by 2005 had sold more than eleven million copies.

III

Miller was a reserved, guarded and withdrawn man who rarely showed his deepest feelings. He was a cool and distant father, had few close friends and eventually broke with his most intimate companions: with Elia Kazan for political reasons and with Norman Rosten for siding with Marilyn after their divorce. Miller also pulled Marilyn away from her own friends. He persuaded her to sever relations with Milton and Amy Greene, and tried to diminish the pernicious influence of Lee and Paula Strasberg.

Miller's dedications shed some light on his limited friendships. Many of his books had no dedications; and sixteen of his twenty-one dedications were given to his family: to his brother, three wives, three children and his third wife's parents (but not to his own father and mother). Of the remaining five dedications, *Theater Essays* was dedicated to his college playwriting teacher Kenneth Rowe; *All My Sons* to Kazan; and *A View from the Bridge* to the writer and translator James Stern "for his encouragement." Two other books were dedicated to people who had recently died: *I Don't Need You Any More* to the memory of his editor at Viking, Pascal Covici, and *The Misfits* "to Clark Gable, who did not know how to hate."

1. Norma Jeane and her
mother, Gladys Baker,
Los Angeles beach, 1928

2. Norma Jeane and
her first husband,
Jim Dougherty, 1943

3. Arthur Miller, Norman Rosten, Hedda Rosten and Mary Slattery Miller, 1940

4. Miller with Mary and his children, Jane and Robert, 1953

5. Marilyn and
Johnny Hyde,
late 1949

6. Marilyn
and Natasha
Lytess, *c.*1952

7. Marilyn and Louis Calhern
in *The Asphalt Jungle*, 1950

8. Marilyn with Anne Baxter, Bette Davis and George Sanders in *All About Eve*, 1950

9. Marilyn and
Joe DiMaggio, 1953

10. Marilyn
entertaining
troops in Korea,
February 1954

11. Marilyn with Milton and Amy Greene, 1955

12. Lee, Paula and Susan Strasberg, 1963

13. Marilyn in airport bathroom,
April 1955

14. Marilyn, signed studio photo, 1956

15. Marilyn in
The Seven Year Itch, 1955

16. Marilyn and DiMaggio
at premiere of *The Seven
Year Itch*, June 1955

Several colleagues were irritated by Miller's characteristic pompous and self-righteous rectitude. Harold Clurman, a founder of the Group Theater and director of Miller's *Incident at Vichy*, observed that "Miller, earnest and upright, is sustained by a sense of mission. . . . For all his unbending seriousness and a certain coldness of manner, there is more humor in him than is generally supposed. He is much less rigid now than he is said to have been in his younger days, when he put people off." Robert Lewis directed Miller's adaptation of *An Enemy of the People*, which starred the married couple, Florence Eldridge and Fredric March. Lewis recalled that on one occasion Miller, who took an active part in the production of his plays and was usually self-controlled, unexpectedly exploded:

> Arthur sensed this wish of Florence's to be loved by the audience. Blowing his top in the middle of a scene one day at a run-through, Arthur yelled up to Mrs. March, "Why must you be so fucking noble?" . . . Florence flew off the stage and into her dressing room, followed by her equally anguished husband. The Marches insisted neither of them would return to the production until Arthur apologized in front of the company. The playwright compromised by offering a private apology, and the Marches finally accepted that.[7]

Kazan shrewdly remarked that after the tremendous success, wealth and fame of *Salesman*, Miller's "eyes acquired a new flash and his carriage and movement a hint of something swashbuckling." Frank Taylor's wife, Nan, added that "Mary, never an extrovert, began to fade into his background, 'meek . . . beside him.'" Lacking insight into Mary's character and their marriage, Miller confessed that "it never occurred to me that she might have felt anxious at being swamped by this rush of my fame." For years Mary had loyally believed in his talent, and helped support him both intellectually and financially. But now that his career had taken off and he had plenty of money, he was less dependent on her. As he developed artistically and socially, and saw sexual possibilities that never existed before, she rather desperately clung to their old way of life.

Long before he met Marilyn, Miller's marriage was strained and unhappy. A crucial incident in 1943, four years before his fame, revealed Mary's puritanical nature. Extremely intolerant and censorious, she took the thought for the deed when he merely fantasized about other women. While discussing the Ernie Pyle project in Washington, Miller was introduced to an attractive war widow, who excited him by confiding that she'd compensated for her loss by sleeping with a number of young sailors. When, Miller wrote, "I blithely told Mary of my attraction to this woman, saying that had I not been married I would have liked to sleep with her," his mild confession "was received with such a power of disgust and revulsion . . . that her confidence in me, as well as my mindless reliance on her, was badly damaged."[8] Mary's reaction to his affair with Marilyn was even more furious; and his next two plays were suffused with his own shame and guilt.

Seven

Secret Courtship
(1954–1955)

I

Toward the end of 1954, after her failed marriage to DiMaggio, Marilyn went to New York to study with Lee Strasberg at the Actors Studio, and to resume her liaison with Miller. She moved from her native city and the fake glamor of the unintellectual movie industry, into a completely different culture – literary, theatrical and highbrow. She understood Hollywood and had made her career there; now, financially and emotionally dependent on Milton and Amy Greene, she was starting again. As she tried to enter this unfamiliar society, she made daily visits to a psychoanalyst and took classes with a famous teacher to improve her acting skills. She was lonely until she met Miller, who belonged to this world and helped – as companion, guide and teacher – to bring her into it. He, in turn, was fascinated by Marilyn's extraordinary power to attract and interest eminent writers.

It was difficult for her to contact him, since he worked at home. The photographer Sam Shaw introduced her to Miller's college friend, Norman Rosten, who told Miller she was in town, and they finally met at one of Strasberg's theatrical parties in June 1955. Miller, meanwhile, still trying to stay out of the emotional vortex and sustain a marriage destroyed by "mutual intolerance," was torn between desire and guilt: "I no longer knew what I wanted – certainly not the end of my marriage, but the thought of putting Marilyn out of my life was unbearable." So he renewed his secret courtship in a series of romantic settings: the Greenes' country house in Weston, Connecticut; the Rostens' summer cottage in Port Jefferson, Long Island; the Strasbergs' summer place on Fire Island; and Marilyn's posh suite high up in the Waldorf Tower.

Mary Miller's reaction to her husband's relationship with Marilyn helped propel him into his eventual marriage to Monroe. Mary had renounced her Catholic faith, shared Miller's left-wing politics, and tried psychoanalysis in an attempt to understand and perhaps solve their problems. In October 1955 she discovered that Miller was having an affair. Their son Robert, then eight years old, later remembered that there was a lot of anger and tension in the air and that he tried in vain to play the peacemaker. Mary, who'd made many sacrifices in the early years of their marriage while her husband struggled for success, was both wounded by his infidelity and furious about his betrayal. She threw him out of the house; and he moved into the Chelsea Hotel, a refuge for bohemians and artists, on West 23rd Street.

Kazan, sympathizing with Miller, described the tense situation that followed: "Month after month he'd begged Mary to take him back, but she couldn't bring herself to forgive her husband. . . . He'd been doing his best to hold their marriage together, but according to him, his wife was behaving in a bitterly vengeful manner." Miller's sister, Joan Copeland, said the break-up of his marriage came as a big surprise:

> I would hear snippets of rumors but I'd just pooh-pooh it because when you're in that position of celebrity, people are going to say and write all sorts of terrible things about you. So I was guarded against any kind of malicious rumor. I just didn't believe it and I didn't ask Mary or Arthur about it. But Marilyn would search me out at the [Actors] Studio and we'd have lunch, talk about scenes. I guess she was trying to curry my favor, or maybe she just liked me.[1]

Miller finally decided to get a divorce in Nevada, which was much easier to obtain than in New York. In order to qualify, he had to reside in the state for six weeks. Saul Bellow was already living out there, divorcing his first wife in order to marry his second. On March

15, 1956, at the suggestion of a mutual friend, Pascal Covici, Miller wrote to Bellow. He asked for advice and, in a bit of one-upmanship, expressed pride in possessing the woman whom millions of other men longed for:

> Congratulations. Pat Covici tells me you are to be married. That is quite often a good idea.
>
> I am going out there around the end of the month to spend the fated six weeks and have no idea where to live. I have a problem, however, of slightly unusual proportions. From time to time there will be a visitor who is very dear to me, but who is unfortunately recognizable by approximately a hundred million people, give or take three or four. She has all sorts of wigs, can affect a limp, sunglasses, bulky coats, etc., but if it is possible I want to find a place, perhaps a bungalow or something like, where there are not likely to be crowds looking in through the windows. Do you know of any such place?

Bellow was then living in one of two isolated cabins on Sutcliffe Star Route, on the western shore of Pyramid Lake, and in due course Miller rented the one next door. Both the cabins and the lake, about forty miles north of Reno, were on the Paiute Indian reservation. In those days there was almost no one else around, and the lunar landscape seemed just the way it was when the world was first created. Ten years earlier, Edmund Wilson had stayed in Minden, south of Reno, while waiting for his divorce. He'd amused himself in that debauched and dehydrated part of the world by exploring the desert, lakes and wildflowers, walking around the pleasant town square and doing a bit of gambling. In a letter to Vladimir Nabokov, he described it as "a queer and desolate country – less romantic than prehistoric and spooky."

A motel near the cabins had once put up people waiting for a divorce, but now housed only the owners, who had the only pay phone between the cabins and Reno. When a call came, they'd drive over to summon one of the self-absorbed writers to the outside world. The companionable highlight of the week was the drive to Reno in Bellow's Chevy to do their laundry and buy groceries for their spartan meals. Bellow stayed longer than the required six weeks, with his new bride Sondra Tschacbasov, in order to continue work on his novel

Henderson the Rain King. (His second marriage lasted only three years, and he would satirize his ex-wife as Madeleine in *Herzog.*)

In a letter of May 12, 1956 to his college teacher Kenneth Rowe, Miller emphasized his strange isolation: "There is no living soul nor tree nor shrub above the height of the sagebrush. I am not counting my neighbors, Saul Bellow, the novelist, and his wife, because they are on my side against the lunar emptiness around us." Miller recalled that Bellow, in a Reichian catharsis, liked to scream into the landscape: "Saul would sometimes spend half an hour up behind a hill a half-mile from the cottages emptying his lungs roaring at the stillness, an exercise in self-contact."

Sondra Bellow – who rode horses from the dude ranch into the hills behind the house – recalled that the two writers did not, as one might expect, have intense and stimulating conversations:

> Miller came out perhaps in mid- or late May for his six-week residency. We overlapped maybe three weeks at most, since we left Nevada the beginning of June. The conversations with Miller at that time were less than fascinating, at least from a literary point of view. He talked a bit about his marriage and how difficult it was to make the decision to get a divorce. But his attention was almost totally focused on Marilyn Monroe. He talked non-stop about her – her career, her beauty, her talent, even her perfect feet. He showed us the now famous photos by Milton Greene – all quite enlightening since neither Mr. Bellow nor I had ever even heard of her before this. To my disappointment, Monroe was filming *Bus Stop* at the time, and never did get to visit Miller in Nevada.
>
> I actually spent more time with Miller than did Bellow, who dedicated much of his day to writing, and believe me, conversation was not at all literary, as you can surmise from the above. Miller occupied himself mornings in his cabin, and also spent a huge amount of time talking (presumably to Monroe) on the only available telephone in the area. This was a pay telephone booth a half mile away on a dirt road used primarily – and rarely – by hunters traveling north. He and I would spend some afternoons together – sightseeing, or going into Reno, or hiking around Pyramid Lake. He generally had dinner with us, during which he repeated all the Marilyn stories he had already told me during the day.

I believe the "bond" between [Bellow and Miller] at this time had much less to do with their being writers, and more to do with their being in somewhat the same place in terms of ending a long-term marriage and starting anew with a much younger woman. I never heard a single literary exchange between them.

They sort of metaphorically circled each other, and pawed the ground. You just knew it from their body language. They told jokes – especially shaggy dog stories with a Yiddish flavor – and gossiped rather than have significant conversation.

Miller had all those Hollywood connections that Bellow would have felt was "selling out." But it was fun to hear his stories. He also thought Miller was not a real intellectual (like the *Partisan Review* crowd). Bellow came from a rabbinical intellectual tradition and Miller's father didn't read or write but had his wife help him.

Miller also was soon to be testifying in Washington before the House Un-American Activities Committee, but there was little substantive discussion about this as well, mostly because Miller was caught up in the Monroe romance, and also, in part, because Bellow and Miller had very different political philosophies. [Bellow was a Trotskyite at the time and Miller was not.][2]

Miller and Bellow were both born in 1915 to Jewish immigrant parents. Bellow had reviewed Miller's novel, *Focus* (1945), in the *New Republic* and thought the sudden transformation of the main character from Jew-hater to a man who accepts his enforced identity as a Jew was unconvincing: "The whole thing is thrust on him. . . . Mr. Newman's heroism has been clipped to his lapel. . . . If only he had had more substance to begin with." Miller accepted the criticism and didn't hold it against him. He published his short story, "Please Don't Kill Anything," in Bellow's little magazine, the *Noble Savage*, and later commended Bellow's work: "I like everything he writes. He still has a joy in writing. . . . He is a genius. . . . He's kind of a psychic journalist – which is invaluable. He's just simply interesting. . . . His work seems necessary, which is high praise. It seems to mark the moment." Bellow won the Nobel Prize, Miller did not, which may account for his rather patronizing tone.

Miller didn't spend all his time with his companions at Pyramid Lake. Marilyn, working on *Bus Stop*, never visited him in Nevada. But

Miller, risking the loss of continuous residence that was required for his divorce, secretly slipped into Los Angeles for a series of romantic encounters on Sunset Boulevard. (The FBI, tracking Miller's movements, knew he was leaving Nevada to see Marilyn.) Amy Greene recalled that "Arthur would come out on weekends . . . they'd lock themselves up at the Chateau Marmont Hotel. He would arrive on Friday, she would go to the Marmont that night, come back to us Sunday night and she would be a mess on Monday. He was still married and she would be upset because she couldn't show this man off to everyone because he still had a wife and two children in Brooklyn."

On June 2, after Bellow's departure, Miller told him that conditions had radically changed at Pyramid Lake and described the intrusive publicity that would both excite and plague them throughout their marriage. Marilyn was protected by the studio, which controlled access by the press. But Miller, though a famous playwright, had never experienced such aggressive attention: "The front page of the [*New York Daily*] *News* has us about to be married, and me 'readying' my divorce here. All hell breaks loose. The [imported] phones all around never stop ringing. Television trucks — (as I live!) — drive up, cameras grinding, screams, yells — I say nothing, give them some pictures, retire into the cabin. They finally go away."[3]

Miller, not Mary, was granted a divorce on the grounds of her extreme mental cruelty, but she exacted harsh terms and made him pay dearly for his betrayal. She "was awarded custody of their two children, Jane (b. 1944) and Robert (b. 1947), child support payments (including rises in the cost of living), the house they had recently bought on Willow Street in Brooklyn Heights, plus a percentage of all his future earnings until she remarried (she never did)." He managed to keep their weekend house in Connecticut, but was responsible for all her legal costs as well as his own. He felt guilty and was willing to pay for his mistakes in order to marry Marilyn. Most of his friends never saw Mary again. She just disappeared and seemed to be wiped out of existence. During our conversation, Mary refused to discuss her contribution to Miller's early success. I told her that she'd been repeatedly characterized as a dull, boring, sexless wife who'd been cast off when someone better turned up. Instead of defending herself, she self-effacingly said: "Maybe I was."[4]

II

Many men had slept with Marilyn, both before and after she'd become a famous sex symbol, and thought nothing of abandoning her the following day, but Miller was devoted to her and always treated her with respect. He perceived her innocence beneath the sexy image, found her waif-like quality appealing and instinctively felt sorry for her. He thought she was opaque and mysterious – not at all the happy, dizzy blonde – and wanted to rescue her from her profound misery. At the same time, he saw her talent and realized he could write material for her and about her. She was a personal and artistic challenge, a tragic muse. She was also fascinating because she was so extraordinarily desirable in the eyes of the world. Miller was famous, but Marilyn was a phenomenon.

Miller was particularly susceptible to Marilyn's lively spirit and devastating charm. He basked in her unqualified adoration, a soothing contrast to Mary's stern disapproval, unremitting criticism and bitter vengeance. He'd met Mary at Michigan and married her when he was twenty-five; he was tortured by shyness in college and felt he'd never experienced real passion in marriage. Marilyn was only the second woman he'd ever known intimately. Miller (like Mary) was rather solemn; Marilyn was funny and her wit released his emotional constraints and made him relish his life with her. He thought he'd discovered hidden depths in Marilyn – and in himself. It flattered his ego to possess the most glamorous movie star in the world. Yet he believed he could spirit her away from her fame and give her a rooted, respectable life; that he could teach, protect and take care of her; and that they could pursue their dramatic careers together.

He called Marilyn "the most womanly woman I can imagine. . . . She's a kind of lodestone that draws out of the male animal his essential qualities." There was also, in his passionate turmoil, a strong irrational element. "Miller was in love," Rosten noted, "completely, seriously, with the ardor of a man released. His first marriage had ended badly; now his second chance had come, and it swept him into channels of newly discovered emotion." When asked if he'd foreseen the problems that would later destroy his marriage and then Marilyn herself, Miller replied, "If I had been sophisticated enough, I would have seen them. But I was not. I loved her."[5]

When Marilyn came to New York she was lost and looking for a savior. Confused, friendless and mentally fragile, constantly exploited, both personally and professionally, she was emotionally needy. She saw safety in Miller's cautious reserve, security in his personal success. In contrast to many alcoholic playwrights – O'Neill, Williams, Inge and Albee – he was sane and sober. Unlike all her other friends, he didn't want to make money out of her. She had always been attracted to older, smarter men, especially to those who wore glasses. Always in search of heroes, she had admired Abraham Lincoln as wise and good, and now saw Miller as an attractive version of Lincoln himself. "He's so gorgeous," she told Lee Strasberg's actress-daughter Susan, "I love to cuddle with him. He's the most beautiful man I've ever seen. . . . And he's so brilliant. He and your father are the two most brilliant men in the world" – which is exactly what Miller wanted to hear. In a dubious compliment, she also said his mind was better than that of any other man she'd ever known. She was pleased that he understood and sympathized with her desire to improve herself. He became her guide, philosopher and friend, and introduced her, partly through his personal example, to the idea of political freedom.

Marilyn believed that Miller had the moral stature to absolve her of her shameful past and the integrity to enhance her self-esteem. In 1950, the year before they met, after a dinner with the Welsh poet Dylan Thomas, Marilyn refused to accompany Thomas to a party at Charlie Chaplin's house. Shelley Winters, her roommate at the time, described her deep-rooted insecurity: "It was a long time before Marilyn ever felt intelligent enough to mix socially with important intelligent people, if she ever did. Maybe that feeling is what was behind her marriage to Arthur Miller. (If you don't graduate from high school – marry an intellectual.)"

Marilyn felt that marriage to Miller would make her a better person and give her a better life. She believed that if she were nothing but a dumb blonde – and she'd always been seen and typecast in this role – he would not want to marry her. Kazan, perceptive as always, explained the feeling of inferiority that only Miller was able to assuage: "What she needed above all was to have her sense of worth affirmed. . . . She wanted more than anything else approval from men she could respect. . . . She deeply wanted reassurance of her worth, yet she respected the men who scorned her, because their estimate of her was her own."[6]

Orson Welles and Rita Hayworth, another unlikely couple, were attracted to each other for the same reasons: "Welles had been drawn to Hayworth because of her sexually iconic quality: conquering her had boosted his image and his ego. He had courted her by gently penetrating beyond the goddess and the star and by urging her to reveal her private hopes, disappointments and dreams. She was attracted to him because he was the first man who seemed willing to listen to her and treat her as something other than a sex-object."

Marilyn admired in Miller all the qualities that she herself lacked: his intellect and culture, his strength and self-discipline, his shrewdness about money and simple way of life. Each one wished to enter the other's world: Miller wanted to write screenplays; Marilyn wanted to become a serious stage actress. He fondly saw them working side by side and drawing inspiration from each other. Marilyn, who'd always wanted to have children, even imagined – while she was making *Bus Stop* and he was in Nevada – that she'd give up her career and settle down as a housewife and mother. She said, "when I married Miller, one of the fantasies I had in my mind was that [through him] I could get out of Marilyn Monroe," a creature invented by the studio. Expressing an unrealistic hope, she told him: "I hate [Hollywood], I don't want it anymore, I want to live quietly in the country and just be there when you need me. I can't fight for myself anymore."[7]

Despite her psychological traumas and sexual scars, their completely different backgrounds, religion and family life, education, tastes and interests, the inhibited Miller and free-spirited Marilyn fell in love. They idealized each other and formed what seemed to be a satisfying complement of mind and body. Their marriage began with physical attraction and the secret thrill of adultery, with a common interest in acting and the theater, with their mutual fame and the narcissistic magnetism of one celebrity for another.

Many playwrights – Eugene O'Neill, Clifford Odets, John Osborne and Harold Pinter, for example – would marry, and divorce, actresses. Several friends, both at the time and with hindsight, thought Miller was making a terrible mistake. Kazan – confirming the set-designer Boris Aronson's devastating question: "That's a wife?" – was astonished by Miller's proposal: "He couldn't be thinking of marrying her! Marilyn simply wasn't a wife. Anyone could see that," except his naïve and inexperienced friend. Miller himself quoted Marcello Mastroianni, who'd appeared in his plays in Italy. Adopting a cavalier attitude, the actor asked him: "'But so much trouble over a woman?' 'Why? What would you do?' 'I would . . . take a walk.'"

The photographer Arnold Newman, brutally frank when interviewed on a television documentary, called Marilyn "the worst woman you'd ever want to get mixed up with; the most unhappy and with the most problems. A very troubled woman." Miller, with more than a touch of arrogance, thought he could get away with what no intellectual had ever dared to do. The actor Brian Dennehy explained Miller's feelings: "Of course Marilyn was not a promising wife, but that didn't matter. She was Helen of Troy, every man's dream. She had a compelling personality and tremendous energy, was powerful beyond reason and hypnotized everyone. Nobody was immune to her, and Arthur was enthralled. He fell madly in love with her and with the idea of her.[8]

III

When Marilyn moved to New York she said she wanted to educate herself, and Manhattan intellectuals were happy to oblige. Celebrities become ecstatic at the sight of other celebrities, though a movie star's fame always trumps a writer's. The local literati, eager to bask in her reflected glory, all wanted to meet her. They soon learned the art of being with and being seen with her – the celebrity dance of being famous together. She had never known any other society but lower-class Hawthorne and Hollywood, and was pleased by all the attention she was getting from prominent people in the cultural capital of America.

Marilyn was twenty-eight years old, emotionally vulnerable but pretty and charming, and everyone wanted to know what she was *really* like. Was she beautiful or vulgar? Genuine or artificial? Sexy or sluttish? Witty or just dim-witted? Voracious publicists and magazine editors looking for sure-fire copy encouraged incongruous, absurd and potentially contentious encounters between Marilyn and highbrow authors she'd never read – nor even heard of. They hoped the beasts would chew each other up and that blood would be shed. Instead, she established a natural affinity with many writers who were, like herself, eccentrics and outsiders, heavy drinkers and drug-takers, physically ill and mentally unstable. She desperately longed for "someone to take me out who doesn't expect anything from me."

She felt more at ease with the homosexuals Truman Capote and Tennessee Williams. Later on she found Montgomery Clift, her co-star in *The Misfits*, a perfect companion. He had no sexual designs on her, no perilous pounce. Filled with self-doubt and neurotic fears, dependent on painkillers and alcohol, he was, Marilyn observed, "the only person I know who's in worse shape than me."

Christopher Isherwood had introduced Marilyn to the notoriously drunken and obstreperous Dylan Thomas in April 1950, when she was still playing bit parts in films. Thomas declared that he'd come to Hollywood "to touch the titties of a beautiful blond starlet," and Marilyn was well qualified to satisfy his fantasies. But when Thomas came to dinner at the flat she was sharing with Shelley Winters, he sensed Marilyn's vulnerability and behaved with unusual propriety. Though he joked with and teased Shelley,

> he was quiet and respectful to Marilyn. Marilyn was so sure things were bound to go awry that I think she unconsciously made things happen to get the waiting over with. I saw her do this time and time again. Dylan Thomas seemed aware that behind the eyelashes and platinum hair and terrific body, there was a fragile and sensitive girl. . . . He was obviously a horny Welshman, but he never once made any kind of pass at Marilyn. Not even a verbal one. I don't think it was because her looks didn't turn him on; he was obviously mad about platinum-blond starlets. I think this poet sensed that she very badly needed not to be thought of as just a tits-and-ass cutie.

She met the Irish playwright Brendan Behan – also notorious for his heavy drinking and outrageous behavior – when he was in New York in 1960 during the successful run of *The Hostage*. He sent her a respectful tribute, clipped to her copy of *The Misfits*: "For Marilyn Monroe – a credit to the human race, mankind in general and womankind in particular."[9] At the beginning and end of her career, she managed to inspire the sympathy and tame the lust of the two Celtic poets.

Capote had met Marilyn through John Huston when she was working on *The Asphalt Jungle*, and she contacted him when she came to New York. Marilyn made dramatic appearances at El Morocco, the Colony and the Plaza Oak Room with Capote and kicked off her high-heeled shoes while dancing with him so she wouldn't be a head taller than her dwarfish consort. A photographer captured Marilyn, in a black dress and with bare arms, turning her eyes to the camera and smiling naturally. Capote – bespectacled and balding, his hair messed up, tie and collar awry, two buttons tightly buttoned on his gray pin-striped suit – holds Marilyn by the wrist. He seems to have trouble keeping up with her and his mouth hangs open like a fish gasping for air.

Two years older than Marilyn, Capote shared her dependence on drink and drugs. Ever the publicity hound, he styled himself her friend and said he wanted Marilyn (not Audrey Hepburn) to play Holly Golightly in *Breakfast at Tiffany's*. With typically disparaging wit he declared that her marriage to Miller would be the *Death of a Playwright*. After Marilyn's death he wrote two crude, self-serving and denigrating essays about her in *The Dogs Bark* (1973) and *Music for Chameleons* (1980).

In his chapter on "Marilyn Monroe," he calls her "just a slob, really" and describes her vulgar mannerisms: "her slippery lips, her over-spilling blondness and sliding brassiere straps, the rhythmic writhing of restless poundage wriggling for room inside roomless décolletage – such are her emblems." Indifferent to her charm, he loathes the lush femininity that her public so admired. He concludes, with pop-psychology and bogus religious imagery, that "she is stained, and illuminated by, the stigmata of orphan-thinking"; that the depth of her anxiety, "her frequent sore-throated indispositions, her nibbled nails, her damp palms, her Japanese-like fits of giggling induces a butter-hearted sympathy." Capote clearly saw the orphan's desperate desire to be liked, but felt no compassion for her wounded spirit.

An outrageous liar who liked to smear straight men, Capote used his second essay on Marilyn to spread obscene scandal about Errol Flynn. In Capote's malicious tale, Marilyn claims that she saw Flynn publicly playing a piano with his prick. Flinging more mud at Flynn, Capote falsely claimed that in 1943 he had had a one-night stand with the handsome Flynn. The title of this essay, "A Beautiful Child," comes from Marilyn's sometime acting teacher Constance Collier, who rightly said, "This beautiful child is without any concept of disci-pline or sacrifice." Capote has Marilyn exclaim, "I like to dance naked in front of mirrors and watch my titties jump around." When she confronts a dimly lit mirror and he asks, "What are you doing?," she cryptically replies, "Looking at Her." But he doesn't connect the two mirror scenes, nor understand that she looked into the mirror in search of herself. Though her tits were reassuringly real, her identity was not.

Capote had called Marilyn a slob in his first essay and he felt obliged to repeat this in the second. Still trying to define her true identity, she remarks, "if anybody asked you what I was like, what Marilyn Monroe was *really* like — well, how would you answer them? . . . I bet you'd tell them I was a slob." In contrast to all the other writers who knew her, Capote portrays a Marilyn insecure about her clothing, confused about her identity, spooked by death, childishly narcissistic and a vulgar slob. Like many of her "friends," Capote exploited her to publicize himself. After her death, when his drinking increased and his career declined, he turned her into salable copy.

Marilyn met Carson McCullers (who was nine years older) in 1954 when they were both staying at the Gladstone, a small, stuffy apartment-hotel on East 52nd Street, off Park Avenue. She accompanied McCullers and Tennessee Williams' mother to a party at the St. Regis Hotel to celebrate the opening of *Cat on a Hot Tin Roof* in 1955, and four years later met Williams again at a publicist's dinner party in Hollywood. McCullers was homely, had had a stroke and lurched around with a cane. Like Marilyn, she drank heavily and gulped down barbiturates, tried to kill herself and did time in the Payne Whitney mental clinic. Virginia Carr wrote that "according to Carson, Miss Monroe had wonderfully admirable attributes."[10] She was capable of instant rapport and conveyed an instinctive warmth to the sickly McCullers.

Like McCullers, the English poet Dame Edith Sitwell, grotesque at sixty-six, was a perfect foil for Marilyn's youthful perfection. Strangely adorned with an elaborate turban, Sitwell was six feet tall, pale-faced and lank-haired, with a distinct curvature of the spine and a long curved nose that resembled an anteater's. The daughter of a wealthy coal magnate, Sitwell claimed descent from the Norman conquerors. Disdaining her work, the critic F.R. Leavis remarked that she belonged "to the history of publicity rather than that of poetry." True to form, when she visited Hollywood in February 1954 she also wanted to meet Marilyn. *Life* magazine, mistakenly convinced that the two women "were born to hate each other, and that their insults to each other 'would cause a commotion when reported,'" brought them together. But Sitwell found her serious-minded and pleasantly shy – that is, suitably intimidated and deferential. They actually had something in common. Sitwell's shallow pretensions and Marilyn's naïve search for meaning in life came together as they talked about the "spiritual doctrines" of the crankish Hungarian anthroposophist, Rudolf Steiner.

When Sitwell returned to England early in 1955, she was annoyed to discover that journalists wanted to talk only about Monroe. Ignoring the fact that *she* was the one who wanted to meet Marilyn (who, of course, had never heard of her) and irritated that Marilyn had upstaged her, Sitwell relegated her to the common herd. She imperiously exclaimed: "I am *not* bringing Miss Marilyn Monroe to England. Is it supposed that I am a publicity agent or a film agent or a press agent? . . . Miss Monroe, like a good many other people, was brought to see me while I was in Hollywood. I thought her a very nice girl, and said to her as I said to others, that if she came to London she should let me know and should come to a luncheon party. There the matter began and ended."[11]

Surprisingly enough, they *did* meet again, in October 1956, when Marilyn was in London making *The Prince and the Showgirl*. Victoria Glendinning described their rather prosaic luncheon at the Sesame Club: "this time Miller and Edith did the talking, while the star sat and listened. The party was spoiled by the intrusion of overexcited photographers and journalists." In his account of the same meeting, Donald Spoto eliminated Miller. He dramatized the encounter and added the exotic costumes, bountiful alcohol and poignant lines of poetry:

> [Sitwell] welcomed Marilyn to her home [i.e. her club] in October. Wearing her usual array of rings on each finger, a medieval gown, a Plantagenet headdress and a mink stole, Dame Edith sat grandly, pouring hefty beakers of gin and grapefruit juice for herself and her guest. During several hours one afternoon, they sat discussing Gerard Manley Hopkins and Dylan Thomas, whose poems Marilyn was reading during sleepless nights that season. For Dame Edith, Marilyn recited lines from one of Hopkins's *Terrible Sonnets* – "I wake and feel the fell of dark, not day [/ What hours, O what black hours we have spent / This night"] – saying that she

understood perfectly the poet's mood of despair. "She's quite remarkable!" pronounced Sitwell soon after.

But even the self-absorbed Sitwell could not miss Marilyn's profound unhappiness and insecurity. She told reporters that the mild-mannered actress had known great poverty and reminded her of a teenage child who had been forced to fend for herself. Sitwell's final judgment was both naïve about Marilyn's recklessly self-destructive sexual life (the virginal poet lacked carnal knowledge) and, with hindsight, poetically precious about her tragic death: "She was very quiet and had great natural dignity (I cannot imagine anyone who knew her trying to take a liberty with her) and was extremely intelligent. She was also exceedingly sensitive. . . . In repose, her face was at moments strangely, prophetically tragic, like the face of a beautiful ghost – a little spring-ghost, an innocent fertility-daemon, the vegetation spirit that was Ophelia." Sitwell gave Marilyn a photo of herself by Philippe Halsman, wearing her elaborate hairdo and huge jeweled rings on several spidery fingers. Marilyn later said, "I expected her to be a real English snob, but she wasn't. She was what my mother would have called a Lady. A grand lady, strong enough to stand up to men."[12] Marilyn and Edith got on well, but completely misunderstood each other's characters. The publicists were wrong to assume that Marilyn would clash rather than sympathize with literary and political celebrities. Though some of them tried to use her, most sensed her vulnerability and admired her sincerity and goodwill.

Eight

New York and the Actors Studio
(1954–1956)

I

Just as Marilyn was confused about her own identity, and let herself be used as a studio property, a piece of "talent" to be traded or exploited, she did not fully understand or accept her limitations as an actress. She had a natural gift for comedy and extraordinary photogenic qualities that made her so striking on film. These were her great strengths, but because they came naturally she did not value them, and could not enjoy her spectacular fame as a movie star. Full of anxiety about the future, and worried that she'd lose her appeal when she lost her looks, she decided to give up almost everything she had achieved and try for an impossible goal: to be a serious stage actress. At the end of 1954 she joined the Actors Studio to study the "Method" under Lee Strasberg, the most influential drama teacher of his time. At this turning point in her life, Marilyn's choice was unwise. Strasberg's teaching, with its emphasis on the actor's inner responses to the role, and his advice that she should undergo psychoanalysis, had a decidedly negative effect on her professional and personal life.

Strasberg had emigrated to America as a child in 1909, and had grown up in a Jewish neighborhood on the Lower East Side of New York. He studied with two of Stanislavsky's disciples, and founded the left-wing Group Theater with Kazan in 1931. His career in Hollywood was brief and disappointing. He spent the postwar years directing trivial screen tests at Fox, which fired him in 1947. In 1951, four years after the Actors Studio was founded, he became its artistic director. He had some famous and charismatic students – Marlon Brando, James Dean and Paul Newman – and their spectacular success made the Method popular with aspiring actors.

Short, thin, intense and extremely critical, Strasberg was stern and distant with his pupils. Like Natasha Lytess, Michael Chekhov and Fred Karger, he was an authoritarian personality who advocated discipline, structure and willpower. A biographer wrote that "Strasberg was revered and deeply feared by the actors. To suffer his wrath, whether it be a masked, stoical iciness or a shrill, maniacally enraged outburst, was each actor's nightmare; to be approved by him, the dream. The limitless power vested in him by these actors for their spiritual life or death was awesome."

Torn between a desire for self-improvement and a habit of self-indulgence, Marilyn seemed an unlikely candidate for this stern tuition. Since she never came to the set on time and couldn't learn her lines, even for a brief movie scene, she seemed to lack the necessary discipline to become a stage actress, memorize three hours of dialogue and give eight performances a week. But Strasberg, delighted to secure such a prominent disciple, bent the credulous Marilyn to his will.

The Studio, located in a deconsecrated Greek Orthodox church with a worn brick façade on West 44th Street, between Ninth and Tenth Avenues, offered several kinds of acting classes. A key part of the discipline was the public presentation of a scene and open discussion and critique of the students' work. Each week at 11 a.m. on Tuesdays and Fridays about a hundred actors would gather to watch two or three of their colleagues act a scene and then explain what they were trying to achieve. Anyone in the audience could comment on or even severely criticize the performance, and at the end Strasberg, the presiding deity, would pass final judgment. Susan Strasberg wrote that Marilyn got special treatment. She "would observe at the studio, work with him at home, sit in on the private classes, and eventually do the exercise work and scenes with the other students."[1] He taught her movement, breath control and projection, and directed her in short scenes.

Strasberg believed, or pretended to believe, in Marilyn's dramatic talent and told her she could transform herself from playing trivial parts in mediocre movies to performing tragic roles on stage. He even said that she could play Lady Macbeth or Cordelia in *King Lear*. Though savage with other actors, he praised her excessively and convinced her that "she was capable of towering achievements, that her motion picture work barely scratched the surface of her latent and untapped talent." Though there was no sign of this genius, even after years of tuition, Strasberg ranked her with Sarah Bernhardt and Eleanora Duse. After her death, he categorically declared that had she lived, "without a doubt she would have been one of the really great actresses of the stage." It is far more likely that he believed Marilyn could help him compensate for his failure in Hollywood and revive his own theatrical career. His biographer wrote that "The Method was known inside the profession. Kazan's movies brought it to national attention. Marilyn made the Studio a household word."[2]

The essential principles of Stanislavsky's Method were rather abstract and confusing, especially to a dreamy, uneducated novice like Marilyn. Maurice Zolotow described Stanislavsky's key terms: "*Justification* requires the Method actor to find some emotional, logical, or factual reason for every action he performs. *Objectification* is relating oneself to the physical objects, the props, in a scene. *Concentration* is the immersion of oneself in the story to such an extent that one achieves a trance-like state, existing entirely in terms of the make-believe world." Another basic concept was "sense memory," the idea that the actor would recall a past experience in his life, translate it into an emotional state and use it to create the character he was playing on stage. But the self-absorbed Marilyn could only be harmed by getting herself into a deeper "trance-like state" and recalling dangerous memories.

Arthur Miller regarded the Method as essentially hostile to the words of the playwright, and felt it encouraged the actors' hermetic egoism and cryptic inwardness:

[Strasberg is] a force which is not for the good in the theater. He makes actors secret people and he makes acting secret, and it's the most communicative art known to man. . . .

The problem is that the actor is now working out his private fate through his role, and the idea of communicating the meaning of the play is the last thing that occurs to him. In the Actors Studio, despite denials, the actor is told that the text is really the framework for his emotions . . . that the analysis of the text, and the rhythm of the text, and the verbal texture, is of no importance whatever. . . . Chekhov, himself, said that Stanislavsky had perverted *The Seagull.*

Joan Copeland, who knew Marilyn at the Actors Studio, thought she was innately a Method actress and that her work revealed how intensely she was driven by inner demons. Marilyn herself believed that Strasberg's teaching was therapeutic, and helped her (as she vaguely said) to "deepen my understanding of my way to approach myself."[3] It was dangerous to tell the emotionally unstable Marilyn, who tended to worship her teachers, to use her pain and use her past. In ordinary life, she couldn't face her pain and tried to suppress her past. When under pressure to perform, she regressed into her childhood stutter.

It was difficult for Marilyn to reveal her inner self and courageous of her to face the criticism of other actors. In February 1956, after studying with Strasberg for a year, she finally appeared with Maureen Stapleton and played the title role in the opening scene of Eugene O'Neill's *Anna Christie* (1921). (Greta Garbo had played Anna in the early sound version of 1930, which had drawn huge crowds with the famous slogan: "Garbo talks.") Anna's past history is revealed in the course of the play. After the death of her mother, Anna had been abandoned by her father and sent to live with relatives. Seduced by a cousin when she was sixteen, she had run away and become a prostitute. In this opening scene the young Anna comes to New York to meet her father, whom she's not seen since childhood and who's been responsible for all her misery.

Strasberg chose this scene, with its clear and psychologically risky parallels with Marilyn's own life, believing that her remembrance of the past would strengthen her performance. Marilyn had also been deserted by her father, been abused by men as a child and worked as a prostitute. In the play Anna says:

> They had to send me to the hospital. It was nice there. I was sorry to leave it, honest! . . .
>
> It's my Old Man I got to meet. . . . I ain't seen him since I was a kid – don't even know what he looks like. . . .
>
> He ain't never done a thing for me in my life. . . . But I ain't expecting much from him. Give you a kick when you're down, that's what all men do.

Kazan described the Actors Studio's rather hostile and resentful attitude toward Marilyn: "The older members had seen that their leader held this movie star, a surprisingly modest girl of modest talent, in awe. They'd believed that he had praised her far beyond her due and no matter how uncertain her work. And that he'd enjoyed his power over her. His raves about her talent they'd considered to be mistaken." But Marilyn gave a surprisingly successful performance. Anna Sten, a Russian actress who'd appeared in Stanislavky's Moscow Art Theater, enthusiastically recalled, "I only ever saw her do one thing at the Studio, when she did *Anna Christie*, and everyone is still talking about it, how magnificent she was." Kim Stanley, an intense, Method-trained stage actress, agreed that Marilyn "was wonderful. We were taught never to clap at the Actors Studio, like we were in church and all that, but it was the first time I'd ever heard applause there."[4] Marilyn may have been impressive, but the actors also clapped because they knew Strasberg would be watching and wanted their public approval. Despite their praise, she never repeated this brief triumph. The result of her year's work at the Actors Studio was not a stage career, but a return to the same mediocre movies in Hollywood. From then on she would have all the Strasbergs' pretentious baggage, and would usually be accompanied by either Lee or Paula as her coach.

II

Strasberg also taught his daughter Susan, who nevertheless felt that her father neglected her and focused on Marilyn. He wisely told Susan to use her natural gifts and follow her intuitive instincts: "What are you doing, darling? You *are* lyrical; for God's sake, don't *act* lyrical. . . . A wonderful actor with no training is better than a bad actor with all the training in the world." Yet he gave the opposite advice to Marilyn. She, too, was a natural actress who followed her instincts and was spontaneously funny without realizing how funny she was. Though Strasberg recognized that "she was already a real actress, but she didn't know it," he forced her to adhere slavishly to his theories. Billy Wilder later explained how the Method had inhibited and nearly extinguished her instinctive spontaneity: "Before going to the Actors Studio she was like a tightrope walker who doesn't know there's a pit down there she could fall into. Now she knows about the pit, and she's more careful on the tightrope. She's self-conscious."[5]

Marilyn sought the training at the Actors Studio to improve her skills, but instead of gaining poise and self-confidence she became completely dependent on Lee and his wife Paula. Kazan, a close observer of both guru and disciple, emphasized Strasberg's lust for power and the gross flattery he devised to gain control of his precious acquisition: "The more naïve and self-doubting the actors, the more total was Lee's power over them. The more famous and the more successful these actors, the headier the taste of power for Lee. He found the perfect victim-devotee in Marilyn Monroe. . . . He encouraged her beyond her gifts in the direction of goals she was not equipped to reach. . . . He soon had her spellbound, feeding her the reassurance of worth she most craved." A minor but significant incident occurred when Strasberg ignored her. It showed how Marilyn, aware of her subservience but too frightened to break away, hung on Strasberg's every word and could be shattered by his silence: "My 'Pope' . . . caused me to run right to my shrink when he didn't say hello in the elevator. That set me back months in analysis. I figure he's unseeing and unhearing me because I'm such a terrible actor. I'm not even worthy of saying hello to."

Once Marilyn had become Strasberg's disciple, he influenced all her decisions and persuaded her to reject an important role in a television drama. She'd always wanted to play the prostitute in Somerset Maugham's powerful story "Rain"; and Maugham himself, "touched and pleased by her desire to be his Sadie [Thompson], said she would be 'splendid.'"[6] But when the executives would not allow Strasberg, who had no experience on television, to direct the adaptation of the story, she withdrew from the project. Marilyn also wanted to appear in John Huston's film biography, *Freud*, but again withdrew when Freud's daughter Anna, a friend of her psychiatrist, Ralph Greenson, didn't want the picture to be made.

Marilyn's mentors and manipulators, Natasha Lytess and the Strasbergs, had a great deal in common. In their doomed effort to turn her into a dramatic actress, they exploited her financially, invited her into their homes, made her dependent upon them, controlled her life, came into fierce conflict with her directors, and aroused the hatred of her husbands and friends. When Miller married Marilyn, he realized that she was pathetically reliant on the Strasbergs and tolerated them to avoid conflict with her. "Lee becomes a guru," Miller said, "and unless he is there, [she] can't move. I never blasted him to

Marilyn because she needed him. I recognized that dependency and as long as she got something out of it, I never said anything. We just didn't discuss him." After their marriage broke up, Miller was more critical of Strasberg's lust for power and damaging theories:

> Strasberg's approach was to force his domination rather than to free up somebody to do without him. . . . She was so vulnerable that she couldn't recover from it. She became more and more addicted to that dependency. . . . She had a natural gift, and she didn't live long enough to absorb any teaching without crippling that gift. . . .
>
> Marilyn, a natural comedienne, seemed distracted by half-digested, spitballed imagery and pseudo-Stanislavskian parallelisms that left her unable to free her own native joyousness. She was being doused by a spurious intellection that was thoroughly useless to her as an acting tool.[7]

Paula Strasberg, who coached Marilyn on her movie sets while Lee ran the Actors Studio in New York, was even more meddling and intrusive. Most established actors did not need a coach; if they did, they took private lessons in the coach's studio. Insecure as ever, Marilyn defied convention by bringing Paula on to the set and into head-on conflict with the directors. Instead of building Marilyn's confidence in her own decisions, Paula – for her own selfish reasons – made her more insecure than ever.

The young Colin Clark, son of the distinguished art historian Sir Kenneth Clark and on the scene during the making of *The Prince and the Showgirl*, described Paula as "short and plump, with brown hair pulled back from a plain, round, expressive face. She has big brown eyes which are usually hidden by big dark glasses – like her protégée. Her clothes are also brown and beige – bohemian but expensive. Her influence over Marilyn Monroe seems to be total. Marilyn Monroe gazes at her continuously and defers to her at all times, as if she was a little Jewish Buddha." For her services, Paula charged Marilyn the extortionate fee of $2,500 a week plus expenses.

Paula earned her keep by putting Marilyn through absurd exercises and by inflating her ego with outrageous praise. To release the tension in her body and loosen her up, she made Marilyn practice a daily ritual of shaking her hands as if trying to detach them from her wrists. Paula did not try to control Marilyn's habitual lateness, but actually encouraged and even justified her prima donna behavior: "What I tell her is, 'You are the one who gets on the screen, not the others, who make the movie. You are the star! Only amateurs watch production costs – that already makes a Grade-B movie.'" Colin Clark explained the secret of Paula's hold over Marilyn – "total, abject syco-phancy, continual flattery, blatant pandering" – and described how Paula melodramatically created expectations that her pupil could not possibly fulfill. She would tell her: "All my life, I have prayed on my knees . . . for God to give me a great actress. And now He has given me you, and you are a great actress, Marilyn. You are."[8]

Paula combined parasitic servility with strict demands that Marilyn slavishly follow her orders. In 1956, after Marilyn had suddenly dismissed Natasha and refused to see her, Paula replaced her as coach in *Bus Stop*. Like Natasha, she fed on her pupil's insecurity, insisted that Marilyn look to her rather than to the director for approval and demanded many takes if she was not satisfied with the scene. Lee, defending Paula, admitted her bulldog tenacity and crude quest for power: "They didn't want Paula there. It is a fact that they tried to get rid of her. However, she spoke right up. She let them know what's what. Paula wasn't shy. It wasn't easy to get rid of Paula. . . . With herself as the front and everybody crawling through her to get to Marilyn, she had developed security and confidence. She was emerging as an overpowering entity." Susan loyally declared that the directors, not Paula, were vain and self-seeking: "their overbearing egos had been threatened by my mother's presence, fearing she would get the credit they wanted." It's significant that Paula developed security and confidence while Marilyn became increasingly insecure and afraid.

Miller, usually more frank and honest when talking to Marilyn's biographer Fred Guiles in 1967 than he was in his autobiography *Timebends* in 1987, bitterly criticized Paula's domination as well as her appalling lack of qualifications:

> Marilyn's feelings were very ambivalent about Paula. Paula rep-resented to her in a very real sense her own mother who wasn't there. Paula was a real kook. She was nutty as a fruitcake . . . but Paula was out in the world functioning. Both Lee and Paula by this time had moved in on Marilyn. They had taken her over, at least her career. . . .

I had no respect for Paula's ability as a dramatic coach. She didn't know any more about acting than a cleaning woman out in the foyer. In this sense, she was a phony, a hoax, but she was successful in making herself necessary to people like Marilyn, she created this tremendous reputation . . . She could cater to the vanities of actresses, to people in the theatre. She had this ability.[9]

When Marilyn came to New York, partly to seek out Miller, he was at the apex of the intellectual and cultural world and she was a complete outsider. Awed by both Miller and the Strasbergs, she naturally felt more insecure than ever. Encouraged by Lee Strasberg and following the current fashion, she went into Freudian analysis. Instead of being helped by this treatment, she became deeply disturbed when probing her troubled unconscious. She had wanted to put her old life behind her, but when she tried to explore the depths of her character and "free" herself for the Method, she dredged up troubling memories of her hideous childhood and her years of sexual degradation in Hollywood. Reliving these experiences undermined her precarious balance, and eventually led to nervous breakdowns and suicide attempts.

Marilyn's psychiatrists continued her deep involvement with European immigrants: Schenk and Hyde, Lytess and Chekhov, Kazan and Strasberg, Lang and Preminger, Wilder and Cukor. The first of her three analysts, Dr. Margaret Hohenberg, was recommended by her patient Milton Greene, and felt no conflict of interest in treating both intricately involved people at the same time. A tall, heavy, fifty-seven-year-old Hungarian immigrant, with white hair braided around her head, Hohenberg had been trained in Budapest, Vienna and Prague. Beginning in 1955, she saw her famous patient five times a week in her office on East 93rd Street. In 1956 she was flown to England, at great expense, to soothe Marilyn when a crisis erupted during the making of *The Prince and the Showgirl*. The following year, when Marilyn severed relations with Greene, she stopped seeing Hohenberg.

Hohenberg was succeeded by Dr. Marianne Kris, who also spoke with a strong accent and whose office was conveniently located in Lee Strasberg's apartment building at 135 Central Park West. The daughter of Freud's friend Oskar Rie, a pediatrician, she had earned a medical degree, married the art critic Ernst Kris and become a member of the Vienna Psychoanalytic Institute. She had been analyzed by Freud himself and worked with his daughter Anna, and was forced to flee Austria after the Nazi invasion in 1938. The New York critic Diana Trilling, who began to see Kris after twenty years of psychotherapy, praised the doctor while expressing the patient's typical dependence on and adoration of the analyst: "Although a refugee from Austria, she employed her new language with exactness and elasticity. . . . I never lay on a couch; we talked facing each other, our facial expressions part of our understanding of what was going on. She was a most remarkable woman, warmhearted, large-minded, sensitive, sensible, imaginative, a great unraveler of emotional knots. She looked wise and she was wise. Her very calm was therapeutic."[10] Trilling also criticized her for intervening in her personal life and giving her bad advice. Kris, later on, would make some terrible mistakes with Marilyn.

III

In December 1955, on behalf of Marilyn Monroe Productions, Greene negotiated a new and infinitely better contract with Fox, and Marilyn finally got the compensation she deserved. She agreed to make four movies with the studio in the next seven years, and (most unusually) had approval of the script, director and cinematographer. She would earn $100,000 plus a percentage of the profits for each film, receive an annual retainer of an additional $100,000 and have a weekly allowance of $500 while filming. Greene would also be paid $75,000 a year as her producer.

The studio discussed the possibility of remaking the classic German film, *The Blue Angel* (1930), with Marilyn playing Marlene Dietrich's role, Spencer Tracy as her co-star and George Cukor as the director. In the screen version of Heinrich Mann's novel, the nightclub singer Lola Lola teases, taunts, seduces, degrades, betrays and destroys the dignified but horribly repressed Professor Unrat. This would have been a great picture for Marilyn. But when Tracy felt Marilyn was using him to strengthen her negotiating position with the studio, he withdrew and the project collapsed.

Marilyn, allowed to make one independent picture a year, completed *Bus Stop* and *The Prince and the Showgirl* in partnership with Greene before their company fell apart. An absurd incident during the shooting of *Bus Stop* in March 1956 revealed how Greene consistently put his own interests before those of his fragile star: "Marilyn suddenly fell from a six-foot ramp. Dazed and in momentary shock before writhing in pain, she lay very near to Milton, who as usual was constantly taking still photographs of every scene. 'He just kept clicking away with his camera without moving to help her,' as [the screenwriter] George Axelrod recalled. 'I was a photographer before I was a producer,' was Milton's reply."

Joshua Logan, the eminent director of *Bus Stop*, had made his name on Broadway as the director of *Annie Get Your Gun*, *Mister Roberts* and *South Pacific*. In 1955 he directed the screen version of *Picnic*, by the playwright William Inge, who also wrote *Bus Stop*. Logan, who'd grown up in Texas and graduated from Princeton, had two special qualifications for working with Marilyn. At the age of twenty-three he had spent a year in Moscow studying with Stanislavsky, and in 1940 he'd had a mental breakdown and spent a year in a psychiatric hospital.

Strasberg's teaching made Marilyn passionately interested in the godfather of the Method. Logan recalled that "she talked constantly of Stanislavsky, and she wanted to know all about my studying with him in Moscow. She wanted to know all about the way actors lived and acted there. How Stanislavsky talked to them and they talked to him – intimate details." Marilyn both amused and irritated Logan by the absurdity of her half-digested psychoanalytical jargon. He wrote that "sometimes she acted as though she had discovered something that no one else knew. Words like 'Freudian slip' and 'the unconscious' and 'affective memory' would appear in her conversation at the oddest time. If they didn't fit in, she made them fit." Logan also described Marilyn's rather pretentious exchange with her co-star Don Murray: "'Don, you made a Freudian slip about a phallic symbol. You see, you were thinking unconsciously of a snake. That's why you said "scaly" [instead of "white"]. And a snake is a phallic symbol. Do you know what a phallic symbol is, Don?' 'Know what it is?' he said. 'I've got one!' "[11]

Murray recalled that Marilyn was emotionally frail, and became more and more so as the movie progressed. (While making the picture she also spent a week in the hospital with bronchitis.) Everyone was always very worried about whether she'd break down in a scene and whether Logan would be able to finish the movie. The tall, youthful-looking, little known, twenty-six-year-old Murray was appearing in his first film, but he had to help *Marilyn* perform. Her year of studying the Method made it more difficult for her to act in a movie. After she kept missing her marks on the set, Logan told Murray, "when you're standing close to her, hold her and move her onto the marks" – and Murray had to guide the superstar throughout the picture.

Marilyn, who had a very short concentration span and couldn't remember more than a sentence at a time, would often say the wrong word or fail to complete her lines. There were many takes for every scene (especially when Paula signaled her dissatisfaction), and Murray had the daunting task of having to be at his best for every one of them. Since Marilyn was unable to sustain an entire scene, they were shot in short pieces and had to be spliced together by the film editor, Bill Reynolds. The professionals in Hollywood, recognizing what Reynolds had achieved, nominated him for an Academy Award.

Murray recalled that they also had problems with censorship. Marilyn showed too much cleavage in her fish-net costume and the designer had to put on a chiffon frill to cover up her bust top. And Marilyn's open-mouthed kisses had to be cut. Kissing scenes (Murray said) were never sexy for him or other actors. The technical aspects, the need to watch the lights and avoid shadows on your face, drained away all the potential excitement. In one intense scene the camera caught a trail of saliva coming out of Marilyn's mouth, but Logan couldn't bear to shoot it yet again and reluctantly allowed the drool to remain in the picture.

Marilyn once lost her temper and got into a fight with Murray. In an emotional moment, he had to grab her and tear off a piece of her tawdry costume. After speaking the line, "Give me back my tail," she unintentionally knocked him off his mark, bounced off his chest and fell flat on her back. When Murray, dropping his cowboy accent, asked, "Are you all right, Marilyn?" she angrily replied, "Can't you improvise?" She then slapped him with a piece of spangled cloth, cut him over the eye and stormed off the set. Murray, who'd been incredibly patient with her, became furious and wanted to tell her off. But Logan, desperate to get through the film, stopped him on the way to her dressing room. Alluding to Scipio Africanus, Logan told him, "Remember the Roman general who won the war by avoiding battles." Later on, Murray was astonished when her make-up man, Whitey Snyder, said it had been her "best-behaved movie."

Murray had a much more pleasant time with Hope Lange, who played Marilyn's confidante during their long bus ride and (though a natural blonde) had to have her hair dyed darker so she wouldn't outshine Marilyn. There were rumors on the set about Murray's romance with Lange. But he'd known her since she was in high school; they became engaged before the picture started and got married while the film was being made.[12]

In *Bus Stop* Murray plays an eager, energetic and innocent cowboy; Marilyn – speaking with an unconvincing Southern accent and wearing a hideous sea-green costume – is an exhausted, petulant and sexually experienced nightclub singer. She confesses, "I've had a real wicked life. I've been going with boys since I was twelve years old." She also tells him, "I'd like to get married and have a family. . . . But maybe I don't know what love is." Murray, hoping to redeem a fallen woman with his love, declares "I like you the way you are." In the repetitive script, she keeps trying to escape and he keeps recapturing her. Following the tedious end-of-the-movie convention, she suddenly falls in love with him and agrees to get married. She doesn't seem to realize that she'll have a hard time adjusting to outdoor life on his rough and remote Montana ranch.

Murray recalled that Logan, who also had to put up with Paula's pretentious interference, was very, very patient with Marilyn. He kept up the enthusiasm, like a football coach yelling "rah rah rah, go go go," and managed to finish the picture, with only a half-day's rehearsal, in twelve weeks. But even after *Bus Stop* was completed, the studio still had problems with Marilyn. In a letter to Buddy Adler, who succeeded Zanuck as head of production at Fox, Spyros Skouras, as if acting in a little Greek tragedy, complained that the picture would be delayed: "Your wire concerning Marilyn Monroe was another blow between the eyes that I received today. In my lifetime I have had many days of bitter experience, but this is one of the worst."

When Logan saw Marilyn the following year on the set of *The Prince and the Showgirl*, she was still furious with him for cutting part of her confessional crying scene on the bus. In this long monologue she confides to Hope Lange about her past experiences and current problems, the men she's known, her disillusionment with life and her desire to go to Hollywood. "Why the hell did you cut out that scene in the bus?," she screamed at Logan. "I'll never forgive you as long as I live. I was going to show it to Arthur and I couldn't. I was never so angry in my entire life, and I'm just as angry now as I was then."[13] Marilyn did not allow Logan to explain that the studio felt the scene was not essential to the story and had cut it despite all his protests. The Strasbergs had taught her to focus on herself instead of cooperating with colleagues, and she continued to believe that her performance was the only one that mattered.

Nine

Betrayal and Guilt
(1950–1956)

I

Miller's major plays of the 1950s, *The Crucible* (1953) and *A View from the Bridge* (1956), had immediate social and political impact. He created powerful situations that dramatized the moral issues and human cost of the communist witch-hunts taking place in America in the 1950s. He analyzed the psychology of the informers who betrayed their friends and the struggle of ordinary men to tell the truth. At the same time, both plays were deeply personal. They portrayed Miller's own anguish and remorse about betraying Mary and his struggle to resolve his conflict between marriage and passion. He anatomized his characters' divided loyalties and forbidden desires, their fear and guilt.

The politics of the 1950s, and the extraordinary fear and anxiety generated by the Cold War, provide the essential context for understanding these plays. In the late 1930s Communist Party cells, which were not illegal, had been set up throughout America. Members agonized over the Spanish Civil War, the rise of fascism in Europe, and the visible suffering of hungry and homeless people during the Depression, when a quarter of the work force was unemployed. A small number of the more intellectual writers, directors and actors felt that capitalism was bankrupt, that America needed a new social system, and joined the Party for brief periods. Many of them soon became disillusioned by the Party's autocratic policies, the Purge Trials in Russia and the cynical Nazi-Soviet Non-Aggression Pact of 1939. Like Miller himself, many left-wing sympathizers, who were not Party members, attended political meetings to raise money and support progressive causes.

World War II ended the Depression and swept Americans into a common cause with their wartime ally, the Soviet Union. But by the late 1940s the Soviets had become a menacing enemy who dominated the whole of Eastern Europe, from Poland on the Baltic to Bulgaria on the Black Sea. In 1949 Mao's Communists defeated Chiang Kai-shek in China; Russia exploded its first atomic bomb; and rumors spread about the Soviets' international spy rings. In America, the Communist Party, once a minor political group that subscribed to poorly understood social theories, was viewed as a seditious movement that threatened to undermine America's democratic form of government and destroy its political freedom. In the atomic age, conservative politicians, eager to reverse the economic and social programs set in motion by Roosevelt's New Deal, generated and thrived in an atmosphere of fear.

The fifties began with three spectacular espionage trials which revealed that the most secret centers of scientific research and the highest echelons of government had been infiltrated by Soviet agents. These spies had damaged American national security and decisively helped the Russians to develop their own atomic bomb. Klaus Fuchs, a German-born British physicist, had worked on the bomb in America during World War II. In 1950 in Britain, he was convicted of selling nuclear secrets to Russia during and after the war, and sentenced to fourteen years in prison. In America, the Ivy-League diplomat Alger Hiss, assistant secretary of state and President Roosevelt's advisor at the Yalta Conference with Stalin and Churchill in 1945, was accused by the former communist Whittaker Chambers of giving him 200 secret state documents. Called before the House Un-American Activities Committee (HUAC), Hiss denied he was a communist. Prosecuted by the young congressman Richard Nixon, who first gained national prominence in the communist witch hunts, Hiss was convicted of perjury in 1950 and sent to jail for five years. The following year Julius and Ethel Rosenberg, who had access to atomic secrets through her brother, a scientist who worked at the top-secret research center in Los Alamos, New Mexico, were accused of selling vital information to the Russians during the war. They were convicted in 1951 and executed by electric chair in Sing Sing prison in 1953.[1] In the early 1950s Hiss and the Rosenbergs, by working for the Soviet Union, seemed to threaten the very existence of the United States. But these convicted spies always maintained they were innocent. Their guilt is still hotly debated and remains in doubt.

In January 1953 Eisenhower became president; in March Stalin died; and in July the Korean War, which had begun in 1950, came to an end. Korea was divided in two, and communist North Korea was allied with China. As the former colonies in Asia and Africa gained independence, communism continued to spread throughout the Third World. John Foster Dulles, the confrontational secretary of state during the volatile Cold War, seemed ready to start a hot war every week. America exploded the first Hydrogen bomb in November 1952 and Russia (again aided by espionage) followed with their own explosion in August 1953. In May 1954 the Viet Cong defeated the French army at Dien Bien Phu. Vietnam, like Korea, was divided and North Vietnam also became Communist. In 1956 Egypt nationalized the strategically vital Suez Canal; and America broke with her traditional allies when Britain and France launched an ill-fated invasion that drove Egypt into the Soviet sphere of influence. That year, Russia brutally suppressed the Hungarian revolution. In 1957 Russia astonished America by suddenly launching Sputnik and surging ahead in the space race. In 1959 Fidel Castro's communist revolutionaries took over Cuba and, despite fanatical American opposition, have remained in power ever since.

A historian explained that in the 1950s, "In a postwar atmosphere suffused with fear and suspicion, opportunities were rife . . . for political persecution and intimidation." After Hiss was convicted, the Republican senator Joe McCarthy, drawing on a deep vein of American philistinism, began to attack intellectuals and universities in an unremitting campaign of vicious smears and half-truths. His senate investigations accused victims, with little or no evidence, and created a paranoid sense of Red menace. He "recklessly assaulted people's integrity, destroyed careers, and used character assassination to seize control of the political process." Miller recalled McCarthy's apparently unlimited powers: "The illusion of an unstoppable force surrounded Senator Joseph McCarthy of Wisconsin at the height of his influence, in the years from 1950 to 1954. He had paralyzed the

State Department, cowed President Eisenhower, and mesmerized almost the entire American press."

Joseph Welch was one of the few people who dared to defy the ruthless and rampaging senator. In 1954 the distinguished attorney represented the U.S. Army during McCarthy's acrimonious investigation of suspected communists in the military. He elegantly put down his abrasive opponent by asking, "Have you no sense of decency, sir, at long last? Have you left no sense of decency?" Eisenhower, who did very little to stop McCarthy when he was destroying the lives of so many innocent people, finally condemned him as the senator began to lose his power. The witch hunts had swept the country on a wave of hysteria and madness that was not understood at the time. "McCarthyism took its toll on many individuals and on the nation," Eisenhower said. "No one was safe from charges recklessly made from inside the walls of congressional immunity. Teachers, government employees, and even ministers became vulnerable. . . . The cost was often tragic."[2]

Membership in the American Communist Party was and still is legal – though generally covert – and its political influence was extremely limited. But the members of HUAC, which had been established in 1945 to investigate and root out communist influence in the United States, believed communism was a national conspiracy. HUAC had the same aims, though less authority and power, as McCarthy's committee in the Senate. HUAC also feared artists and intellectuals, and claimed that Hollywood was filled with subversives who used the propagandistic power of movies to indoctrinate a gullible public. In their attempt to eliminate all liberal content from movies, they used the threat of blackmail, imposed ideological censorship, persecuted people for their political beliefs and often convicted the accused without giving them a chance to defend themselves.

The real aim of HUAC was not to root out communists, whom they knew all about through covert FBI investigations, but to denigrate celebrities and intimidate the Hollywood studios. The American public adored the fantasy figures on the screen, and the hearings became part of its obsession with celebrity. The attack on Hollywood, a riveting public spectacle on radio and in newsreels, captured the attention of the press, justified the committee's existence and advanced many political careers. Leading writers and directors, accused of being Reds or communist sympathizers, appeared before the cameras and blinked in the bright lights. When they tried to defend their right to free speech, they were shouted down by the chairman, who pounded his gavel to silence them. After the hearings, present and former members of the Party, who had not committed any crime, were punished, without evidence or a trial, immediately blacklisted by the studios (which caved into political pressure) and professionally ruined.

Several of Miller's friends and associates – Elia Kazan, Lee J. Cobb and Clifford Odets (as well as Sterling Hayden, who'd acted with Marilyn in *The Asphalt Jungle*) – were desperate to save their careers and willing to compromise their integrity. They appeared before HUAC as cooperative, or "friendly," witnesses and named names of people they knew to be former communists. Notable exceptions in the rush to accuse others were the Hollywood Ten, a group of writers and directors who refused to cooperate, were labeled "unfriendly" witnesses and sent to prison. The historian David Caute explained Kazan's motives and the effect of his testimony:

> Kazan, after refusing to name names, changed his mind on the pretext that the American people needed to know the facts. . . . He appeared before HUAC in public session in April [1952] to name eleven former Communists, including Clifford Odets and the actors J. Edward Bromberg and [Marilyn's old teacher] Morris Carnovsky. . . . Kazan had been a Party member back in the days of the Group Theater, in 1934–35. . . . He had supported the Ten until he became "disgusted" by their "silence" and their "contemptuous attitude." . . .
>
> Kazan's performance before HUAC aroused a greater hostility, a more biting contempt, than that of any other Hollywood informer.

Miller, furious at Kazan's betrayal of his old friends in order to save his skin and continue his career, believed that if he himself had been a communist, Kazan would have denounced him to HUAC. Kazan bitterly recalled that in New York, a few months after his testimony, he ran into Miller and Kermit Bloomgarden, the producer of *Death of a Salesman* and *The Crucible*: "They saw me but didn't acknowledge that they had, either by sound or by gesture. Although I was to work with Art again ten years later, I never really forgave him for that snub." Miller also subjected Kazan to an even greater insult. After he'd sent the typescript of *The Crucible* to Kazan and the director said that he'd be honored to stage such a powerful new work, Miller savagely replied, "I didn't send it to you because I wanted you to direct it. I sent it to you because I want you to know what I think of stool-pigeons."[3]

II

Miller based his historical drama, *The Crucible*, on the witch trials that took place in 1692 in Salem, Massachusetts, and provided a striking analogy to contemporary events. In that small community, men and women were hanged for crimes they could not possibly have committed:"twenty during the year of panic had been executed, nineteen hanged and one (the famous Giles Corey) pressed to death for refusing to plead. Two had died in prison. Eight were under condemnation when [the hysteria subsided and] they were released."

The historian Edmund Morgan wrote that, like HUAC, the judges of Salem denied the legal process, used "phony confessions, inquisitional procedures, and admission of inadmissible evidence. . . . [They] convicted on the basis of spectral evidence alone, evidence offered by a supposed victim of witchcraft to the effect that the devil tormenting him appeared in the shape of the accused." Most important, and again like HUAC, "by releasing defendants who confessed and repented, they placed a terrible pressure on the accused to confess to crimes they had not committed." In the Salem witch trials, "men and women who lied were thus released, whereas those whose bravery and honesty forbade them to lie were hanged." With HUAC, people who testified against their friends were released, while those – like the Hollywood Ten – who refused to betray their friends were cited for contempt of Congress and sent to jail.

Two earlier literary works portrayed the same themes as *The Crucible* and described a small, claustrophobic, narrow-minded community that turns on itself. In Nathaniel Hawthorne's *The Scarlet Letter* (1850), which also takes place in seventeenth-century Massachusetts, the Reverend Arthur Dimmesdale seduces the married Hester Prynne, who nobly refuses to name the father of her illegitimate child. As punishment for her sin, and while the guilty Dimmesdale remains silent, she's forced to stand in the pillory and to wear the scarlet "A" that brands her as an adulteress. Seven years later, after preaching a brilliant sermon on sin and repentance, Dimmesdale mounts the same market-place scaffold where Hester once stood, and makes his long-sought and long-repressed confession. Both Dimmesdale and Miller's hero, John Proctor, are adulterers and both publicly confess their crime.

In his historical account, *The Devils of Loudon* – published in 1952, the year before *The Crucible* – Aldous Huxley also drew analogies between the religious mania and demonic possession in seventeenth-century France and the modern method of demonizing victims to incite and justify political persecution. "In medieval and early modern Christendom," Huxley observed, "the situation of sorcerers and their clients was almost perfectly analogous to that of Jews under Hitler, capitalists under Stalin, communists and fellow travelers in the United States. They were regarded as agents of a Foreign Power, unpatriotic at the best and, at the worst, traitors, heretics, enemies of the people."[4]

In Huxley's book Sister Jeanne, provoked by a malicious mixture of sexual desire and jealousy, accuses Father Grandier of bewitching her. Similarly, in Miller's play, the young Abigail Williams, a servant in the Proctors' household, accuses John Proctor's wife, Elizabeth, of witchcraft. By taking revenge on Elizabeth, who'd dismissed her, she hopes to recapture John, who'd ended their brief liaison. Proctor, known for his truthfulness, tries to save his wife by confessing his adultery and revealing Abigail's treacherous motives. But Elizabeth, lying to protect him, denies his guilt and condemns them both to death. Proctor is offered the chance to save his life by confessing to the crime of witchcraft, but saves his name and his soul by refusing to do so. Like Father Grandier, Proctor is innocent and shows exemplary courage in the face of death.

The play's title is striking and vivid, but Miller later admitted that "nobody knew what a crucible was." Though the word suggests "cruci-fixion," it is actually a vessel for heating substances to high temperatures and thus, a severe and searching test. Miller used it to suggest the burning away of impurities, especially of sexual guilt. To emphasize this theme, he changed the ages of the historical figures – Proctor from sixty to his mid-thirties, Abigail from eleven to seventeen – and invented Proctor's adulterous relations with her. The play's dramatic center, he wrote, then became more personal and concerned "the breakdown of the Proctor marriage and Abigail Williams's determination to get Elizabeth murdered so that she could have John."

In *The Crucible*, in which Proctor and Elizabeth (in one

interpretation) represent Miller and his intransigent wife Mary, Elizabeth has been guilty of coldness toward John, which prompted his lechery, and has punished him for his sin by her emotional and sexual withdrawal. After discovering his infidelity, Elizabeth "has suddenly lost all faith in him." John both accuses her and pleads for mercy by exclaiming: "Spare me! You forget nothin' and forgive nothin'. Learn charity, woman."[5] Miller's friends immediately recognized his confession of guilt in the work. Odets said, "No man would write this play unless his marriage is going to pieces." Kazan agreed that "the central character in it expresses contrition for a single act of infidelity. I had to guess that Art was publicly apologizing to his wife for what he'd done."

Before Miller's affair with Marilyn became public, the contemporary political allegory (which merges with the autobiographical elements) attracted the most interest. The core of the play is Proctor's expiation of his sexual guilt. The characters who falsely confess in the play do so only to save themselves from death. But, as the critic Robert Warshow noted, Proctor's "tormentors will not be satisfied with his mere admission of guilt: he would be required to implicate others, thus betraying his innocent friends." Like his accused townsmen, Proctor must either confess to the imaginary crime of witchcraft or maintain his innocence and hang for it. Thinking of the witnesses who cooperated with HUAC and betrayed their friends, Miller explained Proctor's complex motives: "his pride, and a mixed sense of unworthiness, which is, I suppose, a very Christian idea. Literally, life wouldn't be worth living if he walked out of there having been instrumental in condemning people."[6]

The analogy between the witch trials in Salem and the witch hunts of HUAC, though imperfect, is vivid and convincing. The argument of Miller's play is that those accused of being communists were just as innocent as those accused of being witches, that the American congressmen were as deluded and hysterical as the religious leaders of Salem. The Salem witnesses were eager to confess and incriminated others by telling lies to save their own lives; the HUAC witnesses were pressured to name names and incriminate others. They told the truth to save their own lives. If Proctor confesses he can live; if the communists confess they can work.

Witches did not exist; communists were real, but (with very few exceptions) HUAC persecuted people who had left the Party and were no longer communists. But both governments, driven by mass hysteria, believed the accused people actually *were* a menace to their security. In eighteenth-century Salem and twentieth-century America, the individual was forced to make a moral choice and decide his own fate. In Salem, confessions saved them from hanging; in contemporary America, naming names preserved their careers. But with HUAC, no one was ever acquitted. The victims either betrayed others or refused to testify, were blacklisted as communists and sent to jail.

III

Kazan responded to *The Crucible*, continued his moral debate with Miller and tried to defend his cooperation with HUAC by directing *On the Waterfront* (1955). The film was written by Budd Schulberg and co-starred Lee J. Cobb, both of whom had also named names. Though Miller condemned informing and Schulberg's screenplay justified it, *Waterfront* was strongly influenced by Miller's own screenplay, *The Hook* (1949), which was never produced. Miller wrote that *The Hook* — itself influenced by the solidarity and strike themes and by the rousing speeches to workers in Odets' *Waiting for Lefty* (1935) — "described the murderous corruption in the gangster-ridden Brooklyn longshoremen's union, whose leadership a group of rebel workers was trying to overthrow." The propagandistic theme of his script was "Give them a little organization and they'll come out fightin' . . . and they'll throw all these racketeers in the river."

Though *The Hook* clearly preceded *Waterfront*, Kazan's extremely partisan biographer quoted Schulberg's dubious claim that he had "never read *The Hook*" nor discussed it with Kazan, and maintained that the charge of plagiarism "is absurd."[7] In fact, the similarities of the two scripts are unmistakable. When Miller pulled out of the projected film of *The Hook* after Harry Cohn insisted that the gangsters be changed to communists, Kazan took the idea to his fellow informer, Budd Schulberg. In both *Hook* and *Waterfront* the villains are not communists, but gangsters. Both take place around the New York waterfront, describe the corruption of labor unions by criminals and portray the hero's struggle to lead the longshoremen against the racketeers who exploit them. Both have scenes of desperate dockers gathering for jobs in the cold mist of dawn, a rough crowd fighting for work tokens that are thrown among them, a fatal accident when a winch drops a heavy load on a worker in the hold of a ship, and a man on foot pursued and hunted down by a car. Both have a tender scene set in a park playground, in which the main character sits on a children's swing. Miller's hero, Marty Ferrara, sees his wife Therese (whom he calls Terry) in the park; Schulberg's hero, Terry Malloy (Marlon Brando) courts Edie Doyle (Eva Marie Saint) on the swings of the playground. Both heroes rather bitterly lament that they've never been able to realize their potential and both hope to achieve something better in their lives. Another critic has pointed out that "Farragut, Rocky, and Jack Uptown in *The Hook* are essentially revived in *On the Waterfront* as Big Mac, Charley Malloy, and Johnny Friendly," and that "the ending of *On the Waterfront* owes much to the ending of *The Hook*, in which Miller has a final shot of 'Marty walking, silent, Old Dominick beside him, and the Gang near him. . . . Walking toward us, his face elated, determined, serious . . . and as he walks the crowd of men behind him thickens as they all pour out of the hall. And it keeps thickening, widening . . . FADE OUT.'"

Martin Gottfried speculated that Miller and Kazan came to an understanding about *The Hook* and *On the Waterfront* before the director testified at HUAC. The bargain was that "Kazan would not inform on Miller and in return Miller would not object to his making a movie about labor unions on the waterfront." But this theory fails to note that Kazan was a Party member in 1934–35, when Miller was still a teenager and not yet involved with left-wing organizations. It also fails to explain why Miller never condemned the obvious plagiarism in *Timebends*, in his essays or in his numerous interviews. When questioned directly about this in the 1980s, Miller was unaccountably vague and apparently unconcerned:

BIGSBY: [*The Hook*] sounds remarkably like a film that Kazan did eventually make, *On the Waterfront*.

MILLER: Well, that was later, after his problem with the Un-American Activities Committee.

BIGSBY: Is there a direct relationship between your script and that one?

MILLER: I have no way of knowing. Of course they are both waterfront pictures. The one succeeded the other but they were quite different pictures.[8]

In fact, Miller *did* have a way of knowing and could easily have compared the two pictures, which were very similar and *not* quite different. But he did not wish to criticize Kazan after patching up their friendship and working with him again on *After the Fall*.

In *On the Waterfront* – as in Conrad's *Under Western Eyes* (1911) – the hero, after betraying a friend and causing his death, falls in love with the friend's sister and, risking the loss of her love, feels driven to confess his crime to her. In the film, Terry is torn between a refusal to rat on his friends and (influenced by the saintly Edie) a willingness to testify for a righteous cause and do his duty as a conscientious citizen. At first, Terry refuses to accuse his brother Charley (Rod Steiger), who works for the corrupt union officials. But after the mob kills Charley because he cannot guarantee Terry's silence, Terry redeems himself and tells the big boss, Johnny Friendly (Lee J. Cobb), "I'm glad what I done. . . . I was rattin' on myself all them years and didn't know it, helpin' punks like you." In his autobiography, Kazan maintained that there was a clear analogy between Terry's testifying against the corrupt mobsters and his own testimony before HUAC. Terry's crucial line "was me saying, with identical heat, that I was glad I'd testified as I had."

But the justification for naming names in *On the Waterfront* is specious and corrupt. Terry testifies against a criminal gang, Kazan and Schulberg against their own friends and associates. Terry testifies to send a murderer to jail, Kazan and Schulberg to advance their careers. Terry, at great risk to himself, testifies to help his colleagues, Kazan and Schulberg to destroy innocent people. Unwilling at first to work with the tainted Kazan, Brando was finally persuaded to take the role. He later felt he'd also been betrayed by the director and writer, who "made the film to justify finking on their friends."[9]

A View from the Bridge (1955, revised 1956) – which reprises Miller's portrayal of the informer in *The Crucible* – continued his dialogue with both Mary and Kazan. Miller recalled that the play was inspired by the story "of a longshoreman who had ratted to the Immigration Bureau on two brothers, his own relatives, who were living illegally in his very home, in order to break an engagement by one of them and his niece." In *View* the Italian longshoreman Eddie Carbone is obsessed by a quasi-incestuous passion for his orphaned niece, Catherine, who lives in his house. When the illegal immigrants, Rodolpho and his brother Marco, secretly move in, Catherine falls in love with Rodolpho. Carbone, who becomes increasingly deranged and cannot persuade Catherine to break with her fiancé, betrays them to the immigration officials and is killed by Marco.

In the revised version, Miller deleted the pretentious passages and use of verse, and expanded the original one-act play to a full-length work "by opening up the viewpoint of Beatrice, Eddie Carbone's wife, toward his gathering tragedy." He noted that "both *The Crucible* and *A View from the Bridge* are about the awesomeness of a passion which, despite its contradicting the self-interest of the individual . . . despite every kind of warning, despite even the destruction of the moral beliefs of the individual, proceeds to magnify its power over him until it destroys him."

A View from the Bridge is filled with tragic irony. Eddie, hinting that Rodolpho is homosexual, keeps repeating that he's "not right," but he himself is impotent. Eddie blindly demands a public apology from Marco, whom he's betrayed. Marco, whom Eddie likes, is threatened with deportation and will be jailed for murder. Rodolpho, whom Eddie hates, marries Catherine and remains in America. The play is a study in sexual frustration. Eddie has no sex life with Beatrice; Marco is separated from his wife, who remained in Italy; Eddie does everything in his power to prevent the love affair of Catherine and Rodolpho.

In *The Crucible* Proctor commits adultery because of Elizabeth's sexual coldness; in *View* Carbone's forbidden lust for Catherine (partly based on Miller's love for Marilyn) makes him both guilty and impotent, and he no longer sleeps with his wife (based on Mary). In *The Crucible* Proctor is hanged for refusing to inform on his friends; in *View* Carbone is murdered for betraying Beatrice's cousin. In both plays the revenge and betrayal by Abigail and Carbone are provoked by sexual, not political, motives. In *The Crucible* Proctor remains faithful to his principles; in *View* Carbone betrays not only Rodolpho, but also his wife, his niece and his personal code of honor.

Arguing against the morality of *The Crucible*, *On the Waterfront* praised informers and portrayed them in a self-sacrificial light. *A View From the Bridge*, in turn, challenged that view and revealed the true motives of self-interest beneath the spurious displays of virtue. As Eric Bentley observed of *View* and *Waterfront*, "the climax of both movie and play is reached when the protagonist gives the police information which leads to the arrest of some of his associates. . . . In the movie the act of informing is virtuous, whereas, in the play, it is evil."[10] After taking a passionate stand against those, like Kazan and Schulberg, who named names for HUAC, Miller would himself face that difficult test and make that moral choice when he was also summoned to testify before the committee.

Ten

Witch Hunt
(1956–1958)

I

In 1954 Joe McCarthy was formally condemned by the senate, rashly attacked President Eisenhower and suddenly fell from power. In turn, the House Un-American Activities Committee felt the decline of its own influence and desperately sought public support to maintain its inquisitorial Red-baiting. Miller was not a prime candidate for their inquiries. He had never been a communist, did not work in Hollywood and could not be questioned about communist subversion in the movie industry. But after he and Marilyn resumed their romance in New York, rumors of their liaison became widely known and attracted the attention of HUAC. The committee summoned him to appear during their investigation of passport abuse. They suspected, given his association with left-wing and communist causes, that he might spread anti-American propaganda abroad. After many anxious months, Miller was finally called to testify before the committee on June 21, 1956, and continued his legal battle with HUAC for the next two years.

Miller's political ideas did not focus on any particular party or program. He'd lived through the excesses of capitalism and the disaster of the Depression, and had always sympathized with the working poor and the unemployed. His left-wing activities, limited to supporting various communist enterprises, seem surprisingly naïve. Like many young writers and intellectuals of the 1930s, Miller thought Soviet communism stood for hope, for an ideal of social equality and for opposition to the growing threat of fascism in Spain, Germany and Italy. This idealism blinded him to the true nature of communism in Russia, even after Stalin's monstrous crimes of the 1930s (which had disillusioned many previously hard-line communists) became well known: the forcible collectivization of the peasants that caused widespread famine and death, the political purges, the Moscow show trials, the omnipotent secret police and the millions of innocent victims sent to Siberian prison camps. He kept faith with Russia and continued to support communist-front organizations until the end of the 1940s, despite the cynical non-aggression pact between Hitler and Stalin, the betrayal of the Warsaw rising during World War II and the post-war occupation of Eastern Europe. He added his name to the lists of those supporting the well-intentioned but propagandistic World Youth Festival in Prague in 1947, the World Congress for Peace in Paris in 1948 and the Peace Conference at the Waldorf-Astoria Hotel in New York in 1949 – the latter also endorsed by subversive types like Albert Einstein and Eleanor Roosevelt.

Miller's political activities, innocuous as they were, made him a victim of the general paranoia about leftists and got him into trouble with the authorities on two previous occasions. These incidents also aroused the interest of HUAC. In 1954 the State Department, asserting that it was not in the country's best interests, had refused to renew his passport so he could attend the European premiere of *The Crucible* in Brussels. This refusal prompted Miller's remark, "It didn't harm me, it harmed the country; I didn't need any foreign relations." The following year, when he was asked to write a film script about juvenile delinquency in response to the rise of gang violence in New York, his reputation cost him the job. "I spent the summer of 1955 on Brooklyn streets," he recalled, "wrote an outline and was ready to proceed with the script when an attack on me as a disloyal leftist was opened in the *New York World-Telegram and Sun*. The cry went up that so long as I was the screenwriter the city must cancel its contract with the producer." After the rabid headline of July 22, 1955, declared "Youth Board Filmster Has a Pink Record," the twenty-two city commissioners voted to kill the project.

In 1956, as HUAC continued to attack Hollywood, the most popular films of the year were lavish crowd-pleasers: Mike Todd's wide-screen extravaganza *Around the World in 80 Days*, Yul Brynner as the ruler of Siam in *The King and I* and Charlton Heston as Moses in *The Ten Commandments*. That year Eisenhower, with Nixon as his running-mate, was re-elected president; Nasser nationalized the Suez Canal; Khrushchev denounced the crimes of Stalin; and Russia, intent on maintaining its power in Eastern Europe, crushed the Hungarian revolution.

To defend himself Miller engaged Joseph Rauh, one of the best lawyers in the country. Four years older than Miller and a graduate of Harvard Law School, Rauh was one of the most influential liberals in the postwar era. Active in Democratic politics, he'd worked for two Supreme Court justices and for several agencies in Roosevelt's administration. Throughout his career he had fought for civil rights and represented labor unions. Miller described him as a hero: "A giant of a fellow who somehow looks even broader and taller because of his bow ties, Joe Rauh is a combative lawyer, formerly head of Americans for Democratic Action, a liberal pressure group whose adherents included men like Hubert Humphrey and Adlai Stevenson."[1]

On May 18, testing the waters, Miller applied for a passport, as if he'd never before had trouble with the passport office. He wanted to attend the London premiere of *A View from the Bridge* in October and to accompany Marilyn, who would be making *The Prince and the Showgirl* in England. He also submitted an affidavit that declared he was not a member of the Communist Party. Rauh arranged for him to swear, in return for being granted a six-month passport, that he would return to America if cited for contempt of Congress. On May 22 Miller informed his other eminent attorney, Lloyd Garrison, that his passport application included a letter which stated his business reasons for traveling to England, but did not mention his romance with Marilyn. The clerk, he said, was very nice and did not even try to arrest him. But he was getting tired of holding his breath and wondering what would happen to him in the immediate future, and looked forward to a quiet, uneventful year. This was a vain hope, since peace and quiet would be quite impossible once he married Marilyn.

Miller's FBI file quoted from an article in the *New York Times* of June 22, the day after Miller appeared before HUAC, and reported that the committee questioned him about the signature on a 1947 statement against the outlawing of the CP; a signature on a statement defending [the Red agent] GERHART EISLER before he fled this country to become a top Communist official in East Germany; a statement attacking the HUAC; and statements opposing the Smith Act [of 1940, which made it a criminal offense to advocate the overthrow of the U.S. government]. The article reflected that MILLER stated he had no memory of most of these things but that he would not deny them.

He'd applied to take a course in Marxism in about 1939 and in 1947 attended several writers' meetings sponsored by the Communist Party. But he told the committee that "he came away from CP meetings convinced that his temperament and viewpoints were diametrically opposed to those of Marxists." Another article included in his FBI file, from the conservative *Plain Talk* magazine of June 1947 (the year of *All My Sons*), sneeringly linked Miller and Kazan, who later became political adversaries, saying that "Miller, and his director, Elia Kazan, might both be awarded the Order of Lenin."[2]

All those who faced the committee had to deal with a barrage of negative reporting in the press and on television. To be hauled before them suggested the witness was guilty, and it took great self-possession and expert legal advice to deal with the hectoring questions. HUAC, ironically enough, failed to see that they themselves were playing the role of Grand Inquisitor. They adopted the methods of the Soviet Purge Trials by reenacting the "typical communist scene of [victims] crawling and apologizing and admitting the error of their ways." The informers, by confessing imaginary crimes, joined their accusers and seemed to prove the existence of a secret plot that HUAC felt compelled to investigate. "Only through the humiliating ritual of informing on former colleagues," as David Caute observed, "could the penitent ex-Communist purge and purify himself and so regain the confidence of the inquisition."[3]

Miller, as an unfriendly witness, had three strategic options. He could plead the Fifth Amendment to the U.S. Constitution, which protected him from self-incrimination; he could testify about himself, but be deliberately vague about the names of other people; or he could answer all the questions about himself, but refuse to name names. Miller, advised by Rauh, chose the latter course, invoked the right to free speech and, by implication, the right to silence guaranteed by the First Amendment. Mary McCarthy pointed out that his principled stand was quite unusual and that "he was almost the only prominent figure heard by the committee who did not either tell all or take refuge in the Fifth Amendment."

Miller began by truthfully declaring, "I was never under the discipline of the Communist Party, the communist cause," and "would not support now a cause or movement which was dominated by communists." He openly criticized the committee itself, whose "rather ceaseless investigating of artists was creating a pall of apprehension and fear among all kinds of people." His testimony covered a wide range of political topics. He advocated the repeal of the Smith Act; defended his contribution to a fund that supplied vitally needed medicines to Red China; discussed the ideas of his plays; condemned Ezra Pound's anti-Semitic broadcasts from wartime Italy; and denied that he had any connection with Howard Fast, the American communist writer and winner of the Stalin Peace Prize. When asked if he'd attacked "Kazan because he broke with the Communist Party and testified before a congressional committee," Miller stood firm and declared, "I have never attacked Kazan. I will stand on that. That is it." Instead of trying to deny his former beliefs, he staunchly defended his support of the Loyalists during the Spanish Civil War: "I have always been, since my student days, in the thirties, a partisan of Republican Spain. I am quite proud of it. I am not at all ashamed. I think a democracy was destroyed there."[4]

Miller forthrightly answered all the questions about himself. When provocatively asked, "Do you consider yourself more or less a dupe in joining these communist organizations?" he disagreed. He was idealistic and his political experience had been valuable: "I wouldn't say so because I was an adult. I wasn't a child. I was looking for the world that would be perfect. I think it necessary that I do that if I were to develop myself as a writer. I am not ashamed of this. I accept my life. That is what I have done. I learned a great deal." He also made an important distinction, relevant to the issue of his passport, between his criticism of America at home and overseas: "there is no case that I would say I was ready to support criticism of this country abroad. . . . I do draw a line between criticism of the United States in the United States and before foreigners."

In his profile of Miller, written the following October, the English theater critic Kenneth Tynan pointed out the absurdity of the HUAC's questions: "To clinch its case, the committee confronted him with a revue scene on which he had collaborated in 1938: it presented the committee as a mad Star Chamber where witnesses were gagged, bound and tortured." They read the opening passage of Miller's broadly satiric sketch, *Listen My Children*, written with Norman Rosten, to prove his incorrigible anti-American tendencies: "In the center of room, in a rocker, sits a man. He is securely tied to a chair, with a gag in his mouth and a bandage tied over his mouth. Water, coming from a pipe near ceiling, trickles on his head. Nearby is a charcoal stove holding branding irons. Two bloodhounds are tied in the corner of the room." "Having read the scene," Tynan wrote, "the committee's attorney triumphantly asked: 'Well, Mr. Miller?' Ruminant over his pipe, Miller sharply replied: 'But − that was *meant* to be a farce.' " Tynan's version improved on Miller's reply. He actually said, rather mildly, "I find it amusing. I don't see what is so horrific about that. I think it is a farce. I don't think anybody would take it seriously that way."

Indignant at his effrontery, the committee continued to press Miller about his criticism of their work. They asked him if *The Crucible* was the subject "of a series of articles in the communist press drawing parallels to the investigations of communists and other subversives by congressional committees." Instead of backing down, Miller confirmed the parallel by responding, "I think that was true in more than the communist press. I think it was true in the non-communist press, too. The comparison is inevitable."[5] In this instance, as in the exchange about *Listen My Children*, his quick wit and calm rationality made the committee look absurd.

In October 1947, when the screenwriter Ring Lardner, Jr., one of the Hollywood Ten, was pressured to name names before HUAC, he famously replied, "I could answer the question, but if I did, I would hate myself in the morning." (Lardner was sentenced to a year in jail for contempt and, by an ironic twist of fate, wound up in the same Connecticut prison as the chairman of his investigating committee, who'd been convicted of corruption.) The high point of Miller's testimony came when, remembering Lardner's exemplary statement, he also took his stand and refused to name names:

> I want you to understand that I am not protecting the Communists or the Communist Party. I am trying to and I will

protect my sense of myself. I could not use the name of another person and bring trouble on him. These were writers, poets, as far as I could see, and the life of a writer, despite what it sometimes seems, is pretty tough. I wouldn't make it any tougher for anybody. I ask you not to ask me that question. . . .

I will be perfectly frank with you in anything relating to my activities. I take responsibility for everything I have ever done, but I cannot take responsibility for another human being. . . .

My conscience will not permit me to use the name of another person. . . . My counsel advises me that there is no relevance between this question and the question of whether I should have a passport.[6]

On September 27, 1956, the FBI summarized the main charges against Miller: "He admitted signing many appeals and protests issued by 'Red front groups in the last decade' but denied he was ever under communist discipline. MILLER, when asked if he signed an application to join the CP in 1939 or 1940, stated he had signed what he thought to be an application for a 'study course' in Marxism. He refused to name persons he had seen at CP Writers meetings."

Despite these damaging accusations, the "pipe-smoking playwright," self-assured and dignified, made a good impression and was treated with respect. One historian wrote that his "appearance was notable for its air of sober amiability. . . . Despite a certain [deliberate] fuzziness on a number of points, Miller had been a credible witness. He was responsive, collected, and only moderately sententious." David Caute added that "up to a point Miller was a cooperative witness, wordy rather than eloquent, less at home with the spoken than the written word." Mary McCarthy explained why he was punished for resisting the committee: "when it came to giving names he balked, and this balking, in the view of his questioners, amounted to a limitation on Congress' power to investigate." The committee of course already knew all the names, but wanted him to accept "the *principle* of betrayal as a norm of good citizenship." When he refused to do so, on July 25, 1956 "the contempt citation against him was voted eventually by the House of Representatives − 373 to 9."[7] Miller's staunch opposition to HUAC firmly established his image as a man of courage and integrity. Comparing the two old friends, Victor Navasky noted how "Kazan emerged in the folklore of the left as the quintessential informer, and Miller was hailed as the risk-taking conscience of the times. . . . In his life, his politics, and his art, [Kazan] has done as much to defend the naming of names as his old colleague Miller has done to challenge it."

Not everyone admired Miller's performance. The playwright Lillian Hellman, who'd also been defended by Rauh when she was summoned by HUAC, had pleaded the Fifth Amendment and stated, "I will not cut my conscience to fit this year's fashions." She was jealous of his success and did not see anything courageous about his testimony. Alluding to *The Crucible*, he'd told HUAC that he'd "been to hell and back and seen the devil." Hellman wisecracked that he "must have gone as a tourist." She meant that he had come back safely from Washington, that he was merely self-dramatizing his appearance and that "he was too cozy with the committee for her taste, too willing to grant their right to ask questions in the first place." In 1964, when Miller's autographical play *After the Fall* was being performed in New York, Hellman (using her own name instead of Miller's) published a wicked parody that mocked his role as noble martyr:

> "Buy My Guilt" was written by Lillian Hellman and is now being performed in the converted tiger cages of the Bronx Zoo on a most advanced thrust-retreat stage. . . . Miss Hellman claims the play is not autobiographical, but the editors must point out that the events of the play follow closely on her life. . . .
>
> The play concerns itself . . . with Miss Hellman's appearance before the House Un-American Activities Committee, her inner struggles, her unselfish concern with weaker and less fortunate friends, her final admirable admission that all of us must stand trial for the rest of us.[8]

By pleading the Fifth Amendment Hellman had avoided the charge of contempt. But, as Navasky noted, Miller took a greater risk by opposing HUAC: "Miller made a decision, in spite of an awful lot of advice the other way. People said, 'You are blowing your career.' Either he was braver or smarter than they were or he could not be in the company of corrupt men for too long and live well with himself." On July 8, about three weeks after the hearings and before he was cited for contempt, Miller described his reaction to the ordeal in a letter to Saul Bellow: "The slightly amazing thing to me is that I never felt scared at all. Something's snapped in me – the connections of fear. I guess I have reached that ancient and dangerous stage when one just doesn't give a shit."[9]

II

Miller maintained that he was not subpoenaed for his left-wing views, but "because I was engaged to Marilyn Monroe. Had I not been, they'd never have thought of me. They'd been through the writers long before and they'd never touched me. Once I became famous as her possible husband, this was a great possibility for publicity." Congressman Francis Walter, the chairman of HUAC, hoped that Marilyn, concerned about maintaining her popularity with the public, would support the committee. Wanting above all to get re-elected, he actually telephoned Joseph Rauh and (Miller said) promised "that if Marilyn would take a photograph with him, shaking his hand, he would call off the whole thing. It's as simple as that. Marilyn would get them on the front pages right away."

Miller refused to allow Marilyn to kiss the frog – and then staged his own publicity feat. In the midst of his testimony, to take the heat off and generate sympathy, he unexpectedly announced the real purpose of his visit to England: "The objective is double. I have a production which is in the talking stage in England of *A View from the Bridge*, and I will be there with the woman who will then be my wife. That is my aim." Learning from Marilyn about how to manipulate the media, Miller pulled off a brilliant *coup de théâtre*. Marilyn was surprised and delighted by his public announcement. Reacting as if Miller were the great man and she the unworthy consort, she told Norman Rosten: "He announced it before the whole world! He told the whole world he was marrying Marilyn Monroe. Me! Can you believe it? You know he never really asked me. We talked about it, but it was all very vague. I mean, really ask *me* to marry *him*!"[10]

Like Miller, Marilyn was pressured by well-intentioned but misguided friends who urged her to protect her career and stay out of the political controversy. The Strasbergs, intervening on her behalf, pressed Miller to be a "friendly" witness and purge his "guilt" for Marilyn's sake. He rejected their self-serving advice, which was prompted by their own dubious history. Miller recalled that "Paula had been a friendly witness. She had been named by Kazan when he was called in 1952, and named persons who were members. Her attitude was that of a very cooperative person and I was [also] expected to be cooperative."

At the same time that the Strasbergs were offering their advice, Spyros Skouras was trying to keep his biggest star out of trouble. Marilyn, who'd shrewdly rejected the studio's advice about the nude calendar scandal and their warning about breaking her contract to go to New York, now ignored their instructions to dissociate herself from Miller and remain aloof from the struggle. Thinking of Marilyn, Miller once remarked that "whatever psychological security one has had better come from within, because the social support for it is very chancy." Marilyn had very little psychological security and no social support from her friends or the studio. But, braver and smarter than her advisers, inspired by her love for Miller, she stood by him.

The HUAC investigation put intense and unremitting pressure on both Miller and Marilyn just before and during the first two years of their difficult marriage. Always sympathetic to the underdog, she was naturally influenced by his left-wing political views. When questioned, later on, about the communists, she relied on her instincts and said, "They're for the people, aren't they?"[11] Realizing perhaps that she'd unintentionally aroused HUAC's interest in Miller, and identifying with him as a victim, she was absolutely determined to use all her considerable power to defend him.

Coached and encouraged by his lawyer, she told the press, "I'm fully confident that in the end my husband will win his case." She also confirmed, while alluding to Skouras, that when "Miller was on trial for contempt of Congress, a certain corporation executive said either he named names and I got him to name names, or I was finished. I said, 'I'm proud of my husband's position, and I stand behind him all the way.'" Marilyn's loyalty during this crisis was their finest hour, and they would never be as close and as happy again. Impressed by Marilyn's performance, Miller jokingly told Rauh that she would make a fine vice president, though the senators would not be able to concentrate on their work.[12]

A sympathetic newspaper article in Miller's FBI file, published after he was indicted, suggested that his relations with Marilyn had made things more difficult for him. His marriage, "and not his brilliant plays, have made him 'hot copy' and fair game for any semi-literate hick politician who wants to make a hit with the folks back home by proving that he can push Marilyn Monroe's husband around." Yet the opposite was also true. Miller admitted that "to marry me in my situation was a disaster" for Marilyn. But the intensely romantic and highly publicized marriage greatly enhanced his image and actually took the pressure off Miller. The courts finally decided it was best not to imprison the husband of America's most glamorous and desirable woman.

Miller had testified on June 21; he married Marilyn eight days later, on June 29; and they flew to London on July 13, faced with the distinct possibility that he would be convicted and sent to jail. The FBI never forgave Marilyn's loyalty to Miller and kept a file on her for the rest of her life. They recorded that she had applied for a Soviet visa in 1955, had been taken on a tour of Brooklyn by a communist photographer in April 1956 and "associated closely with certain members of the American Communist Group in Mexico" while on vacation in March 1962.[13]

On February 18, 1957 (after their return from England) a federal jury indicted Miller on two counts of contempt of Congress, for twice refusing to name writers suspected of communist sympathies. Each count was punishable for up to a year in prison and a $1,000 fine. Rauh drafted Miller's public statement, which indicated the basis of his appeal, and argued that questions about suspected communists had nothing to do with inquiries about the abuse of passports:

> The contempt citation for which I must now stand trial was based on my refusal, on grounds of conscience, to name certain persons who were present at a meeting of authors nine years ago. I answered fully all the questions regarding myself and asked only that I not be forced to name other people whom I believed to be innocent of wrong-doing.
>
> I was advised by my counsel that the questions regarding the identity of the authors were not relevant to the investigation of passport abuses, which was the subject-matter of the investigation. I was further advised that a refusal to answer irrelevant questions is not punishable. I understand that this will be among the defenses which counsel will urge on my behalf in seeking dismissal of the indictment.

On May 14 Miller was tried, without a jury, before Judge Charles McLaughlin in the federal district court, and on May 31 was convicted of two counts of contempt and faced a year in prison. On July 19 the judge reduced his conviction to one count, suspended his one-year prison term and fined him $500. A year later, on June 28, 1958, in the U.S. Court of Appeals for the District of Columbia, Rauh stated that Miller, an honest and cooperative witness, had "answered all but two of the 200 questions. The two questions he refused to answer concerned those present at certain meetings of Communist Party Writers he attended in 1947." In his *Paris Review* interview, Miller explained the principles that sustained Rauh's successful appeal:

> My legal defense was not on any of the Constitutional amend-
> ments but on the contention that Congress couldn't drag people
> in and question them about anything on the Congressman's
> mind; they had to show that the witness was likely to have infor-
> mation relevant to some legislation then at issue. The committee
> had put on a show of interest in passport legislation. I had been
> denied a passport a couple of years earlier. Ergo, I fitted into
> their vise. A year later I was convicted after a week's trial. Then
> about a year after that, the Court of Appeals threw out the whole
> thing.[14]

In August 1958 Rauh triumphantly announced that Miller had followed his conscience, "refused to inform on others and won his case" – which was reversed on a technicality. The Court of Appeals ruled that HUAC had not given him sufficient warning of the risk of contempt. At the same time, Miller publicly stated that he "hoped to stop the inhuman practice of making witnesses inform on long past friends and acquaintances." In another letter Rauh explained how Miller's courageous example had provided a legal precedent that fatally weakened HUAC's oppressive power: "As more people like Arthur refuse to 'inform' and are acquitted . . . more and more people will stand up against the committee and ultimately the prin-ciple will receive vindication."[15]

In August Miller also wrote Rauh that the workers renovating his Connecticut house had followed his case, and celebrated his victory with a bottle of whiskey and several cartons of beer. He couldn't resist quoting a hypocritical letter he'd just received from Spyros Skouras – the "spiral staircase" himself: "Let me be the first to congratulate you on your acquittal by the U.S. Court. I am delighted with this outcome to your long ordeal and I certainly admire the courage and perseverance with which you met it. I cheerfully must concede that I was wrong in my advice to you. Seriously, it is wonderful to know that you have won out in the contempt proceedings." Miller, punning on the title of Ibsen's play and calling Skouras a pillow of society, was amused by this groveling if insincere apology and said the son of a bitch must feel proud of his magnanimity.

Miller continued to correspond with Rauh for the next few years. In November 1957, between his conviction and his successful appeal, he agreed to introduce Rauh's speech to the American Civil Liberties Union meeting in New Haven, Connecticut. He invited Rauh to stay with him in his country house in Roxbury, and mentioned that if Rauh flew up from Washington in a small plane, he could land on a private airfield about a mile away. Miller said he'd gone back to his writing and that Marilyn, who was also eager to see Rauh, sent her extreme best regards.

In 1959, Miller finally sent a check for half his legal bill. He mentioned how difficult it was to estimate his taxes because NBC had tentatively offered to pay a small fortune for television rights to *Death of a Salesman* and he didn't know if the deal would actually come through. He said that after their successful appeal, other witnesses had been convicted for contempt of Congress and that the committee was once again looking for blood. He urged Rauh, if John Kennedy were elected president in November, to accept a high judicial appointment and use his liberal influence in the courts. In a letter of 1960, sent from Reno, Nevada, Miller apologized for the late payment of Rauh's fee and promised to send it in the next few days. He thought the Democratic presidential convention had been a bit of a disaster, that Adlai Stevenson had seemed too intellectual and other-worldly, but felt that Kennedy had been a good choice. Both he and Marilyn were working hard on the filming of *The Misfits* and hoped all their efforts would turn out to be worthwhile.[16]

Caught up in one of the most bizarre and disgraceful episodes of American political history, Miller said his battle with the committee was "a fraud and a farce, except it cost me a fortune [$40,000] for

lawyers and a year's time lost in the bargain, worrying about it and
figuring out how to react to it." When he was invited to Kennedy's
inauguration in January 1960, he joked that "it seemed strange to be
going [to Washington] without a lawyer."[17]

Eleven

Marriage and England
(1956–1957)

I

Though it seems unlikely, Marilyn's two famous husbands had quite a lot in common. DiMaggio was born in 1914, Miller a year later, and both were more than a decade older than her. They were tall and handsome, capable and conventional men, who felt sorry for Marilyn and wanted to help and protect her. Both were powerful authority figures who seemed able to provide the security she needed as well as absolution for her illegitimate birth and sexual history. Miller's theatrical triumphs from *All My Sons* to *The Crucible* were the equivalent on Broadway of DiMaggio's spectacular hitting streak in Yankee Stadium. But Marilyn's fame was greater than theirs. Her marriage to DiMaggio had been good for *her* career; her marriage to Miller would help *his*.

Both men took an active interest in her professional affairs. Though they often had to hang around, with very little to do, while Marilyn worked, she criticized them for ignoring her. She complained that DiMaggio constantly watched television and that Miller was completely immersed in his work – even when he was writing a screenplay for *her*. DiMaggio thought Marilyn had no talent and resented her absorption in acting. Miller admired her ability, encouraged her and even participated in her career – though he hated Strasberg as much as DiMaggio hated Lytess. Marilyn failed to interest

DiMaggio in serious books, but eagerly learned a lot about books from Miller. She found DiMaggio too boring, Miller too intellectual; she was too serious for DiMaggio, too ignorant for Miller.

DiMaggio loathed Marilyn's sexy outfits and wanted to keep her entirely to himself. Miller liked her to reveal her sensual body and was proud to share her with the public. "Why shouldn't she show off her God-given attributes?" he asked. "Why should she have to dress like her maiden aunt?" Marilyn seemed to want with Miller the kind of life that DiMaggio had wanted with her. "I hate [Hollywood]," she told Miller. "I don't want it anymore. I want to live quietly in the country and just be there when you need me. I can't fight for myself anymore." She became close to her husbands' families, and after her divorce from Joe traded spaghetti and pizza with the DiMaggios for matzo balls and gefilte fish with the Millers.

DiMaggio was intensely jealous and even worried about imaginary lovers; Miller ignored and tolerated her infidelities. DiMaggio sometimes lost his temper and slapped her around; Miller always contained his anger under the most extreme provocations. Like the glamorous but essentially unhappy contemporary marriages of Jack and Jackie Kennedy, Prince Rainier and Grace Kelly, and (later on) Prince Charles and Diana Spencer, the Miller-Marilyn marriage would have one spouse who was notoriously unfaithful.

At the time of their wedding the thirty-year-old Marilyn was no longer the unknown starlet whom Miller first met in January 1951. Since then she'd become a world-famous superstar, been married to a wealthy baseball hero, formed her own production company – and was used to getting her own way with everyone. Except for brief periods with Lytess, Karger, Shelley Winters, Greene and DiMaggio, Marilyn had always lived alone. Her radical adjustment from a solitary to a married life, and Miller's from a private to a very exposed existence, was difficult for both of them.

After Miller announced their impending marriage, rumors quickly spread about where and when it would take place, and the press pursued them to rural Connecticut. In late June, Mara Scherbatoff – a forty-eight-year-old Russian princess and New York bureau chief of the French weekly magazine *Paris-Match* – was killed in a car accident on a winding country road close to Miller's house. He wrote that Scherbatoff's teenaged driver, chasing them at high speed, lost control of his car: "Inquiring for my house from a neighbor, he had mistaken a passing car for mine, roared off in pursuit, failed to make this turn and collided with the tree. . . . Returning home later in the afternoon, we came on a Chevrolet askew in the road a quarter of a mile from the house, its front end mangled around this tree. We stopped, and I got out and looked and saw a woman, stretched out on the front seat, her neck obviously broken."

Miller ran back to help and Marilyn – hypersensitive to pain and suffering – followed before he could stop her from witnessing the grisly scene. They saw "the boy crumpled beneath the steering wheel. Scherbatoff, in the passenger's seat, had been hurled partway through the windshield. Her face was sliced open from the middle of her lip to her forehead. Teeth were missing. Her chest was crushed, her legs broken. Blood gushed from a severed artery in her throat. She was crying softly." Marilyn helped pull the mangled reporter from the car and got bloodstains on her clothes. A photo of the crash, taken before the ambulance arrived, showed the smashed-in car, the dazed and bloodied driver sitting on the ground near the tree and the dying Scherbatoff stretched out under a blanket.[1] Marilyn, hysterical and horrified, had to be reassured that the accident was not her fault.

Miller was furious at the press for hounding them so recklessly. He told Bellow that photographers with telescopic lenses were perched in (and nearly falling out of) the trees across the road from his house. To put an end to the circus they decided to get married right away. Their marriage, announced with the headline: "Egghead Weds Hourglass," began with this fatal omen. Six hours after the car crash, on June 29, 1956, the civil ceremony took place in the courthouse in White Plains, New York. Two days later, they were married again in a Jewish ceremony in the home of his longtime agent, Kay Brown, in Katonah, New York.

By marrying Miller, Marilyn embraced a new Jewish identity that was already familiar to her. Many of Marilyn's closest associates were Jewish: not only Natasha Lytess, Joseph Schenck and Johnny Hyde, but also Sidney Skolsky, Lee and Paula Strasberg, Milton Greene, Norman Rosten, her agent Charles Feldman, her publicist Arthur Jacobs, her three analysts and most of her doctors. The actresses Carroll Baker and Elizabeth Taylor had (or soon would) set a fashionable precedent by changing their religion when they married Jewish husbands, and Amy had converted when she married Milton Greene.

Marilyn told Susan Strasberg, "I can identify with the Jews. Everybody's always out to get them, no matter what they do, like me." Acutely aware that she did not have a family of her own and eager to join the families of her husbands and friends, she converted to Judaism to express her loyalty and get close to both Miller and his parents.

Miller recalled that Marilyn's tuition in the mysteries of the Jewish faith by Rabbi Robert Goldberg (who also married them) was brief, superficial, even surreal:

> The rabbi was a reformed or liberal rabbi and he sat with Marilyn for a couple of hours and that was it. I'm not religious, but she wanted to be one of us and that was why she took some instruction. I don't think you could say she became a Jewess, but still she took it all very seriously. I would say she wanted to join me and become part of my life. But her interest in talking to the rabbi had about it an unreality to me.

Marilyn's perfunctory conversion resembled Rex Mottram's pro forma conversion in Evelyn Waugh's *Brideshead Revisited* (1945). In a great hurry and not particularly concerned with the finer points of doctrine, Rex tells the priest: " 'I'll become a Catholic. What does one have to do? . . . I don't pretend to be a very devout man, nor much of a theologian, but . . . a man needs a religion. If your Church is good enough for [my fiancée] Julia, it's good enough for me.' . . . So Rex was sent to Farm Street to Father Mowbray, a priest renowned for his triumphs with obdurate catechumens."

Marilyn took the sacred vow from the Book of Ruth (1:16), one of the most moving passages in the Old Testament, and swore fidelity to the faith of her husband: "whither thou goest, I will go; and where thou lodgest, I will lodge; thy people shall be my people, and thy God my God." Her Certificate of Conversion stated that "Marilyn Monroe, having sought to join the household of Israel by accepting the religion of Israel and promising to live by its principles and practices, was received into the Jewish faith on July 1, 1956."[2] While married to Miller she'd sometimes sprinkle her talk with Yiddish expressions – Hi *bubeleh*, *oy veh*, what *tsures* (rhymes with Skouras) – to confirm her conversion and sense of belonging. When describing her nude calendar, she said "there I am with my bare *tuchas* out."

None of Marilyn's family or Hollywood friends attended the Jewish ceremony, as she stood under the bridal canopy and Miller crushed the symbolic glass with his foot, nor appeared at the wedding reception – at which, though strictly prohibited by Jewish law, lobster was served. Lee Strasberg, a surrogate father, gave the bride away. Norman Rosten, originally asked to be best man, was awkwardly replaced at the last minute by Miller's brother, Kermit. The guests included Miller's parents, his two children, Jane and Robert; Kermit and his wife, Miller's sister Joan Copeland and her husband; his cousin Morton and his wife; the Rostens, Greenes and Strasbergs, the agent Kay Brown and designer John Moore. The "exclusive photos" were, as always, by Milton Greene.

Marilyn called herself a "Jewish atheist." After her divorce from Miller, her Judaism was pretty much confined to a *mezuzah* on the door frame and a rather kitschy "brass-plated musical menorah for Hanukkah whose base played 'Hatikvah,' the Israeli national anthem." When Marilyn converted to Judaism, Egypt retaliated by banning all her movies. But in April 1961, right after her divorce, the United Arab Republic – hoping to catch the biggest act since Verdi's *Aida* celebrated the opening of the Suez Canal – sent an urgent telegram to Skouras requesting her presence "for inauguration light and sound of pyramids and sphinx. All expenses to be borne by government."

On July 8 Miller wrote Bellow that Marilyn, trying hard to lead a normal life, had turned into a real Hausfrau – cooking, waxing floors and (for an all-too-brief moment) treating him like an oriental pasha. He added that his children, aged twelve and nine, were both in love with the exciting movie star and reluctant to go back to their mother when the weekend was over. Miller's father and children (his possessive mother was more distant) loved Marilyn till her death. Marilyn, who adored old people and children, fully returned their affection.

Despite the fatal car accident, the beginning of their marriage seemed propitious. Marilyn had gone from Hollywood to New York to prepare for a career on stage; Miller in turn would go from New York to Hollywood to work on her film script. She had a brilliant, famous and supportive husband; loved Miller's family; belonged to the Jewish community; soon became pregnant with a child of her own; was decorating their apartment in New York and country house in Connecticut; and was planning to collaborate with him in *The Misfits*.

Interviewed during her first year with Miller and emphasizing her emotions, Marilyn said that marriage had assuaged her vulnerability and relieved her sense of solitude: "I love being married to Arthur Miller. All my life I've been alone. Now for the first time, the really first time, I feel I'm not alone any more. For the first time I have a feeling of being sheltered. It's as if I have come out of the cold. . . . There's a feeling of being together – a warmth and tenderness. I don't mean a display of affection or anything like that. I mean just being together."[3] Their marriage also had a powerful impact on Miller. Her intense emotions released many of his inhibitions, made him less stiff and self-conscious, and enhanced his poise and self-confidence.

II

At the outset, *The Prince and the Showgirl* (1957), like *Bus Stop*, seemed to be a prestigious project. It would be the screen version of a successful play by an important dramatist and would have a distinguished director. It was therefore highly ironic – even absurd – that when Marilyn formed her own production company she chose mediocre plays that had exactly the kind of part she'd always been trying to avoid. She'd been playing a poor chorus girl who captures a wealthy upper-class man ever since her dreadful early movie, *Ladies of the Chorus* (1948).

In March 1955 the English playwright Terence Rattigan, author of *The Sleeping Prince* (1953), was flying from London to Hollywood to discuss the screen adaptation of his play with the director William Wyler. When Rattigan stopped in New York, Marilyn and Greene summoned him to a conference and offered to pay a much higher price for the rights. When Wyler failed to make a definite offer, Rattigan accepted her bid of $175,000 and agreed to write the screenplay. They considered various titles – "A Night in Love," "The Purple Pillow" – before settling on *The Prince and the Showgirl*, which named both leading roles.

Richard Burton, then a hot property, was originally considered for the leading role. In April Marilyn told Charles Feldman that "she would love to sleep with the Prince if his name were Richard Burton." She also considered appearing with Noël Coward and having costumes created by Cecil Beaton. She finally pulled off a coup by convincing Sir Laurence Olivier, the leading Shakespearean actor of his time, to appear in and direct the Ruritanian fantasy. Marilyn became, rather awkwardly, both his co-star and (as head of Marilyn Monroe Productions) his employer. They were an odd couple, but there seemed to be some advantages for both of them. Olivier wanted money, glamor and international recognition; Marilyn wanted respectability, prestige and recognition as a serious actress.

In February 1956, at the press conference at the Plaza Hotel in New York that announced their surprising joint venture, Marilyn's delicate dress strap, straining under its burden, broke right on cue. The photographers went wild and she stole the show from Olivier. Though she'd captured Olivier, there was still a problem with funding. That year the Fox producer Buddy Adler, responding to rumors, wrote Skouras, "it is evident that she is in desperate need of this cash and is hoping that we will advance it" and back the film. In the end, Olivier became the producer, Milton Greene the executive producer; Warner Bros. put up the money and became the distributor.

Olivier was then experiencing a severe personal crisis. His wife, Vivien Leigh, had played the showgirl part on the London stage, with Olivier as her co-star and director, and resented Marilyn taking over her role. She'd recently had a melodramatic and well-publicized affair with the handsome English actor Peter Finch. She announced her pregnancy (by Olivier) on July 12, a few days before Miller and Monroe arrived in England; and had a miscarriage on August 12, while Olivier was making the movie. Her miscarriage and depression led to one of her recurrent mental breakdowns. She was declared schizophrenic and subjected to electro-shock treatments. She finally divorced Olivier in 1960.

Marilyn had flown to Tokyo just after her marriage to DiMaggio, and flown to London right after her marriage to Miller. While married to DiMaggio, she'd entertained troops in Korea and made *The Seven Year Itch*. While married to Miller, she had a classier act. She appeared in *Showgirl* with Olivier and was presented to Queen Elizabeth at the Royal Command Performance of a war movie. The young Queen, eager to meet Marilyn, had asked Rattigan about her. As Marilyn curtsied, the Queen graciously mentioned that they were now neighbors at Windsor.

While she was making the film, Miller and Marilyn lived in Parkside House, in Surrey, a magnificent mansion rented from Lord Moore, the publisher of the *Financial Times*. Rosten wrote that it was "an hour from London and an hour's drive to the studios where Marilyn was to begin work. It contained a dozen rooms, a staff of six or seven, several acres of lush green lawn, inimitable English rose gardens, and its backyard was enclosed by an iron fence and a gate that opened on Windsor Park, the private property of Her Majesty the Queen." Marilyn, enthusiastic about England, found it a striking contrast to Los Angeles. She wrote to a friend that "Compared to California, England seems tiny and quaint with its little toy trains chugging through the miniature countryside. . . . I am dying to walk bareheaded in the rain. I want to eat real roast beef and Yorkshire pudding. . . . I want to buy a tweed suit. . . . I want to ride a bicycle, and I'd like someone to explain the jokes in *Punch* – they don't seem funny to me."[4] A Hungarian couple who worked for them as domestic servants were bribed by the press to report their conversations and activities. When they were found out the Millers forgave them, but the police threatened them with deportation if they ever revealed another word.

With no official role in the production of the movie and nothing much to do, Miller roamed nervously about the mansion, so different from his own modest home. He played the piano, wrote a bit, filled up Marilyn's scrapbooks with press cuttings and read film scripts that had been sent to her. An unidentified London friend wrote that Miller seemed ill at ease in his new role and was having trouble living up to his romantic image: "Arthur makes a bad impression here. Cold as a refrigerated fish in his personal appearance. Not like a hot lover, more like a morgue keeper left with a royal cadaver." The tabloids called him "Mr. Monroe" and "Marilyn's Boy."

Miller did, by all accounts, seem to satisfy Marilyn. Colin Clark, an assistant on the set, described them watching the daily rushes: "When we got into the viewing theatre, to everyone's embarrass-ment, they went into the back row and started snogging as if they were on a date!" An actor in the film confirmed both Miller's awkward manner and Marilyn's adoration: "She'd just married Arthur Miller and this sort of tall weird man used to come onto the set just looking on, and she would run over and jump into his arms and wrap herself around him and they would disappear into the dressing-room for about ten minutes – and then she would reappear again 'refreshed.'" After attending the London premiere of *A View from the Bridge* on October 12, Miller proudly wrote Rosten that Marilyn wore a garnet-colored velvet gown, halted traffic as far north as Liverpool and conquered everyone. She was so worried about the play's success that she squeezed his hand throughout the performance whenever things went well or looked shaky.[5] They enjoyed John Osborne's daring new play, *Look Back in Anger*, at the Royal Court Theatre in Sloane Square, the first shot in a battle that eventually drove playwrights like Rattigan off the English stage.

Paula Strasberg, who disliked Miller, noted their physical attraction and emphasized his devotion: "I have never seen such tenderness and love as Arthur and Marilyn feel for each other. How he values her! I don't think any woman I've ever known has been so *valued* by a man." Even Olivier – sophisticated, emotionally remote and married to the porcelain beauty Vivien Leigh – could not resist (at first) Marilyn's overpowering allure. After meeting her in New York, he gushed (while puffing their picture) that "she was so adorable, so witty, such incredible fun and more physically attractive than anyone I could have imagined, apart from herself on the screen." In London he could scarcely contain his enthusiasm as he described her essential skill as an actress: "She has the extraordinarily cunning gift of being able to suggest one minute that she is the naughtiest little thing, and the next minute that she is beautifully dumb and innocent."

Olivier's enthusiasm disappeared once they began shooting and he realized that Marilyn was not only adorable but also impossibly difficult. On the first day she appeared at Pinewood Studios (west of London, near Heathrow airport) with her full palace guard: hairdresser and make-up man, secretary and cook, two publicists and bodyguards, as well as the inevitable Paula who would, as always, cause a great deal of trouble. Colin Clark was shocked to discover that Marilyn, the famous beauty, "looked absolutely frightful. No make-up, just a skirt, a tight blouse, head scarf and dark glasses. Nasty complexion, a lot of facial hair, shapeless figure and, when the glasses came off, a very vague look in her eye. No wonder she is so insecure." The dazed look would trouble cameramen for the rest of her career. But when she appeared on the screen, there was "an incredible transformation. Now MM looked like an angel – smooth, glowing, eyes shining with joy . . . perfect lips slightly parted, irresistible."[6]

Marilyn and Olivier were worlds apart intellectually and immediately clashed over their very different approaches to acting. The Method emphasized psychological realism. British actors, trained in more classical and impersonal speech and movement, were more oriented to the stage than to film. Olivier emphasized the contrast by stating, "My own way is an extremely external one: starting with the image of the person and working inwards. This is against the modern trend which works the other way round." Using the Method for the frivolous *Showgirl* seemed like taking a deep dive into a shallow pool. When Olivier, as director, urged Marilyn to "be sexy," she took this as an insult. The caviar-eating scene required no less than two whole days, thirty-four takes and twenty jars of the costly sturgeon roe.

The cameraman, Jack Cardiff, noted that Paula's instructions confused Marilyn and interfered with her work:

> There was something unreal about it all. The great Olivier, magnificently costumed in heavy military felt, cumbersome medals, epaulettes, belts, riding boots and thick make-up, with his hair plastered down and a monocle wedged in his eye, would be all ready to shoot a scene. Having wearily rehearsed Marilyn for ages, he would be about to say "Roll the camera" when Marilyn would go over to Paula in the shadows and talk again, while Larry waited – in sweat and silent fury.

Paula would then tell Marilyn, '"Now remember, darling, think of Frank Sinatra and Coca-Cola." At last Marilyn entered into the scene – and forgot her lines." When Olivier inevitably contradicted Paula's instructions, Marilyn immediately sent for Greene, and he complicated matters by calling Lee Strasberg in New York.

Miller felt that Olivier's dual roles as co-star and director had put the actor in an impossible position, and that the picture would have been much better with a different English director. Marilyn felt Olivier had become a fallen idol, and she never recovered her faith in him: "She was terribly disappointed in Olivier. Olivier turns out to be an actor instead of a great person – in Marilyn's mind – the collapse of the great God image. To her, they didn't use creativity but seemed to work by the numbers, by the book. It was a big letdown. This collapse of her respect for Olivier was the most direct reason for her inability to sleep at night."[7] Marilyn's support group – Miller, Greene, Paula and Hedda Rosten (who'd been a psychiatric social worker and had been brought to England as a secretary and companion) – attempted to encourage her performance and control her conflict with Olivier. But they all made the mistake of trying to provide what she wanted instead of giving her the discipline she needed.

Olivier despised Marilyn's pretentiousness and lack of professionalism, her "lateness, her stupidity, her aggravating behaviour, her lack of respect for him and her complete unconcern for studio-time and studio money." Maliciously condemning her performance, he said, "teaching her to act was like teaching Urdu to a marmoset." Clark added that she "doesn't really forget her lines. It is more as if she had never quite learnt them." She, in turn, loathed Olivier's hypocrisy and disdain. She angrily told her maid that "he gave me the dirtiest looks, even when he was smiling. I was sick half the time, but he didn't believe me, or else he didn't care. . . . He looked at me as if he had just smelled a pile of dead fish. Like I was a leper, or something awful. He'd say something like, 'Oh, how simply ravishing, my dear.' But he really wanted to throw up."[8]

Marilyn could not tolerate any disagreement with her own point of view. Speaking of Hedda Rosten, but also alluding to his own difficulty in dealing with Marilyn, Miller said, "by declining to support everything Marilyn believed, she risked the charge of unfaithfulness, and yet she could not in principle reinforce her friend's unhealthy illusions." Speaking of his own problems with Marilyn, Miller (like Jack Cardiff) again emphasized the illusory aspect of her already unreal life as an actress. He suggested that she'd lost confidence in him, as well as in Olivier, when they were forced to oppose Paula and Greene: "in order to keep reality from slipping away, I occasionally had to defend Olivier or else reinforce the naïveté of her illusions; the result was that she began to question the absoluteness of my partisanship on her side of the deepening struggle." When Olivier disappointed her and Miller tried to present a more realistic view of the situation, Miller became another god that failed.

Marilyn, a limited actress, came under intense pressure when acting with the high-powered Olivier. The more controlled and icy his behavior, the more upset she became. Despite Miller's love and emotional support, she gave in to her addiction to alcohol and drugs, and established a destructive pattern that would plague her for the rest of her life. She started to drink in the morning and, Miller explained, the barbiturates intensified her distortion of reality, her insecurity and her guilt:

> [She was] bedeviled by feelings she couldn't name. Just a generalized feeling of threat. She was trying to immunize herself against feeling too much by taking pills during the day. She was

like a smashed vase. It is a beautiful thing when it is intact, but the broken pieces are murderous and they can cut you. . . .

The management on the film called me and the pressure was on me to help her get [to the studio]. She couldn't sleep and began taking the pills and when she got up, she was very depressed and, of course, it was difficult to get her on her feet. She began to identify me with the management.

My regret was enormous. I had the illusion that I could help her, could work something out. I made her feel guilty that she had made me feel this way. She wanted to be of help to *me* really, to be a "good wife."

Though Miller tried to keep the production from collapsing, she resented his paternal interference. As they fought fiercely on the set, he was caught in the crossfire between Marilyn and Olivier, and felt that she was "devouring" him.

The crisis deepened, whether by accident or by intent, when Marilyn found her husband's private diary and read what he had written about her (an episode Miller omitted from *Timebends*). Despite his awareness of her years of failure and guilt, her frail ego and fears of being abandoned, her extreme sensitivity to criticism, Miller probably left his diary out on purpose. It was a way of telling her how he felt, of confessing that he couldn't take much more emotional punishment. In any case, she read the fatal entry which, Miller said, "had to do with Olivier and her. She was aware of a grinding frustration in me and in that note there was an allusion to the fact that I was unable to help her and I was not of any use to her or myself." Miller must have wondered how he had ceased to be a playwright and become the diva's servant.

Marilyn told Lee Strasberg that Miller's diary described "how disappointed he was in me. How he thought I was some kind of angel but now he guessed he was wrong. That his first wife had let him down, but I had done something worse. Olivier was beginning to think I was a troublesome bitch and Arthur no longer had a decent answer to that one."[9] She also told Susan Strasberg, more frankly and forcefully, that Miller "was ashamed of me, ashamed to love me. . . . Her problems with Olivier [were] her fault because she was a bitch." Though Miller merely mentioned, and did not exaggerate, her self-destructive faults, her reaction "was horror. You know, a woman wants her husband to bolster her up, not magnify her flaws." In yet another version of this incident, Miller is supposed to have written, "The only one I will ever love is my daughter." Marilyn responded to Miller's diary with five stark words, written on her initialed notepaper and found after her death, "he does not love me."[10] She seems to have lost, early on, the feeling of being sheltered in his warmth and tenderness.

Following this crisis, which took place halfway through the shooting, Miller flew to New York, supposedly to visit his sick daughter ("the only one I will ever love"). When Paula also had to return to New York, Marilyn's analyst, Dr. Hohenberg, was flown over to England at great expense to provide psychological help, alleviate Marilyn's depression and reduce her dependence on drugs.

On October 13, when he'd returned to London, Miller wrote Rosten that he and Joshua Logan had seen the first fifty minutes of the "spectacular" movie and had been "bowled over" by it. The picture does have some amusing topical allusions. Olivier, referring to HUAC, accuses his political enemies of "Un-Carpathian Activities." Marilyn's dress strap breaks during her first meeting with Olivier (the Prince Regent) just as it did during their press conference in New York. There are references to her habitual lateness as she dresses for a seductive midnight supper with Olivier. When she enters the ornately furnished Carpathian embassy, she speaks personally and declares, "All I can say is give me vulgarity." As they're about to kiss for the first time, she notices his excessive pomade and punctures his romantic image by observing, "There's a lot of funny stuff in your hair." The Olivier character also hurls a dart at Marilyn by remarking, "We are not dealing with a supervised adult, but with a moody child."

Miller was whistling in the dark about the movie. The trivial plot concerns Marilyn's conquest of the stiff and formal Olivier (whom she calls "Your Grand Ducal"), who's visiting London in 1911 for the coronation of King George V. The picture retains the verbosity and staginess of the original play, and most of the characters enter and exit through the main set, the salon of the embassy. Marilyn doesn't always look her best, and her chorus-girl song comes out of nowhere. Worst of all, Marilyn and Olivier are more an awkward couple than a sensational match. Olivier is very cold, they have no personal magnetism or emotional spark, and don't seem as though they could ever fall in love with each other. They appear to be acting in two different movies.

In his disputes with Marilyn, the English cast and crew naturally sided with the greatly respected Olivier, and were also quite bitter about her unprofessional behavior. Their anger erupted at the end of the shooting when she set out her parting gifts on a trestle-table: bottles for the gentlemen, identical purses for the ladies. One man disgustedly threw his bottle into a huge rubbish bin and "Immediately one of the ladies followed and threw in her purse. There was a sort of rippling murmur of anger and assent, and then everyone followed suit. Quite soon the bin was literally overflowing with bottles and purses, still wrapped and labelled – 'Thank you from Marilyn Monroe.'"

After seeing the second and final version of the movie, Marilyn (perhaps advised by Miller) sent Jack Warner a very shrewd professional analysis of its faults, and made specific suggestions about how to improve the pace, plot, comedy, editing and music:

> It is not the same picture you saw in New York last winter, and I am afraid that as it stands it will not be as successful as the version all of us agreed was so fine. Especially in the first third of the picture the pacing has been slowed and one comic point after another has been flattened out by substituting inferior takes with flatter performances lacking the energy and brightness that you saw in New York. Some of the jump cutting kills the points, as in the fainting scene. The coronation is as long as before if not longer, and the story gets lost in it. American audiences are not as moved by stained-glass windows as the British are, and we threaten them with boredom. I am amazed that so much of the picture has no music at all when the idea was to make a romantic picture. We have shot enough film to make a great movie, if only it will be as in the earlier version. I hope you will make every effort to save our picture.

Marilyn was as angry with Olivier after *Showgirl* as she'd been with Joshua Logan after *Bus Stop*. When the picture was released, Olivier visited the Actors Studio and Marilyn took refuge in the ladies' room until she was sure he had left. Shelley Winters "asked her if the shooting of *The Prince and the Showgirl* had been that rough. She blinked and smiled and said, 'English actors are ashamed of their feelings and hate the idea of expressing themselves with our Method work. They prefer to act with technique.'"[11]

The acrimony over *Showgirl*, the second and last picture made with Milton Greene for Marilyn Monroe Productions, destroyed her friendship with her partner. Miller, believing her contract with Greene was extraordinarily disadvantageous, was eager to get Marilyn out of it. But he realized, since Greene had not always separated his own purchases from company expenses, that dividing company assets would be complicated. Miller declared that Milton and Amy "bought antiques in London and charged them to the company. . . . The financial affairs of the company were in a mess." Greene had, however, financed her luxurious lifestyle in New York. "It would be hard to say how much was owed Milton at the time. He was paying for nearly everything for Marilyn" from the time she left Hollywood until she went to work on *Bus Stop* and *Showgirl*. "I think this period when he was giving her money began in 1955. It continued when she was living in the Waldorf."

In April 1957, after a series of angry legal conferences, Greene was forced to sell his stock to Marilyn for $100,000. This was his payment for establishing the profitable company, working for her during their partnership and paying most of her expenses for more than a year. Marilyn, relieved to break their agreement, said, "my company had not been organized to parcel out 49 percent of my earnings to Mr. Greene for seven years." Miller maintained that Greene "swindled" Marilyn and "did nothing but live off her work. She prevented him from getting majority control, and then had to pay $100,000 to get rid of him." Greene's son saw things rather differently and declared, "Miller fucked my family."[12]

Twelve

Heading for Disaster
(1957–1960)

I

While married to Mary and before he met Marilyn, Miller had led a structured and productive life. For Marilyn's sake he gave up a great deal – not only his long-term marriage and children, but the privacy, peace and secure way of life that had sustained his greatest work. Like Orpheus, he descended into a troubled underworld to rescue his Eurydice, and he, too, was doomed to fail. Miller thought he'd been unhappy with Mary, but now found himself far worse off. Exposed to the glare of publicity and scrutiny of the media, swept into Marilyn's chaotic life and tormented by a woman who was impossible to please, he became what Norman Mailer called "the most talented slave in the world."

After returning from England in November 1956, Miller took Marilyn back to his country house in Roxbury, Connecticut, where he hoped they could lead a normal life. The two-story house, built in 1783 during the colonial period, had huge ceiling beams. It was surrounded by 325 acres of land and planted with fruit trees. There was no other house in sight, and a cool breeze blew through a row of maples. The back veranda, with its view of endless hills, led to a swimming pond with water so clean you could drink it.

It soon became clear that they would have trouble combining their habits, tastes and interests. The contrast between Marilyn's lofty dreams and reckless indifference to money and Miller's down-to-earth realism and notorious frugality became obvious that autumn when she asked Frank Lloyd Wright to design a new house. Though Miller told Wright that they wanted to live rather simply, Wright's grandiose plan included, Miller wrote, "a circular living room with a dropped center surrounded by ovoid columns of fieldstone some five feet thick, and a domed ceiling, the diameter no less than sixty feet, looking out toward the view over a swimming pool seventy feet long with fieldstone sides that jutted forth from the incline of the hill." This gigantic pleasure-dome, suitable for an oriental potentate, fulfilled Wright's own fantasies but ignored his clients' needs. It had "only a single bedroom and a small guestroom, but did provide a large 'conference room' complete with a long boardroom-type table flanked by a dozen high-backed chairs." In the end they rejected his concept as far too impractical and outrageously expensive and decided to preserve the old house. They modernized the rear part, put in sliding doors, and built a garage and a separate one-room study for Miller.

For Marilyn the housewife's routine had no charms. Life in a run-down house with a husband who spent the mornings reading and writing in his study and the afternoons replacing rotten timber and putting in plumbing must have come as a shock. Mailer satirized the homespun Miller as "the complacent country squire, boring people with his accounts of clearing fields, gardening, the joys of plumbing ('Nothing like taking a bath in water that comes through pipes you threaded your-self')." Miller was self-sufficient, fully occupied and used to solitude. Marilyn – who'd been taught almost nothing as a child – had no useful skills or diverting pastimes, and focused entirely on her own appear-ance. She had nothing to occupy her empty hours in the country, and soon got tired of rearranging the furniture and playing with Hugo, Miller's sluggish and incontinent basset hound. She wanted her husband's absolute attention but, as Miller observed, "physical admiration threat-ened to devalue her person, yet she became anxious if her appearance was ignored." The screenwriter Nunnally Johnson noted the abyss that had opened between them: "I think she bored the hell out of every-body. She just didn't have the intelligence, but she was aware she didn't have it. . . . My guess is she just wasn't enough for Arthur Miller. After you've married the sex goddess – nobody finds it very difficult to talk before you get into the hay, but what do you say afterwards? Marilyn was like a child, she thought a lay was the answer to everything."

Soon after their wedding Marilyn invited the Strasbergs for a country brunch, and their strange visit revealed the anxiety and chaos that reigned in Roxbury. The Strasbergs arrived punctually at 11 a.m. Marilyn and Miller seemed to have quarreled and he'd left all the preparations to her. She was unprepared for her guests and he was indifferent, even hostile. No one had done any shopping. "In her terrycloth housecoat, Marilyn appeared to have just awakened. Nobody else was there, not even a maid. Nobody made moves toward the kitchen. Tension floated in the air. It was apparent something was awry. Miller didn't . . . offer even a glass of water. An hour and a half went by." When the uneasy guests said they were hungry after the long drive from New York, Marilyn "panicked. 'Come inside.' She ran into the kitchen. She pulled open the freezer, put her hands on a frozen steak and stammered nervously, 'I'll g-get you s-something to eat right away.'"

The friend who'd driven them up from New York tried to ease the tension by bringing hostilities into the open and rather awkwardly saying:

> "Hey, try to relax. We all know Arthur doesn't like Lee, but even if Lee doesn't like Arthur he respects him, so relax, willya? Nothing's going to happen. Take it easy."
>
> Marilyn didn't answer. She opened the refrigerator. Nothing was there except a bottle of milk. Back at the freezer she pulled out the frozen steak. "Here," she said.
>
> "This won't work. What else do you have?"
>
> Marilyn began to claw at the trays. She pulled out frozen strawberries, frozen peas.[1]

Finally, the guests escaped to a nearby restaurant.

A few years later, Frank Taylor, Miller's friend and publisher, was invited to Roxbury with his family to hear Miller read the script of *The Misfits*. Always seductive, Marilyn asked Taylor's four boys, aged seven to seventeen, "Who wants to lie on the hammock with me?" They all raced to cuddle up with her – all together, if possible; serially, if not. Curtice Taylor recalled how, as a self-styled "weird pre-adolescent," he wanted to see Marilyn on his own. Later on he got permission to visit his horse, Ebony, which the Taylors had not been able to keep and had given to the Millers. As he hung around the house, the Millers must have thought, "what the hell is this kid doing here?" Though Curtice felt awkward with Marilyn, she lavished affection on him. Curious about her sexual life, he was strangely disturbed when he looked through the door and saw the twisted sheets in the bedroom.

Curtice also recalled another tense and sad incident, involving Marilyn's love of animals (except the minks in her coat), which seemed straight out of *The Misfits*:

On another weekend, when we Taylors were visiting the Millers, my brother Mark and I were playing around in the pastures when we came upon a newborn calf being tended to by its mother. We knew Marilyn would love this, so we went and got her. Indeed, she did love it, and cooed about the mother licking it clean as it struggled to get up. We were all laughing and having a fine time when we saw the farmer who rented the pasture coming across the field. He gruffly greeted us, went over to the calf and unceremoniously opened its legs. Getting the information he needed, he strode away, only to return a few minutes later with a large gunny sack. When he picked up the struggling creature and started to stuff it into the bag, Marilyn went ballistic! "How could you take it away from its mother? It was just born and is innocent." Then, just like in *The Misfits*, she said, "I'll buy it from you. How much do you want for it?" She was on the border of hysteria. After stuffing the calf into the bag, the farmer proceeded with his task, despite her protestations, and said to Marilyn: "Mrs. Miller, I will not sell you this calf. It's a male calf and I run a dairy. I will now raise him for veal. This is what I do. This is how it works." He put the squirming sack over his shoulder and walked away. Arthur was waiting for us as we brought a sobbing Marilyn back to the porch. The day was ruined and she withdrew into seclusion.

The Millers' life in New York was equally unreal. At first they lived in Marilyn's apartment at 2 Sutton Place, a posh street not far from the United Nations, with views of the East River and the Queensboro Bridge. Its décor looked like an albino stage set. Her maid condescendingly wrote, "It seemed half-finished, half-furnished, and reminded me of a hotel. There was a white piano, some nondescript white sofas, and wall-to-wall white carpeting marred by many stains. The view of the buildings across the street was gloomy. Floor-to-ceiling mirrors were everywhere."

The larger, 13th-floor flat at 444 East 57th Street, where they moved in 1957, had a living room with bookcases, a fireplace and a piano; dining alcove with a mirrored table; kitchen and study; main bedroom and bathroom; guest bedroom, with floral designs on the white porcelain doorknobs. An interviewer, satirizing the overdone décor, called the place "unexpectedly MGMish: white sofas and spreading ice-cap expanses of white fitted carpet. There is, in fact, a sharp division when you enter Mr. Miller's work-room. . . . The stokehole below the first-class lounge" revealed his different taste and symbolized his humble status.[2]

As she tried to adjust to her third marriage, Marilyn projected an image of a successful union, of shared interests and mutual support. She told the press that they talked, read and listened to music at home; went to movies, saw friends and walked in Central Park. The young poet Sylvia Plath, married to the English poet Ted Hughes and trying to be a writer, a wife and a mother, identified with Marilyn's apparently ideal life. Plath also suffered from depression, had mental breakdowns and committed suicide five months after Marilyn's death. Conned by Hollywood publicity, she had no idea of Marilyn's troubles. She imagined Marilyn as a model of married perfection, an intimate and optimistic companion. In a journal entry of October 1959 Plath recorded how she dreamed about being groomed and encouraged by the actress, who fulfilled her youthful fantasies: "Marilyn Monroe appeared to me last night in a dream as a kind of fairy godmother. . . . I spoke, almost in tears, of how much she and Arthur Miller meant to us, although they could, of course, not know us at all. She gave me an expert manicure. I had not washed my hair, and asked her about hairdressers, saying no matter where I went, they always imposed a horrid cut on me. She invited me to visit her during the Christmas holidays, promising a new, flowering life."

In reality, Marilyn was restless and unhappy. When she was not preparing for a public appearance or playing Marilyn Monroe in the movies, she retreated into her protective cave and wondered what to do with all her energy and talent. She often spent her hours and days doing absolutely nothing – wandering around her flat, peering into the kitchen, stumbling pointlessly from room to room. In movies she'd seen sophisticated stars like Fred Astaire and Ginger Rogers, Cary Grant and Katharine Hepburn, feasting on caviar and drinking champagne. When Marilyn became a star she imitated these movie fantasies and tried to live a luxurious life. She acquired cases of her favorite drink, Dom Pérignon champagne – named for the seventeenth-century Benedictine monk who discovered how to put sparkle into still wine – to prove she had achieved success and could have anything she wanted in the world.

Miller spent all day in his study. The maid noted that "Bobby and Jane would come by to see their father after school in the afternoons. But [unlike the Taylor boys] they seemed far less interested in their father's famous new wife than in the hamburgers, Cokes, candy, and other goodies Hattie [the cook] stocked for them." Meanwhile, as the observant maid wrote, Marilyn led a rather narcissistic and lonely life:

> Her doctors' appointments . . . and her acting lessons were virtually all she had to look forward to. She spent most of her time in her little bedroom, sleeping, looking at herself in the mirrors, drinking Bloody Marys or champagne, talking on the phone, which seemed to be her greatest pleasure. . . .
>
> I never saw her read a book or a newspaper. Once in a while she would thumb through the pictures of high-fashion models in *Vogue*. She didn't own a television [which had obsessed DiMaggio], never listened to the radio. Marilyn did seem to enjoy playing jazz and blues records on the small hi-fi set next to her bed.

The Millers seemed happier in the summer of 1957 in Amagansett, renting a house on the Atlantic shore at the eastern end of Long Island. They spent time riding in a dune-buggy, fishing and swimming, running on the beach and leaning lovingly against each other. Like Paula Strasberg, a friend noticed that "Arthur was so attentive, so concerned. He hung upon her every word. . . . He seemed so concerned for her that, if he could have, he would have physically *merged with her* and taken on her sadness."[3]

II

In New York, as in England and Hollywood, Marilyn, often accompanied by Miller, continued to meet distinguished writers, heads of state and even royalty. In February 1959, when the seventy-four-year-old Danish author Isak Dinesen – wasted, skeletal and ravaged by syphilis – expressed a desire to meet them, Carson McCullers invited the actress and playwright to lunch at her house in Nyack, New York. Dinesen, keen to secure the Nobel Prize, wanted all the exposure and publicity she could get while in America and felt that Marilyn could easily be exploited for this purpose. McCullers recalled that "Marilyn was very timid and called me three or four times about the dress she was going to wear, and wanting to know if it should be low-cut or not. I said that anything she wore would be beautiful on her. She actually wore a dress cut very low that showed her lovely bosoms. Marilyn sat and listened while [Dinesen] talked."

McCullers served oysters, white grapes, soufflés and champagne on a black marble table. Virginia Carr noted that "Monroe, who had a marvelous sense of humor and whom the guests found charming, entertained the group with an anecdote from her own kitchen. She told with much cleverness a tale on herself involving some homemade noodles she had tried to create one night for her husband like his mother [who was actually born in America] used to make in the 'old country.' The conglomeration was such a failure that she was afraid she had lost not only a meal, but a husband." Judith Thurman added an amusing detail to Marilyn's story: "it got a little late, the company was arriving, and the pasta wasn't ready, so she tried to finish it off with a hair dryer."[4]

Referring to Dinesen by her familiar name, McCullers described how Miller questioned her rather pedantically about her strange diet and received a stern rebuke: "Tanya ate only oysters and drank only champagne. . . . Arthur asked what doctor put her on that diet. . . . She looked at him and said rather sharply, 'Doctor? The doctors are horrified by my diet but I love champagne and I love oysters and they agree with me.' . . . Arthur mentioned something about protein and Tanya said, 'I don't know anything about that, but I am old and I eat what I want and what agrees with me.' Then she went back to her reminiscences of friends in Africa."

McCullers' memoir gives the flavor of this bohemian gathering. The Southern writer recalled that her own black help reminded Dinesen of her African servants: "It was a great delight for her to be with colored people. Ida, my housekeeper, is colored, and so are my yardmen, Jesse and Sam. After lunch everybody danced and sang. A friend of Ida's had brought in a motion picture camera, and there were pictures of Tanya dancing with Marilyn, me dancing with Arthur, and a great round of general dancing." In McCullers' account Marilyn seems happy – talking freely, making fun of herself, enjoying the affection and attention of two eminent ladies.

Thurman mentioned that Tanya "was photographed in New York with Marilyn Monroe, and that image was more 'typical' of the old Isak Dinesen: twisted smile, elegant gray suit, head swathed in a turban, body muffled in a fur." Dinesen's account of Marilyn's appearance and character shows that she understood, better than McCullers, her complex and disturbed personality. Using words like "incredibly" and "unbelievable" to emphasize Marilyn's hyper-reality, but with a novelist's insight, she compared her to an apparently harmless but quite dangerous wild animal. "It's not that she is pretty," she said, "although of course she is almost incredibly pretty – but that she radiates at the same time unbounded vitality and a kind of unbelievable innocence. I have met the same in a lion cub that my native servants in Africa brought me. I would not keep her."[5] Underlying her beauty and apparent innocence, which fascinated Miller and everyone else, was the traumatically damaged orphan.

In the spring of 1956 Saul Bellow had spent six weeks next door to Miller as they waited for their divorces, but he did not meet Marilyn until later on. In 1959, when she was in Chicago for the premiere of *Some Like It Hot*, they dined together at the Ambassador Hotel. Bellow was intrigued by the details of her life, and admired the way she dealt with the intrusive demands of publicity. He found "the star surrounded by an entourage that included a manicurist and a bodyguard, who left the door open when he went to the bathroom. 'He's not supposed to let me out of his sight,' Monroe explained. After dinner at the Pump Room, she signed the guest book, 'Proud to be the guest of the Chicago writer Saul Bellow.' In a star-struck letter to [his editor Pascal] Covici the next day, Bellow reported: 'Marilyn seemed genuinely glad to see a familiar face. I have yet to see anything in Marilyn that isn't genuine. Surrounded by thousands, she conducts herself like a philosopher.'" Bellow, who had an eye for women and married five times, called her a very witty woman, and spoke rapturously of the golden glow and luminous incandescence of her skin. He must have been besotted, indeed blinded, to find Marilyn, the essence of Hollywood artificiality, as "genuine." In recent years she'd suffered miscarriages and had several nervous breakdowns. She'd attempted suicide and made Miller's life a misery. She was more like the mad philosopher Nietzsche than the conventional Immanuel Kant. Her friends and colleagues, not Marilyn, had to be philosophical.

After Marilyn's death, with greater insight into her character, Bellow found her more tragic than amusing: "I always felt she had picked up some high-tension cable and couldn't release it. She couldn't rest, she found no repose in anything. She was up in the night, taking pills and talking about her costumes, her next picture, contracts and money, gossip. In the case of a beautiful and sensitive creature like that, it was a guarantee of destruction."

Marilyn had always hero-worshipped Abraham Lincoln and, when she first met Miller, was fond of comparing him to the upright president. Lincoln's biographer, the monkey-faced Carl Sandburg, had left school at thirteen and tried many proletarian jobs before becoming a poet and writer. Much anthologized, Sandburg was a beloved if limited poet, a fixture of the fifties. Robert Frost, always annoyed, even infuriated, by the way Sandburg combed his long silky hair *into* his eyes, exclaimed: "You know the way he dresses, that hair of his and those [string] ties. Everything about him is studied – except his poetry."[6]

The eighty-one-year-old Sandburg met Marilyn during the filming of *Some Like It Hot* in 1958, and again during the shooting of *Let's Make Love* in 1960, when he came to Hollywood to write additional dialogue for the biblical epic *The Greatest Story Ever Told*. He liked to visit her New York apartment and give her informal literary tutorials. Marilyn established immediate rapport with the poet and enthusiastically praised his energy and curiosity: "Carl Sandburg, who's in his eighties – you should see his vitality, what he has contributed. Why, he could play the guitar and sing at three in the morning," which suited her insomniac hours. "You can meet Carl Sandburg and he is so pleased to meet you. He wants to know about you and you want to know about him. Not in any way has he ever let me down." She bought a ten-inch bust of Sandburg by the American sculptor Joseph Konzal and enshrined him in her flat.

Donald Spoto wrote that Sandburg "found her 'warm and plain' and charmed her by asking for her autograph. 'Marilyn was a good talker,' according to Sandburg, 'and very good company. We did some mock playacting and some pretty good, funny imitations. I asked her a lot of questions. She told me about how she came up the hard way, but would never talk about her husbands.'" The lonely old man and lonely young woman were photographed doing invigorating exercises and drinking champagne.

After her suicide Sandburg was interviewed in *Look* magazine. The reporter described Sandburg's "longish white hair flapping like skeins of corn silk" and noted that Marilyn had bonded with the poet by bleaching her platinum-blond hair "the exact shade" of his. In a string of reassuring banalities posing as pearls of wisdom, Sandburg said she was "a great actress," "had a genuine quality" and "had some faith in me." Though Marilyn "had a hard time with her sleep," he "saw no signs of despondency" and felt, reasonably enough, that "thirty-six is just too young to die."[7] Unlike Dinesen, Sandburg, ever the aged smiling public man, ignored the dark side of her personality.

On May 20, 1959 Miller was awarded the Gold Medal for Drama from the American Academy of Arts and Letters, and the rather formal ceremony was sparked into life by Marilyn's stunning appearance. A historian dutifully recorded: "if the award was certainly deserved, the speech was dependable. Miller, on occasion, managed to be witty when he spoke, but you could always count on him to be pious in the last sentence of the first paragraph: 'An honor which the artist perhaps would not part with, but never truly takes as his own, because labor freely given and the joyful misery of creating cannot be translated into a prize.' Nevertheless, his presence was an event: Marilyn Monroe, then his wife, was in the audience."

Miller, well aware of her habits, arrived on time and without her. Marilyn came very late and at the very end of the luncheon. She was placed next to the seventy-eight-year-old Irish writer, Padraic Colum, who hadn't minded the empty seat and truthfully claimed that he'd never heard of Marilyn Monroe. Wearing a very tight and very décolleté black dress, with three strands of pearls and long white gloves, she sat demurely among the spectators. She knew she was on display – all eyes, as always, were riveted on her – and was smiling, charming and self-possessed. The intellectuals and academicians were tremendously excited by her presence. Everyone was thrilled to be there and fought to get near the deity. Abandoning their customary reserve, they swarmed around her and swooned like a bunch of love-sick schoolboys. While Miller gave his pious speech, Marilyn quietly stole the show.

Marilyn also impressed several heads of state. She curtsied to Queen

Elizabeth of England and to King Paul of Greece, dazzled Sukarno and charmed Nikita Khrushchev. Sukarno, mad about movies, refused to attend a party at the Beverly Hills Hotel unless she was there. Bowing to diplomatic pressure, she turned up on her thirtieth birthday, June 1, 1956, while filming *Bus Stop*. Throwing her arms around Sukarno, she exclaimed, "I'm so glad to meet the president of India." He then explained that he was the president of Indonesia.

Au courant with the latest gossip, Sukarno asked (four weeks before her wedding) if she were going to marry Mr. Miller. She shrugged and giggled; he encouraged her by expressing his approval. Aware of her publicity value and ignoring the Muslim prohibition of nudity, Sukarno flattered her by stating, "you are a very important person in Indonesia [also in India]. Your pictures are the most popular of any that have ever played in my country. The entire Indonesian population is interested in my meeting you." The attractive couple were clearly drawn to each other. Rosten wrote that Marilyn, witty as always,

> had been thrilled. She recalled that he was handsome and courteous despite the fact that "he kept looking down my dress, you'd think with five wives he'd have enough." She liked him, she liked his fez [i.e., his Malay cap], she liked his public admittance of his five (or was it four?) wives, all of whom he referred to endearingly. In Marilyn's eyes, that was machismo, romanticism, poetry, and whatever helped explain man's devotion to women.[8]

The following year, when Sukarno's life was in danger after an attempted coup, Marilyn wanted to rescue the dashing hero (and his harem) by offering him a safe haven in America. Miller, though touched by her habitual compassion, refused to welcome the volatile leader into their household.

Twentieth Century-Fox still regarded her as its property. When Nikita Khrushchev visited the studio in September 1959, president Spyros Skouras felt the contrast between beauty and the beast would provide a great photo opportunity. He told Marilyn to wear her tightest, sexiest dress and invited her to sit at the main table in their lavish commissary. For the first time in her life Marilyn arrived early, which prompted Wilder to suggest that Khrushchev ought to direct her next picture.

Khrushchev was a crude, powerful, larger-than-life character, whose visit had an enormous political impact. Robert Frost admired his homely proverbs, sense of humor and peasant's smile, and called him "very good-natured, hearty, jolly, rough in a way, you'd call it coarse." After the band played "The Star-Spangled Banner" and "The Internationale," the studio staged a fake shooting of the musical *Can-Can*, starring Shirley MacLaine, with no film in the camera. Invoking Soviet puritanism to condemn the dissolute American society, Khrushchev called her dance "immoral," fit only for an "insatiable" audience, and added that "a person's face is more beautiful than his backside."

As the music faded, Darryl Zanuck unexpectedly announced that the right-wing Walt Disney "has informed us that he does not think that premier Khrushchev and his family should go to Disneyland this evening, as he cannot guarantee their safety." Keen to see that fantastic place and used to exerting absolute authority, the great dictator was furious. He seized the opportunity to condemn both America's warmongering and its dangerous criminals: "Just imagine, I, a Premier, a Soviet representative . . . told that I could not go. . . . Why not? . . . Do you have rocket-launching pads there? . . . Or have gangsters taken hold of the place? . . . If you won't let me go to Disneyland, I'll send the hydrogen bomb over."[9] There was just enough hysteria in his voice to suggest that if he couldn't see Mickey Mouse he might overreact and destroy Southern California. Frank Sinatra, trying to defuse the explosive situation, told David Niven, who was sitting next to Khrushchev's sturdy wife, "Screw the cops! Tell the old broad you and I'll take 'em down this afternoon."

The director George Cukor called it "an extraordinary occasion and you had to find it funny, but [Marilyn] couldn't make any connection with it." But Marilyn did make a striking connection with Khrushchev himself, who seemed to find her backside as beautiful as her face. When Skouras told his oft-repeated story of how he had progressed from barefoot immigrant to studio head, Khrushchev "countered that he was the son of a poor coal miner and was now the head man of the whole Soviet Union. Marilyn thought that a fantastic reply; like her, Khrushchev was odd man out." Skouras presented her to Khrushchev "as a great star. The Soviet chairman was obviously smitten with her, and she in turn liked him for his plainness."[10]

Natalie Wood, whose parents were Russian and who spoke the language fluently, had prepped Marilyn for her momentous encounter. Natalie taught her to say "We the workers of Twentieth

Century-Fox rejoice that you have come to visit our studio and country." The luminaries chatted through an interpreter about *The Brothers Karamazov*. The eminent pianist Emil Gilels, who'd met Marilyn at Carnegie Hall in October 1955, had urged her to travel to Russia and assured her that everyone there would be delighted to see her. She now seemed eager to accept Khrushchev's invitation to visit his country and have a *tête-à-tête* in the Kremlin. He promised to take her to the Moscow Art Theater and let her see the Method performed at its sacred source.

Gratified by her ability to charm, she later told friends that she'd impressed the repulsive, bone-crushing premier, who'd been brought up on Soviet propaganda films featuring the muscular heroines of industrial labor: "He didn't say anything. He just looked at me. He looked at me the way a man looks at a woman. That's how he looked at me. . . . I could tell Khrushchev liked me. He smiled more when he was introduced to me than for anybody else at the whole banquet. . . . He squeezed my hand so long and hard that I thought he would break it. I guess it was better than having to kiss" the man who was "fat and ugly and had warts on his face and growled."[11] Marilyn had done her share of couch-casting during her early years in Hollywood and knew exactly what it was like to kiss disgusting old men. Even at the peak of her career, her beauty remained a prize to be exhibited and shown off before visiting dignitaries.

Marilyn was a touchstone that revealed the character of the writers she met. Unsure of her own identity, she identified with others. She was warmly responsive to those who showed an interest in her, and the most perceptive authors appreciated her human qualities. The Russian novelist Vladimir Nabokov was as handsome and sophisticated as Nikita Khrushchev was coarse and crude. He met Marilyn at a Hollywood party while he was working on the screenplay of *Lolita* in the spring of 1960, and examined her as if she were one of his exquisite butterflies. Stacy Schiff wrote that "in Vladimir's recollection, 'She was gloriously pretty, all bosom and rose' – and holding the hand of [her co-star and current lover] Yves Montand. Monroe took a liking to Vladimir, inviting the [Nabokovs] to a dinner, which they did not attend." But he called her "one of the greatest comedy actresses of our time. She is simply superb."

Nabokov didn't care about Marilyn's publicity value. But he saw her with a shrewd novelist's eye and imaginatively recreated her in two novels: *Ada* (1969) and *Pale Fire* (1962). Ada's absurd lessons from Stan Slavsky satirized Marilyn's rather futile lessons at the Actors Studio. In the title poem of *Pale Fire*, Nabokov celebrated Marilyn's "bosom and rose" in watery imagery. The last line's "corporate desire" puns on the public lust for her sensual body and on the dominant studio that controlled so much of her life:

> The famous face flowed in, fair and inane:
> The parted lips, the swimming eyes, the grain
> Of beauty on the cheek, odd gallicism,
> And the soft form dissolving in the prism
> Of corporate desire.[12]

With poets as wild as Thomas and Behan, addicts as troubled as Capote and McCullers, eccentrics as strange as Dinesen and Sitwell, intellectuals as antithetical as Bellow and Sandburg, characters as different as Khrushchev and Nabokov, Marilyn — always searching for her identity, her real self — knew how to excite important writers through her radiant warmth and intuitive sympathy.

III

Marilyn and Miller had fallen in love despite their great differences in background, education and experience. Temperamentally they were miles apart. She was egoistic, mercurial, full of self-doubt; he was devoted, consistent, secure. Early on, Miller believed he could compensate for these inequalities by giving her the love and attention she needed. Though he tried his best, their marriage gradually fell apart. Attempting to explain the source of their difficulties, Marilyn said that "when you're both famous, it's a double problem — even when you're famous in different ways, like Arthur and I were." Her fame was much greater, yet more illusory and evanescent. Miller needed an orderly and coherent world, felt he had to be in control of his life and was accustomed in his first marriage to having his own way. He wanted privacy and silence; she needed attention and adulation. Since she was more dominant and inflexible, he had to adjust to her mode of life. But he was not well suited to be the domestic handler of a turbulent star and felt vulnerable when subjected to her increasingly irrational demands.

At first Marilyn tried to be a good wife, converting to Judaism and performing domestic chores while Miller briefly played the pasha. But she couldn't be an equal partner in marriage and needed the kind of unconditional support that a child demands from an adult. She resented his self-absorption (as he resented her egoism) and declared, "I think he is a better writer than a husband. I'm sure writing comes first in his life." She was also disturbed, when married life seemed to compromise her glamor and make her seem ordinary, by the disparity between her image on the screen and her image in private life. She felt she could not be Mrs. Miller and a sex goddess at the same time. *Variety*, the trade newspaper, commented that "the two images began going in different ways when she married Arthur Miller. It made people say 'Who is she really? We thought she was someone else.' For box office purposes, it put her in an image limbo."[13]

The cook and maid in New York, more sympathetic to Marilyn than to Miller, both provided an insider's view of the household. He seemed to ignore Marilyn as they drifted from the passionate excitement of their first years, through disillusionment and silent indifference, to anger and hostility.

> He stays as far away as he can. Gets up before she does and usually doesn't say two words to her all day. I don't know what that man does in that room for so long. Whenever I go in there to bring him his food, he's just sitting there, staring off into space.

> They sat at the table and ate without speaking for the longest time. Marilyn looked at her husband admiringly and longingly, as if she were dying for some attention. He just ate quietly and did not look at her. . . .

> Mr. Miller was the cause of many of her current problems. As a great intellect and playwright, he was too big a challenge for her. In trying to win his respect, she had become obsessed with the "serious dramatic actress" goal.

She still didn't seem to understand Miller's need to be alone, thinking about his work and staring into space. She admitted that she didn't know what to do with herself, but complained that he ignored her and blamed him for her unhappiness: "I'm in a fucking prison, and my jailer is named Arthur Miller. . . . Every morning he goes into that goddamn study of his, and I don't see him for hours and hours. I mean, what the fuck is he doing in there? And there I am, just sitting around; I haven't a goddamn thing to do."[14]

Marilyn absorbed some of Miller's approaches to drama, and he taught her how to analyze a script. She also adopted one of Miller's carpentry metaphors to describe her aims as an actress: "You're trying to find the nailhead, not just strike a blow." He always valued her work and acknowledged her exceptional gifts, and dedicated his *Collected Plays* (1957) "To Marilyn." But the intellectual abyss opened before them as they struggled to find something significant to talk about. Marilyn said that when they discussed American politics, she always felt ignorant: "Arthur was always very good at explaining, but I felt at my age I should have known." As he assumed the role of teacher, she seemed like a self-conscious and inadequate pupil. She told friends, "I don't think I'm the woman for Arthur. He needs an intellectual, somebody he can talk to[15]. . . . He makes me think I'm stupid. I'm afraid to bring things up, because maybe I am stupid. Gee, he almost scares me sometimes." Their mental disparity brought out the differences in their background and education, and revealed his unintentionally condescending attitude toward her. Elia Kazan, speaking for himself as well as for Marilyn, noted that she "expressed revulsion at [Miller's] moral superiority toward her and much of the rest of the world."

While they were married, Marilyn would sometimes be confronted by her squalid past and treated as if she were still a sluttish starlet. "There were times," she recalled, "when I'd be with one of my husbands and I'd run into one of these Hollywood heels at a party and they'd paw me cheaply in front of everybody as if they were saying, *Oh, we had her.* I guess it's the classic situation of an ex-whore."[16] This crude and degrading behavior, which would have made DiMaggio explode into violence, was tolerated by Marilyn, who felt guilty, and by Miller, who always avoided confrontation.

Taking out her frustrations on her husband, Marilyn emasculated Miller by subjecting him to both public humiliations and private abuse. Maureen Stapleton, who acted with Marilyn in the scene from *Anna Christie*, remarked that "Arthur was becoming a lackey. He was carrying her make-up case and her purse, just doing too much for her, and I had the feeling that things had gone hopelessly wrong."

Susan Strasberg provided some excruciating details: "In front of other people, strangers, she treated him terribly – contradicting him in a combative manner, insulting him. He took it, seething silently. . . . They were arguing about something, and finally she screamed at him, 'Where's my mink coat? Get me my mink!' As if he were her slave. Arthur fled from the room to get her coat." Attempting to defend her behavior, Marilyn declared, "You think I shouldn't have talked to him like that? Then why didn't he slap me? He should have slapped me." Marilyn knew she was behaving badly and deserved to be punished, but Miller merely increased her fury and forfeited her respect by suppressing his anger and refusing to respond to her insults.

In 1959, between completing *Some Like It Hot* and beginning *Let's Make Love,* Marilyn expressed her frustration and dissatisfaction by declaring, "I want to have a real career. I want to act. I want friends. I want to be happy. I want some respect."[17] There were many reasons, apart from her difficulties with Miller, for her unhappiness. She could not have a child, she drank too much, she took too many pills, she was not helped by her psychiatrist, she was reclusive, she did not take advantage of life in New York, she had no close friends to rely on (except for the pernicious Lee and Paula Strasberg) and she could not achieve her goal of becoming a serious dramatic actress.

Fond of the Rostens and eager for their company, Marilyn wrote them (in an undated letter): "Please tell me when you're in town, I'd love to see you. Come up to my place to rest when you're spending the day in the city or we could eat or do something – whatever you want." Rosten had won the prestigious Yale Younger Poets prize in 1940 and was awarded a Guggenheim fellowship; he published poetry in the *New Yorker* and wrote a successful stage adaptation of Joyce Cary's African novel *Mister Johnson,* but he never quite fulfilled his early promise. In 1956 Miller helped him revise his play *Mardi Gras,* which failed in tryouts and never reached New York; but he did write the screenplay of Miller's *A View from the Bridge* (1962). The two college classmates drifted apart as Miller's career took off, and Miller finally broke with his two closest friends: with Elia Kazan for betraying his friends, and with Rosten for invading his privacy by writing two books about Marilyn. Toward the end of his life Miller, heaped with honors and living on his royalties, rather bitterly said that Rosten "now lived on his pretensions."

The emotional turbulence with Marilyn and his guilt after her death impeded Miller's writing during his nine-year "silence" between *View from the Bridge* (1955) and *After the Fall* (1964). Apart from the screenplay of *The Misfits*, he did not complete a major work during those years. But he could not, and did not, stop writing entirely. In that relatively fallow time he published a charming children's book, *Jane's Blanket* (1963); five of the stories in *I Don't Need You Any More* (1967); and most of the major contributions to *The Theater Essays of Arthur Miller* (1978), which ponderously tried to explain and justify his own work.

After Marilyn's death Norman Mailer wrote one of the most perceptive accounts of her self-destructive character. Like Sylvia Plath, he fantasized about her – the very name of Norma Miller was close to Norman Mailer – and was characteristically frank and amusing about his dreams and obsessions. "Movie stars fascinate me," he said. "Their lives are so unlike anyone else's. You could almost postulate they come from another planet. The way of life of the movie star speaks of another order of existence. The lack of connection between a movie star's life and our lives is greater than the points of view we have in common." The much-married Mailer believed the famous actress deserved a charismatic writer as a husband. He felt that *he*, and not Miller, was the appropriately supercharged consort for La Monroe – "the Stradivarius of sex."

Mailer revealed how he planned to seduce Marilyn, replace Miller and write a work especially for her: "I lived five miles away from him in Connecticut, so I kept waiting for the moment for Miller to pick up the phone and say: why don't you come over to dinner? The call never came. . . . I just would have tried to make her fall in love with me. . . . I would have thought of writing a play in which she would star."[18] Rosten explained that Mailer's devious stratagem was foiled when Miller, suspecting the base motives of his would-be rival, froze him out: "Miller didn't want to set anything up with Mailer. He just didn't like the idea. Miller is a rabbi, and he didn't want this strange guy powering in. He wasn't a buddy of Mailer's, and they'd always had a vague sort of animosity toward each other ever since the late forties in Brooklyn Heights. . . . Miller didn't want to risk his bride being contaminated by Mailer or – while I didn't say it then – maybe getting fucked by Mailer."

In his idiosyncratic book on Marilyn, Mailer suggested that Miller – whom he loathed and mocked – did not satisfy her. He also conceded

that he himself did not have the patience and tolerance to support
and protect her, and that he and Marilyn would have torn each other
apart. (He'd once stabbed one of his wives; Marilyn might have stabbed
him.) Describing himself, Mailer wrote: "One of the frustrations of
his life was that he had never met her. . . . The secret ambition, after
all, had been to steal Marilyn; in all his vanity he thought no one
was so well suited to bring out the best in her as in himself. . . . It
was only a few marriages (which is to say a few failures) later that
he could recognize that he would have done no better than Miller
and probably been damaged further in the process."[19]

IV

Throughout her adult life Marilyn was plagued by serious physical
illness and often incapacitated by pain. She was hospitalized twenty-
four times and (apart from her early abortions) had at least twelve
operations (see Appendix). Despite the physical hardships, illness had
a certain appeal for Marilyn, who seemed to enjoy hiding out in
hospitals and having a kind of medical holiday. Once there, the star
patient had a kind of careless freedom, a comfortable routine with
no responsibilities, and received from the doctors and nurses all the
protection, care and lavish attention she never had in childhood.
Nevertheless, when still pale and weak, she was mobbed by fans and
forced to smile at the crowd as she left the hospital.

Marilyn's difficulties with Miller and with her colleagues, as well
as her addiction to drugs, can best be understood in their medical
context. The fear and insecurity when she was awake caused insomnia
at night. At two or three in the morning, when she had a lot to drink
but couldn't sleep, she'd get on the phone and wake up friends who
were asleep. She started to take sleeping pills in the early 1950s. Her
main suppliers were two men she thought were her friends: the journalist Sidney Skolsky, who had an office in Schwab's drugstore and
could get whatever drugs he wanted without prescriptions, and Milton
Greene, who later succumbed to catastrophic addictions. During the
day Benzedrine and Dexedrine suppressed her appetite, kept her awake
and induced a mild euphoria. At night, barbiturates – sedatives and
hypnotics like Seconal and Nembutal – eventually put her to sleep.
As her tolerance increased, she took as many as twenty pills a day,
and would pierce the capsules with a pin to speed up the effect. Susan

Strasberg, a sympathetic friend, gave a horrific account of Marilyn dragging herself on all fours through the family's apartment after she'd overdosed, and whimpering for help:"She had taken too many sleeping pills one night after drinking champagne, and awakening groggy and dazed, needing help and unable to stand up, she had crawled on her hands and knees to my parents' doorway, scratching at it with her fingernails. . . . I hid so she wouldn't have to know that I had seen her that way, helpless and vulnerable."

Marilyn had sloppy habits (which disturbed both DiMaggio and Miller), especially when there were servants to pick up after her. The sharp-eyed Billy Wilder described the chaotic back seat of her prized Cadillac convertible:"There [are] blouses lying there and slacks, dresses, girdles, old shoes, old plane tickets, old lovers for all I know, you never saw such a filthy mess in your life. On top of the mess is a whole bunch of traffic tickets." But dirtiness, especially in a woman who spends most of the day beautifying herself, was a sure sign of mental illness. When depressed she even went out in public with menstrual stains on the back of her dress.

Marilyn's most persistent medical problems were gynecological, most probably the result of her dozen illegal abortions. These back-alley procedures may have caused infections and adhesions that either prevented pregnancy or led to miscarriages. She also had endometriosis, a condition found in 10 to 15 percent of women from their mid-twenties to mid-forties, in which the tissue lining the uterus grows unnaturally outside the womb, scarring and distorting the ovaries and Fallopian tubes. It causes painful coitus, agonizing periods, severe bleeding, and infertility from either spontaneous abortion or ectopic pregnancies (when conception occurs in the Fallopian tube instead of in the uterus). Marilyn had operations for endometriosis in November 1954, May 1961 and July 1962, but the surgeons in Cedars of Lebanon Hospital in Los Angeles were unable to correct the problem.

In the summer of 1956, soon after marrying Miller, Marilyn sent a panicky and surprisingly clinical letter to the Rostens. She described her symptoms, mentioned the risks she'd been taking (despite her delicate condition) and asked *their* advice instead of rushing to her doctor:

> I think I've been pregnant for about three weeks or maybe two. My breasts have been too sore to even touch – I've never had that in my life before, also they ache – also I've been having

cramps and slight staining since Monday – now the staining is increasing and pain increasing by the minute.

I did not eat all day yesterday – also last night I took 4 whole ambutal sleeping pills – which was by actual count really 8 little ambutal sleeping pills.

Could I have killed it by taking all the ambutal on an empty stomach? (except I took some sherry wine also).

What shall I do?

If it is still alive I want to keep it.[20]

Though Marilyn wanted a child more than anything else in the world, she worried that it might damage her career and feared she would not be a good mother. Susan Strasberg, another confidante, noted Marilyn's anxiety about having the baby she dearly wanted – but whose life she was willing to risk by her addictions: "How would she have patience for a child twenty-four hours a day? Then there was her fear of the pain of childbirth and what it might do to her body. She'd insinuated that her inability to conceive now might be a punishment."

Marilyn's recurrent mental breakdowns were closely connected to her gynecological ailments, and her joy in marriage was tragically overshadowed by her inability to have a child. She *did* conceive three times when married to Miller, but could not carry the baby to term. She had her first miscarriage (shortly after her letter to the Rostens) on August 19, 1956, while making *The Prince and the Showgirl*, and had an ectopic pregnancy – which caused severe abdominal pains, sent her into a hospital and had to be aborted – on August 1, 1957, shortly before starting *Some Like It Hot*. Despite her doctors' warnings, she continued to drink alcohol and take as many as four barbiturates a day. As Miller feared, she suffered her second miscarriage on December 17, 1958, soon after completing *Some Like It Hot*.

Marilyn believed that having a child would compensate for her abortions, provide the family she never had, redeem her womanhood, prove herself as a wife and mother, and strengthen her bond with Miller. Her abortions, which had sacrificed unwanted babies, now prevented her from having one with the husband she loved. She had failed in the most elemental biological act and, as her long-suppressed religious feelings emerged, clearly saw this failure as retribution for the sins of her past. Her inability to have a child intensified her psychological problems, her depression, her dependence on drugs and her feelings of worthlessness, and irreparably damaged her marriage.

Marilyn punished herself and tried to commit suicide after her second and third loss. Miller was home during her first attempt and heard her strange respiration:"There is a word to describe her breathing when she was in trouble with the pills. The diaphragm isn't working. The breathing is peaceful, great sighs. It took an awfully long time before I knew what was coming on." Despite the delay, he rushed her to the hospital in time for the doctors to pump her stomach and save her life. The attempts to kill herself, strangely enough, seemed to test Miller's love and bring them closer together: "After she was revived, she would be extremely warm and affectionate to me because I had saved her."[21]

Thirteen

Billy Wilder and Yves Montand (1958–1960)

I

In August 1958, as she started work on Billy Wilder's *Some Like It Hot* (1959), Marilyn's status in Hollywood, where you're only as good as your last picture, had taken a downward turn. *The Prince and the Showgirl* had been a failure and she no longer had her own production company. Once again she was working for a big studio, with almost no say in the script or the part. In fact, she was playing yet another dumb blonde. Her physical and psychological condition was deteriorating, and her behavior on the set was maddening. Yet *Some Like It Hot* turned out to be enduringly funny, a perfect vehicle for her comic talent, one of the finest pictures she ever made. Marilyn's high-wire act seemed best when she was standing over a precipice, even if she tortured everyone else.

Wilder's scripts have irony, wit and an inventive use of his third language (he'd learned English as an adult, after German and French). Back in 1957, Wilder had sent Marilyn a two-page outline of *Some Like It Hot*, whose title refers to the hot jazz of the 1920s as well as the two desperate jazz musicians, in danger and on the run. The fast-paced plot takes off when the impulsive Joe (Tony Curtis), who plays the saxophone, and the more cautious Jerry (Jack Lemmon), on the bass fiddle, accidentally witness a real event: the St. Valentine's Day Massacre of February 14, 1929. During a gang war in the Prohibition era, six members of Bugs Moran's gang and a car mechanic who happened to be on the scene were lined up inside a garage on Chicago's North Side and gunned down by Al Capone's men.

The comic essence of the movie is disguise and mistaken identities, where almost everyone pretends to be different than he really is. To escape the gangsters, Curtis and Lemmon dress up as "Josephine" and "Daphne" and get jobs with an all-girls' orchestra that's about to leave for Florida. On the train going south, Curtis falls in love with Marilyn, or Sugar Cane, the band's ukulele-playing singer.[1] Though frustrated by his own disguise, Curtis manages to get Marilyn to confide in him. He learns that she's had a series of affairs with penniless sax players and now hopes to land a rich husband. In Miami, Curtis intermittently drops his female persona. Posing as an oil baron, he lures Marilyn onto a yacht and challenges her powers of seduction by pretending that he's both extremely rich and mysteriously unresponsive to the female sex. Curtis becomes more masculine and Lemmon more feminine as the yacht's real owner, Osgood Fielding (played by Joe E. Brown), zealously courts the irresistible "Daphne." When Lemmon announces *his* engagement and Curtis asks, "Who's the lucky girl?", he delightedly replies, "*I* am." After the gangsters arrive for their convention, the musicians' cover is blown and they all escape in the yacht. The movie transforms the clichéd situation of the gold-digger in search of a rich man (and the rich man hoodwinked by a girl), satirizes the mobsters and combines hot music with true love.

Marilyn hesitated at first about playing a blonde who's dumb enough to believe that two guys are really girls. But their disguise is transparent and obvious; and their absurd wigs, cloche hats and clownish make-up, their mincing walk, falsetto voices and coy gestures are all part of the comedy. When the designer John Orry-Kelly teased Marilyn by saying, "You know, Tony's ass is better-looking than yours," she replied: "Oh yeah? Well, he doesn't have tits like these!" Her doubts about taking the part were assuaged by a fee of $100,000 and 10 percent of the gross earnings. Her share eventually came to $1.5 million; Curtis and Lemmon got $100,000 each. Curtis later recalled a pompous moment when Miller and Marilyn met the two screenwriters to finalize the deal: "Miller put one arm around Wilder, the other around [I.A.L.] Diamond, and began, in a pedantic tone: 'The difference between comedy and tragedy is . . .' Everybody rolled their eyes."

After all the difficulty Marilyn had in making the film, her glowing performance is extraordinary. Her fear and insecurity prevented her from learning her lines and every scene needed costly retakes. She would start to cry after each bad take, and caused yet another expensive delay when they had to apply a new coating of make-up. She drank and took drugs to ease her pain, constantly came late, and was often rude and snappy. When an assistant director was sent to her dressing room to fetch her to the set, she told him that she'd just decided to wash her hair. On another occasion, though she wanted to maintain good relations with the crew, she dismissed him, while reading Tom Paine's *The Rights of Man*, with a curt "Fuck You!" Mocking her egregious fault, the exasperated Wilder declared that "if she has to go to school, why doesn't she go to Patek Philippe in Switzerland and learn to run on time?"[2]

Once on the set, she blew the simplest lines and, Wilder said, seemed completely unaware of the problems she created: "We spent quite a few takes getting 'It's me, Sugar!' I had signs painted on the door: IT'S. ME. SUGAR. 'Action' would come and she would say, 'It's Sugar, me! [or even 'Sugar, it's me!']. I took her to the side after about take fifty, and I said, 'Don't worry about it.' And she said, 'Worry about what?'"

Jack Lemmon emphasized her absolute selfishness: "Marilyn didn't give a damn about the director, the other actors, or anything else. . . . She knew she was limited and goddamned well knew what was right for Marilyn; and she wasn't about to do anything else." Lemmon also told the producer Walter Mirisch about the worst nightmare he ever had. In his dream he was shooting a scene with Marilyn and had gone through fifty-five takes. She finally got it right – and he blew his lines. After Marilyn's death, when Lemmon had a greater understanding of her inner torments, he became more tactful, more sympathetic and more impressed by her transformation on screen. He said, "She was a sweet lady who was clearly going through some kind of hell on earth. I don't know all the reasons, but I saw she was suffering – suffering and still producing that magic on film. It was a courageous performance. . . . It was infuriating for us, at times, but I was really fascinated to watch her work."[3]

Some Like It Hot was shot in San Diego at the grand Hotel del Coronado. It was built in 1888, and its Victorian turrets and cupolas effectively replicated a Miami hotel in the late 1920s. The picture is laced with delightful allusions to classic films. It opens with police cars chasing a black hearse filled with bootleg liquor, which recalls the racing police car, with sirens wailing, in the opening scene of Wilder's *Sunset Boulevard* (1950). The car chase signals the astonishing pace and speed of the film. Curtis and Lemmon race to escape a raid in a speakeasy, the massacre in the garage and the gangsters who recognize them in Miami. Curtis and Marilyn both race to the yacht on bicycles. Sugar Cane, whose real name is Kowalczyk,[4] first appears on the railroad platform in Chicago and seems to parody the dramatic appearance of Anna Karenina in *her* railway station. A cloud of steam shoots out of a locomotive and recalls the rush of hot air from the subway that lifted Marilyn's skirt in *The Seven Year Itch*.

The girls in the band, who squeeze into one berth of the sleeping car for a late-night drinking party, recall the mass of people comically crammed into a small closet in the Marx Brothers' *A Night at the Opera* (1935). Edward G. Robinson, Jr., with a toothpick in his mouth, imitates George Raft's signature mannerism in *Scarface* (1932) by flipping a coin. Raft (playing Spats Colombo, the gangsters' boss) asks him, "Where did you pick up that cheap trick?" Raft threatens to shove a grapefruit into his henchman's face just as James Cagney actually does to his girlfriend in *White Heat* (1949).

At the convention of the Friends of Italian Opera (a cover for the gangsters' meeting) their leader Little Bonaparte – with bald head, jutting jaw (and hearing aid) – looks and acts like Benito Mussolini, just as Jack Oakie does in Charlie Chaplin's *The Great Dictator* (1940).[5] Marilyn's pretentious claim that she spent three years at the Sheboygan Conservatory of Music alludes to the remark in *All About Eve* that she was a graduate of the equally absurd Copacabana School of Dramatic Arts. Her midnight supper in luxurious surroundings, where she's the seducer, recalls a similar scene in *The Prince and the Showgirl*, where Olivier tries to seduce *her*.

Wilder originally wanted Cary Grant to play Tony Curtis' part. When he pretends to be a wealthy oilman Curtis, wearing glasses and a yachting outfit, imitates Grant's accent and mannerisms as both he and Marilyn fake their background, social position and wealth. (When he saw the film, Grant missed Curtis' exaggerated tour de force and stiffly insisted, "I don't talk like that!") Like Horner in William Wycherley's Restoration comedy *The Country Wife* (1675), Curtis

beguiles Marilyn by pretending to be impotent. Despite his notorious remark that making love to Marilyn was like "kissing Hitler,"
their seduction scene is superb. He regretfully tells her: "My family
did everything they could – hired the most beautiful French upstairs
maids – got a special tutor to read me all the books that were banned
in Boston – imported a whole troupe of Balinese dancers with bells
on their ankles and those long fingernails." He even, to no avail, "spent
six months in Vienna with Professor Freud – flat on my back." Marilyn
then innocently asks, "Have you ever tried American girls? . . . I may
not be Dr. Freud or a Mayo brother or one of those French upstairs
girls but could I take another crack at it." Curtis replies, "All right –
if you insist."

Though Marilyn (playing Sugar) calls herself "not very bright,
I guess . . . just dumb" and Lemmon compares her to "Jello on
springs," her character has surprising depth. In contrast to all
the deception around her, Marilyn's Sugar is genuine and
sincere, naïve and trusting. After being badly wounded by a
number of men, she's retreated to the protection of an all-girls'
band. Her songs – "Running Wild," "I Want To Be Loved By You"
and "I'm Through With Love" – are (for once) well integrated into
the story and beautifully sung. They suggest the three stages of her
love-life – promiscuity, romance and renunciation – as well as her
difficulty in finding the right man. She alludes to Miller and long-
ingly notes, "Men who wear glasses are so much more gentle and
sweet and helpless."[6] She has a *thing* about saxophone players and
always falls for the wrong man. As she laments in a famous line,
"That's the story of my life. I always get the fuzzy end of the
lollipop." But the fuzzy and the sweet end are the *same*, since the
fuzz always adheres to the sweet and no one ever licks the end of
the stick.

In her longest, poignant speech, Marilyn gives a brief history of
her involvement with a series of parasitic and unfaithful men:

> You fall for them and you love 'em – you think it's going to
> be the biggest thing since the Graf Zeppelin – and the next
> thing you know they're borrowing money from you and spending
> it on other dames and betting the horses. . . . Then one morning
> you wake up and the saxophone is gone and the guy is gone,
> and all that's left behind is a pair of old socks and a tube of

toothpaste, all squeezed out. . . . So you pull yourself together and you go on to the next job, and the next saxophone player, and it's the same thing all over again. See what I mean? — not very bright. . . . I can tell you one thing — it's not going to happen to me again. Ever.

Marilyn's reference to the *Graf Zeppelin* suggests the depths of her disappointment. The German dirigible, built in 1928 and the biggest airship of the time, was suddenly retired in 1937 after another dirigible, the *Hindenburg*, crashed in New Jersey, burst into flames and killed thirty-five people.

Before they escape together on the yacht, Marilyn begins to weep about her past disappointments with men and Curtis, still dressed as Josephine, consoles her by saying, "None of that, Sugar — no guy is worth it." Yet Curtis himself, a hardened gambler who loses his money on the dogs, seems just the sort of unreliable guy she's been trying to avoid. Sugar, like Marilyn, is emotionally battered but still dreamily romantic. At the end of the film, the musicians have lost their cover and their jobs and are still being hunted by the surviving gangsters. Though Marilyn and Curtis are both poor, and he's not yet revealed that he's a complete fraud, they fall for each other and plan to get married. Though everything in the film is a fake, love (even with the deceitful Curtis) is still real.

The final scene, still making fun of fakery and self-deception, ends with a brilliant non sequitur. Lemmon tries to squirm out of his engagement with a series of absolutely honest excuses while Brown is unrelenting in his forgiveness:

JERRY (*firmly*):   We can't get married at *all*.

OSGOOD: Why not?

JERRY: Well, to begin with, I'm not a natural blonde.

OSGOOD (*tolerantly*):   It doesn't matter.

JERRY: And I smoke. I smoke all the time.

OSGOOD: I don't care.

JERRY: And I have a terrible past. For three years now, I've been living with a saxophone player.

OSGOOD: I forgive you.

JERRY (*with growing desperation*):   And I can never have children.

OSGOOD: We'll adopt some.

JERRY: But you don't understand! (*he rips off his wig; in a male voice*) I'm a Man!

OSGOOD (*oblivious*):   Well — nobody's perfect.

Curtis' puzzled question, "Why would a guy want to marry a guy?" resonates even more powerfully today.[7] Though Lemmon captures the millionaire whom Marilyn had hoped to find in Florida, he can't marry him. Even the lecherous Brown isn't at all what he seems to be. He's unnaturally attached to his mother and, though married and divorced seven or eight times, may actually be more interested in men than in women.

II

In August, as filming began, Miller received some good news from his lawyer. His citation for contempt of Congress had been reversed on appeal. Rauh had successfully argued that Miller had not been informed about why he had to answer HUAC's questions nor told about the penalties that would be imposed if he refused to do so. Though his legal problems were over, Miller was on the scene for a lot of the filming and inevitably became entangled in Marilyn's professional conflicts. Acknowledging his vital support, Marilyn wrote Norman Rosten from San Diego, "Arthur looks well though weaker — from holding me up." During the shooting of the film, Miller wrote his friend James Stern that Marilyn demanded his total attention, yet expected him to go on writing. After having been in Hollywood "for ten days, until two weeks ago, I found it impossible. . . . All she wants is to see work pouring out of me, so I'm back [in New York] but I'll visit there every so often."

Perceiving Miller's repressed anger and impatience with his wife, Wilder remarked that "in meeting Miller at last I met someone who resented her more than I did." Zolotow wrote that Marilyn had forced Miller into the embarrassing role of mediator between actress and director: "It was a humiliating position for him — but he bore it gracefully and never criticized Marilyn. He always defended her to Billy. He found excuses for her. She put Miller through literal hell. He knew no peaceful hours either awake or asleep. . . . Even though she was a destroyer of those around her, she made them feel guilty." Wilder's co-author, Izzy Diamond, realized that Marilyn had also put

Wilder into an impossible situation. But he still sympathized with Miller: "Miller conducted himself with reasonable dignity. He did not make suggestions as to dialogue changes. He never criticized the rushes. He only tried to be a peace-maker. Once, he came to Wilder – this was around November 1 – and said, 'My wife is pregnant. Would you go easy with her, Billy, please? Could you let her go at four-thirty every day?'" Wilder angrily said that she never arrived until eleven-thirty and wasn't ready to work till one, and that he still didn't have a take at four o'clock: "You get her here at nine, ready to work, and . . . I'll let her go at noon."[8]

As Miller feared, Marilyn suffered her second miscarriage in December 1958, six weeks after completing the movie. An essentially good-hearted woman, she was quite capable of spite and cruelty. Wilder had seen her at her worst. After the film was finished he unleashed his anger and frustration in a series of bitter but amusing recriminations. Referring to his constant battles with Marilyn, he declared, "There have been more books on Marilyn Monroe than on World War II, and there's a great similarity." He savagely condemned her total lack of consideration for her colleagues: "She was rude, mean, discourteous and completely selfish. She wouldn't show up on time, and she didn't know her lines. She was the most unprofessional person I ever met."[9] He called her "a continuous puzzle, without any solution" and, attempting to explain her troubled character, added, "She never found anyone who understood her, and she was completely incapable of normal communication. She was a mixture of pity, love, loneliness and confusion." Asked if he would ever make a third film with Marilyn, Wilder replied, "I have discussed this project with my doctor and my psychiatrist, and they tell me I am too old and too rich to go through this again." Yet, like everyone else, Wilder was astonished that she could act so brilliantly, relying on intuition and spontaneity, under the worst possible conditions: "Anyone can remember lines, but it takes a real artist to come on the set and not know her lines and give the performance she did."[10]

Despite his own exasperation with Marilyn, Miller was infuriated by Wilder's caustic comments and gallantly rushed to his wife's defense. After Wilder's remarks were published in a frank interview with the Hollywood columnist Joe Hyams, Miller (deadly serious) and Wilder (typically ironic) exchanged a bitter series of telegrams. Ignoring all the problems Marilyn had caused on the set, Miller portrayed her as a dedicated martyr and unfairly blamed the "cruel" and "unjust" Wilder for her miscarriage – which did *not* begin immediately after the picture was finished:

> Dear Billy: I cannot let your vicious attack on Marilyn go unchallenged. You were officially informed by Marilyn's physician that due to her pregnancy she was not able to work a full day. You chose to ignore this fact during the making of the picture and worse yet, assiduously avoided mentioning it in your attack on her. Fact is, she went on with the picture out of a sense of responsibility not only to herself but to you and the cast and producer. Twelve hours after the last shooting day her miscarriage began. Now that the hit for which she is so largely responsible is in your hands and its income to you assured, this attack upon her is contemptible. I will add only that she began this picture with a throat infection so serious that a specialist forbade her to work at all until it was cured. She went on nevertheless. Your jokes, Billy, are not quite hilarious enough to conceal the fact. You are an unjust man and a cruel one. My only solace is that despite you her beauty and her humanity shine through as they always have.

Refusing to take responsibility for her miscarriage, Wilder answered with an angry blast that emphasized her unprofessional behavior and her complete indifference to the feelings of the cast and crew:

> Dear Arthur: This is a small world with very sharp ears. Ever since the early days of shooting, when rumors of Marilyn's unprofessional conduct first leaked out, I have been besieged by newspapermen from as far as London, Paris and Berlin for a statement. I have staved them off, I have avoided them, I have lied to them. As for the story in the *New York Herald Tribune* the conclusions reached by the columnist from his own research would have been twice as vicious had I not submitted to the interview. Of course I am deeply sorry that she lost her baby but I must reject the implication that overwork or inconsiderate treatment by me or anyone else associated with the production was in any way responsible for it. The fact is that the company

pampered her, coddled her and acceded to all her whims. The only one who showed any lack of consideration was Marilyn, in her treatment of her co-stars and her co-workers. Right from the first day, before there was any hint of pregnancy, her chronic tardiness and unpreparedness cost us eighteen shooting days, hundreds of thousands of dollars, and countless heartaches. This having been my second picture with Marilyn, I understand her problems. Her biggest problem is that she doesn't understand anybody else's problems. If you took a quick poll among the cast and crew on the subject of Marilyn you would find a positively overwhelming lack of popularity. Had you, dear Arthur, been not her husband but her writer and director, and been subjected to all the indignities I was, you would have thrown her out on her can, thermos bottle [which she filled with vermouth] and all, to avoid a nervous breakdown. I did the braver thing. I had a nervous breakdown.

Respectfully.

Chastened, somewhat, by the ferocity of Wilder's response, Miller restrained his rage, shifted his argument and stated that Wilder should have been grateful for, rather than critical of, Marilyn's undoubtedly fine performance:

That others would have attacked her is hardly a justification for you to have done so yourself. The simple truth is that whatever the circumstances she did her job and did it superbly, while your published remarks create the contrary impression. . . . In the light of the results you could see every day on the screen, you should have realized that her way of working was valid for her, completely serious and not a self-indulgence. . . . She has given your picture a dimension it would not have had without her and this is no small thing to be brought down with a quip. . . . The basic reason for my protest [is] at the injustice not only toward her as my wife but as the kind of artist one does not come on every day in the week, after all. She has created something extraordinary, and it is simply improper for you of all people to mock it.

Believing that he was right and had won the argument, Wilder quoted his own script and concluded the duel with a mock apology:

"Dear Arthur. In order to hasten the burial of the hatchet I hereby acknowledge that good wife Marilyn is a unique personality and I am the Beast of Belsen but in the immortal words of Joe E. Brown quote Nobody is perfect end quote." Not satisfied by the conclusion of the dispute, Marilyn called Wilder and dispensed with Miller's eloquence. When Wilder's wife picked up the phone and told her that Billy wasn't at home, Marilyn said, "Will you give him a message for me? Please tell him to go fuck himself."[11]

III

Wilder and Diamond's acid wit and black-and-white recreation of the 1920s had turned the stock figures of the dumb blonde, shady musicians and wealthy tycoon into a quartet of original characters. Marilyn's vulnerability and lush femininity were a poignant contrast to the three parodic males. But the vapid, Technicolor *Let's Make Love* (1960), which she made next under her new contract with Fox, put her right back into the utterly predictable role she had played and replayed in almost every movie she'd ever made. Marilyn embodied the ancient stereotype, repackaged by Hollywood, of the humble girl who captures a wealthy and often Old World gentleman. "By the mid-'50s," as one critic noted, "she stood for a brand of classless glamor, available to anyone using American cosmetics, nylons and peroxide."

Marilyn's history of atrocious behavior on the set, no secret in Hollywood, made it difficult to find a co-star, and the leading role in *Let's Make Love* was turned down by Yul Brynner, Cary Grant, Charlton Heston, Rock Hudson and James Stewart. Gregory Peck took it on, but dropped out after Marilyn's role was expanded and his own diminished. She then suggested Yves Montand, whom she'd seen singing and dancing in a triumphant one-man Broadway show, and who looked a lot like Joe DiMaggio.

Five years older than Marilyn, Montand was born Ivo Livi into a poor anti-fascist family in a village in Tuscany. In 1922, after Mussolini seized power, they fled to Marseilles. He grew up in France, left school when he was eleven and worked in many humble jobs before starting his singing career at the age of eighteen. Montand first became famous by appearing in French nightclubs with Edith Piaf. In 1953 he emerged as a powerful actor in *Wages of Fear*, an exciting film about driving a truckload of nitroglycerine to an oilfield in the Central American jungle. That year he married the famous French actress Simone Signoret, whose family was also anti-fascist. Her Jewish grandfather had fled to London during the Nazi occupation of France and joined the Free French government of Charles De Gaulle. Montand and Signoret played the adulterous John Proctor and his betrayed wife Elizabeth in the French stage and film version (with a screenplay by Jean-Paul Sartre) of Miller's *The Crucible*. In the French adaptation, the Puritan judge–inquisitor stood for the Nazis and John Proctor for the wartime Resistance. Montand and Signoret were Miller's personal friends, and their roles in *The Crucible* foreshadowed their personal lives.

Montand was enormously popular in France as a singer and actor, and he and Signoret were a famous and well-respected couple. Signoret was a compelling, though not conventionally beautiful actress, with an emotional depth that transformed the material she played. She had just starred with Laurence Harvey in the excellent *Room at the Top*, a British film version of John Braine's popular novel that made her known to English-speaking audiences. *Let's Make Love*, Montand's first Hollywood venture, was a mediocre movie, but his appearance with Marilyn, and the scandal that surrounded their affair, made him an international star.

During the making of the film the Millers and Montands lived in one of the detached bungalows set among the towering palm trees, lush lawns and tropical gardens of the Beverly Hills Hotel. Each bungalow had four apartments of five rooms and two bathrooms, and the two couples lived on the second floor, across the hall from each other. Shooting began in January and on the first day Marilyn signaled her intentions by toasting Montand and saying, "Next to my husband and Marlon Brando, I think Yves Montand is the most attractive man I've ever met."

Marilyn was attracted to Montand's Italian origins, shared his impoverished background and admired his political commitment. His extreme uneasiness about acting in English – a language that he (unlike Signoret) could barely speak – made him especially appealing. Though she still had to be dragged out of her dressing room, Marilyn tried to put him at his ease. As they began to work together, she warned him, "You're going to see what it means to shoot with the worst actress in the world," and he confessed, "So you're scared. . . . Think of me a little bit. I'm lost." He later noted that "In Marilyn there was without any doubt a constant and obsessive awareness of her limitations, the conviction that she was not the great actress she longed to be." In a notebook entry, made while shooting the picture, she anxiously asked herself, "What am I afraid of? Why am I so afraid? Do I think I can't act? I know I can act but I am afraid."[12] In practice she guarded her talent and stayed within her limits, but she also dreamed of transcending them.

A crisis occurred in the midst of the shooting, when the Screen Writers Guild went on strike. Despite the strike, Marilyn pressured Miller to rewrite the final scenes of Norman Krasna's weak script. Miller later recalled that the movie "had no story," which added to the strain Marilyn felt. "Before production," he said, "I did some rewriting of a couple of scenes. I tried to give some point between these two featureless figures. When they talked, there was no character, no motivation, so I stepped in and did what I could for the script. But we were beating a dead horse. It was obvious that all this didn't help any. It was an additional load to bear." In *Timebends*, Miller did not mention either breaking the strike or the $25,000 he was paid for his work. Despite his somewhat humiliating and ultimately useless script-doctoring, Miller sadly wrote, "it was plain that her inner desperation was not going to let up, and it was equally clear that literally nothing I knew to do could slow her destructive process."

Miller then returned to New York, just as he'd done during a similar crisis in *Showgirl*, leaving Marilyn alone with Montand. Miller later acknowledged his motives for leaving when he said, "I guess our marriage was deteriorating." Marilyn, he noted, continued the recurrent pattern with many men in her life: hero-worship, followed by disillusionment: "Marilyn was looking at Montand rather idolatrously and she couldn't realize that he was not this tower of strength. At any period of her life, the oncoming stranger was vitally important. He or she was invested with immense promise, which of course was smashed when this person was discovered to be human."

One day, after Montand had spent hours preparing for a difficult scene and Marilyn, without notifying him, had failed to turn up for work, he slipped an angry note under her door. Deeply upset, Marilyn called Miller in Ireland, where he had gone to work with John Huston on the script of *The Misfits*. Like a distant nanny, he then called the Montands and begged them, "Please do me a favor and go knock on Marilyn's door. She's there, she's told me all about it, she doesn't know what to do. She's ashamed." When they confronted her, Marilyn wept and confessed, "I'm bad, I'm bad, I'm bad. I won't do it again, I promise!"[13]

Signoret won an Oscar that year for her role in *Room at the Top*. She stayed on in Hollywood to attend the ceremony on April 4, and soon after returned to Europe to make her next film. The sudden disappearance of Signoret and Miller put Montand in an enticing yet awkward position, with Marilyn in the dominant role. As Montand told a friend, "He's leaving me with Marilyn and our apartments are adjoining. Do you think that Arthur doesn't know that she is beginning to throw herself at me? After all, I'm a man and we're going to be working together, thrown together on the set, and I don't want the responsibility. I can't alienate her because I'm dependent upon her good will and I want to work with her." Montand, a well-known philanderer, also explained his feelings for Marilyn and her need for affection as her marriage began to break up:

> What contributed enormously to bringing us together was, first, that we both came from poor backgrounds and, second, Marilyn's behavior during the witch hunt, when she wholeheartedly supported Miller, to the fury of the studios. But there was also something deeper. My affection for her grew once I realized her vulnerability, her lucidity, her true sadness at not being given a real part to play in our movie

—though Montand's part was even worse than hers.

According to Montand, their emotions reached a fever pitch when the ubiquitous Paula Strasberg, playing the role of procurer, urged them on. She wanted to regain complete control of Marilyn by replacing Miller with the more amenable Montand. "'Go and say goodnight to Marilyn,' Paula said. 'It'll make her feel better. It's bothering her that she can't rehearse.'" As he entered Marilyn's room, Montand wrote, the flame suddenly ignited:

> I sat on the side of the bed and patted her hand. "Do you have a fever?" "A little, but it'll be okay. I'm glad to see you." "So am I, I'm glad to see you." "How was your day?" "Good, good." The dullest exchange you can imagine. I still had a half-page to work on for the next day. I bent down to put a goodnight kiss

on her cheek. And her head turned, and my lips went wild. It was a wonderful, tender kiss. I was half stunned, stammering. I straightened up, already flooded with guilt, wondering what was happening to me. I didn't wonder for long.

Signoret, a woman of the world, believed that winning her Oscar had "delighted" Marilyn. But Marilyn, who was not nominated for *Some Like It Hot*, explained why she really fell for Montand: "I think it was when she got the Oscar. I was so jealous. I wanted to say, 'You've got the Oscar, but I've got Yves.'"[14]

Their well-publicized affair lasted from April to late June 1960. Miller, far more complaisant than Joe DiMaggio, lost Marilyn's respect by refusing to fight for her, by tolerating and even passively encouraging her affair with Montand. After the affair was reported in the newspapers, Marilyn both accepted responsibility for her behavior and tried to justify it: "No wonder they all feel sorry for Arthur. It makes me look like a tramp. And Arthur looks so pitiful, too; God, I don't blame them for hating me. I know he'd never hurt me – he'd do anything [for me]. But we're wrong, the two of us – this marriage is all wrong."

On August 22 the English author Christopher Isherwood, who lived in Los Angeles, recorded that "Signoret had been visiting [the English actress] Mary Ure, and moaning because Yves [has had] this affair with Monroe. Arthur Miller doesn't care, it seems. But Simone and Mary shed tears and got drunk." Both actresses understood that intense but shallow affairs during the staging of a play or the making of a film were common in their profession. But if you were the injured party, it hurt just the same. In her surprisingly generous and sympathetic portrait of Marilyn, Signoret wrote that "she irritated me" and "it was a bit tedious to listen to her," but "I never detested her."[15] Like Miller, Signoret was hurt more by the public humiliation than by her spouse's infidelity.

When Marilyn, always subject to romantic delusions, told Miller that Montand was going to leave Signoret and marry her, he gently said, "You know that isn't true." Montand confirmed this and then, with Gallic *savoir vivre*, speculated (like Mailer) about the dubious prospects of life with Marilyn: "Not for a moment did I think of breaking with my wife, not for a moment; but if she had slammed the door on me, I would probably have made my life with Marilyn.

Or tried to. That was the direction we were moving in. Maybe it would have lasted only two or three years. I didn't have too many illusions. Still, what years they would have been!" Montand was caught in the same net of pity and love that ensnared Miller, but managed to extricate himself in time. And like Miller, Montand seemed willing to risk everything for Marilyn.

When the filming was over, Montand left Hollywood. Unwilling to accept reality, Marilyn (as she so often did) played the role of pursuer and seducer. On June 30 she intercepted him, en route to Paris, at the New York airport. She'd booked a nearby hotel room and filled it with flowers and bottles of champagne. "[Montand] turned down the hotel but accepted the champagne. He and Marilyn said farewell in a rented Cadillac limousine, slumped for three or four hours in the back of a heavy, air-conditioned vehicle, nibbling caviar and sipping champagne. Montand kissed Marilyn and told her gently that he had no intention of leaving Simone." Throughout that summer and fall Marilyn – sad, lonely and *désolée* – tried to recapture him. She sent endless letters and telegrams, made desperate phone calls summoning him to New York and threatened to turn up in Paris. But Montand, across the ocean, securely back with his wife and pursuing his career in Europe, was now immune to her temptations. Marilyn's unhappy marriages were punctuated by her unhappy love-affairs.

The plot of *Let's Make Love*, a heavy-handed romantic comedy, stuffed with tedious song-and-dance numbers that seemed antiquated the day they were choreographed, is absurd even by Hollywood standards. Marilyn plays an aspiring actress in an off-Broadway musical that satirizes Montand, a French-born New York business tycoon. Distressed about the bad publicity in the show, he attends the rehearsal incognito and is hired as an actor to play himself. He falls in love with Marilyn, who at first refuses to believe he's really a billionaire, but finally succumbs to his irresistible mixture of charm and cash.

The movie begins with a long prologue, spoken by a narrator and illustrated by cartoon drawings, about the history of Montand's family's fortunes. In a double entendre, his ancestor (like Montand) "was interested in balloons of every kind." Montand appears wearing an incongruous derby hat, has a strong French accent and – though he supposedly speaks six languages – seems uneasy in English. Like William Powell in *How to Marry a Millionaire*, he owns a skyscraper with his name on the façade.

Marilyn first appears in a long violet sweater over black tights and slides down a fireman's pole onto the stage. A slightly chubby, adult Lolita, she renders "My Heart Belongs to Daddy" with bump-and-grind movements and exaggerated infantile gestures. Her character has some obvious similarities to Marilyn herself. Always eager to learn, she takes night classes, and uses Yiddish words, learned from Miller, like "*mishugenah*." Miller contributed an old vaudeville joke which falls terribly flat: Montand tells a doorman "Call me a taxi" and the doorman says "You're a taxi." When Marilyn is deceitful, she imitates Jack Lemmon's urgent reminder in *Some Like It Hot* – "I'm a girl, I'm a girl, I'm a girl" – by repeating, "I'm a louse, I'm a louse, I'm a louse."

The dialogue also reflects the stars' real life entanglement. Echoing his pleas for assistance, Montand asks Marilyn, "I hope you'll help me. I've never been on stage before" and begs her to "Give me some acting pointers. I know you can help me." The scenes in which Bing Crosby and Gene Kelly (in cameo roles) are hired to teach Montand (a great star in Europe) how to sing and dance are meant to be funny, but are merely embarrassing. In the movie Montand tells the serene and sweet young woman, "You seem 'appy. At 'ome wherever you are," whereas he is really addressing an emotionally unstable Marilyn, whose marriage to Miller he was helping to destroy. Frankie Vaughan, Marilyn's boyfriend in the movie, is finally replaced by Montand, who actually supplanted Miller.

In contrast to his furious telegrams to Wilder, Miller praised the director George Cukor for his sympathetic treatment of Marilyn during the shooting. Miller knew the picture was important to her and to Cukor, but "the precious days and weeks of her life which your patience and skill and understanding have made humanly meaningful to her" were even more important. Miller had never known her so happy at work, so hopeful about her prospects, so prepared to forget the worst of her doubts. Cukor, he wrote, "must know now some of the reasons why she is so precious to me" and would understand Miller's sincere respect for him.[16] The end result, however, had little to do with the director's treatment of the star. Despite Wilder's anger and Cukor's benevolence, *Some Like It Hot* is a great film and *Let's Make Love* is a dud.

Let's Make Love was another stage in Miller's *via dolorosa*. Marilyn constantly forced him into intolerable positions: go-between with directors, non-stop worker on her behalf, script-scab, defender in telegrams, long-distance apologist, writer of thank-you notes – and public cuckold. Frequently and knowingly manipulated, he seemed willing to take almost anything – though he occasionally managed to escape to New York or Ireland. He still loved Marilyn, despite her faults, but was as obsessed with his career as she was with hers. He wanted to remain loyal to her and continued to work on his beloved script of *The Misfits*.

Fourteen
Making The Misfits
(1960)

I

In the screenplay of *The Misfits*, Miller focused on two main elements of the story: his fascination with Marilyn's traumatized personality and his interest in the rough cowboys he had known in Nevada. He first used each subject separately in two short stories. Eventually, he found a way to unite the two elements in a screenplay and novel, relating the characters to each other and setting them in the context of Reno and the Nevada landscape.

Miller captured an essential quality of Marilyn's character, and the hold she had on his heart, when he portrayed her as the heroine of his story, "Please Don't Kill Anything." In *Timebends* he described the vivid incident that inspired the tale, which took place during the summer of 1957 in Amagansett, a year after their marriage. Marilyn perplexed the local fishermen "by running along the shore to throw back the gasping 'junk' fish they had no use for and had flung from their nets. There was a touching but slightly unnerving intensity in her then, an identification that was unhealthily close to her own death fear."

The heroine of the story – tense, startled and afraid – expresses her own vulnerability and pain by a neurotic sensitivity to the cruel treatment of the doomed yet still living fish. As she tries to throw them back, a retriever, following his natural instinct, shows the futility of her efforts by fetching them out of the water and bringing them back to the shore. The man (or husband) in the story "worshiped her fierce tenderness toward all that lived." But he also knows she must learn that "she did not die with the moths and the spiders and the fledgling birds and, now, with these fish." He tries to teach her that "victims make other victims," that fish, a part of the natural cycle, must die so that men can eat, and must be allowed to die in peace or agony. Still unconvinced by his arguments and unwilling to "make other victims," she naïvely claims that some of the fish, if thrown back into the sea, will "live as long as they can." He manages to tease her out of this notion by personifying the fish and ironically agreeing that "they'll live to a ripe old age and grow prosperous and digni-fied." The story, told from the man's point of view, suggests that the woman's reverence for life is hysterical and absurd, yet poignant, humane and endearing. But her failure to learn and acknowledge the principle of survival makes her dangerously neurotic and threatens the future of their marriage.

A.J. Liebling's "The Mustang Buzzers," which appeared in the *New Yorker* of April 3 and 10, 1954, two years before Miller went to Nevada, was an unacknowledged source for the film. It described the essen-tial background of *The Misfits*, which mainly takes place forty miles north of Reno, at Pyramid Lake:

> There are herds of wild horses in the mountains north of the lake, and a mustanger catches them for the horse-meat market. . . .
>
> [An airplane pilot] would cruise through the canyons until he spotted a band of mustangs – usually an old stallion with some mares and young horses. Then he would buzz them and start them off in the general direction of the corral, steering them from the air and firing a shotgun at their tails when they seemed disposed to dally. In the end, after a run of from fifteen to twenty-five miles, he would edge them toward the open end of the corral.[1]

Liebling's cheerful title and mannered diction ("disposed to dally"), indifference to the shotgun and suggestion that there were plenty of horses to fill the corral are quite different from Miller's emphasis on the fate of the desperately galloping horses and the tragic futility of the hunt.

In the spring of 1956, while waiting out his divorce in the Nevada desert, Miller met some real mustangers and watched their round-up. After only six weeks, the urban easterner developed an intuitive feeling for the western cowboys and wrote a story, "The Misfits," which realistically portrayed their speech, thought, work and values. This version focuses on three vulnerable, lonely men and their hunt for wild mustangs. Two of them are ordinary cowboys with rather fancy names: Gay (for Gaylord) Langland and Perce (for Percy or Percival) Howland. The similarity of their last names seems to connect them and emphasizes their relation to the wild and empty land. Their backgrounds are briefly sketched. Gay, aged forty-five and older than the others, has an ex-wife and two children living nearby, whom he hasn't seen for several years. He discovered her having sex with a man in a car, beat him up and got divorced. Perce, the youngest, is an expert bronco rider. He's deeply attached to his mother, and wants to phone her and reassure her that he's not been injured in the rodeos. Sympathetic yet lacking self-confidence, he admits, "I'm never goin' to amount to a damn thing." In the story Perce is Gay's unequal rival for Roslyn, who's merely mentioned and doesn't actually appear. Guido Racanelli, a widower who'd been a bomber pilot in Germany during the war, flies the plane that drives the wild horses out of the mountains. Though a man of action, he was unable to save his pregnant wife, who died suddenly at home, and hasn't wanted a woman since then.

Up in the air, in a battered old plane that flies perilously close to the mountains, Guido shoots eagles (because they kill lambs), and uses a shotgun to frighten the mustangs and keep them racing toward their doom. Once the horses reach the lake, the men pursue them in an open pickup truck, with Guido driving and Gay and Perce lassoing them when they get close enough to throw the rope. The cowboys anchor them with heavy truck tires tied to the ropes and, in a risky maneuver, bind their rearing legs. They leave the horses trussed up on the desert floor, to be collected the next morning by the butcher.

Miller describes the setting of the hunt as "a prehistoric lake bed thirty miles long by seventeen miles wide, couched between the two mountain ranges." Echoing Genesis 1:2, "And the earth was without form, and void," he writes, "It was a flat, beige waste without grass or bush or stone." He also uses biblical diction and rhythm to suggest the archaic nature of both the lake and the hunt: "When there was something to be done in a place he stayed there, and when there was nothing to be done he went from it." Gay wrestling with the stallion to test and prove himself suggests Jacob wrestling with the angel of the Lord in Genesis 32:24.

As always Miller is interested in how his male characters struggle, and often fail, to make a living. These men, misfits who have no families and can't fit into conventional society, prefer this highly skilled but low-paying work to tamely slaving away in a grocery store or gas station. "Anything," they repeat, "is better than wages." The skinny horses are also misfits. They're too small for adults to ride, can't run cattle and cost more to ship than they're worth. Even the spooky desert landscape is a geographical misfit, good for nothing but capturing and killing.

Guido is fully committed to the hunt, but Perce and Gay realize the futility, even absurdity of their quest. Perce, who belongs nowhere, voices the fundamental objections by remarking, "These mountains must be cleaned out by now. . . . I never feel comfortable takin' these horses for chicken feed. . . . Just seems to me they belong up there." Gay tries to answer him, but evades the real issue. He rather weakly asserts that someone else will capture the horses if they don't, that they're eating good grazing grass and that they'll be shot if the cattle ranchers find them.

After the horses are finally captured, Gay echoes Perce's objections, anticipates Roslyn's sympathy for the captured colt and admits that they've worked three days for only thirty-five dollars each. Even Gay's dog, like the retriever in "Please Don't Kill Anything," senses a violation of the natural order. She quivers nervously, as if the ground were filled with hidden explosives, when the horses approach the dried-out lake. The snarling dog has eaten horse meat and will eat it again. Perce, compressing the whole ghastly process of turning vital mustangs into dog food, and stressing moral over monetary values, regretfully says, "There's wild horses in the can." Despite all his doubts and his inability to explain his own feelings, Gay still believes the hunt has gone "the way it ought to be even if he could never explain it to her or anyone else."[2] He drives home feeling content and with his values intact. The great irony of the story is that the apparently free men, subjected to economic pressures, are forced to work like slaves for whatever low price the dog-meat canners will pay. Miller's story is characteristically framed in social and economic terms, but his love for Marilyn had stimulated his interest in the moral dimensions of hunting wild creatures and killing them for profit.

II

Miller worked intensely and created most of his plays in a rush of inspiration. He wrote *Death of a Salesman* in five weeks, *The Crucible* in seven weeks, *A View from the Bridge* in three weeks, *After the Fall* in a year and *The Creation of the World and Other Business* in six weeks. Though he had written an earlier screenplay, *The Hook*, he had a great deal of trouble with *The Misfits* (his first script to be made into a film), and worked on it for three years. Miller lost a lot of time because he was no longer in total control of his work. In this collaborative effort he had to defer to the director, John Huston, who was nine years older and infinitely more experienced in making movies. Huston knew, far better than he, how to transform words and ideas into images and action. Miller also had difficulty writing a script especially for Marilyn. She craved his attention and knew she'd inspired him, but objected to playing a role that seemed to analyze and expose her real self. Alternately encouraging and berating him, she was never satisfied with the finished product, and constantly criticized his portrayal of the character as they were filming.

On July 14, 1958, Miller sent a description of his story to Huston at his Irish country home, St. Clerans, in Galway: "I'm writing to you to offer you an original screenplay I've written. . . . The setting is the Nevada back country, concerns two cowboys, a bush pilot, a girl, and the last of the mustangs up in the mountains. . . . The script is an early draft. If you are interested I'd want to sit and talk over my notions of further developments and of course would like to hear yours." Miller also mentioned that Marilyn would star in the film and, in a rather muddled apology, blamed Milton Greene for hurting her relations with Huston, who'd directed her first significant picture, *The Asphalt Jungle*: "Marilyn is available for the girl and since her break-up with one Milton Greene she has sometimes wanted somehow to let you know she was put in a position vis-à-vis you which was not of her doing and for which she felt and still feels badly. Tell you the truth I can't recall what it was all about but it probably no longer matters anyway."

Huston was drawn to the rough life of the competitive but closely bonded male characters and to the challenge of shooting the exciting scenes with wild horses. He read the script and, eager to direct the film, cabled back a single word: "Magnificent." On October 5, Miller, with a bit of forced enthusiasm and an unrealistic view of the future, told Huston: "Not since *Salesman* have I felt such eagerness to see something of mine performed. . . . I have a sense that we are all moving into one of those rare productions when everything touched becomes alive. . . . What started as a revision [of an earlier work] became a door opening into what was for me a strange and quite exhilarating new world. . . . Marilyn asks to be remembered to you, as always; she is slowly getting onto tiptoe for the great day."

On June 16, 1959, after a year of revisions, Miller – in another rather strained letter – tried to reassure Huston about the value of the script. He said he was newly enamored with the story and, after making it more personal, no longer approached it from a telescopic distance. He felt his characters had come alive and that the movie would break the heart of the audience. He was continuing to revise and was now very keen to do the work.[3] In the spring of 1960, when Marilyn was shooting *Let's Make Love* and about to become involved with Montand, Miller flew from New York to Ireland to work on the script with Huston. A French journalist on the scene optimistically wrote, "Miraculously and all at once, these two completely different and often opposed characters are marvelously in agreement in the clear, quiet and hard-working atmosphere of St. Clerans."

Angela Allen, Huston's script supervisor, recalled that he had a far stronger personality than Miller and knew much more about films. Though Huston had called the screenplay "magnificent," he always prodded and pushed his writers to revise the script. Huston himself was a superb screenwriter, but he wouldn't rewrite an author he respected and made Miller do the work himself. Driven by Huston and exhausted by Marilyn, whenever he reached an impasse Miller would exclaim, "I can't think of anything else." But they went on and on, month after month, year after year, trying out many different endings but not improving the script. During the shooting Huston insisted that Miller revise the dialogue every day and late into the night (which made it much more difficult for Marilyn to memorize the constantly changing lines). Miller even continued to revise some scenes that had to be reshot *after* the film was finished.

Once Marilyn was secured and Huston agreed to direct, the other pieces fell into place. Lew Wasserman, the powerful head of the MCA agency that represented both Miller and Marilyn, launched the project with United Artists. The budget was $3.5 million, but overwhelming problems made the picture run forty days over the ninety-day schedule and half a million dollars over budget. It was, at the time, the most expensive black-and-white film ever made. Miller was paid $225,000; Marilyn and Huston got $300,000 each. Clark Gable was fifty-nine, had a heart condition and hadn't made a good movie since his military service in World War Two. But he got a great deal: top billing and a spectacular $750,000, plus $48,000 a week overtime.

The writers' strike had delayed the completion of *Let's Make Love*, so the cast and crew arrived in the desert at the hottest time of the year. They stayed at the Mapes Hotel on North Virginia Street in Reno, and began the first stage of shooting on July 20. As sand blew into their eyes and into the cameras, they worked in Nevada until September 21 in temperatures of 110° Fahrenheit. There was a lot of dusty driving, in real life and in the film, from Reno to the distant locations. They piled into cars, trucks and busses, and drove through the desert for the mustang hunt at Pyramid Lake. The scenes in the unfinished house were shot in Quail Canyon, about twenty miles from the lake, and the rodeo scenes were filmed in Dayton, about twenty miles southeast of the city. The rest of the film was completed in the Hollywood studio.

In those days Reno was still a frontier town pushing into the edge of the desert, and the film reflects the crude atmosphere of the city, the fierce emptiness of the land and the harsh rigors of the climate. The French photographer Henri Cartier-Bresson, working on the scene for Magnum, noted the contrast between the lively activity in Reno and the empty, barren hills surrounding it.[4] Reno was famous for its waves of well-heeled women visitors, who gambled in the casinos and slept with the local studs during their six-week wait for a divorce. The town fathers, always on the make, seeded the Truckee River under the Virginia Street bridge with old wedding rings, encouraging the new divorcées to cast off the symbols of their bondage and contribute their gold to the city. At the beginning of the film Gable (Gay) bids a hasty farewell at the train station to a stylish divorcée (played by Huston's former mistress Marietta Tree) with whom he's had a brief fling. After getting her divorce, Marilyn (Roslyn) hesitates and then decides not to throw her ring into the river. On August 20 the dry heat of the summer intensified when a natural disaster hit Reno, and the sky was blackened with smoke from two huge forest fires in the western mountains. The flames cut the only power lines and the town went dark – except for the big gambling casinos, lit by auxiliary systems – for three days. The film crew ran special electric lines to Miller's room so he could continue to turn out the words.

The rodeo and round-up were difficult and dangerous to shoot, and both Gable and Clift were injured in these scenes. Directors almost never allowed movie stars to do their own stunts – the risk was far too great. If an accident occurred, the actors would not be covered by insurance and the costs would be catastrophic. But both Huston and Gable were swaggering machos. Despite his illness and the warnings of his fifth wife, pregnant with his son, Gable insisted on doing some of his stunts in the exceptionally fierce heat. Though it seemed in the picture as if the wild stallion was dragging him across the dry lake bed, he was actually holding on to a rope attached to a moving camera truck. When the driver asked Huston how fast he should go, Huston – enjoying the spectacle of Gable's discomfort and testing his strength – replied, "About thirty-five, the speed of a horse, or until Clark begins to smoke." Gable was covered with an armor of "chaps, shoulder pads, gloves and a sort of all-over corset to be worn underneath . . . to protect him from bruises and sand burns." But it was extremely tough work, and he was cut and bruised.

The horses were vital actors in the film, in which they are meant to look terrified and traumatized. When the film came out a number of people complained about their cruel treatment. Huston, who himself took the trouble to write a long, angry and abusive response to one of them, declared, "I have received low-minded letters before and misinformed letters – occasionally even vicious letters, but never have I seen one single missive contain all of these qualities – and in such abundance." In his review of *The Misfits* J.M. Coetzee noted the cruelty to the animals, and lamented the "exhaustion and pain and terror one sees on the screen." But officials were on the scene to make sure the animals were treated properly; and the mustang captured at the end by Gable was a trick horse, specially trained by the studio to rear up in Hollywood movies.

There was, however, one unfortunate accident when the 1939 Meyers biplane was driving the mustangs through the narrow canyon to be captured on the desert lake. The cameraman asked the daredevil pilot "to keep the plane as close as possible to the horses" and he "buzzed them with a foot or so to spare. But one of the mares heard the plane at the last moment and raised her head. The left wing . . . struck the mare, breaking her neck, and causing [the plane] to veer sharply off to the left. [Ken] Slater found himself flying ninety degrees from his original course and barely recovered the controls without crashing."[5] Though Huston regretted the accident, he loved this kind of daring and danger.

The drama off the set of *The Misfits* was as great as the drama portrayed in the film. The searing heat and arduous drives, forest fires and power cuts, difficulties with shooting the rodeo and the wild mustangs, reckless pilots and fragile planes were external factors that Huston could not control, and he handled them as best he could. But he also had to deal with the actors, always on the edge of a crisis. Gable's health was a serious concern, Montgomery Clift indulged in lethal drinking bouts and Paula Strasberg constantly interfered with Huston's direction. Marilyn caused frequent delays and huge cost over-runs, and her wrangles with Miller led to endless revisions of the script. Despite all the chaos, Huston's intuitive understanding of his cast as well as his own commanding presence and creative temperament kept the whole show together. He extracted brilliant performances from all the actors and created a superb film.

Huston believed in taking advantage of every film location to lead a risky way of life. He gamely rode in an exciting Labor Day camel race. He often stayed up all night gambling in the casinos, losing as much as $10,000 in one session; Marilyn stayed up all night with insomnia. Huston turned up on time for work the next morning (his stylish clothes always neatly pressed); Marilyn, still in a drugged state, did not. But Huston sometimes fell asleep on location. When he woke up and forgot what scene he was directing, he'd say, as if still in control, "now we'll shoot scene twelve." Angela Allen would whisper, "we've already done that one" and he'd casually declare, "Fine, then we'll do the next one."

Marilyn thought Huston was the only director who gave her the proper respect and treated her like a serious actress. He did not discuss motivation and provided minimal direction, but was always gentle – the only way to deal with her – and encouraged her by saying, "that's okay, darling." The photographer Eve Arnold recalled, "in the love scene on a bed with Gable, when he, fully dressed, woke her with a kiss, she, nude and covered only in a sheet, sat up and dropped the sheet, showing her breasts. . . . Huston let her finish the scene her way, didn't say 'Cut' to the cameraman until she was through, but he did cut it in the editing. And when she looked at him for approval, all he said was, 'I've seen 'em before.'" Truman Capote, with some exaggeration, declared, "My old friend John . . . he hated Montgomery Clift. And he hated Marilyn Monroe. But if you ask him, he'll just say (*imitating Huston's deep voice*): 'Oh, I just love Marilyn, I put her in her first picture and in her last.'" But Huston was actually more sympathetic than hostile. "There was something very touching about her," he observed, "one felt protective about Marilyn. . . . You felt that she was vulnerable and might get hurt, and she damn well did."[6] Her four best films – *The Asphalt Jungle, All About Eve, Some Like It Hot* and *The Misfits* – were all shot in black and white.

Frank Taylor, the unflappable producer of the film, was an old friend of Miller and shared his intellectual interests and political views. From a Catholic family in upstate New York, near the Canadian border, he'd graduated from Hamilton College in 1938. He'd been an editor at Reynal & Hitchcock, where he hired Miller's first wife as his secretary, and published *Focus* and *Situation Normal*. In 1948 he was invited to become a Hollywood producer by Louis Mayer, who wanted to bring some class and intellectual prestige to MGM. Taylor later moved to Fox to work for Darryl Zanuck, but during the McCarthy era he was blacklisted for his political activities and forced to leave Hollywood. He returned to publishing, founded Dell Books, and brought out both classics and serious contemporary works. Producing *The Misfits* united his love of literature with his interest in film. Miller, who admired Taylor's style, taste and intelligence, called him "a gaunt, sophisticated man of great height, an imaginative mixture of aggressive entrepreneur and aficionado of literature."

In 1957, three years before appearing in *The Misfits*, Montgomery Clift smashed up his handsome face in a near-fatal car crash and had to have it rebuilt. In the film, the scars from his plastic surgery fitted his character, and seem to have come from his frequent falls and fractures in the rodeos. He reassures his mother, on the telephone, that she'll still recognize him after all his injuries. A covert homosexual and heavy drinker, with a tortured personal life, the fragile Clift was delicately balanced on an emotional high wire. Huston said, "he was a mess; he was gone," and called him "the male counterpart of Marilyn

– of that thing in her that touched people . . . a sense that she was headed for disaster."[7] Nevertheless, his performance was perfect.

The rough-hewn Eli Wallach, a distinguished stage actor and leading exponent of the Method, had known Marilyn in New York. He'd made his screen debut as the unscrupulous seducer in Elia Kazan's *Baby Doll* and had been the bandit leader in *The Magnificent Seven*, a popular western based on the Japanese *Seven Samurai*. The raspy-voiced, Brooklyn-born Thelma Ritter, who played Roslyn's friend Isabelle, was twenty years older than Marilyn. She appeared as Bette Davis' maid in *All About Eve* and was greatly valued as a cynical, wise-cracking character actress.

A revealing group photo was taken during the shooting of *The Misfits*. Marilyn – shoulders thrown back, breasts thrust out and wearing a white dress patterned with red cherries – sits at the center of a triangle. The three main male characters – Clift, Gable and Wallach – are placed around her. With one hand on her hip and the other on Clift's shoulder (who's also wearing white), Marilyn suggests their emotional bond. Gable, his booted foot on a crate, leans possessively toward her. Wallach, sitting sideways, hints at his outsider's role in the film. Huston, Miller and Taylor, all unusually tall and slim, form a second triangle around the actors. Huston, the presiding genius, is centered above Marilyn. Miller, balding and with thick spectacles, stands outside the charmed circle. Taylor, looking rather apprehen-sive, grips the edge of a high triangular ladder that seems to trap him under it.

III

Marilyn's mental state had a greater impact on the making of *The Misfits* than all the other problems put together. Often sick and depressed, drinking heavily and addicted to prescription drugs, she was usually four or five hours late. After the assistant producer had picked her up at the Mapes Hotel in Reno, he'd drive ahead of her chauffeured car to announce her imminent arrival. But the cast and crew were astonished to find that after she got to the site she needed yet another hour to get ready to appear. They were forced to wait patiently and never dared utter a word of criticism. Marilyn's coming late, forgetting her lines and needing infinite takes cost the studio a great deal of money (though it was no longer Marilyn's money), and

her entire entourage was on the payroll. She had, a journalist satiric-
ally noted, "ten people to take care of her: a masseur for her body;
a drama coach for her psyche; a make-up man for her face; a make-
up woman for her limbs; a secretary for her affairs; a maid for her
convenience; a lady to comb her hair; three wardrobe women for her
clothes."

Her masseur, Ralph Roberts, four years older than Marilyn, was a
big, gentle, slow-moving Southern gentleman. He'd studied the
Method, was a friend of the Strasbergs, massaged Susan, and became
Marilyn's close friend and confidant. He played a bit part as the ambulance attendant at the rodeo. Her secretary, the petite, mild-mannered
May Reis, had worked for both Kazan and Miller before being annexed
by Marilyn. Intelligent, well-organized and capable, a great supporter
of liberal causes, she had no family and (like Roberts) was absolutely
devoted to Marilyn. Besides this extensive support group, she had
Miller, Huston and Taylor, who tried to please her on location, as
well as Lee Strasberg and Dr. Ralph Greenson, who were on call to
solve dramatic crises and nervous attacks.

Ignoring all the difficulties, caught up in the excitement of making
the movie and seeing his words come to life on film, Miller sent
some optimistic bulletins to Saul Bellow. He said that he stood behind
Huston all day and was exhausted at night; felt as if he were in a
surrealistic state as his dreams materialized before his eyes; and praised
Marilyn's fabulous acting, which broke everyone's heart. Marilyn,
however, was filled with her usual fears, doubts and insecurities. Like
a boxer tensed up in the corner between rounds, she waited nervously to be called for the next scene.

Marilyn's notes on the script repeated the principles of the Method.
She prodded herself to achieve her goals, described her character in
the film and explained her motivation:

Nightclub – I'm not ashamed of that / hold onto . . . that / as
Lee says of my acting / say it to myself . . . don't act results /
let it occur . . . observe / react / let it happen. . . .

   The important thing – The dance [around the tree near the
unfinished house] – I can do it. How will I start it? That's all –
I've done it before so I can. . . . Do things that have not been
done on the screen. . . .

   [Roslyn has a] strange lovely quality / not bitter / not

blaming / realizing / no pressure now / I hoped so much that things would be different. . . . She kisses [Gable] because she could say that she's lonely – then, when he doesn't seem to respond, she's hurt, then glad for the interruption.[8]

Paula Strasberg, now on the payroll at $3,000 a week, dressed entirely in black in the torrid climate. Puffed up with self-importance and secure in her position, she always rode to the set in Marilyn's limousine so they could rehearse her lines en route. To enhance her prestige, Paula also demanded and got her own chauffeured but empty limousine that pointlessly followed them through the desert. As she constantly sought direction from Paula and relied entirely on her judgment, Marilyn's conflicts with Huston and Miller intensified. Paula would hold up bizarre, simple-minded signs, meant to guide her disciple, which said, "You're a branch on a tree. . . . You're a bird in the sky." When Marilyn did something as simple as walking down a staircase, she looked to Paula (not Huston) for approval. If Paula didn't like the way she walked, they'd have to shoot the scene over and over again. When the conflicts became insoluble, Lee Strasberg was summoned from New York to sort things out. In contrast to Paula and her funereal costume, Lee, the Jewish greenhorn trying to fit into the Nevada desert, appeared in a ludicrous western get-up. The guru, Miller wrote, "was dressed in a stiff brandnew cowboy outfit – shiny boots, creased pants, ironed shirt with braided pockets and cuffs – but with the same whitish intellectual face and unexercised body."[9]

When Lee failed to encourage Marilyn and solve the disputes between Paula and Huston, Marilyn sought refuge in drugs. She asked the young Irish doctor who worked for the film company to provide her with pills and he had the guts to refuse. After trying to fire him for insubordination, she eventually got her supply from a doctor in Reno. She took Benzedrine or speed for uppers, Nembutal or tranquilizers (a strong dose of four pills a night) for downers. Angela Allen recalled, "She ate pills like children eating candy. She built up such a tolerance for them, they didn't do much good, and then she would take more. It had affected her mind. No one really resented her lateness or her behavior . . . they all understood she had problems." Huston confirmed, "Often she would not even know where she was. Her eyes had a strange look. She was definitely under the influence. She had apparently been on narcotics for a very long time. . . . It seemed so hopeless."

Blaming Miller for Marilyn's addiction, Huston told him that it was irresponsible, even criminal, to allow her to take any drugs. But he soon realized that that she wouldn't listen to Miller and he couldn't control her. One morning, Frank Taylor's wife, Nan, went to their hotel suite "and found Arthur sleepless, his nerves raw. He was shaking with fatigue. He'd been up all night with Marilyn. Marilyn was in no better shape, but everyone was very protective toward her, very considerate. . . . We watched those two tearing themselves to bits." Marilyn was so high in one scene that Huston, after trying a few takes, gave up.[10]

In late August 1960, suffering from complete physical exhaustion, Marilyn had a nervous breakdown, took an overdose of sleeping pills and collapsed on the set. Huston sent for medical help and took personal responsibility for getting her off the drugs. She was rushed to Westside Hospital in Los Angeles, and while there, saw her psychiatrist every day. She also tried unsuccessfully – by telephone and telegram – to revive her affair with Montand, who'd returned to France. The film shut down for ten days, with everyone on full pay, and tensions continued to mount. The doctors managed to reduce her dependence on barbiturates, but she was experiencing withdrawal symptoms and still taking Demerol when she returned to Reno. Miller later realized that "she was very badly ill a lot of the time, as she was for most of her life. . . . More ill than I knew." But the press ignored her tragedy. Emphasizing her happiness after her release from the hospital, a reporter made a grotesque attempt at black humor. He jokingly wrote that he'd phoned the film's publicity office and said, "We're just calling to check a news flash that Marilyn Monroe has committed suicide." They replied, "That's impossible! She has to be on the set at 7:30! . . . Besides, Paula Strasberg would never stand for it!"[11]

IV

Marilyn's marriage to DiMaggio had broken up just after *The Seven Year Itch* and she knew that Miller would leave her at the end of *The Misfits*. Their anxiety and conflict were palpable. Wounded, bitter and still obsessed with Montand, Marilyn took out her anger and frustration on Miller and often humiliated him in public. When he brought the English journalist W.J. Weatherby back to their suite, she coldly exclaimed, " 'Thank goodness you've brought someone home. . . . You never bring any company. It's so dull,' and she disappeared into the bedroom." Weatherby noted that "Miller looked as if he'd been struck. I felt sorry for him." Marilyn also became absurdly jealous of Angela Allen, who had to work closely with Miller. "I hear you're Arthur's girlfriend now," she said. "Are you enjoying it?" She constantly sent Miller on degrading errands and, if he objected, called him "Old Grouchy Grumps." Miller admitted that he'd become "a guardian who 'slept [next to] her and counted her pills.' "[12]

Huston, tough with women and allied with Miller in their struggle against Paula and Marilyn, squirmed when Marilyn used her tyrannical power to insult Miller in public:

> She'd talk out against Arthur Miller right in his presence, to me, and with others around. And say things that embarrassed me, and certainly must have made him cringe. He would pretend he wasn't listening. And all my sympathies were with him. . . . I didn't like what she was doing to him. . . . I saw him humiliated a couple of times, not only by Marilyn but by some of her hangers-on. I think they hoped to demonstrate their loyalty to Marilyn by being impertinent to Arthur. On these occasions Arthur never changed expression. One evening I was about to drive away from the location – miles out in the desert – when I saw Arthur standing alone. Marilyn and her friends hadn't offered him a ride back; they'd just left him. If I hadn't happened to see him, he would have been stranded out there. My sympathies were more and more with him.

Angela Allen called her behavior "despicable."

Even if he couldn't help Marilyn, Miller understood her better than anyone else. Half-apologizing for her ferocious temper, he called it "slashing, out to destroy. She didn't remember later the kind of fury she would project, and she would be sweet to the same person, Billy Wilder, for instance, and they [like Miller himself] would be puzzled and surprised."[13] Seething within but unwilling to provoke her, self-controlled, disciplined and determined to complete the film, Miller swallowed the toad and remained outwardly quiet and calm. But his very tranquility enraged her.

In *The Misfits*, dressed in the cowgirl's jeans she'd first worn in *Clash By Night*, Marilyn far surpasses the dramatic parts she'd tried to play in *Don't Bother to Knock* and *Niagara*. But she didn't fully realize that her complex and vulnerable character in *The Misfits*, written for her and clearly based on her own life, was very different from her previous parts as a comical dumb blonde and predatory chorus girl. Like Zelda Fitzgerald, she felt she was being exposed and exploited in her husband's work. "When I married [Miller]," she declared, "one of the fantasies in my mind was that I could get away from Marilyn Monroe through him, and here I find myself back doing the same thing, and I just couldn't take it." Her greatest opportunity and most difficult role was to play herself. The Method had taught her to explore her deepest emotions when creating a character, but this was the last thing she wished to do. She was afraid of revealing her inner self and wanted, if possible, to escape from herself. Miller had always hoped to restore Marilyn's self-confidence. In his endless revisions, he enhanced her role and made her character more and more appealing. He had the Gable, Clift and Wallach characters fall in love with her, and express their admiration for her sweetness, charm and beauty. Yet, in a terrible psychological bind, Marilyn lost all trust in Miller, hated her role and believed she was being victimized. As the shooting progressed, the marriage of Gay and Roslyn, which ran counter to the heartbreaking events in real life, seemed bitterly ironic to the actors and crew. Gable, Miller's surrogate, wins Marilyn at the very moment that Miller loses her.

The script became the battleground between Marilyn and Miller. She found it difficult to distinguish between Roslyn's character and function in the screenplay and her own life and personality, and constantly fought with Miller about the way he portrayed her. Her publicist Rupert Allan explained that Marilyn was "desperately unhappy at having to read lines written by Miller that were so obviously documenting the real-life Marilyn. . . . She felt lonely, isolated, abandoned, worthless, that she had nothing more to offer but this naked, wounded self. And all of us who were her 'family' – well, we did what a family tried to do." Before shooting started she'd called a crucial scene "lousy" and told Norman Rosten (whom she tried to enlist as an ally against Miller), "I object to the whole stupid speech. And he's going to rewrite it!" She was rejecting Miller as she rejected his script. "She was giving him the business, making him eat the Hollywood shit even as they made her eat it for so long. She was fighting the pain and humiliation of another rejection, of one more failure in love."

Marilyn complained that in the scene when she tries to persuade the cowboys not to kill the wild mustangs, "I convince them by throwing a fit, not by explaining why it's wrong. I guess they thought I was too dumb to explain anything. So I have a fit. A screaming, crazy fit. . . . And to think, *Arthur* did this to me. . . . He was supposed to be writing this for me. He could have written me *anything* and he comes up with *this*. If that's what he thinks of me, well, then I'm not for him and he's not for me."[14] Blinded by Paula, alienated from Huston and hostile to Miller, she did not fully understand the dramatic needs of the screenplay or Gay's reasons for freeing the horses. Though Marilyn was mentally and physically ill, looked slightly chubby in the swim scene, affectedly twitched her lips and had great trouble remembering her lines, she gave a poignant portrayal of a wounded woman who understands suffering. In an agonizing blend of reality and fiction, Marilyn – herself hypersensitive, intuitive and naïve – played a lost soul who struggles to prevent the cruel treatment of the mustangs. Her confrontation with defeat and despair had its own artistic energy. The more she suffered, the greater her performance. She never understood how good she was in *The Misfits*.

As soon as one battle was over, new hostilities would break out. As Marilyn struggled with Huston and Miller about her interpretation, Paula encouraged her to dig down into her own subconscious. But the influence of Method acting now became psychologically damaging. She was so self-involved that she believed her emotions, rather than Miller's words, were paramount. Each take became torture as she tried to act out her own personal feelings instead of portraying Roslyn's character.

Wallach described a typical emotional explosion during a crew member's birthday party. Marilyn suddenly screamed at Miller: "'You don't understand women! I am a film actress and I know what I'm doing. Stop interfering. Why don't you let John direct?' Miller lowered his head and stared at his plate as the entire room went silent. Later that evening I ran into Marilyn in a hallway of the hotel, and she lashed out at me. 'Oh, you Jewish men,' she said, walked down the hall and slammed the door to her room." Her outburst was painfully ironic. Her dependence on Paula proved that she did *not* know what she was doing; and it was Paula, not the scapegoat Miller, who constantly interfered with Huston's direction.

Though Miller and Huston would have done *anything* to finish the picture, and were extraordinarily tolerant of her behavior, Marilyn felt they were her enemies. She exclaimed, "Arthur said it's *his* movie. I don't think he even wants me in it. It's all over. We have to stay with each other because it would be bad for the film if we split up now. I don't know how long I can put up with this. I think that Arthur's been complaining to Huston about everything he thinks is wrong with me, that I'm mental or something. And that's why Huston treats me like an idiot."

Everyone wanted photos of Marilyn and Miller, but she refused to pose with him. Yet Inge Morath, a Magnum photographer who later married Miller, saw them in their hotel room and captured a telling moment in the dissolution of their marriage. Marilyn, wearing a low-cut black dress, has pulled aside the gauzy curtains. She turns away from Miller and looks out at the tacky town, shrouded under a smoky sky. A huge ugly lamp stands between them. A gaunt Miller, cigarette in his mouth and hands in his pocket, stares mournfully at her. The dream had gone; the artistic triumph had become a personal disaster.

In *Timebends* Miller admitted that toward the end of the film he could neither speak to nor help Monroe – who could not help herself – and that his very presence provoked her fury: "I had no inkling of what to do or say anymore and sensed she was in a rage against me or herself or the kind of work she was doing. She seemed to be filling with distrust not only for my opinions of her acting, but also for Huston's." Miller wrote that when he came into her room as a doctor was injecting her with Amytal, a barbiturate sedative, "She saw me and began to scream at me to get out. . . . The screaming was too terrible, and her distress in my presence canceled out any help I could hope to give."[15] Paula, exacerbating the conflict for her own advantage and achieving absolute authority over Monroe, persuaded her to move out of Miller's hotel suite and live with her.

Rosten, noting the roles Miller had assumed, wrote that he'd once been Marilyn's "teacher, lover, protector, father, and man of integrity to shield her against the world's assaults, real or imagined." But he was unable to sustain this impossible burden. He may have been too paternal; she may have over-idealized him. As Clift observed, "All idols fall eventually. Poor Marilyn, she can't keep anyone for long." Their unhappiness was even greater because they could not separate. Everyone knew they were intensely miserable and had to remain together until the ordeal was over. Miller remarked, "I didn't even ride home with her on the last day."[16] When they finally completed the film in Hollywood on November 4, 1960, Marilyn appeared at the end-of-shoot party and Miller drove back alone to the Beverly Hills Hotel. When a journalist later asked if Marilyn was pleased with the film, Miller replied, "I really don't know. I couldn't tell you. By [the time the film was completed], we were hardly able to speak to each other." Even Huston, at the end, was forced to communicate with Marilyn through Paula.

The novelist and screenwriter James Salter observed that with movie stars, "their temperament and impossible behavior are part of the appeal. Their outrages please us. The gods themselves had passions and frailties . . . modern deities should be no different." Miller sadly observed, "I had written it to make Marilyn feel good. And for her, it resulted in complete collapse. But at the same time, I am glad it was done, because her dream was to be a serious actress. . . . I had seen this film as a gift for her, and I came out of it without her."[17] Miller and Monroe were as mismatched as his misfit characters. The happiest days of their marriage were the first and the last.

Fifteen

The Misfits: *Life into Art* (1960)

I

The Misfits was a transitional work for Miller. He wrote it between his early, hugely successful social plays, where the actors represent large moral themes, and his later work, which is more personal, more character-driven. He worked and reworked the material for three years, combining, with considerable skill, the heroine of "Please Don't Kill Anything" with the cowboys in his story "The Misfits" to make the expanded film script of 1960. As he worked on the script he developed the biographical parallels between himself and Gay, Marilyn and Roslyn. He returned to the script again in 1961, when he turned it into a novel, adding more description and dialogue to deepen the connection of the characters and develop the dominant themes.

Some details of Gay's life are based on Miller's experience. When Saul Bellow lived next door to Miller at Pyramid Lake, he'd relieve his tension by roaring into the wilderness. Gay and Roslyn echo this strange habit by yelling across the prehistoric lake and calling into the emptiness. Miller regretted the loss of his children, Robert and Jane, after he was divorced from Mary and married Marilyn. After his marriage breaks up, Gay regrets the loss of his children, another boy and girl, who turn up for a moment at the rodeo and then suddenly disappear into the crowd before he can introduce them to Roslyn.

The name of Gay's daughter, Rose-May, is close to Ros-lyn, who replaces Rose-May, and becomes both Gay's daughter and lover.

Miller had shown his love for Monroe by devoting several years of his life to writing the film script for her. Gay, who has never done anything for a woman before, expresses his love for Roslyn by doing all the chores around their house. Like the handy Miller, he cleans it up, repairs the fireplace, windows and fence, mows the grass, plants flowers and starts a vegetable garden. He buys the food, cooks it while she sleeps late and serves her breakfast when she gets up. He wakes her in the house and puts her to sleep in the desert. Gay asks in *The Misfits*, as Miller recalls asking Monroe in *Timebends*, "What makes you so sad? I think you're the saddest girl I ever met." Like Miller, who hoped to rescue and rehabilitate Marilyn, Gay is completely committed to Roslyn. He tries to teach her how to live and plans to stay with her for ever. But Gay's bitter discovery that his best friend was sleeping with his wife recalls Miller's humiliation over the affair with Montand.

Guido, the most hypocritical and self-serving of the three cowboys, comes from a Mediterranean background, has a foreign name and is physically unattractive. These qualities suggest Miller's close friend and early rival for Marilyn, the Greek born in Turkey, Elia Kazan, who managed to sleep with her before Miller did. In the film, Guido expresses his frustration and bitterly condemns women with words that Miller often thought and felt, but never allowed himself to use with Marilyn. When the drunken Guido pounds the crooked boards into the side of his unfinished house (which looks like an open-walled stage set and suggests his unwillingness to become domesticated), he seems deranged and doomed. When Roslyn rejects him, he erupts with fury about his inability to please her, despite all he's done for her: "[Women are] all crazy! . . . You try not to believe it. Because you need them. You need them but they're crazy! . . . You struggle, you build, you try, you turn yourself inside out for them, but nothing's ever enough! It's never a deal, something's always missing. It's gotta be perfect or they put the spurs to you! I know – I got the marks!" The spur that digs into the horse and noose that remorselessly chokes the mustangs suggest Miller's own sense of pain, entrapment and suffocation with Marilyn.

In the earlier story Gay thinks fondly and apprehensively of the Eastern and educated Roslyn, who never actually appears. In the film,

Miller makes her Midwestern and uneducated to have her resemble the real life Marilyn, and she becomes the main character. There are many biographical parallels between Roslyn and Marilyn, which both disturbed her and inspired her performance. Like Marilyn, Roslyn has never had a real father or mother, misses her mother, and has never finished high school. Despite her charm and warmth, Marilyn couldn't maintain a stable relationship, constantly moved from place to place and didn't know where she belonged. She felt she had no real friends, that everyone was trying to exploit her and that she was completely alone in the world. Roslyn's life, like Marilyn's, is a shambles. Her room is chaotic and she can't memorize her lines for testimony in the divorce court. Her assertion that her previous husband "persistently and cruelly ignored my personal rights and wishes" echoes her charge against DiMaggio. And Roslyn desperately wants to have children.

Marilyn saw herself as a tragic victim and often complained about her troubles. In a sly allusion to Marilyn, Roslyn, speaking of Guido's uncomplaining wife, says that a little complaining sometimes helps. (Gay's wife, like Guido's, had never complained about him.) Marilyn moved into and decorated a new house with Miller in Roxbury, just as Roslyn does with Gay. Miller once told me, as we looked over the grounds of his house, "You know, Marilyn lived here." I asked, "Was she happy?" and he replied, "Nothing could make Marilyn happy." At the end of the film, furious about the imminent slaughter of the mustangs, Roslyn screams at Gay, "*I hate you!*" which reflects Marilyn's public anger at both Miller and his script. Instead of using a traditional close-up, Huston filmed her in a long shot as a tiny figure, standing alone amid the sun-charred and eroded rocks of the lunar landscape. She rages not only against the cowboys, who need all this wilderness to feel free, but also against the hostile universe. Emphasizing the similarities between Marilyn and Roslyn, Miller remarked, "Off-screen she was a lot like on-screen excepting when she got angry. She wouldn't show that, excepting I had her do it in the last scene of *The Misfits*, when she was furious at them for capturing the horses. Then she was quite a different person, and she became herself: quite paranoid."[1]

II

J.M. Coetzee observed that Miller wrote *The Misfits* at the "end of a long literary tradition of reflecting on the closing of America's western frontier, and the effects of that closing on the American psyche." Miller called the film an "Eastern Western" that described the meaninglessness of our lives. He portrays a debased rather than triumphant version of two archetypal Western experiences: the rodeo and the round-up. In the rodeo, where a bucking-strap with nails digs into the horse's belly and makes him furious, Perce gets thrown and battered, and Gay finds but immediately loses his children. In the round-up, where the last cowboys kill the last mustangs – both are a dying breed – the beautiful wild horses are transformed into dead meat. The critic Leslie Fiedler noted that Miller also reverses the archetypal plots of Gary Cooper's westerns, from *The Virginian* (1929) to *High Noon* (1952). In these movies, "a conflict between a man and a woman, representing, respectively, the chivalric code of the West and the pacifism of Christianity, ends with the capitulation of the woman, and the abandonment of forgiveness in favour of force."[2]

Roslyn is not only modeled on Marilyn but also recalls the character of Cherie, whom Marilyn played in *Bus Stop*. Both women live with a lady friend in a boarding house; have worked as exotic (or striptease) dancers in cheap nightclubs; can't bear the cruelty and danger when watching the rodeo; inspire the love of cowboys who are determined to marry them; and are kissed by their fully dressed lovers while naked in bed. *The Misfits* reframes *Bus Stop* in a modern context. Though Bo in *Bus Stop* is a real cowboy, with his own ranch and cattle in Montana, he's a shallow and one-dimensional character. His values are those of the western myth of hard work, limitless land and the promise of prosperity. Gay and Perce, transcending the western clichés of the earlier movie and showing how hard it really is to make a living, have unusual complexity and depth.

In the beginning of *The Misfits*, at the courthouse and in the casino, Roslyn wears a black hat, black dress and high heels; at the end, acclimatized to the rough house and sweltering desert, she has pigtails and western clothes. None of the men understand the naïve yet enigmatic Roslyn, but they all fall in love with her. Anxious, frightened, suffering, angry and in pain, she expresses simple, sometimes simple-minded, New Age wisdom. She says that the garden seeds, though tiny, "still know they're supposed to be lettuces!" and that "Birds must be brave to live out here. Especially at night. . . . Whereas they're so small, you know?" Intuitive rather than rational, sympathizing with all hunted creatures and haunted men, she passionately undermines the mustangers' macho beliefs. She makes the cowboys, whom Roslyn's friend Isabelle calls the last real men left in the world, feel guilty about expressing their primitive instincts and taking part in the exhilarating hunt.

Roslyn's rapturous dance around the tree near Guido's house reveals Miller's physical passion for Marilyn. It portrays, Coetzee wrote, "a diffuse and . . . forlorn sensuality, to which neither Guido's sexual predatoriness nor Gay's old-fashioned suave courtliness is an adequate response." This lyrical scene, to everyone's surprise, provoked the overzealous film censors. Marilyn's reputation (created by the studios) as a hot, sensual woman was too much for the Catholic Church. Miller recalled, "the gravest displeasure was expressed with a scene in which Marilyn Monroe, in a mood of despair and frustration – fully clothed, it should be said – walks out of a house and embraces a tree trunk. In all seriousness this scene was declared to be masturbation."[3]

The Misfits is artfully structured and the thematic parallels are as forceful as the biographical ones. The tender-hearted Roslyn repeatedly pleads to save all living creatures from harm: the reckless, self-destructive Perce, the vegetable-nibbling rabbits, Gay's dog that trembles and snaps at her as the horses approach, and finally the captured mustangs themselves. In the story, Gay's dog is a bitch called Margaret. In the film, the dog is a male, ominously named Tom Dooley after a man who's murdered his girlfriend and is hanged for the crime. In touching scenes, Roslyn first comforts the bandaged, drunken Perce near a garbage heap outside the bar, and then consoles the drunken Gay after he loses his children, climbs onto a car and collapses in the street. Her sympathetic bond with Perce seems even stronger than her sexual union with Gay. After winning a lot of money from bets on her dynamic paddleball performance in the bar-room (one of the best scenes in the film), Roslyn tries to pay Perce, who's been thrown and injured by the bucking bronco, not to ride the bull in the rodeo. She also tries to buy the captured mustangs from Gay. Both men proudly reject her well-intentioned but humiliating bribes. Guido and Perce both offer to free the mustangs in order to please Roslyn and win her love. Gay knocks Roslyn out of the way as he's trying to rescue Perce from the wild bull and again as she pulls at the rope he's using to tie up a wild mustang. Gay watches Perce get battered by the bronco and the bull; Perce watches Gay get battered by the stallion in the desert.

Like the characters in Hemingway's *The Sun Also Rises* (1926), wounded and traumatized by the Great War, the pathetic and lonely men in *The Misfits* are psychologically damaged and unable to adjust to ordinary life. (Courage is tested in the novel by the bullfight and in the film by the mustang hunt.) "The striking thing about these characters," Miller said, "was they were internally drifting without it being painful to them. They had a wonderful independence and at the same time they weren't tough." All the characters suffer from disappointed ambitions. Guido had wanted to be a doctor, Perce a rodeo champ and rancher, Gay a husband and father, Roslyn a serious dancer until it got "changed around into something bad." Their domestic life has been destroyed. Guido has lost his wife and baby in childbirth; Perce has lost his father in a hunting accident. Gay was betrayed by his wife, who divorced him; Perce by the step-father who stole the family ranch. Even Isabelle was divorced by her husband, who married her best friend. They all feel, like Hamlet, that the time is out of joint.

All the men try to prove their masculinity: Perce by riding a bronco in the rodeo, Gay by lassoing mustangs from a truck, Guido by daredevil flying in his decrepit plane. But Perce is a physical wreck; and Guido's plane leaks oil, needs repairs, and like Gay's truck, is falling apart. Guido, who'd been an Army Air Force pilot, now performs a parodic reprise of his glorious exploits. Guido sees his military combat as heroic; Roslyn, unimpressed by his wartime missions, equates bombing with mustanging. Both, in her view, butcher helpless victims. Using machines – a plane and a truck – to capture the six mustangs, makes the vital animals seem helpless and tragic. Gay echoes Roslyn and voices their desperation by exclaiming, "it just got changed around, see? I'm doin' the same thing I ever did. It's just that they . . . they changed it around. . . . They smeared it all over with blood, turned it into shit and money just like everything else."[4]

All three men, in Miller's tribute, keep telling Roslyn that she's beautiful, innocent and desirable. They all want to marry and protect her. She transforms all of them, and even revives Guido's neglected house. Shy, for once, instead of suave or swaggering, Gay tells the luminous Roslyn, "It's almost kind of an honor sittin' next to you. You just shine in my eyes." He can't bear the idea of losing her and "wouldn't know how to say goodbye." Even Guido, deeply moved by her, tells Roslyn, "You just walk in, a stranger out of nowhere, and for the first time it all lights up. . . . You have the gift of life." Instead of replacing Guido's dead wife, as he hoped she would; Roslyn moves into Guido's house with Gay. But Roslyn, still a lost soul despite all the adoration, is confused about what to do and how to act. Natural yet self-conscious, she asks the fundamental question: "how can you . . . just live?"[5] To Gay, sometimes just living means being free; at other times, it means killing animals.

Gay's stoical acceptance of the inevitable is directly opposed to Roslyn's desire to change the world. He explains (like the man in "Please Don't Kill Anything") that you can't live unless you kill. He promises to show her real life when they go into the desert to hunt the horses, but his idea of life is her idea of death. They may be "the last real men" but to her they all seem dead. As the conflict mounts between respect for his values and submission to her wishes, he tells her, "I don't want to lose you. You got to help me a little bit, though. Because I can't put on that this is all as bad as you make it." Guido's torn jacket, patched-up plane and derelict house suggest his blind commitment to a meaningless quest. In this contemporary Western – like Dalton Trumbo's *Lonely Are the Brave*, made the following year – cowboys have no place in the modern world.

The Misfits reaches its emotional and dramatic climax in the mustang hunt, and Huston, as always, is brilliant when filming horses. Gable, Marilyn's idol and father figure, said "I didn't like the original ending of the screenplay (in which the stallion defeats Gay and leaves him lying on the lake bed, arousing Roslyn's compassion) but I didn't know the solution. I think Arthur's new ending is the answer." Like Hemingway in *Green Hills of Africa* (1935), the mustangers bond in male friendship and express their love for wild creatures by slaughtering them. The stallion, mares and colt (which parallel Roslyn and her three "stallions") are called a "family." When they are freed, Roslyn urges them to "Go home." At the end Gay, after being dragged across the burning desert while trying to tie up the stallion, captures him by himself to prove his manly power. He then cuts him loose to show his love for Roslyn and gain her respect. Though the horses are freed, the men, whose freedom is an illusion, are still trapped.

At the beginning of the film, Gay refuses to become entangled with women; in the end, he commits himself to Roslyn. Roslyn, in Reno to get divorced, replaces the rich and elegant woman whom Gay first saw off at the train station. By doing so, she rescues him from his two degrading roles: decorative gigolo and supplier of dog food. Roslyn knows that she belongs with Gay and has learned how to live with him. Despite his feckless behavior and her unstable background, they decide to overcome their doubts and get married. Gay never thought about marriage "in daylight," but he decides to marry at night when they head for the big star — Venus, named after the goddess of love, the brightest in the sky — with the highway right under it. As Wallace Stevens wrote, "The lines are straight and swift between the stars."[6] Gay says they'll follow the star that will take them home, though neither has a home, and "home" is the last word in the film.

Roslyn and Gay are poignant in their loneliness, and their love becomes a forlorn poetry uniting their solitudes. When Gay chooses love for Roslyn over a roving life and freedom with horses, he returns to domestic and economic responsibility. This is especially difficult for Gay, who has no way of earning a living (apart from escorting wealthy divorcées) and will be forced into humiliating work in a supermarket, laundromat or service station. The finale of the film, like the end of the story, is ironic. Marriage, like mustanging, had better be "better than wages" because Gay will need wages to provide for his wife and the children they hope to have. Gay transforms Roslyn, who finds herself and discovers she has the "gift of life," just as Miller had hoped to transform Marilyn. *The Misfits* ends positively. But, like all the works Miller wrote about Marilyn, it portrays, in Guido's blast against women and Roslyn's desert screaming scene, his inability to satisfy her emotional demands.

The Misfits finished shooting on November 4, 1960, and the following day Clark Gable had a heart attack. He entered a Hollywood hospital and, after a second massive attack almost two weeks later, died on November 16. After his death, his wife rather bitterly told the Los Angeles *Mirror-News*: "It wasn't the physical exertion that did it. It was the horrible tension, that eternal waiting, waiting, waiting." But Gable himself, who was paid a fortune for working overtime, said that he didn't mind waiting. He told Miller that *The Misfits* was the best picture he ever made.

Marilyn had fantasized that her real, handsome, mustachioed father looked like Gable, and as a child had kept a photo of the star in her bedroom. After helping to kill her "secret father," she felt guilty about it, just as she had about the fatal accident of the French journalist on her wedding day. "I kept him waiting," she told Sidney Skolsky, "kept him waiting for hours and hours on that picture. Was I punishing my father? Getting even for all the years he's kept me waiting?" There were other casualties soon after *The Misfits* was completed. Marilyn never made another movie. Clift made three more pictures but also died of a heart attack, at the age of forty-five, in 1966.

In the midst of making the picture, Miller told Bellow that if it was not a success, it would be the most highly publicized failure in history. The United Artists' publicist in New York prepared a twenty-minute featurette, *The Making of "The Misfits"*, to promote the film around the world, and the backstory helped sell it. The narrator emphasized the congenial atmosphere and warm camaraderie of the writer, director, cast, crew, cowboy riders and bush pilots. The short showed the stars talking together – conversation was "the favorite leisure-time activity"; Miller and Eli Wallach playing football and softball; Marilyn riding a horse, Clift (or his double) in the rodeo, Wallach (or his pilot) flying the plane; the actors and technicians having "a quiet meal cooked over an open flame." The short mentioned that seventy-five tons of equipment were transported to the Nevada desert; that the internationally famous Magnum photographers had also publicized the film; and that the picture, most unusually, was shot in sequence to develop the complex characters and themes. It revealed that Robert Mitchum had been considered for Gable's part, and that Gable had died just after the film was completed.

When Miller had a chance to publicize the film, he focused rather ponderously on himself and bored the audience to death. According to the *Hollywood Reporter* of January 31, 1961, "Miller was scheduled to discuss *The Misfits*, but though he had a wonderful captive audience in the crowded Grand Ballroom of the Waldorf, eager to hear his personal observations about his first exposure to movie-making, he didn't make a single reference to the film. . . . Instead, he went into a serious discussion of the intellectual, drugged in illusion" – as he himself had been deluded about Marilyn.

The Misfits, an unusually serious western, did not match the expectations of the audience. Though respectfully received by the critics, it was not a commercial success. *Variety* (February 1, 1961) remarked that Marilyn's Method acting conveyed exactly the opposite effect than she intended: "Monroe's familiar breathless, childlike mannerisms have a way of distracting, of drawing attention away from the inner conflicts and complexities of the character itself." But the *New York Daily News*, in an appreciative notice, justly praised the acting of the two stars: "Gable has never done anything better on the screen, nor has Miss Monroe. Gable's acting is vibrant and lusty, hers true to the character as written by Miller. . . . The screen vibrates with emotion during the latter part of the film, as Marilyn and Gable engage in one of those battles of the sexes that seem eternal in their constant eruption. It is a poignant conflict between a man and a woman in love, with each trying to maintain individual characteristics and preserve a fundamental way of life."[7]

III

As Marilyn predicted, her marriage ended with the completion of the film. She had overcome formidable obstacles to become a great star, but like many self-made people she could not fully realize her ambitions. She wanted to be so much more than she could be, yet did not believe she deserved her astonishing success. Miller loved her wit and humor, her warmth and beauty. He wanted to cherish her, comfort her, help her achieve her dreams. She believed he would be her salvation, and when he failed her, she turned on him. Sentimental yet tough, she loved and hated with equal intensity. Miller believed she was responsible for her own destruction by seeing herself – despite years of intensive psychoanalysis – as the helpless victim of her unfortunate background, her friends and colleagues, her lovers and husbands. "She needed a miracle," he said, "and none [was] available. She was a basically serious person who had hopes for herself [as a dramatic actress] but did not have time to develop." Her wounds, he thought, "were self-inflicted, mostly. She had very little confidence in herself. She had been exposing herself as an actress . . . and this brought to a head all her sense of unworthiness. She felt she was being a faker."

Miller tried hard to save her. "All of my energy and attention," he said, "were devoted to trying to help her solve her problems. Unfortunately, I didn't have much success. . . . I represented betrayals and misplaced trust. And there was no possibility of erasing that from her mind." Finally, he was faced with the conflict – which he portrayed in his early novel *Focus* and his play *After the Fall* – between responsibility to another person and the need for self-preservation: "She was beyond help. There was simply nothing but destruction that could have come, my own destruction as well as hers. A person's got to save himself." He felt responsible for her and was afraid she might break down and commit suicide if he left her. But, as he once wrote to me about Katherine Mansfield, with Marilyn and himself in mind, "I'd only question whether any husband or anyone else could have saved her. . . . She is one of those tragic persons launched on a short trajectory, the self-consuming rocket."[8]

Thinking no doubt of Marilyn and wondering why he ever married her, Miller poignantly observed that "love is difficult to explain after it has subsided, probably because it draws away the veils of illusion as it disappears." But his illusions were certainly dispelled when she unleashed her pitiless anger and vengeance. Her psychiatrist believed that Marilyn harbored a "venomous resentment" toward Miller. In a series of unjust accusations, she claimed that he was "attracted to other women, and dominated by his mother. She accused Miller of neglecting his father and not being 'nice' to his children." While Miller pondered the reasons for their lost love, Marilyn blamed him for the collapse of their marriage.

In several extraordinarily honest and perceptive confessions, Marilyn acknowledged the conflict between her different selves and the confusion about her real identity. She told the English cinematographer Jack Cardiff that "Arthur saw the demon in me. . . . A lot of people like to think of me as innocent, so that's the way I behave to them. . . . If they saw the demon in me they would hate me. . . . I'm more than one person, and I act differently each time. . . . Most of the time I'm not the person I'd like to be – certainly not a dumb blonde like they say I am; a sex freak with big boobs."[9]

If she was a self-confessed demon with Cardiff, she became a monster with the English journalist W.J. Weatherby. Repeating what Miller had said about *her*, she remarked that he'd also shifted from idealization to disillusionment as she adopted the false roles he expected her to play. She wanted the journalist to pity the monster as well as the victim:

> When we were first married, he saw me as so beautiful and innocent among Hollywood wolves that I tried to be like that. I almost became his student in life and literature. . . . But when the monster showed, Arthur couldn't believe it. I disappointed him when that happened. But I felt he knew and loved all of

me. I wasn't sweet all through. He should love the monster, too. But maybe I'm too demanding. Maybe there's no man who could put up with all of me. I put Arthur through a lot, I know. But he also put me through a lot."

Beneath Marilyn's glowing persona, Norma Jeane Baker was still wondering who she really was. In yet another revelation, Marilyn specified Miller's faults: "He's a cold fish. . . . I thought he was Lincoln, but Lincoln had a great sense of humor. Arthur's got no sense of humor. I'm living with a dead man. You know the most frightening part? He reminds me now of a Nazi."[10] It was cruelly ironic that Marilyn began by likening her idealized husband to Lincoln and (as a Jewish convert) ended by comparing her Jewish husband to a Nazi.

Miller, who lasted longer than any of Marilyn's lovers or husbands, called their marriage "a calamity – to me. It was for her, too, I suppose, but she was more accustomed to it. Her life as a whole was full of calamity." Explaining why the marriage failed, he said:

> I really could not manage that kind of life, finally. I live a very quiet existence, despite appearances, and that whole show business thing was more than I could take. And she was on her way. She wanted to do other things. She could not quite be happy settling down into a domestic kind of situation – nor should she have. But I think it was also that her attitudes toward herself were ripening, so to speak. There was a very destructive thing going on in her.

In the end, he had to decide whether to save Marilyn or save himself, and he felt she was beyond help: "There was simply nothing but destruction that could come, my own destruction, as well as hers. The point comes when you cannot continue anymore. There is no virtue in it, there is nothing positive, and your hope is that she can find some other means of saving herself."[11]

Like many couples, Marilyn and Miller seemed happier in their secret courtship than in their marriage, which brought very little joy and a great deal of pain. It's easier to note the reasons for failure than to explain why they married in the first place. They suffered the intense glare of publicity, the ill-omened death of the French reporter on their wedding day and their inability to lead a normal

17. Miller and
Marilyn on their
wedding day,
with his parents,
June 1956

18. Miller and Marilyn,
July 1956

19. Miller and Marilyn in English garden, July 1956

20. Marilyn and Billy Wilder making *Some Like It Hot*, 1958

21. Marilyn with
Isak Dinesen and
Carson McCullers,
February 1959

22. Miller and Marilyn with Simone Signoret and Yves Montand, January 1960

23. Marilyn with
President Sukarno, 1956

24. Dr Ralph Greenson, *c.*1960

25. John Huston, Marilyn and Miller on the set of *The Misfits*, 1960

26. Frank Taylor, Miller, Eli Wallach, Huston, Montgomery Clift, Marilyn and Clark Gable on the set of *The Misfits*, 1960

27. Gable and Marilyn in *The Misfits*, 1960

28. Miller and Marilyn estranged in Reno hotel room, 1960

29. Marilyn's crypt, Westwood Memorial Park, 1962

30. Miller and
Elia Kazan, *c.*1963

31. Barbara Loden
and Jason Robards
in *After the Fall*, 1964

life. Marilyn's disillusionment after reading his private diary in England was the first nail in their coffin, the first acid of suspicion that corroded their life. She fell under the spell of the Strasbergs, was frustrated by appearing in many mediocre movies and hurt by her bitter break with Milton Greene. Miller hated her drama teachers and business partner, was frustrated by his inability to write and could not meet her impossible demands. Sexually frigid and unable to match her lover's expectations, she was tormented by gynecological illness and could not have a child. Tortured by psychological problems and drug addiction, she had (while with Miller) three mental breakdowns and three suicide attempts. Despite her aspirations to fidelity, she was unfaithful to all three husbands. She humiliated Miller, and despised him when he passively accepted her intolerable behavior. He tried to save her; she nearly destroyed him. He had to escape from her alluring scalpel, lick his wounds and start a new life.

John Huston "was absolutely certain that Marilyn was doomed." He agreed with Miller that "she was incapable of rescuing herself or of being rescued by anyone else." In 1960 he correctly predicted, "she'll be dead or in an institution within three years." Huston also provided an incisive analysis of her character, her poor judgment and her talent as an actress: "People say Hollywood broke her heart but that is rubbish – she was observant and tough-minded and appealing but she adored all the wrong people and she was recklessly willful. . . . You couldn't get at her. She was tremendously pretentious (she'd done a lot of shit-arsed studying in New York) but she acted as if she never understood why she was funny and that was precisely what made her so funny. . . . In certain ways she was very shrewd. . . . If she was a victim, it was only of her own friends."[12]

The end of *The Misfits* was also the end of Marilyn's marriage. She had left Dougherty and DiMaggio, but Miller left her. In their divorce proceedings of January 1961, echoing Miller on Mary Slattery and John Proctor on Elizabeth in *The Crucible*, Marilyn called him "cold and unresponsive." In late July 1961, soon after her gall bladder operation, Marilyn went to Roxbury for the last time to bring back some of Miller's possessions and pick up some things she'd left in the Connecticut home. She'd been recently reunited with her half-sister, Berniece, who reported that Miller was still extremely solicitous: "Arthur asks Marilyn question after question about her health; he's happy that she's well enough to be up and about, and says he wants her to feel truly well. 'How are you sleeping? Better? Are you taking pills?' "

After his divorce from Marilyn in 1954, DiMaggio continued to see her, remained a close friend and helped her through her psychological crises. Their marriage had lasted less than a year, yet he remained emotionally involved with her to the end. Miller was married to her for five years, a longer connection than she'd had with anyone else, and had been in love with her since 1951. More deeply committed and more deeply hurt by the way she'd treated him, he broke completely with her to protect himself. Explaining their divorce, he said he'd endured as much as he could take and declared, "if I hadn't done this, I would be dead."[13] Miller had acted honorably toward Marilyn, and had held her life, career and finances together. After her visit to Roxbury, he never saw her again.

Sixteen

Something's Got to Give
(1961–1962)

I

George Cukor, who directed Marilyn's last, unfinished movie, said, "I think she was quite mad" and then added, "she adored and trusted the wrong people." Her closest and most trusted friends did the most damage. Sidney Skolsky and Milton Greene provided unlimited supplies of drugs. Elia Kazan got her pregnant, persuaded her to enter the Actors Studio and pushed her into analysis. Lee Strasberg made her self-conscious and destroyed her natural spontaneity as an actress. Without Miller's presence in her life, Marilyn depended more than ever on drugs and doctors to keep her afloat. She had been seeing her Hollywood analyst, Dr. Ralph Greenson, since June 1960, and consulted him constantly during the making of *The Misfits* and the break with Miller. But her years of psychoanalysis did little to relieve her anxieties, and his therapeutic methods actually hastened her tragic end.

Greenson, born Romeo Greenschpoon in Brooklyn in 1911 and known as Romi, was the son of a doctor. (His twin sister, a concert pianist, had the matching name of Juliet.) After graduating from Columbia University, he earned his medical degree at the University of Berne in Switzerland, where he met his future wife, Hildi Troesch. He was analyzed – a sort of laying on of hands – by Freud's disciples Wilhelm Stekel and Otto Fenichel, and by Freud's personal physician,

Max Schur; and he became a friend of Freud's daughter, the analyst Anna Freud. During the war, as a captain in the Army Air Force, Greenson ran a military hospital in Denver, Colorado. After the war, he practiced psychiatry in Los Angeles, became a professor at UCLA medical school, and attracted celebrity patients like Frank Sinatra, Peter Lorre and Janet Leigh. Greenson, with a dark complexion, graying hair, assertive nose and continental mustache, was dynamic, charismatic and sexually attractive, a great lecturer and an amusing raconteur. Anna Freud's biographer described him as "a hard-living man of passionate enthusiasm and even flamboyance, a man for whom psychoanalysis was . . . a way of life."

Greenson would become famous for his textbook, *The Technique and Practice of Psychoanalysis* (1967), and his Hollywood clients, notorious for his unorthodox practice and dubious methods. Beginning in June 1960, when she was in Los Angeles, he saw Marilyn every day, sometimes in sessions that lasted as long as five hours, and in her home rather than in his office. He taped her sessions and (setting himself up as the ideal of normal life) invited her into his own home. He encouraged her to become part of his family by eating meals with them and by sleeping overnight in their guest room. Marilyn even modeled her new Spanish-style house on his residence. Greenson's use of "adoption therapy" appealed to Marilyn's deep-rooted need for a surrogate family, and continued her previous attachment to warm and welcoming Jewish clans: the Strasbergs, Greenes, Millers and Rostens.

In his lecture on "Drugs in the Psychotherapeutic Situation" (1964), Greenson contradicted a fundamental principle of psychoanalysis and medical ethics: the doctor's duty to maintain a professional distance between himself and the patient. Instead, he argued, psychiatrists "must be willing to become emotionally involved with their patients if they hope to establish a reliable therapeutic relationship." He explained his method – or narcissistic intrusion – in a letter to a colleague, which advocated rather than discouraged transference: the transfer of feelings about a parent to an analyst: "All of our patients come to us with varying degrees of mistrust and anxieties; they have to overcome their mistrust and we must help them (a) by interpreting the neurotic distortions from his past which he repeats with us in the transference reaction; (b) we try to become and remain reliable human beings whom he can trust . . . by being whole persons who also have emotions and frailties."[1]

Marilyn spent her short life trying to find her real self. But this real self may have vanished or been better left in obscurity. Her analysts believed that Marilyn could overcome her problems by confronting her memories, facing her resentments and understanding her past. Yet repression, in her case, would have been more helpful than revelation. During her years with Greenson, as with Hohenberg and Kris, while her mental health continued to decline, she discussed the fear and insecurity that came from the insanity in her family, abandonment by her parents, sexual abuse, forced early marriage, prostitution, promiscuity, abortions, and exploitation by almost everyone who knew her.

Marilyn craved a strong man in her life (though no husband was strong enough), and put her complete trust in Greenson. But, like Strasberg, he took advantage of his professional position to dominate every aspect of her life. After ferreting out her most intimate secrets, Greenson used them to prey on her weakness and exploit her child-like dependence, to enhance his reputation and increase his income. In Greenson she finally found someone whose ego was even bigger than her own. The doctor, in this case, was more disturbed and dangerous than the patient.

Greenson, sure that his treatment should be paramount, sought complete control over Marilyn's life. He forced her to break with her masseur, driver and confidant, Ralph Roberts, and banish him to New York. "He had tried to get rid of almost everyone in her life," Roberts ruefully said, "and she didn't have that many people to begin with." Greenson then filled the void with his own cadre. His brother-in-law Mickey Rudin became Marilyn's lawyer; his friend Harvey Weinstein became the producer of her next film – with Greenson as paid adviser; his colleague Hyman Engelberg became her internist. "You're both narcissists," Greenson told her, "and I think you'll get along fine together."

Greenson also introduced a spy into Marilyn's household. Eunice Murray – under the guise of housekeeper, companion and nurse – told Greenson almost everything Marilyn said and did. Murray, who never finished high school and had no medical qualifications, made a terrible impression on Marilyn's loyal entourage. Her make-up man Whitey Snyder called Murray "a very strange lady. . . . She was always whispering – whispering and listening. She was this constant pres-ence, reporting everything back to Greenson, and Marilyn quickly realized this." Her publicist Pat Newcomb agreed: "I did not trust Eunice Murray, who seemed to be always snooping around. . . . I just didn't like her. She was sort of a spook, always hovering, always on the fringes of things." Her hairdresser George Masters confirmed, "She was . . . a very weird woman, like a witch. Terrifying, I remember thinking. She was terrifically jealous of Marilyn, separating her from her friends — just a divisive person."[2]

It's quite astonishing that an egoist like Greenson, who behaved in this outrageous manner, could achieve such eminence in his profession. Not surprisingly, Greenson himself admitted, "I had become a prisoner of a form of treatment that I thought was correct for her, but almost impossible for me. At times I felt I couldn't go on with this." Miller, who'd also been analyzed, condemned the whole process. He believed that analysis had made Marilyn "conscious of how unhappy she was, [and] she was unhappy nearly all her life. . . . She tried to be real, to face enemies as enemies, and it simply tore her to pieces. . . . Psychiatrists can't help most of the people who go to them. A case could be made for Whitey Snyder's opinion that they did Marilyn harm. Her life began to fall apart. You could see her analysis was a failure because she died."[3]

II

On February 7, 1961 — eight months after she began to see Greenson and only a few weeks after her Mexican divorce from Miller on January 20 — Marilyn, all alone in the world, had the worst moment of her life. In New York for the disappointing premiere of *The Misfits*, she fell into a deep depression and had another mental breakdown. Terrified that she would lose her reason, like her mother, and lapse into permanent darkness, she tried to kill herself. Dr. Kris committed her to the Payne Whitney Hospital (on East 68 Street, near the East River) without telling her that it was a locked-ward psychiatric clinic. When the full horror of her situation sank in, Marilyn naturally felt betrayed by her doctor.

Though Marilyn checked in under the name of Faye Miller (a name curiously close to Nathanael West's hysterical Faye Greener), everyone in the hospital knew who she was. Describing the horrific conditions to several friends, she told Susan Strasberg that she was still performing in a new role: "It's crazy, isn't it? I can't even have a nervous breakdown in private; everybody wants to be there, like it's a show. I ought to charge." Jane Russell recalled, "The attendants, the whole damn hospital staff would come and peer into the glass in her door, staring at her like she was some kind of strange bug in a cage." In a traditional sanctuary, where it was absolutely essential to have peace and security, her privacy was invaded and she was put on display. She was put in the ninth-floor security ward, her clothes were taken away, her room was locked on the outside and it was almost impossible to make phone calls. Though frightened by her forced confinement, she took strange comfort from the most extreme cases and told friends, "There were screaming women in their cells. . . . Those people were really nuts. I knew I wasn't *that* crazy."[4]

Three well-known women novelists, also graduates of Payne Whitney, left vivid accounts of their confinement that illuminate Marilyn's experience. In June 1938, after a mental breakdown and physical fight with her husband Edmund Wilson, Mary McCarthy was placed in the psychiatric hospital without being told where she was going. She was led into a small, cell-like room, searched and stripped. Left alone in the dark cubicle, she listened to the clicking sound as the staff opened and closed the wooden shutter of the tiny window to spy on her.

Jean Stafford, then married to the manic-depressive poet Robert Lowell, voluntarily entered the hospital in November 1946. But she felt frightened and humiliated at being institutionalized (a nurse watched her while she bathed), and thought the clinic was more like a prison than a sanctuary. Stafford, too, was frightened by the screams of the more violent inmates:

> I knew the doors would be locked and that they would take everything away from me . . . that I could not get out once I had signed myself in, that the pain of the analysis was going to be excruciating. That first night, I lay perfectly motionless in my bed, fighting off terror by repeating . . . "I must resign myself." I could hear the really disordered patients on the floor above screaming, beating their heads on the floor.

Carson McCullers, whom Marilyn had met in New York and saw throughout the 1950s, spent three weeks in Payne Whitney in March

1948. She'd also been deliberately misled, and felt betrayed, vulnerable and ashamed. Her biographer wrote:

> Never before had she felt such utter helplessness and abandonment. Perhaps worst of all, she acknowledged, was the feeling that her mother had used trickery in effecting her confinement. Nothing seemed more devastating to her than that. Encapsulated, it seemed, in a vacuum, unable to try to help herself or to read or write undisturbed, allowed no veil of privacy, she felt stripped bare, defenseless, exposed to the marrow.[5]

Marilyn's letters about her experiences in Payne Whitney were introspective, articulate and incisive. In a letter to the Strasbergs, close to her in New York, she said the clinic itself was driving her mad and pleaded for help:

> Dr. Kris put me in the hospital under the care of two idiot doctors. They both should not be my doctors. I'm locked up with these poor nutty people. I'm sure to end up a nut too if I stay in this nightmare. Please help me. This is the last place I should be. I love you both. Marilyn.
>
> P.S. I'm on the dangerous floor. It's like a cell. They had my bathroom door locked and I couldn't get the key to get into it, so I broke the glass. But outside of that I haven't done anything that is un-cooperative.

Committed by Dr. Kris in New York, she turned for sympathy to Dr. Greenson in Los Angeles. After her release, she described her incarceration as if she were a character in a novel by Franz Kafka – or the only actual Marilyn Monroe in captivity:

> There was no empathy at Payne Whitney – it had a very bad effect on me. They put me in a cell (I mean cement blocks and all) for *very disturbed*, depressed patients, except I felt I was in some kind of prison for a crime I hadn't committed. The inhumanity there I found archaic. They asked me why I wasn't happy there (everything was under lock and key, things like electric lights, dresser drawers, bathrooms, closets, bars concealed on the windows – and the doors have windows so the patients can be

visible all the time. Also, the violence and markings still remain on the walls from former patients). I answered, "Well, I'd have to be nuts if I like it here!"

To protest her helplessness and draw attention to her plight, Marilyn resorted to threats and violence, and gave Greenson a different explanation of why she broke the glass in the bathroom door. She behaved in the madhouse as if she were a psychopath in a movie. Her *role* as psychopath was, in fact, just as real to her as her experience as a patient:

I got the idea from a movie I once made called *Don't Bother to Knock*. I picked up a light-weight chair and slammed it against the glass, intentionally — and it was hard to do because I had never broken anything in my life. It took a lot of banging to get even a small piece of glass, so I went over with the glass concealed in my hand and sat quietly on the bed waiting for them to come in. They did, and I said to them, "If you are going to treat me like a nut, I'll act like a nut." I admit the next thing is corny, but I really did it in the movie except it was with a razor blade. I indicated if they didn't let me out I would harm myself — the farthest thing from my mind at the moment, since you know, Dr. Greenson, I'm an actress and would never intentionally mark or mar myself. I'm just that vain.

In her long, sad and brave letter to Greenson, Marilyn also described how she sought but failed to find some consolation in nature. Unconsciously alluding to her doctor, she contrasted the "promise" and "hope" of the *green* grass, bushes and trees, as they lay under a shroud of snow and bare branches. Suspended in an unreal state, she lost track of the time, and ended with bitter tears and troubled insomnia:

Just now when I looked out the hospital window where the snow had covered everything, suddenly everything is kind of a muted green. There are grass and shabby evergreen bushes, though the trees give me a little hope — and the desolate bare branches promise maybe there will be spring and maybe they promise hope. . . .
As I started to write this letter about four quiet tears had fallen. I don't know quite why.

Last night I was awake all night again. Sometimes I wonder what the night time is for. It almost doesn't exist for me.[6]

Marilyn's letter to Jack Cardiff was the most revealing of all. Exploring her deepest fear about the very core of her identity – whether she was really mad – she mentioned the history of insanity in her family, and repeated that her harsh confinement might actually drive her crazy: "I was *afraid* – I still am. . . . There's my mother – paranoid schizophrenia . . . and *her* family – all destroyed by the same thing – insanity. Was I a nut, after all? There I was, in a cell like I was mad. . . . I was hysterical – who wouldn't be? And they were going to put me in a straitjacket. I knew that if I stayed there for long, I really would be mad." Dr. Kris later confessed, "I did a terrible, terrible thing. Oh God, I didn't mean to, but I did." But Marilyn was the one who suffered for her doctor's mistake.

After four days in Payne Whitney, Marilyn was finally rescued by Joe DiMaggio, who'd come back into her life after her divorce from Miller. Storming the citadel with his intimidating physical presence and barely restraining his fury, he threatened the hospital authorities by shouting, "I want my wife. . . . And if you do not release her to me, I will take this place apart – piece of wood, by piece . . . of . . . wood."[7] This was a long speech for the laconic athlete, who meant what he said. The administrators, afraid of provoking a violent confrontation that would attract a storm of unfavorable publicity, agreed to his demands – though Marilyn was not, of course, his wife. She was transferred to the Neurological Institute of Columbia University Presbyterian Hospital, on West 168th Street in Morningside Heights, and recovered there from February 11 to March 5.

DiMaggio was a frequent visitor when Marilyn returned to her apartment on East 57th Street. Her half-sister described his angry reaction to an incident that would also have exasperated Miller. She noted that DiMaggio was still looking after Marilyn's interests – though he could not contain her extravagance – and that she must have resented his discovery of her habitual carelessness: "Joe spies a discarded bill and idly fishes it out [of the trash bin]. He scans over the list of household supplies and wines that have been delivered in the afternoon. He grumbles loudly, 'This bill is not right! It's added up nearly double! Doesn't someone check these things when they are delivered?'" DiMaggio gave a great deal to Marilyn and took nothing from her.

In her last, unfinished letter to DiMaggio, found after her death, Marilyn wrote, "If I can succeed in making you happy, I will have succeeded in the biggest and most difficult thing there is – that is, to make *one person completely happy*. Your happiness means my happiness, and . . . "

She continued to be plagued by medical problems. On June 28, 1961, still only thirty-five years old, Marilyn entered the hospital for the fifth time in the last ten months. She'd had a nervous breakdown during *The Misfits* in August 1960; been confined in Payne Whitney and in Columbia Presbyterian in February – March 1961; had a second (unavailing) operation for chronic endometriosis in May; and had her gallbladder removed in June. When she left the Polyclinic Hospital on West 50th Street in New York on July 11, she was assaulted by devoted and deranged fans (short for "fanatics"). "It was scary," she wrote. "I felt for a few minutes as if they were just going to take pieces out of me. Actually it made me feel a little sick. I mean I appreciated the concern and their affection and all that, but – I don't know – it was a little like a nightmare. I wasn't sure I was going to get into the car safely and get away!"[8]

III

Attempting to achieve a sense of stability and security, Marilyn bought her first house in February 1962 for $77,500, paying half in cash and taking out a mortgage for the rest. 12305 Fifth Helena Drive was on a short cul-de-sac off Carmelina Avenue, between Sunset Boulevard and San Vicente, in the Brentwood district of Los Angeles. Unlike the glamorous houses of most Hollywood stars, it was a modest, personal refuge. Marilyn bought some essential furniture on shopping trips to Tijuana and Mexico City: tiles for the kitchen, tin masks and mirrors for the walls, and textiles depicting Aztec figures. But the house was sparsely furnished and her phonograph remained on the floor. The small, 2,900-square-foot, one-story, L-shaped, Spanish-colonial home had adobe walls and a red-tile roof, and was protected by a high wall. It had two bedrooms, a small guest house, an oval swimming pool and a large garden. The interior had white stucco walls, white carpeting, cathedral-beamed ceilings, and tiled fireplaces in both the living room and master bedroom.

She called it "a cute little Mexican-style house with eight rooms," and regretfully added, "I live alone and I hate it!" She loved animals and had always been fond of pets, who soothed her loneliness. She had had Tippy, the stray puppy of her childhood, who was shot by a neighbor; Josefa, a Chihuahua, named after its donor Joseph Schenck; and Hugo, Miller's basset hound, who helped pass her idle hours in Roxbury. Frank Sinatra now gave her a poodle called Maf (short for "Mafia"), whose name recalled his mob connections. Proud of the house and the improvements she made, she keenly showed visitors around and called it "a fortress where I can feel safe from the world".

After her divorce from Miller, Marilyn attempted to fill the emotional emptiness in her life with a number of love affairs – all of them unhappy. She'd met the attractive and electrifying Frank Sinatra, a familiar mixture of vulgarity and glamor, through his friend Joe DiMaggio. When DiMaggio broke with Sinatra after the farcical Wrong Door Raid, Marilyn became sexually involved with her favorite singer. Sinatra loved luxury, was a lavish spender and tried to live up to his romantic reputation. But his seductive promises about marriage had recently deceived the sophisticated Lauren Bacall. She "said that she 'loved' her good times with Frank but that he could become 'ice cold'; she admitted that it was 'quite terrifying to be a victim of that.' . . . At a New Year's Eve party, Bacall said, Sinatra got drunk and became abusive, bringing her to tears."[9] Resenting the pressure to marry, Sinatra publicly dumped Bacall when he got fed up with her. Notorious for his abrasive personality, Sinatra could be equally cruel with Marilyn. When she was talking to friends and dramatizing her orphaned childhood, Sinatra interrupted her by exclaiming, "Oh, not that again!" His boorish comments recalled Fred Karger's cruel put-downs. When she bored him, Sinatra (no great brain himself) would shout: "Shut up, Norma Jeane. You're so stupid you don't know what you're talking about."

In January 1962, Sinatra discarded her and became engaged to the dancer Juliet Prowse. As usual, Marilyn hopelessly pursued the man who'd jilted her. The following month, Eunice Murray told the FBI that Marilyn was "very vulnerable now because of her rejection by ARTHUR MILLER and also by JOE DiMAGGIO and FRANK SINATRA. She telephoned SINATRA to come and comfort her and he would not do it." Marilyn would spend the last weekend of her life at Lake Tahoe in Sinatra's Cal-Neva Lodge, where the line dividing the two states cut through the public rooms and swimming pool. She was invited by the actor Peter Lawford to hear Sinatra sing and discussed future projects with Dean Martin. But she spent most of her time (quite separate from Sinatra) with DiMaggio.[10]

With Ralph Roberts banished and Eunice Murray hostile, Marilyn turned for comfort to her West Coast publicist, Pat Newcomb. Four years younger than Marilyn, she came from a wealthy and prominent Washington, D.C. family – her father was a judge, her mother a psychiatric social worker – and had graduated from Mills College in Oakland, California. Blond and attractive, she had the classy look of the Kennedy sisters. Marilyn's maid described Newcomb as "an eager, efficient college girl who didn't threaten Marilyn at all. Pat was all business, seeing her role as mainly one of shielding Marilyn from the press, setting up interviews and photography sessions, making sure all her travel plans went smoothly." Newcomb accompanied Marilyn to Mexico for her divorce from Miller, and helped her find and furnish her new house. On the last day of Marilyn's life, Newcomb unintentionally infuriated her insomniac boss by sleeping overnight in the house for twelve long hours.

IV

Living in her isolated, makeshift way in Brentwood, Marilyn was courted and discarded by various unscrupulous men. In one of the most bizarre episodes of her life, she became involved with the president of the United States. Peter Lawford, John Kennedy's brother-in-law, introduced Marilyn to him and his brother Robert, the attorney general. Their womanizing father, Joseph Kennedy, had had a well-known liaison with the actress Gloria Swanson; Presidents Roosevelt and Eisenhower both had mistresses. The youthful, handsome, wealthy Kennedy, complete with elegant wife and pretty children, followed an even more promiscuous path. A historian of Hollywood politics noted that Kennedy's "dalliance with Marilyn Monroe chiseled into the culture the assumption that power's rewards included access to the iridescent life of the famous, with its code of license barred to ordinary men and women." In those days the press protected the randy president, who cavorted with naked beauties in the White House swimming pool, and the public knew nothing about the private life of the remarkably idealized man. But there was always the danger of scandal to add drama and excitement to his seductions. He did not have much time for protracted liaisons, but enjoyed flirting with his lovers on the phone. The Oval Office telephone tapes recorded "much explicit talk of a sexual nature with Monroe."[11]

The journalist Seymour Hersh stated that the Marilyn–Kennedy affair began in the mid-1950s and lasted into the presidency, and that she once visited his family estate on Cape Cod. But their main venues were Lawford's beach house in Santa Monica and the Carlyle Hotel (Kennedy's favorite) in New York. Both Marilyn and Kennedy knew how it felt to be irresistibly attractive and adored by millions. Arthur Schlesinger, Jr., the Harvard historian and Special Assistant to the president, revealed that Marilyn could seduce intellectuals as well as the mass of ordinary men. He found her ravishing, but (like Natasha Lytess, Nunnally Johnson and George Cukor) noted her remote, withdrawn and detached "under water" quality:

> The image of this exquisite, beguiling and desperate girl will always stay with me. I do not think I have seen anyone so beautiful; I was enchanted by her manner and her wit, at once so masked, so ingenuous and so penetrating. But one felt a terrible unreality about her – as if talking to someone under water. Bobby [Kennedy] and I engaged in mock competition for her; she was most agreeable to him and pleasant to me, but one never felt her to be wholly engaged. Indeed, she seemed most solicitous to her ex-father-in-law, Arthur Miller's father, a baffled and taciturn man whom she introduced to the group and on whom she constantly cast a maternal eye.

Like an overeager pupil, Marilyn may have bored Kennedy with some liberal ideas that she'd picked up, second-hand, from Miller. The FBI, without (as usual) establishing the reliability of its informant, reported that Marilyn had met Kennedy at the Lawfords': "She was very pleased, as she had asked the President a lot of socially significant questions concerning the morality of atomic testing and the future of the youth of America. She already had been asked by LAWFORD to appear at the President's birthday party." Her maid reported, more persuasively than the FBI, that Marilyn was completely unaware of contemporary political events: "To Marilyn, Castro was a convertible sofa, not a dictator. Because she didn't read the paper or listen to the radio, she didn't know the Bay of Pigs invasion [of April 1961] ever occurred."[12]

In any case, Kennedy had no time for sexual niceties, let alone political pillow talk. When dallying with her, Marilyn said, "he wouldn't indulge in foreplay, because he was on the run all the time." Her sometime neighbor, the minor actress and trick-shot golfer Jeanne Carmen, gave a crude but convincing account of Marilyn's galloping connection with the president:

> To John Kennedy, Marilyn was just another fuck. I don't think he ever really cared about her the way Bobby did, and I don't think she was ever really in love with him. And he wasn't even good in bed; I can tell you that firsthand, because I had him too. I don't know too many women out here who *didn't* sleep with Jack. He was a two-minute man. I think sex to him was just about another conquest.
>
> Now, Bobby was a different story. He was sweet, cute and playful, and he really cared about Marilyn. . . . I think he was in love with her, in his own little way.

When John sent his brother to break off his affair with Marilyn, Robert quickly succumbed to her charms and had his own affair with her. In this negative version of vicarious courtship, the envoy replaced the lover he was supposed to represent. Since Marilyn could no longer have John, she maintained her glamorous connection to Washington by taking Robert as his surrogate. The young attorney general, the nation's chief prosecutor and notable family man, was equally dazzled by the Hollywood star.

Marilyn first met Robert at Peter Lawford's house of assignation on February 1, 1962. The next day she sent Miller's teenage son a girlishly enthusiastic letter describing how she had spoken up for the "youth of America":

> Oh, Bobby, guess what. I had dinner last night with the Attorney General of the United States, Robert Kennedy, and I asked him what his department was going to do about Civil Rights and some other issues. He is very intelligent, and besides all that, he's got a terrific sense of humor. I think you would like him. Anyway, I had to go to this dinner last night as he was the guest of honor, and when they asked him who he wanted to meet, he wanted to meet me. So I went to the dinner and I sat next to him, and he isn't a bad dancer, either. . . . He asked if I had been attending some kind of meetings (ha ha!). I laughed and said, "No, but these

are the kind of questions that the youth of America want answers to and want things done about." Not that I'm so youthful, but I feel youthful. But he's an old 36 himself, which astounded me because I'm 35. It was a pleasant evening, all in all.

Their sporadic affair lasted only a few months, though Robert saw her on the last day of her life. A friend later recalled that in January 1964 Robert "handed me a packet of letters – maybe a dozen or so – and told me to 'get rid of them.' . . . He admitted to me later that they were love missives both he and Jack had received from Marilyn Monroe."[13] She undoubtedly wrote to the Kennedys, but it seems highly unlikely that Robert would give the volatile letters to a friend instead of simply destroying them himself.

The FBI – along with the Kennedys, the corrupt union leader Jimmy Hoffa and the executives at Fox – had all wired Marilyn's house and tapped her phone. In January 1965, the FBI (run by Robert's fierce enemy, J. Edgar Hoover) turned up some evidence about the liaison: "An alleged relationship between the Attorney General and Marilyn Monroe had come to the Bureau's attention previously." After Fox cancelled her contract, Marilyn Monroe phoned Robert Kennedy at the Department of Justice "to tell him the bad news. ROBERT KENNEDY told her not to worry about the contract – he would take care of everything. When nothing was done, she again called him from her home to the Department of Justice, person-to-person, and on this occasion they had unpleasant words. She was reported to have threatened to make public their affair."

Marilyn never quite understood, even after three divorces, that many men wanted to sleep with her but very few wanted to marry her. Miller had left his wife for Marilyn; Montand and the Kennedys would not. (Jackie Kennedy's imitation of Marilyn's breathy, whispering voice may have been an attempt to make herself more attractive to her husband.) These sophisticated men had casual affairs with Marilyn and then abandoned her. She fell in love and expected them to marry her. When they rejected her and told her the affair was over, she pursued them and made her wound more bitter. Complaining to Lawford about a recurrent pattern in her life, she said angrily that the Kennedys "use you and then they dispose of you like so much rubbish." The super-star also told another man that she'd been treated like a whore: "I feel passed around! I feel used! I feel like a piece of meat!"[14]

V

Marilyn's last project, *Something's Got to Give*, was the greatest disaster of her career. The shooting began on April 23, 1962, and recapitulated in a more intense way all the problems of her previous movies. It was a remake – almost always worse than the original – of the Cary Grant-Irene Dunne comedy, *My Favorite Wife* (1940), in which a female explorer, presumed dead seven years after her shipwreck, suddenly turns up on the day her husband has finally remarried.

Peter Levathes, the new head of production at Fox, came (like Skouras) from a Greek background. A lawyer, formerly head of the television department of a New York advertising agency, he'd replaced Zanuck and was supposed to reverse the studio's alarming financial decline. The director Jean Negulesco described him as "a tall, dark man, nervous and with the faraway look of a man with responsibilities beyond his understanding or ability." Hoping to prevent Marilyn's notorious lateness, Levathes instantly met all her demands. At her insistence, he dismissed the producer David Barry and replaced him with Harvey Weinstein, a New York stage and television producer who (under Greenson's guidance) was supposed to be able to control her. Levathes agreed to have the script extensively rewritten. He also hired Marilyn's first choice, Dean Martin, as her leading man, but this too caused conflict. Martin (who spent most of the time practicing his golf strokes) made $300,000 plus 7.5 percent of future profits. Marilyn, still under the stringent Fox contract, got only $100,000. When she became dissatisfied with the director Frank Taschlin, Levathes – at a cost of $250,000 – replaced him with George Cukor, who'd directed *Let's Make Love*.

Nunnally Johnson, who wrote the fatuous scripts of Marilyn's *We're Not Married* and *How to Marry a Millionaire*, completed the screenplay and left for Europe. In true Hollywood style, six other writers then worked on the script, constantly changing but never improving it. To conceal their handiwork and deceive Marilyn, they had the secretaries retype the pages on white paper instead of the blue normally used for rewrites. In the end, there were only four pages left of Johnson's screenplay. Marilyn, naturally confused and upset by all the changes, was angry about not being consulted or respected.

Finally, Walter Bernstein, a bright Dartmouth graduate and once-blacklisted writer, was brought in to do a "final polish" – or revive the corpse. As he discussed the script with Marilyn, Bernstein found "her manner at once tentative, apologetic, and intransigent." When they disagreed about a scene, she exclaimed, "Don't be such a *writer*." She thought that Bernstein, like Miller, was too defensive about his script and too unreasonable in expecting the words to be spoken as he'd written them. She also, playing the operatic diva and repeating Paula Strasberg's grandiose notions, referred to herself in the third person: "Remember, you've got Marilyn Monroe. . . . You've got to use her." Glad to have the job, Bernstein added one scene in the bedroom. But he thought Johnson's original script was fine and that there was no real reason for all the changes. They merely made Marilyn even more insecure and unhappy.[15]

When shooting finally began, Marilyn, pleading poor health, turned up for only thirteen of the first thirty work days. "If she did show up," Bernstein recalled, "it was like the Second Coming. Everybody bowed down and genuflected." In six weeks, Cukor, running a million dollars over budget, managed to turn out only seven-and-a-half minutes of usable film. From her infrequent appearances it was clear to him that she could no longer function as an actress. *Something's Got to Give* (in its few completed scenes) is an awful movie and Marilyn is quite awful in it. She's stiff and unnatural with her "cute" Hollywood children, who are playing in the pool when she returns home as a stranger and is reunited with them.

Marilyn's megalomania was combined with – perhaps stimulated by – her feelings of fear, inadequacy and worthlessness. Without Miller to reassure and restrain (if not control) her, she was now even more difficult to deal with. Bernstein said the studio had a big investment in Marilyn, one of the very few stars who could "open a picture" and draw an audience to see *her* movie. But no one knew how to handle her. Levathes was weak, Weinstein weaker. Everyone was scared, and Marilyn filled the power vacuum. Fox conceded too much and gave in for too long. Like a child with a loaded gun, Marilyn was out of control and got away with outrageous demands. Zanuck, much tougher than his successors, would never have indulged her.[16] Yet once more, production halted because she was sick.

In the midst of this crisis, Marilyn suddenly recovered her health and flew to New York to appear at President Kennedy's forty-fifth birthday party. She was thrilled to know that her idol, Jean Harlow, had attended President Roosevelt's birthday ball in 1934. But Levathes, furious at her absence, failed to see that this extraordinary event – which combined politics and power with celebrity and fame – was a superb opportunity to publicize her latest picture. On May 19, in Madison Square Garden – along with Maria Callas, Ella Fitzgerald, Peggy Lee, Henry Fonda and Jack Benny – Marilyn performed before 15,000 faithful Democrats, who contributed a million dollars to the party. As she was being sewn into her shimmering, skin-tight dress, the actor Peter Lawford, punning on her habitual fault and foreshadowing her fate, introduced her as "the late Marilyn Monroe." She turned "Happy Birthday, Mista Pwes-i-dent" into a breathy, even orgasmic tribute, rated PG for parental guidance, not suitable for children's parties.

Kennedy, with ironic wit, said he was pleased that "Miss Monroe had sung happy birthday to him in such a wholesome way." Few people in the wildly enthusiastic audience knew that Marilyn had been Kennedy's mistress and was publicly expressing her love. Adlai Stevenson, echoing Arthur Schlesinger and perhaps in the know, wrote a friend about his " 'perilous encounters' that evening with Marilyn, 'dressed in what she calls "skin and beads." I didn't see the beads! . . . Robert Kennedy was dodging around her like a moth around the flame.' "

Marilyn was eager for even more publicity to strengthen her hand in the struggle with Fox. On May 28 she posed for nude photos in the swimming pool on the set, which was modeled on Cukor's luxurious house. The photos showed that her body was still sensuous and beautiful. But all her serious ambitions, all her lessons at the Actors Studio, had led to a rotten movie and another display of her body.

Speaking of disputes during production, Billy Wilder once told me, "If there's a serious conflict halfway through a film, the actor stays, must stay, and the director must go." Cukor, increasingly bitter and angry about Marilyn's behavior, urged the studio to replace her. Instead, he was replaced by Jean Negulesco, who'd directed *How to Marry a Millionaire*. When asked by the critic Kenneth Tynan what food Marilyn resembled, Cukor unkindly compared her to "a three-day-old Van de Kamp Bakery angel cake."[17] Interviewed later on, he repeated the "under water" image that had struck previous colleagues, blamed yet pitied Marilyn and admitted that the whole project had been a disaster:

> Monroe had driven people crazy with her behavior during filming and had finally gone "round the bend." We have shot for seven

weeks and we have five days' work. And the sad thing is that the five days' work are no good. She's no good and she can't remember her lines. It's as though she were under water. She's intelligent enough to know it's no good. And there's a certain ruthlessness, too.

The studio has given in to her on everything. She's tough about everything. She's so very sweet with me. I am enormously sorry for her. Even her lawyer is baffled. She's accusing him of being against her. I think it's the end of her career.

Cukor (contradicting his statement about her sweetness) also resented Marilyn's "plotting and bullying everybody with her outrageous demands" and concluded, "Fox was weak and stupid and deserved everything it got."[18]

The crises on *Something's Got to Give* coincided with Fox's even more disastrous production in Rome of Elizabeth Taylor and Richard Burton in *Cleopatra*. Fox had lost $61 million in the past three years; and *Cleopatra*, budgeted at $5 million, eventually cost $25 million. The studio, inextricably committed to *Cleopatra*, could not afford the excesses of both Elizabeth and Marilyn. On June 7, ten days after she posed for the nude photos, Marilyn was fired for her absence, lateness and impossibly poor performance. Fox also sued her to recover $750,000 in excessive costs. Like the hostile crew at the wrap-party of *The Prince and the Showgirl* in England, the Fox crew felt that Marilyn had neither appreciated their work nor treated them with respect. They placed an ad in *Variety* that sarcastically thanked her for the loss of their jobs at a difficult time.

Fox had always treated Marilyn maladroitly. Schenck and others had forced her into couch casting; Zanuck, slow to recognize her talent, gave her many mediocre parts; the executives dropped her when her first contract expired; denied her a star's dressing room; kept her to an extremely unfair contract when she earned more than anyone else for the studio; suspended her in 1954 for refusing to appear in the inferior picture, *The Girl in Pink Tights*; and failed to exploit the publicity value of her birthday tribute to President Kennedy. They also did more harm than good by indulging her. They tolerated her drama coaches on the set, put up with her lateness, failed to give her the proper treatment for drug addiction and waited far too long to fire her from *Something's Got to Give*. Walter Mirisch, the experienced producer of *Some Like It Hot*, thought Marilyn was clearly not well enough to perform, and that the studio should have shut the picture down in less than thirty days.

Marilyn, used to getting her way with everything, was devastated. She and everyone else thought her career was ruined. She spent hours and hours staring at herself in the mirror, looking for telltale wrinkles and signs of old age. Like the bosomy Hollywood columnist Sheila Graham, she slept with her bra on to prevent her breasts from sagging. Being fired made her even more unsure of her identity. When the photographer George Barris introduced Marilyn to his maid, who said, "I can't believe it. Are you really Marilyn Monroe?" she replied, "I guess I am. Everyone says I am."[19]

Marilyn was replaced by Lee Remick. But Dean Martin, who had a contractual right to approve his co-star, said "no Marilyn, no picture." Then, on July 25, the executives at Fox, who still didn't know what they were doing, suddenly changed their minds. They dropped the lawsuit and asked, even begged Marilyn to come back. On August 1, only four days before her death, she signed a new contract for $250,000 – two-and-a-half times her original fee. Marilyn, insecure as ever, was still in a precarious emotional state, but the new contract seemed like a second chance, a promising turn of events.

Seventeen

Suicide
(1962)

I

In 1962 Marilyn's physical and mental health was deteriorating, her personal and professional life was failing, and she was increasingly lonely, ill and frightened. The circumstances of her death were muddled and mysterious, and people inevitably speculated on its causes. Who or what destroyed her – the men who abused her, the doctors who bungled her care, or her own craving for release? She may have died of an accidental overdose, she may have been a deliberate suicide or (as some think) the victim of a politically motivated homicide: we'll never know for sure.

Richard Meryman, who interviewed her for *Life* magazine the month before her death, recently wrote, "I do not believe that she deliberately killed herself. There was no indication of such a degree of despair. It is my strong opinion that her death was an involuntary overdose of narcotics." Several circumstances suggest that her death was accidental. She did not seem depressed and did not alarm most friends who saw her during the last days of her life. She loved her new house and was absorbed in decorating it. She was still, as her last photos show, luminously attractive. She had contracted with Fox to resume work on *Something's Got to Give*. There was a vague possibility of remarrying DiMaggio, though they had still not resolved the essential conflict between her domestic life and her career. She also had a high tolerance for drugs and thought she could handle them. After muddling her brain with barbiturates, she may have forgotten how many pills she'd already taken.

But the evidence suggests that Marilyn did in fact commit suicide. Her emotional difficulties – sexual frigidity, insomnia, drug addiction and depression – were getting worse. She feared yet another mental breakdown and permanent insanity. More immediately disturbing factors were Kay Gable's accusation that Marilyn was responsible for Clark's death; Marilyn's third divorce, from Miller, and the disconcerting news that his new wife, Inge Morath, was pregnant; the failure of her third operation for endometriosis and inability to have children of her own (Murray told the FBI that Marilyn felt like a "negated sex symbol"); the failure of her psychoanalysis; her cruel rejections, within a few months, by Sinatra and both Kennedys; her persistent anxiety that she was growing older and losing her looks; her fear that she'd never be able to change from comedy to drama, and that, despite the new Fox contract, her career was (or soon would be) over.

The process of aging – as the Gloria Swanson character revealed so memorably in Wilder's *Sunset Boulevard* (1950) – is especially hard for a once gorgeous and idolized woman. For an actress who derives all sense of self-worth from her looks, it is tragic. When Clara Bow, for example, failed to make a comeback, she gained weight and grew reclusive, became depressed and suffered a series of breakdowns. Joseph Mankiewicz noted, as early as Marilyn's appearance in *All About Eve*, how she obsessively examined her face in the mirror. When she looked at herself in 1962 and saw a spot, a sag, a deepening of wrinkles, she knew her days as a beauty were ending. After her latest film fiasco, many male stars (and some outstanding directors) were unwilling to work with her. As Robert Frost wrote in "Provide, Provide": "No memory of having starred / Atones for later disregard / Or keeps the end from being hard."[1]

Lack of true friends and soul-piercing loneliness also contributed to Marilyn's suicide. Even when living with a husband and working with colleagues, she tended to exist in a self-enclosed world of her own. Abandoned in childhood by her parents, she was finally abandoned by her friends. She felt she could buy rather than earn friendship, and therefore had no one to rely on. She was a beautiful woman who couldn't keep a man and didn't have a date on her last Saturday night. Peter Lawford called her at 7 p.m. to invite her to a dinner party, but she refused, in a voice that was thickened and nearly inaudible from drugs. Her last, foreboding words to him were, "Say goodbye to Pat [his wife]. Say goodbye to Jack. And say goodbye to yourself because you're a nice guy." There was no need to say goodbye to Bobby: she'd just seen him. Naturally alarmed about Marilyn, Lawford called his manager, who advised him not to get involved. So Lawford ignored the danger and did nothing to help her. His last wife (also named Pat), wrote, "He was haunted by her death, maintaining a sense of personal responsibility for her loss for the rest of his life. . . . If anyone 'killed' Marilyn Monroe, it was Peter and his manager, who failed to act in a constructive manner."

Many people not only claimed that they'd phoned Marilyn on her last day, but also insisted that they were the last one to speak to her. Peter Lawford, Ralph Greenson, Sidney Skolsky, Joe DiMaggio, Jr., Ralph Roberts, the New York businessman Henry Rosenfeld, her hairdresser Sidney Guilaroff, Jeanne Carmen (who called, she said, to arrange a golf date!), her Mexican lover José Bolaños and Norman Rosten all seemed to be worried about her, but none of them assuaged or responded to her solitude, depression and despair. Rosten retrospectively realized that she was deceiving herself and living in a dream world: "[Marilyn said] she was in great shape (not true); she was planning to begin a film in the fall (fantasy); her house was almost furnished (never to be); . . . she was getting film offers from all over the world (doubtful)." Rosten wondered if there could be "a life for her outside the dream? Marriage and motherhood – that crucial reality – had faded away. Was there any other for her? It seemed improbable that a new life could be found in the land of the scorpions."[2]

After severing ties with most of her family, ex-husbands, friends and employees, Marilyn had almost no one left. Lawford had pimped for the Kennedys, who'd jilted her. Pat Newcomb was apparently following their orders, and Eunice Murray spied on her. Greenson exploited his celebrity patient. DiMaggio was in San Francisco. Her New York friends were too distant or too self-absorbed to help. That great portrayer of solitude, Joseph Conrad, described her condition when he wrote, "We live, as we dream – alone."

Like Sylvia Plath, Marilyn had narrowly survived several suicide attempts, from her late teens until the year before she died (see Appendix). Her marriage to Miller did not prevent her from attempting suicide, but did prevent her from succeeding. After he cut loose from her, she was on her own and heading for the rapids. Overwhelmed by her psychological crises, Marilyn was now willing to destroy her beauty and talent. Ever since she'd posed for photographers as a pretty teenager, she had learned to become "Marilyn Monroe" and had lived, in a strange dissociation, as two women. One was the ordinary girl who wanted a stable domestic life, with friends, marriage and children; the other was the movie idol and sex goddess, with the hourglass figure, glistening lips and crown of blond hair. She no longer wished to maintain her unreal self, and may have thought, at the end: whoever finds my body can do whatever they like with it. I don't want it any more.

Finally, she took control of her life by ending it. Her suicide was a form of revenge against the living, a tacit accusation that the survivors had not done enough to save her, a way to punish the false friends and treacherous lovers who'd failed and abandoned her. She wanted to make them feel guilty about her death and to take her suffering seriously. As she sadly prophesized in her memoir, "I was the kind of girl they found dead in a hall bedroom with an empty bottle of sleeping pills in her hand."[3]

II

Marilyn's doctors were partly responsible for her death. Well aware of the danger, Greenson said he wanted to make "a drastic cut in Marilyn's use of drugs . . . and keep strict control over the medication, since [he] felt she was potentially suicidal." Greenson also said that he brought in the internist Hyman Engelberg to help Marilyn reduce her dependence on drugs, and that the two doctors promised to keep in close contact about the dosage. In fact, as Greenson's wife revealed, the doctors gave her whatever she wanted: "The idea was that she was never to be said no to when she wanted a prescription, because the only thing that would happen was she would procure medication elsewhere and not inform her primary physicians about it. So whenever she asked for a drug she would usually get it." Both Greenson and Engelberg, without consulting each other, recklessly prescribed potentially fatal drugs for her, and were willing to risk her suicide rather than lose her as their patient.

Greenson's forceful personality had made Marilyn slavishly dependent on him, and he knew that she was "depressed and agitated, i.e. rejected and tempted to act out" during her conflict with Fox about *Something's Got to Give*. But he abandoned her by leaving on May 10 for a five-week summer vacation in Europe, and placated her with a new prescription. In his weirdly egotistic manner, he described this treatment as a kind of pharmaceutical fellatio that would fill her mouth with his essence:

> I prescribed a drug which is a quick-acting anti-depressant in combination with a sedative – Dexamyl. I also hoped she would be benefited by having something from me to depend on. . . . I felt that she would be unable to bear the depressive anxieties of being alone. The administering of the pill was an attempt to give her something of me to swallow, to take in, so that she could overcome the sense of terrible emptiness that would depress and infuriate her.[4]

The autopsy report stated that Monroe, "a thirty-six-year-old, well-developed, well-nourished Caucasian female . . . had swallowed forty to fifty Nembutals and a large number of chloral hydrate pills. . . . The blood test showed 8.0 mg.% of chloral hydrate, and the liver showed 13.0 mg.% of pentobarbital (Nembutal), both well above fatal doses." The cause of death was "Acute barbiturate poisoning. Ingestion of overdose." Barbiturates first numb the brain and then shut down the respiratory system, and prevent the victim from breathing. Engelberg insisted that he'd never prescribed chloral hydrate, a hypnotic and sedative, which Marilyn could have bought on her recent shopping trip to Mexico City. But he freely admitted, without any sense of remorse or guilt, that he'd prescribed fifty Nembutals on Friday August 3, knowing that if Marilyn took them all at once, they would certainly be fatal. She bought the pills that day, and the bottle was found empty beside her deathbed. John Huston, who'd helped save her in Reno, stated the real cause of Marilyn's death: "The star system had nothing to do with it whatsoever. The goddamn doctors killed her. They knew the girl was a pill addict."[5]

The circumstances surrounding Marilyn's death have been fiercely disputed, but it's possible to establish the basic facts about what actually happened. In the afternoon of Saturday August 4, Robert Kennedy apparently visited and quarreled with her. Greenson (who'd returned from Europe on June 6) also saw her for several hours and found her despondent. Between 10 and 11 p.m. Arthur Jacobs, Marilyn's chief publicist and Newcomb's boss, was summoned from a concert at the Hollywood Bowl – though it's not clear how he was found among the thousands of people in the audience. Murray, who didn't usually stay overnight, was the only other person in the house.

The accounts of both Murray and Greenson, who found the body, were incongruous and inconsistent. At first Murray said she suddenly awoke at midnight, saw a light shining under Marilyn's door and found the bedroom locked. But the new thick carpet prevented any light from being seen outside the room; and Marilyn, especially after her forced confinement in Payne Whitney, *never* locked her door. Murray said she then phoned Greenson, who told her to use the fireplace poker to part the draperies through the grille of the open bedroom window. In fact, the drapes were nailed across the window to ensure darkness and had no parting in the middle. Yet, according to Murray, she managed to see Marilyn's naked body (in a grotesque parody of the nude calendar) sprawled prostrate and angled across the bed. Greenson rushed over to the house from Santa Monica. With the same poker, he broke an unbarred window at the side of the house and climbed into the bedroom.

Marilyn's room looked like a cubicle in a cheap motel. There was no furniture, apart from the bed, a simple mattress and box-spring, with its twisted sheets. There was one light fixture on the wall and a tiny lamp on the bedside table, which was full of empty pill containers. Her few possessions, scattered around the carpeted floor, gave the impression that she'd just moved in.

Marilyn's doctors did not call the police for several hours, and gave Murray time to tamper with the scene. Greenson summoned Engelberg who, at 3:50 a.m. on Sunday August 5, declared Marilyn dead – though she probably died between 10 p.m. and midnight on August 4. The police, finally summoned at 4:20 a.m., arrived ten minutes later. They were surprised to find Murray cleaning up the bedroom and running the washing machine in the middle of the night. After questioning her and the two doctors, they searched for and failed to find a suicide note. Murray – vague, evasive and contradictory – changed the time she discovered the body, from midnight to 3 a.m., to explain the delay in calling the police. Inez Melson, Marilyn's business manager, then arrived and removed her personal papers. Newcomb also appeared to answer the numerous phone calls and help control the press and the crowd that began to gather at the house.

At 5:30 a.m. Marilyn's corpse was taken to the Westwood Village Mortuary; at 8 a.m. it was moved to the City Morgue; and at 10:30 a.m. Dr. Thomas Noguchi, the deputy coroner, did the autopsy. Noguchi specified that Marilyn's "liver, kidney, *stomach and contents*, urine and *intestine* [should be] *saved for further toxicological study*." But most of her organs were destroyed by his superiors before they could be analyzed. Marilyn's death seemed to make self-destruction fashionable. In Los Angeles in August 1962 suicides increased by 40 percent.

The studios had carefully created the glamorous Marilyn through a series of aesthetic improvements. The autopsy carved her up and took her apart. Dr. Noguchi, a well-respected pathologist, wrote, "I began my examination by searching painstakingly with a hand-held magnifying glass for any needle marks which would indicate that drugs had been injected. . . . I found no needle marks, and so indicated." But he allowed the possibility of an injection by adding, "punctures made by fine surgical needles, such as Dr. Greenson used, heal within hours and become invisible. Only fresh punctures can be discovered."

Noguchi also asked and answered the two vital questions that would trouble investigators for years:

—If Marilyn Monroe swallowed dozens of sleeping pills, why was there no evidence of pills in her digestive tract?
—Her stomach was familiar with those pills, and they were digested and "dumped" into the intestinal tract.
—The yellow dye on the Nembutal she swallowed should have stained her stomach. And yet you found no evidence of staining. How can that be?
—Nembutal is made with a capsule whose color does not run when it is swallowed.

Considering the forty to fifty pills that Marilyn swallowed, Noguchi definitively concluded, "In Monroe's case, an accidental overdose of that magnitude was extremely unlikely." His conclusion was confirmed by the suicide panel that studied her case and also "had no doubt that she had killed herself."[6]

The autopsy report seemed conclusive. But it was clear from the many lies, contradictions and irregularities surrounding Marilyn's suicide that there had been a cover-up between 11 p.m., when Jacobs arrived, and 4:30 a.m., when the police arrived. This cover-up was meant to conceal any foul play that might have caused Marilyn's death and to hide her intimate connection with the Kennedys. (There is no trace of Marilyn in the John F. Kennedy presidential library.) The attempt to conceal the truth has spawned many wildly implausible conspiracy theories, fueled by political fanaticism or a crass desire for publicity and money. The leading theories were: Greenson, Marilyn's lover and in a jealous rage, murdered her with a fatal injection or a fatal enema. Or Greenson, acting as an agent for the Kennedys, killed Marilyn, who threatened to expose her affairs with them. The other usual suspects were the CIA, the FBI and the Mafia, who killed her either to prevent her from disclosing top secret information or to discredit, frame and incriminate the Kennedys.

There's absolutely no evidence that Greenson was Marilyn's lover. In any case, with no apparent motive, he would never have risked his career, reputation and life by murdering her. Noguchi had explained why there was no residue of pills or dye in Marilyn's digestive tract and stomach. But David Heymann, in a hostile and sensational attack on Robert Kennedy, argued with false logic that the lack of residue "proved" that Greenson not only gave her a fatal injection or enema, but also that "the attorney general of the United States very likely had conspired in the murder of his former lover." Some authors even claimed that Robert Kennedy actually smothered Marilyn with a pillow. By contrast, Noguchi convincingly argued that "Almost every allegation has been followed up and found to be without basis so far as the DA's office was concerned, ranging from the mysterious missing 'diary' to the 'doctor' who had administered a 'killing' shot."[7]

Though the Kennedys did not kill Marilyn, they did attempt to hide their affairs with her. Newcomb has never revealed anything about her friendships with Marilyn or the Kennedys. Immediately after Marilyn's death, she was flown to the Kennedy compound on Cape Cod, sent on a long trip to Europe and then given a job at the United States Information Agency. Murray quickly disappeared on a long, gift-wrapped cruise around the world. But an FBI report of July 9, 1963, quoting the early release of a *Photoplay* magazine article of August 1963, said a "married man had an affair with Marilyn and 'caused' her suicide when he rejected her." The "clues" to the identity of her lover, obviously Robert Kennedy, were "that the man is happily married and has children; . . . that he is a great man, famous, known the world over; . . . and that he is considered a 'truly honorable man.'"

Robert Kennedy's rejection was a factor in Marilyn's suicide. But the theory that the Kennedys were responsible for murdering her, because she was going to reveal top secret political information or expose their affairs with her, does not bear close examination. The Kennedys would never have discussed sensitive material with such an unstable and indiscreet woman (John didn't even have time for foreplay). And Marilyn's "secret knowledge" that Jimmy Hoffa was hostile to Robert and that Fidel Castro hated John was obvious to everyone.

If the Kennedys were seriously worried about a sexual scandal involving Marilyn, they would not have kept the Oval Office tapes of their indiscreet conversations about her nor asked someone else to destroy her potentially damaging letters. The risk of killing her was infinitely greater than the risk of her revelations. Their affairs with her might actually have increased their prestige (as it increased Miller's) and helped rather than hurt their political careers. The Kennedys were also skilled at crisis management. If Marilyn had publicly revealed her affairs with John and Robert, they could have denied them. The public would not have believed the wild accusations of a suicidal woman, who'd recently been confined in a psychiatric hospital, against the word of the apparently honorable and happily married Kennedys. Most important, Marilyn, loyal to the Kennedys, conclusively told Greenson, "Bobby would do absolutely anything for his brother and so would I. I will never embarrass him."

The Kennedys' chauffeur remembered the mood on Cape Cod when the family learned that Marilyn had died: "[On] the day we heard the news that Marilyn Monroe had been found dead in California, I remember the strange silence that came over everybody who was there. . . . It was such a curious reaction. . . . Years later, when the rumors came out about Marilyn Monroe and John Kennedy, and then Robert Kennedy, I remembered the silence that August afternoon."[8] The Kennedys did not grieve for Marilyn, but felt guilty about the way they'd treated her and relieved that she was no longer a problem.

III

Greenson had much more reason to feel guilty. From the beginning of July until her suicide, he saw Marilyn almost every day. (She also had many medical problems and Engelberg saw her thirteen times during her last month.) Greenson's letters to his mother confessor, Anna Freud, written before Marilyn's death and not mentioning her by name, were characteristically self-centered. He complained about his interrupted holiday in Europe and alluded to, but did not explain, her traumatic dismissal by Fox: "I had to interrupt my trip and return home alone because of the difficulties of one of my patients. Since I returned home she felt much better and was able to resume work. Nevertheless, the studio fired her the day after I returned for a variety of other reasons. This was a most frustrating experience, since now I was back home and she was feeling fine, but she no longer had to work and therefore I was free to return to Europe, which was impossible."

Anna Freud, using the childlike euphemism "acting up," attempted to comfort him and (in contrast to Greenson) expressed concern about Marilyn: "I have tried to follow your fate in the newspapers and I saw that your patient was acting up. But I did not realize that this would interrupt your holiday and I do feel sorry for this. I wonder what will happen to her and with her. There must be something very nice about her from what I understood from Marianne Kris."

Marilyn's suicide and his own failure were a personal loss as well as a public humiliation for Greenson. With hindsight and remembering her panic in Payne Whitney, he wrote Rosten, ten days after her death, "I should have played it safe and put her in a sanitarium, but that would have only been safe for me and deadly for her."[9] Writing to Marianne Kris at the same time, Greenson admitted (after all their analytic sessions) that he had not been able to provide professional insights and had offered kindness instead of therapy: "I was her therapist, the good father who would not disappoint her and who would bring her insights, and if not insights, just kindness. I had become the most important person in her life. I also felt guilty that I put a burden on my own family. But there was something very lovable about this girl and we all cared about her and she could be delightful. . . . She was a poor creature I tried to help, and I ended up hurting her" – as Kris had done.

On August 20, Greenson wrote again to Anna Freud. He admitted the all-too-obvious failure of his so-called "science." Then, shifting the blame from himself to the hypocritical world (that is, Hollywood), he focused as usual on his own tender feelings. He never mentioned, of course, that he and Engelberg had supplied the drugs that Marilyn had used to kill herself:

> This has been a terrible blow in many ways. I cared about her and she was my patient. She was so pathetic and she had had such a terrible life. I had hopes for her and I thought we were making progress. And now she died and I realize that all my knowledge and my desire and my strength were not enough. God knows I tried and mightily so, but I could not defeat all the destructive forces that had been stirred up in her by the terrible experiences of her past life. Sometimes I feel the world wanted her to die, or at least many people in the world, particularly those who after her death so conspicuously grieved and mourned. It makes me angry. But above all I feel sad and also disappointed. It is not just a blow to my pride, although I am sure that is present, but also a blow to my science of which I consider myself a good representative. But it will take me time to get over this and I know that eventually this will only become a scar. Some good friends have written to me some very kind letters and this helps me, but it hurts to remember; and yet it is only by remembering that I shall some day be able to forget it.

In January 1963 Greenson, suffering from bronchitis and feeling lonely after his two children had moved out of his house, wrote Anna Freud about his current emotional state and mentioned that he'd had some informal therapy with two other mentors: "I personally am beginning to feel better and think that I have overcome the worst of my grief about Marilyn Monroe. I saw Marianne Kris and Max Schur in New York in a recent meeting and it was very helpful to talk to them." Finally, ten months after her death, Greenson announced that he was cured: "I have overcome my grief and depression about the M.M. affair."[10]

In his collection of essays, *Explorations in Psychoanalysis* (1978), Greenson gave a patronizing and self-aggrandizing account of how he'd successfully treated a young woman. Though he never mentioned her name, readers were clearly meant to see that he was discussing Marilyn Monroe. He said she'd developed an exceptionally close and clinging relationship to him, but did not admit that he'd encouraged it in every possible way. He wrote that she'd tried to compensate for his forthcoming absence in Europe by choosing a primitive fetish to represent him:

> I told an emotionally immature young woman patient, who had developed a very dependent transference to me, that I was going to attend an International Congress in Europe some three months hence. We worked intensively on the multiple determinants of her clinging dependence, but made only insignificant progress. Then the situation changed dramatically when one day she announced that she had discovered something that would tide her over [during] my absence. It was not some insight, not a new personal relationship, it was a chess piece. The young woman had recently been given a gift of a carved ivory chess set. The evening before her announcement, as she looked at the set, through the sparkling light of a glass of champagne, it suddenly struck her that I looked like the white knight of her chess set. The realization immediately evoked in her a feeling of comfort, even triumph. The white knight was a protector, it belonged to her, she could carry it wherever she went, it would look after her, and I could go on my merry way to Europe without having to worry about her.

He noted that Marilyn had used it as a good luck charm during her performance – evidently at John Kennedy's birthday party:

> The patient's major concern about the period of my absence was a public performance of great important to her professionally. She now felt confident of success because she could conceal her white knight in her handkerchief or scarf; she was certain he would protect her from nervousness, anxiety, or bad luck. I was relieved and delighted to learn, while in Europe, that her performance had indeed been a smashing success.

But her sense of security was tenuous, and she needed the magical presence of her analyst:

> Shortly thereafter, however, I received several panicky trans-atlantic telephone calls from her. The patient had lost the white knight and was beside herself with terror and gloom, like a child who has lost her security blanket. A colleague of mine who saw her in that interval said that all his interventions were to no avail and he reluctantly suggested that I cut short my trip and return. I hated to interrupt my vacation and I doubted whether my return would be beneficial. Surprisingly, it was. I no sooner saw her than her anxiety and depression lifted. It then became possible to work for many months on how she used me as a good luck charm rather than [as] an analyst.
>
> The talisman, the chess piece, served her as a magical means of averting bad luck or evil. It protected her against losing some-thing precious.[11]

Turning the "science" of psychoanalysis into a bit of mumbo-jumbo, Greenson concluded that the incongruous fetish, a shining white knight, protected her from "losing something precious" – the analyst himself. This story seems to be a self-serving fantasy. Marilyn did not go in for chess and never mentioned the chess piece, and she was not clutching it during her performance. If the story were true, Greenson did not consider that Marilyn might have deliberately lost the white knight in order to free herself from his bondage. In fact, as he well knew, the fetish neither averted evil nor protected her against losing something else that was far more precious – her very life. His essay never mentioned that the anonymous patient killed herself while under his care.

IV

DiMaggio flew down from San Francisco to make the funeral arrange-ments. He still loved Marilyn, who looked absolutely ghastly after the autopsy, and sat up all night in a morbid death watch, gazing into the open coffin and clasping her fingers in a final farewell. The simple funeral took place on August 9 in the small Westwood Memorial Park at 1218 Glendon Avenue, now hidden away behind the tall buildings on Wilshire Boulevard. The thirty-one mourners were DiMaggio, his sidekick George Solotaire and Joe, Jr. (in his Marine dress uniform); Marilyn's half-sister Berniece Miracle; Lee and Paula Strasberg; the Greensons and their two grown children. From Marilyn's Los Angeles past were her sometime foster parents, the Knebelcamps; Fred Karger's mother and sister; and her acting teacher Lotte Goslar. The rest were all on her payroll: Murray and Newcomb, two lawyers, business manager and her husband, make-up man with his wife and daughter, three hairdressers, masseur, secretary, chauffeur and maid. Sinatra and the Lawfords were particularly excluded. When the Hollywood lawyer protested that DiMaggio was keeping out a lot of important studio executives, directors and stars, Joe bitterly said, "Tell them if it wasn't for them, she'd still be here." When Marilyn's mother (institutional-ized yet again) heard of her death, she also blamed Hollywood and disingenuously said, "I never wanted her to become an actress."

At the service the Lutheran minister from a Westwood church read Psalm 23: "The Lord is my shepherd; I shall not want"; John 14: "Let your heart not be troubled: ye believe in God, believe also in me. In my Father's house are many mansions. . . . I go to prepare a place for you"; Psalm 46: "God is our refuge and strength, a very present help in trouble. Therefore will not we fear"; and the especially apt Psalm 139: "I will praise thee; for I am fearfully and wonderfully made: marvelous are thy works; and that my soul knoweth right well." Lee Strasberg delivered the brief but touching eulogy. To comfort the mourners he called Marilyn's death an accident, and described her as "a warm human being, impulsive and shy, sensitive and in fear of rejection, yet ever avid for life and reaching out for fulfillment. . . . She had a luminous quality – a combination of wistfulness, radiance, yearning – to set her apart and yet make everyone wish to be part of it, to share in the childish naïveté which was at once so shy and yet so vibrant."[12] The coffin was carried across the wide lawn and placed in crypt 24 in The Corridor of Memories.

Though Marilyn had severed relations with Marianne Kris because of her "terrible mistake," she made Kris and the Strasbergs the major beneficiaries of her will, which named the following people:

—Berniece Miracle: $10,000
—Norman and Hedda Rosten: $5,000 (for the education of their daughter, Patricia)

—Michael Chekhov's widow, Xenia: $2,500 a year
—Marilyn's mother, Gladys Baker: $5,000 a year (from a $100,000 trust fund)
—Marilyn's secretary May Reis: $10,000 plus 25 percent of the balance (not to exceed $40,000)
—Dr. Marianne Kris: 25 percent of the balance (to be donated to the psychiatric institution of her choice)
—Lee Strasberg: 50 percent of the balance (in addition to all Marilyn's personal effects and clothing).

Legal obstacles caused delays for a decade and the first payments were not made until December 1971. Despite her husband's bequest, the insatiable Paula claimed that she was owed an additional $22,000 for "coaching."

Ten years after her death, when Marilyn's estate was finally settled and her possessions unpacked, they turned out to be a random collection of cheap and tacky objects, battered by her frequent moves. She had no interest in material things and left very little money. But her clothes and cosmetics revealed the two sides of the character she was always trying and failing to connect:

[There were] books of poetry with underlined passages. A Golden Globe statuette, cracked, with the lead filling visible. Bone-color stationery embossed with "Marilyn Monroe." Unmailed letters dated '59. . . .

A whole room . . . crammed with Marilyn's ordinary furniture. A gooseneck reading lamp with the paint chipped off. A plain wooden desk. . . . Plastic dishes. . . .

Stuffed into grocery cartons were black fur outfits, leopard hats, white mink muffs, ermine coats, double-skin white fox boas with silk between and piles of heavily beaded professional gowns. . . . Such stage wardrobe as was worn at the Circus opening or at President Kennedy's birthday party bore the theatrical labels: "Marilyn Monroe from *Gentlemen Prefer Blondes*." In one box of her personal clothing a moth flew out.

Monroe had two of everything. One set for *the* Marilyn Monroe, the other for when she was herself. The theatrical make-up in a black case initialed M.M. held bright greens and blues for her eyes, not the kind of make-up worn at the supermarket.

Although Marilyn denied she wore bras, she had two sets. For Marilyn Moviestar she wore décolleté special no-bra bras that looked like nothing. Her personal brassieres were the simplest and plainest and poorest.

The offstage dresses went to thrift stores anonymously. The stage gowns met with a tragedy. A burst pipe spewed raw sewage onto them.

Marilyn was right: everyone wanted a piece of her. At her death her possessions seemed intrinsically worthless, but decades later, as divine relics, they fetched high prices. In October 1999 Christie's auctioned them off for $13.5 million. Lee Strasberg's second wife, Anna (who never knew Marilyn), got the money and still earns well over $2 million a year in licensing fees. As a result the Strasberg Institute on East 15th Street in New York, now separate from the Actors Studio, is assured of support. It includes a Marilyn Monroe Theater and Marilyn Monroe Museum, under the "surveillance" of Anna Strasberg.

Marilyn fulfilled the American dream of success, but suffered the American tragedy of losing it all. As Samuel Johnson wrote of such ephemeral celebrities: "They mount, they shine, evaporate, and fall."[13] Like famous beauties of the past, she was painted by leading artists, but her most famous images were deconstructed rather than commemorated. Willem de Kooning's portrait is built from modernist fragments, a fitting evocation of her shattered life. Andy Warhol's silkscreen print series confirmed her iconic photographic image and keeps it current. But the real, warm Marilyn is buried under layers of color. In Warhol's variations the fluffy blonde expression remains fixed, yet seems to vary from a smile to a grimace, from exuberant joy to misery and tears.

When the publicist Arthur Jacobs informed Miller of Marilyn's death, the playwright, wishing to detach himself entirely and relieved that he was no longer responsible for her, merely said, "It's your problem, not mine." Asked if he planned to attend the funeral, he cryptically replied, "She won't be there." Miller, on the East Coast, did not attend and may not even have been invited, though he and his children sent flowers. He had suffered enough. His response seemed callous, but he was determined to protect himself from further pain.

Still paternal and protective eighteen months after they parted, Miller "had the feeling, amounting often to tearing guilt, that the divorce had helped her toward her death and that he should have been able to do something to save her." But he later commented that Marilyn's fate seemed predestined: "It had to happen. I didn't know when or how, but it was inevitable."[14] Having tried to help her, Miller believed her problems were intractable: "I know now that it wasn't a matter of the individuals around her that brought her to that end. It would have happened even if she hadn't been in movies." Noting a basic contradiction in Marilyn's character, he suggested that she behaved recklessly and, like a real goddess, thought she was immortal: "Marilyn never believed she was going to die. She just kept pushing the boundaries further and further." At other times she felt that she was destined to die as a final tribute to her fans: "[Her] conviction was that she was meant to be a sacrifice and a victim." Miller also observed that the death-haunted Marilyn had always been vulnerable and sad: "Beneath all her insouciance and wit, death was her companion everywhere and at all times, and it may have been that its unacknowledged presence was what lent her poignancy, dancing at the edge of oblivion as she was."[15]

Eighteen

Miller's Tragic Muse
(1964–2004)

I

In 1852, the poet Charles Baudelaire vented his rage against Jeanne Duval, the mistress and muse who'd been tormenting him for the previous ten years. He bitterly wrote how he had learned "To live with a person who shows no gratitude for your efforts, who impedes them through clumsiness or permanent meanness, who considers you as a mere servant, as her property, someone with whom it is impossible to exchange a word about politics or literature, a creature who is unwilling to learn a single thing, although you've offered to teach her yourself, a creature who *has no admiration for one* and who is not even interested in one's studies." Baudelaire's description of Jeanne was more vituperative than anything Miller ever wrote about Monroe, but it suggests the depths of his degradation and the bitterness of his wounds.

Miller made his name as an intellectual playwright who used characters and stories to embody his ideas and make moral arguments. A critic has noted that in his early plays – *Death of a Salesman*, *The Crucible* and *A View from the Bridge* – the wife "is a fine woman who is not in the least sexually interesting." But "Miller's implicit indictment of sex as a wicked influence is remarkably consistent and emphatic." He makes illicit sex "both the root and symptom of his heroes' disorders." After he became involved with Marilyn, his work changed focus and became more autobiographical. For ten years, from 1951 until their divorce in 1961, her willful, passionate, unstable temperament fascinated, inspired and humiliated him. Marilyn was a ready-made tragic muse, whom he knew better than anyone else in the world. Her character and his suffering during their marriage obsessed him for more than fifty years: from their first meeting until the very end of his life. Miller wrote three short stories, a screenplay, a novel and four plays with sad, neurotic heroines. He recreated Marilyn in two of his best works: Roslyn in *The Misfits* and Maggie in *After the Fall* (1964). She was also Sylvia in *Broken Glass* (1994), Cathy-May in *Mr. Peters' Connections* (1999) and Kitty in his last, still unpublished play, *Finishing the Picture* (2004).

Though he had rationally absolved himself of blame, his failure to arrest Marilyn's slide into breakdown and death continued to haunt him. He had repeatedly taken responsibility for her, and finally had to give up. He was able to close this episode in his life, but not in his art. The great division in his dramatic works was Marilyn's suicide in 1962. In his four autobiographical plays he tried to explain his response to her enchanting and maddening character, to justify his own behavior and to depict the destructive environment of the modern mass-entertainment business.

The germ of *After the Fall* came from Miller's unfinished play of 1951, *An Italian Tragedy*. Quentin, the autobiographical hero, has recently had an adulterous adventure that makes him realize how much he hates the restrictions of married life. His wife (based on Mary Slattery) refuses to forgive him and insists that he suppress his adulterous desires. He wants to remain married, but doesn't want to give up his new-found erotic ecstasy. The heroine, Lorraine (based on Marilyn), is a precursor to Maggie in *After the Fall*. She is naïve, sexy, insecure, self-destructive and fatal to men who get involved with her. In *Timebends* Miller described Lorraine in rather vague and contorted prose:

> With her open sexuality, childlike and sublimely free of ties and expectations in a life she half senses is doomed, she moves instinctively to break the hold of respectability on the men until each in his different way meets the tragedy in which she has unwittingly entangled him. . . . Like a blind, godlike force, with all its creative cruelty, her sexuality comes to seem the only truthful connection with some ultimate nature. . . . She has no security

of her own and no faith, and her liberating promise is finally
illusory.[1]

After the Fall was Miller's first full-length play in eight years. Starting
with the Lorraine character and writing furiously, he had no clear
idea of where he was going. His first draft amounted to 5,000 pages,
which he drastically cut down to the final version of 180 pages. Even
so, it seemed a work in progress. Jason Robards, who appeared as
Quentin, thought Miller gave a terrible reading when he first presented
it to the cast.

The play, directed by Elia Kazan, opened in New York in January
1964. The work reunited Miller with the man who'd directed his
early works and had once been his closest friend, and their collaboration reopened old wounds and continued their old quarrel. Miller
clearly based the character of Mickey, who's named names, on Kazan.
In his director's notes Kazan analyzed Mickey's character – and exalted
his own: "Mickey: The Guiltless Man (as vs. Quentin). A great and
natural hedonist, full of energy and pleasure . . . because he is not
crippled with puritanism and consequent guilts." He is "troubled,
talking to himself, arguing it out with himself. He's still trying, and
will be for years, to figure out whether he did right or did wrong."
To make matters even more incestuous, Miller was relying on Kazan,
the man who had slept with Marilyn while Miller himself was still
shyly courting her, to direct the play. Kazan had casually dropped
Marilyn, while Miller had let himself in for five hellish years of
marriage. In a further twist of fate, Kazan's wife had died in December
1963, leaving him free to marry his mistress, Barbara Loden – who
was cast as Maggie. Kazan seemed to be taking possession of Marilyn
all over again. But the play had been chosen to be the opening production of the new Lincoln Center Repertory Company, and Kazan
certainly had an unusually intimate understanding of the play. So
Miller and Kazan, who needed each other, managed to overcome
their personal and political animosity.

The intensely personal nature of Miller's material demanded a new
dramatic technique. He cast the story of his autobiographical hero
Quentin and the disintegration of his relationship with Maggie in
the form of a confession. This sometimes confusing method was a
new departure for Miller. The play portrayed his own consciousness
and conflicts, and attempted to heal his damaged psyche. He wrote

that "the action takes place in the mind, thought, and memory of Quentin. . . . With stream-of-consciousness evocations of characters, abrupt disappearances, and transformations of time and place, the play often verged on montage" – a combination of disparate elements intended to form a unified whole.[2] The Listener, whom Quentin addresses with the free associations of a psychoanalytic patient, is God, his own conscience and the audience in the theater.

Act One sets out the social context of Quentin's life and the historical events that provide the backdrop of his mind: the financial ruin of his father in the Depression, the effects of the Holocaust and the destruction of innocent people's lives in the Communist witch-hunts of the 1950s. Quentin and Holga (an idealized character based on Miller's third wife, the Austrian photographer Inge Morath) visit an extermination camp, whose tower rises above the set. In Act Two Miller focuses on the failures of Quentin's first marriage to Louise (Mary) and of his second marriage to a popular singer, Maggie (whose name suggests DiMaggio and is clearly modeled on Marilyn).

The critics, then and now, have obsessively focused on Maggie and neglected Louise, a complex character who vividly reveals the moral and sexual conflicts in Miller's first marriage. If Maggie is the id, Louise is a savagely critical superego, urging her husband to rise above his baser instincts and filling him with guilt. Suggesting that his first wife was even more self-righteous than he was, Miller told Kazan that Quentin "made Louise the custodian of his conscience and just to look at her sometimes in her rectitude arouses his sense that he is guilty." In a hectoring tone that condemns Quentin's behavior, Louise moves from self-effacement to self-assertion. His disloyalty provokes her to insist on her own individuality and worth:

> I did contribute; I demanded nothing for much too long. . . .
> 　　The moment I begin to assert myself it seems to threaten you. I don't think you *want* me to be happy.

She also defends her right to be valued as an intelligent woman:

> The way you behave toward me. I don't exist. People are supposed to find out about each other. I am not all this uninteresting. Many people, men *and* women, think I *am* interesting. . . .
> 　　I don't intend to be ashamed of myself any more. I used to

think it was normal, or even that you don't see me because I'm not worth seeing. But I think now that you don't really see any woman.

This last speech is highly ironic in view of Quentin's passion for Maggie, but it also suggests Louise's tragedy, her sense of loss and betrayal. Quentin feels (like Miller when describing this real-life episode in *Timebends*) that he might as well have extramarital sex if Louise damns him for merely thinking about it. Louise admits, "I did overreact, but it's understandable. You come back from a trip and tell me you'd met a woman you wanted to sleep with." To which Quentin defensively replies, "And for damn near a year you looked at me as though I were some kind of monster who could never be trusted again."[3]

Miller tried to integrate the major economic, historical and political themes with the intensely personal ones through the character inspired by Inge Morath, who had endured the difficult and dangerous war years. As a child she "moved to Germany with her parents, Protestant liberals and research scientists. At the outbreak of World War II she was studying languages at Berlin University. When Morath refused to become a Nazi supporter, she was assigned to forced labor, assembling airplane parts at Tempelhof airport, a site that was repeatedly bombed by the Allies. She escaped from Tempelhof when an air raid blew open the gate, and found her way through war-torn Europe back to her family in Austria." Inge had close relatives in Nazi ministries, and had also been a courier for those involved in the unsuccessful plot to kill Hitler in July 1944. But she was not Jewish and was not a survivor of the camps.

The most poorly integrated material in the play came from Miller's experience as he was writing it. In a weirdly jarring and intimate revelation about Inge's first child with Miller – their son Daniel, born in the fall of 1962 – Holga mentions that he had Down's Syndrome and was immediately placed in an institution: "I had a child . . . and it was an idiot, and I ran away." In fact, it was Miller – not Inge – who ran away. Right after Daniel was born, Miller told the producer Robert Whitehead: " 'He isn't right.' . . . Arthur was terribly shaken – he used the term 'mongoloid.' . . . 'I'm going to have the baby put away.' "[4] Daniel was placed in the Southbury Training School, near Roxbury, a home for the mentally retarded. Inge visited him weekly for the next forty years. Miller never did.

The relation of social responsibility to personal (especially survivor's) guilt is a dominant theme in Miller's plays from *All My Sons* and *Death of a Salesman*, through *The Crucible* and *A View from the Bridge*, to *After the Fall*. At the beginning of his early novel *Focus* (1945), the hero, Newman, is awakened in the middle of the night when a woman, assaulted by a drunken man, cries out for help. Hearing her Puerto Rican accent and assuming she's a prostitute, Newman ignores her scream and does not try to help her. *Focus* anticipates the theme of Albert Camus' *The Fall* (1956), which in turn influenced both the title and theme of *After the Fall*. In Camus' novel the confessional narrator is walking along the Seine late at night: "I had already gone some fifty yards when I heard the sound – which, despite the distance, seemed dreadfully loud in the midnight silence – of a body striking the water. . . . I heard a cry, repeated several times, which was going downstream; then it suddenly ceased. . . . I was still listening as I stood motionless. Then, slowly under the rain, I went away. I informed no one."

The Fall discusses the burden of guilt in a world where it is no longer possible to be innocent and where there is no redemption for the guilty. The novel blends the theological fall of man, the physical fall of the drowning woman and the moral fall of the narrator, who (like Newman) refuses to help her. Thinking about himself and Marilyn when discussing the moral choice in Camus' novel, Miller wondered how far a man could be responsible for someone else's life: "what if he had attempted to rescue her, and indeed managed to, and then discovered that he had failed in his mission – to overcome his own egoism which his action may even have expressed; that there were innumerable complications about rescuing somebody as a pure act of love?"

Before his fall from grace, Miller believed he could sustain his love for Marilyn. *After the Fall* portrays the death of their love. The play has essentially the same biblical theme as Milton's *Paradise Lost*: the loss of prelapsarian innocence; the curse of sin, guilt and death; the possibility of salvation. Holga, the resister and survivor of cosmic evil, ultimately redeems Quentin. His mother also suggests the theme of salvation by alluding to Christ's words in John 8:12: "I am the light of the world" and by twice telling her son, you are "a light in the world!"[5]

The Misfits and *After the Fall* are like the heaven and hell panels in a Renaissance diptych. Marilyn was vulnerable, sweet and appealing in the former; neurotic, drugged and destructive in the latter. In *The Misfits* Miller had focused on Roslyn and explained why he'd married Marilyn. In *After the Fall* he focuses on his less devoted and adoring, more defiant and critical self. When he wrote the film script for Marilyn, he had to portray the positive aspects of her character and provide an (ironically) happy ending. In the play, he dramatizes the charming and attractive side of her character when they first met and, five years later, when they married. But he also portrays her irrational, selfish, irresponsible side, her sense of being victimized, her lack of personal responsibility and her inevitable doom. The play's title and hero suggest the emphasis is on Miller himself. The play is about the process of falling and its author is living "after the fall," after his loss of innocence and crushing emotional defeat.

Miller builds on Roslyn's melancholy moods and quaint speech to characterize Maggie. Both women long for their lost mothers; both feel that they're a joke and that people laugh at them. Roslyn uses the uncolloquial "Whereas" to describe the small birds of the desert and people's indifference to whether her dancing is real or fake; Maggie uses this characteristic and slightly pretentious word five times in the play. Like Gay with Roslyn, Quentin tells Maggie that "I almost feel honored to have known you!" and that "Your eyes make me shiver."[6]

Marilyn was alive when Miller began *After the Fall* and had died by the time he finished it. Her death and apotheosis, as well as Barbara Loden's blond wig and imitation of Marilyn's mannerisms, emphasized the play's autobiographical source and the many intriguing parallels between Marilyn and Maggie. In *The Seven Year Itch* the girl, played by Marilyn, keeps her panties in the refrigerator to cool off during the hot summer. In *After the Fall* one of her fans keeps Maggie's "hot" records in the fridge to prevent them from melting. The wounding entry in Miller's private diary, which Marilyn read in England and Maggie discovers in the play, is identical: "The only one I will ever love is my daughter." Miller said that Maggie, like Marilyn, was "a slave to the idea of being victimized" and "had an inexorable lust for destruction."[7]

Quentin's first two scenes with Maggie portray Marilyn's troubled background and appealing qualities. Maggie has never known her father, who abandoned her as an infant and refused to see or even talk to her when she later tracked him down. Her grandmother once tried to smother her with a pillow. She didn't finish high school, but is interested in books and wants to improve herself. Miller captures Marilyn's naïve and childish directness when – in an amusing and charming non sequitur – Maggie says that she'd like to have a dog "if I had a way to keep it, but I don't even have a refrigerator."

Miller had seen how Marilyn's physical beauty and palpitating sexuality made men treat her like a cheap tart and constantly proposition her. In her Marx Brothers' movie, *Love Happy*, Marilyn tells Groucho: "Men keep following me all the time!" and he knowingly replies, "Really? I can't understand why." After Maggie is propositioned in *After the Fall*, Quentin asks: "That happen to you very often?" and she admits, "Pretty often." By contrast Quentin, like Miller, is shy and "polite." He encourages and sympathizes with her instead of trying to seduce her.

Like Marilyn, who'd posed for the notorious nude calendar, Maggie's name floats "in the stench of locker rooms and parlor-car cigar smoke!" She has a similar history of promiscuity and has generously offered herself to callous men who gave her nothing in return. Maggie becomes the pupil of the famous coach Ludwig Reiner (based on Lee Strasberg), and is engaged to Quentin when he appears as a defense lawyer before HUAC (as Marilyn was engaged to Miller when he was subpoenaed). Under Quentin's influence, Maggie adopts left-wing political views and absurdly tells him that the much reviled communists are "for the poor people. Isn't that what you believe?"[8] Maggie's singing at the London Palladium recalls Marilyn's acting with Laurence Olivier in *The Prince and the Showgirl* and singing at Kennedy's birthday party. Maggie does not know how to take care of herself and has no close friends. She's been exploited by agents and lawyers, and has signed several disadvantageous contracts. In a useful summary, a critic wrote that both Marilyn and Maggie "are the illegitimate daughters of disturbed mothers; both are vain, exhibitionistic, neurotic, and infantile, yet idolized and desired by millions; both quit high school, have an affair with a senior professional associate, and are forbidden by his family to visit him on his deathbed; both suffer from addiction to alcohol and tranquilizers, are in psychoanalysis, and work on their chosen craft with a fabled teacher; both end as suicides."

Despite all this (and the blond wig to top it off) the blindly self-absorbed Miller maintained that "he failed to notice in time that the actress who plays the role identified by many playgoers with Marilyn Monroe could so obviously be identified." Shortly before the play opened, Miller nervously told Robert Whitehead, "It just hit me. I'm awfully worried that this is going to seem like a play about Marilyn." The stunned producer inevitably replied, "Of course they're going to think it's a play about Marilyn. How could they not?" Though the connection between Marilyn and Maggie was obvious, Miller looked foolish when he disingenuously insisted in *Life* magazine that Maggie "is not in fact Marilyn Monroe."[9]

In his analysis of Maggie's character, Kazan, noting her change of attitude toward Quentin, wrote that she "feels that Quentin is the first person, the first and only, who has ever aroused in her a sense of worth. And a sense of her potential as a human" being. She is "an orphan looking for support. She . . . [wanted] to join a family, to belong . . . and hoped for a miracle from Quentin (saviour). Then no miracle happened. Quentin didn't live up to *what she thought he was*." In his autobiography, Kazan added that in the play Miller was unusually honest and self-critical: "he put into the mouth of Maggie precisely what Marilyn had thought of him, particularly her scorn for him at the end of their marriage. This character is true and has an interesting dramatic development from adoration to contempt. Art is rough on himself, giving us all that Marilyn said in her disappointment and resentment."[10]

The marriage begins to fall apart halfway through Act Two as Maggie, unstable and insecure, turns on Quentin. She reads his criticism of her character in his private diary and, revolted by his moral superiority, begins to hate him. She becomes jealous of other women and quarrels with her mother-in-law. Though deeply in debt, she's wildly extravagant, and fakes sickness when she needs money but doesn't feel like working. She constantly attacks him, claiming he's emotionally cold and sexually unresponsive; that he doesn't defend her interests and cares only about cash. Though he devotes half his time to her, instead of concentrating on his own work, she blames him for all her betrayals and broken hopes. She forces him to fire an innocent musician. When he protests that "I've fired three others in three other bands," she humiliates him by replying: "Well, so what? You're my husband. You're supposed to do that. Aren't you?" Brutal with her colleagues and employees, she's come a long way from sympathizing with poor people and underdogs.

Maggie begins to add pills to her heavy drinking, and Quentin saves her twice from suicide. She's unable to face the consequences of her actions and demands much more than he's able to give. She wants to die and to destroy him as well. In a dramatic reversal of his earlier love for her, Quentin realizes that he can no longer help her and must try to protect himself. The whole play leads up to this moment of severance, the split that leads to the Fall. In his crucial speech Quentin, finally pushed to the limit of his endurance, urges her to stop acting like a victim and accept responsibility for her faults: "if you could only say, 'I have been cruel. . . . I have been kicked around, but I have been just as inexcusably vicious to others, called my husband idiot in public, I have been utterly selfish despite my generosity, I have been hurt by a long line of men but I have cooperated with my persecutors.'"

After the Fall, Miller's most innovative and underrated work, dramatizes Marilyn's radical change from trusting to suspicious, from adored to contemptible, from saint to succubus. Her transformation is signaled by a cutting-blade metaphor. At first, Quentin protectively tells Maggie, "they're carving you." Later on, she assumes the dominant role and tells him, "you don't see the knives people hide."[11] She begins as a victim, he as a protector; in time she becomes a monster who victimizes him. Finally, unwilling to face her failures and overwhelmed by her demons, Maggie kills herself. In this cathartic play, Miller tried to portray Marilyn, soon after her death and for the first time, with all her contortions of mind and complexity of suffering. He also wanted to justify himself: to show how deeply he had loved her and how cruelly she had treated him. Miller also reaches beyond the merely personal dimensions of the drama to illuminate a recurring pattern in our sexualized entertainment. Actors and singers who achieve great fame remain friendless, lonely, compelled to seek oblivion in drugs and early death. Those whom the pop-culture gods love, die young.

The drama critics resented Miller's astonishing success and glamorous marriage, his years of silence and exalted reputation, his uncharacteristic boldness and lack of restraint. Most critics censured the play as a vulgar, hypocritical and megalomaniacal attack on the martyred actress. His old adversary Robert Brustein, writing in the *New Republic*, believed Miller had exploited and sensationalized Marilyn, and then ungallantly blamed her for their disastrous marriage. Brustein dismissed the play as "a three and one half hour breach of taste, a confessional autobiography of embarrassing explicitness." Maggie begins "as a giddy, simpleminded, generous creature who only wants to love" and develops into "a raging, screaming, suicidal shrew. . . . He has created a shameless piece of tabloid gossip, an act of exhibitionism which makes us all voyeurs." Brustein felt, as Bertrand Russell remarked of D.H. Lawrence's intimate revelations in *Look! We Have Come Through!*, "They may have come through, but I don't see why I should look."

Richard Gilman, another influential critic, agreed that Miller engaged in "self-justification which at any time is repellent but which becomes monstrous in the absence of any intelligence, craft or art." The English playwright Noël Coward, equally severe in his private diary, criticized Miller's personal, intellectual and artistic qualities more than his exploitation of Marilyn:

> The play is a three-and-a-half-hour wail about how cruel life has been to Arthur Miller. What it does *not* mention is that the cruellest blow life has dealt him is that he hasn't a grain of humour. He is capable of writing one or two fairly effective 'theatre' scenes. His philosophy is adolescent and sodden with self-pity. His taste is non-existent. The Marilyn Monroe part of the play is really vulgar beyond belief. Out of all this pretentious, turgid verbosity emerges the character of a silly, dull man with a mediocre mind.

But Coward (who was himself condemned for satirizing friends in his plays) was mistaken when he claimed, "It has, needless to say, been hailed as a masterpiece and treated with the greatest possible reverence."[12]

Miller made matters worse by trying to defend *After the Fall*, and sabotaged himself with his pitiful lamentations and portentous rhetoric. Instead of denying the obvious autobiographical elements, he should have admitted that he began with a personal impulse and transformed it into art. When he said "I honestly feel that I have nothing to complain about," his interlocutor cheekily reminded him, "But you're always complaining." Thinking of O'Neill, Odets and Tennessee Williams, as well as himself, Miller maintained, "The story of American playwrights is . . . celebratory embraces soon followed by rejection or contempt." He tended to blame the critics and whine about the condemnation of his play instead of trying to explain his method and ideas. He told the Italian journalist Oriana Fallaci that he'd been deeply wounded: "I did not expect such a narrow-minded reaction; so cruelly and miserably mean. I did not expect such incredible and degrading short-sightedness."[13] In his *Paris Review* interview he attacked, without vanquishing, his unnamed enemies: "The ironical thing to me was that I heard cries of indignation from various people who had in the lifetime of Marilyn Monroe either exploited her unmercifully . . . or mocked her viciously, or refused to take any of her pretensions seriously." He didn't seem to realize that pretensions could not be taken seriously. But Miller triumphed over his critics by continuing to write serious plays until he was eighty-nine and by leaving an estate worth nearly twenty million dollars.[14]

The critical condemnation of the play permanently damaged Miller's reputation in America, and toward the end of his career prevented his new work from being produced on Broadway. In *After the Fall* Miller may have been narcissistic, self-justifying and provocative, but he made an effective drama out of this fascinating material. He explored his love for Marilyn, their marriage and the reasons for his failure with self-lacerating honesty.

II

Later in life, despite a happy third marriage and successful career as a playwright, Miller, as if probing a wound, returned to his obsession with the ideal and real Marilyn. His marriage to Inge Morath inspired his exploration of the holocaust theme in *After the Fall*, *Incident at Vichy* (1965), *Playing for Time* (1980) and *Broken Glass* (1994). But the last play is also a vehicle for exploring his relationship with Marilyn. In *Broken Glass* she reappears as Sylvia Gellburg, Miller himself is the model for Sylvia's husband, Phillip, and Ralph Greenson is portrayed as Harry Hyman (whose surname is the first name of Marilyn's internist, Hyman Engelberg). The title of the play refers to *Kristallnacht* (the Night of the Broken Glass) on November 9–10, 1938, when the Nazi government encouraged mobs throughout Germany to burn synagogues, break the windows of Jewish stores and ransack Jewish homes. On that violent night 30,000 Jews were arrested and sent to concentration camps. A newspaper photograph, showing elderly bearded Jews forced to crawl on their hands and knees and to scrub filthy gutters with toothbrushes, has traumatized Sylvia. She suffers from a psychosomatic illness that has paralyzed both legs.

Dr. Greenson was in his early fifties when he treated Marilyn. Dr. Hyman is "in his early fifties, a healthy, rather handsome man, a determined scientific idealist." Greenson received his medical education in Berne; Hyman got his medical degree in Heidelberg. Both doctors see patients in their homes and use extremely unconventional methods. Hyman, like Greenson, admits, "I don't know. I'm out of my depth! I can't help you." But Hyman is actually in love with Sylvia – a warm, buxom woman with a strong body and beautiful (though inert) legs – and openly expresses his sexual desire for her. He excites her by ecstatically declaring, "I haven't been this moved by a woman in a very long time," that "Your body strength must be marvelous. The depth of your flesh must be wonderful." Though Sylvia has not slept with her impotent husband in twenty years, Hyman tells her, "I want you to imagine we've made love" and kisses her on the mouth. One scene ends as she "lets her knees spread apart."[15]

Like Marilyn, Sylvia is hypersensitive to the suffering of others and fears she'll be put away in an insane asylum. Her paralysis is a way to harm both herself and her husband. At one point Miller conflates Phillip Gellburg's authoritarian behavior at his grandmother's funeral with DiMaggio's imperious behavior at Marilyn's funeral. Hyman's wife describes him as "a dictator, you know. . . . He stands outside the funeral parlor and decides who's going to sit with who in the limousines for the cemetery. 'You sit with him, you sit with her.' And they obey him like he owned the funeral!"

Like Miller with Marilyn, Gellburg realizes that Sylvia is "trying to destroy me!" Thoroughly disillusioned with the pernicious doctor (as Miller was with Greenson), he screams at Hyman, "Since you came around she looks down at me like a miserable piece of shit!" At the end of *Broken Glass* Gellburg, looking into the mirror of unbroken glass, begs Sylvia "not to blame me anymore."[16] In a dramatization of what might have happened to Miller himself if he'd stayed with Marilyn, Gellburg dies, Sylvia walks – and recovers at his expense.

III

Marilyn makes a startling appearance as Cathy-May, the eponymous hero's dead lover, in Miller's little-known late play, *Mr. Peters' Connections* (1999). Harry Peters, a retired airline pilot, turns up in an abandoned New York nightclub. As people from his past appear and disappear, he tries to bring together the strands of his experience and make sense of his life. Cathy-May appears twice, with and without clothes, and seems more vivid to him when dead than when she was alive. Miller's italicized descriptions, interwoven with his characters' comments, portray her as sexually alluring and irresistible, as well as naïvely self-deprecating: "*Cathy-May comes to him; she is naked, in high heels; a big smile breaks onto his face as she approaches. She is giggling.* Ah yes, how proud of your body." In her second appearance she's dressed in virginal white and even more seductive and alluring than when naked: "*Cathy-May enters. She is in a tight white miniskirt, transparent blouse, carries a white purse. . . . and wears a dog collar. . . .* Case I get lost" – though it's not clear where she lives and to whom she belongs.

When Peters sees her, his passion flares up once again. Cathy-May's ex-husband Larry (crudely based on DiMaggio) and Peters' brother Calvin both respond, as Miller himself did, with gustatory and almost orgasmic lust: "She's juicy. A prime sirloin. A ripe pomegranate. A Spanish blood orange. An accordion-pleated fuck. . . . She looks perfect. With a white angora sweater. And pink plastic spike-heel shoes. A little on the pudgy side but not too fat . . . just . . . you know, perfect." Cathy-May, a lost soul who has no identity or real life of her own, merely exists as Peters' sexual fantasy. He remembers that she'd once loved him, but she's now forgotten all about him. He wonders if her past anger has subsided and if, under the right conditions, their love could have succeeded. Despite her tarted up appearance, Peters insists "she's not really a common slut."

Marilyn was notorious for wearing no underwear; Cathy-May's underwear has been stolen, sold or given away. At the end of the play her ex-husband Larry expresses his outrage at her exhibitionism – an allusion to DiMaggio's outrage when Marilyn's skirt flew up to her waist and exposed her panties in *The Seven Year Itch*. Though no longer married to Cathy-May, Larry thinks he still owns her and asks "Where is your underwear, stupid!!" Obsessed by the need to publicly humiliate and symbolically rape the woman who's dominated him with her sexual power, Larry acts out the violence that Miller would never dare to express. Larry throws her down on the floor and exposes her sexual parts: "*With a sweeping gesture he sends her onto her back, legs in the air, and looks under her skirt; she is struggling ineffectually to free herself.* You see underwear, Mister? Look, everybody! *He is trying to spread her legs apart.* . . . Take a look at this! How can this belong to anybody!"[17]

Mr. Peters' Connections is more bitter and savage than Miller's previous works about Marilyn, and Peters' response to Cathy-May suggests Shakespeare's Sonnet 129, in which passion degrades man's soul: "The expense of spirit in a waste of shame / Is lust in action." Peters realizes that his overwhelming physical desire for Cathy-May has deceived him about the possibility of loving and living with her. Larry's brutal and vengeful anger, her shameless dress and provocative behavior, shatter Peters' idealized image. She's a temptress, if not a slut; she's corrupted by the phony world of the movies and can't really belong to any man. Like a damned soul in a gothic tale, she destroys anyone who gets close to her, but begs men to "pity the monster."

Miller also alludes to Marilyn in his late story "The Bare Manuscript" (2002), in which Clement, a prize-winning but now blocked novelist, tries to spark his creativity by paying a woman to let him write a story with a felt-tip pen on her naked body. Like Monroe, Clement's wife Lena had an insane parent who was confined to an asylum, and she herself has had several abortions. Subject to violent mood swings, she's confused about her identity and doesn't even understand why she's alive. Despite all these problems, Clement still loves her. In *The Misfits*, Gay Langland says to Roslyn, "You shine in my eyes." In "The Bare Manuscript," Clement tells Lena, "you glow like a spirit." Clement writes his story as "a kind of paean to her as she once had been" and optimistically wonders – as Miller did when he wrote *The Misfits* for Marilyn and as Peters does when Cathy-May reappears – "would she recognize herself and be reconciled?"[18] Miller's love for Marilyn, and the pain she inflicted, never died.

IV

The black comedy *Finishing the Picture*, Miller's last play and last attempt to portray her character, ended his half-century fascination with Marilyn. Performed at the Goodman Theatre in Chicago in October

2004, four months before his death in February 2005, it was criticized as too talky, repetitive and undramatic. It never reached Broadway
and has not been published, but it does reveal the interesting backstory about the making of *The Misfits*.

The play has no cowboys or mustangs, no actors based on Clark
Gable or Montgomery Clift. The Marilyn character, who did not
appear in "The Misfits" story and took centerstage in *The Misfits* film,
is central to the action but almost entirely silent in *Finishing the Picture*.
Kitty, a dysfunctional actress with a starring role in a movie, is unable
to work during the filming. Her erratic behavior threatens to close
down the over-schedule and over-budget production. As with *After
the Fall*, Miller denied that the play was about Marilyn. This time, as
if to prove his point, he made the heroine a brunette instead of a
blonde.

Kitty speaks a few words offstage in Act One, and doesn't actually
appear until two-thirds of the way through the play. She then lies
drugged and naked in bed, either silent and stupefied or screaming
(like Marilyn) at her husband. She speaks only one more offstage
word, an unconvincing "Yes." She's a ghostly presence, stripped down
to her elemental weakness, and has to be rehabilitated. As Kitty wanders
naked through the hotel corridors, she's rescued and put into the
producer's bedroom. All the characters try to get her out of bed and
back to work. They all plead with Kitty, who doesn't answer them
directly: her responses are implied in their speeches. Everyone sees
something different in her striking yet opaque personality and everyone
fails to reach her. She has no real identity, and needs pills much more
than people.

Like Kitty, the characters are transparently based on real models.
Phil Ochsner, the sympathetic producer (played by Stacy Keach), came
from the trucking business – just as the real producer, Frank Taylor,
came from the publishing business – when his company merged with
Bedlam Pictures. (*Ochsner* in German is a driver of oxen, a precursor
to a driver of trucks.) His character is based on both Taylor and Miller.
Edna Meyers, Kitty's devoted personal assistant, has an impulsive affair
with the widowed Ochsner, which suggests Inge's love affair with
Miller. Paul (who has no surname and was played by Matthew Modine)
is the screenwriter as well as Kitty's disillusioned and defeated husband.

Derek Clemson, the director, is obviously based on John Huston.
Edna says he's "very macho and doesn't really relate to women."

He loves horses and has directed Kitty's first important film (Marilyn's *The Asphalt Jungle*). He courts danger by losing thousands of dollars when gambling all night and by smuggling Pre-Columbian artifacts from Mexico. Terry Case, the cameraman, is based on Russell Metty. He carefully examines Kitty's unfocused eyes, her peculiar stare and characteristically "spooky underwater" look to see if she can perform, then concentrates his lens on her "perfect ass."

Miller finally retaliates by satirizing Lee and Paula Strasberg. The acting coach Flora Fassinger is dressed entirely in black and hangs several watches around her neck. Egotistical, foolish and inept, she's mainly interested in the size of her hotel suite and her chauffeured limousine. A Tartuffian hypocrite and perfect fraud, she's not only failed to help Kitty, but also confused and depressed her. Flora's husband Jerome, Kitty's New York acting guru, wears a comical cowboy outfit (as Lee actually did) for his cameo appearance in Nevada. He agrees, for a first-class airplane ticket and an exorbitant per diem fee, to try to encourage Kitty. But he repeatedly says he will not take responsibility for her failure to perform. Realizing disaster is imminent, he immediately flies back to New York. Like Flora, Jerome has hurt rather than helped Kitty by cultivating her pathological reliance on him and by making her intensely self-conscious. As Terry Case says, "You had a bird here who naturally sang. Then they started to teach her how to sing, and so naturally she can't sing anymore." By making the Strasbergs absurd, Miller missed the chance to portray their malign influence on Marilyn.

As Phil Ochsner searches for a solution to their problem, each character suggests a different way to help Kitty. Edna Meyers believes she needs consideration and kindness, Paul thinks she needs love, Derek Clemson appeals to her sense of honor, Terry Case urges toughness and threats, Flora Fassinger wants her to rest, Jerome encourages her with the inspiring example of the great Italian actress Eleanora Duse. (In *Timebends*, Miller records Marilyn ordering him "to sit down right now and listen to a tape of Lee's lecture on Eleanora Duse.") Ochsner has three choices: rousing Kitty so she can immediately return to work (the entire crew has been summoned and is waiting in the lobby), letting her rest in the hospital for a week or shutting down the picture. Saving the film means saving Kitty–Marilyn. If they shut down the picture she won't be able to get insurance and will never again be able to work.

As Paul tells Derek, it might even drive her to suicide: "That would devastate her. It could kill her."

Miller subjects Kitty's haunted character to intense scrutiny. Derek Clemson says, "She is a case of terminal disappointment. With herself, her husband, the movies, the United States, the world." Alluding to the title of his play of 1994, Miller writes: "She's had a frightful life . . . she's been stepping on broken glass since she could walk." Kitty can never recover from her childhood fears of being exploited, mocked and abandoned: "She has ghosts sitting on her chest; ghosts of things she's done, or [have] been done to her; she can't breathe, can't sleep, can't wake [without] fleeing the hounds of hell."[19] Life has Kitty by the throat. She thinks she's a fake, wonders if she really exists, and feels as if somebody has got inside her and stolen her identity. Fearful, resentful and angry, she has no one to depend on. She's tormented by a sense of "spiritual outrage" and by the "condition of her soul." Propelled by a monstrous but well justified mistrust of people and taking some kind of "power trip," she tries to humiliate everyone.

Psychoanalysis, encouraged by her teachers, has also confused and depressed her. She's left two of the best analysts in the country baffled and "talking to themselves." Terry Case bitterly calls her treatment "the world's most expensive fertilizer." Miller doesn't mention that her analysts, like her internist, freely prescribed the addictive pills that killed her. Kitty's character is fully explored, but since she rarely speaks, everything we learn about her comes secondhand from the people around her.

Insomniac, unpleasant, manipulative, irrational and frightening, Kitty takes no responsibility for herself and allows no one to take responsibility for her. She can't stop blaming people and it's impossible to stop her from destroying herself. All Paul's love cannot help Kitty and all her love for him has, through suspicion and mistrust, turned to hate. Fatalistic and beaten, Paul finally accepts the inevitable and is even relieved that their marriage is finished. In his final speech, he confesses to the character based on Inge:

> She doesn't *like* me, Edna. And how could she – I didn't save her, I didn't do the miracle I kind of promised. And she didn't save me, as she promised. So nothing *moved*, you know? It was like we kept endlessly introducing ourselves to one another. I'm afraid of her now – I have no idea what she's going to do next.

I wonder if maybe there was just too much hope; we drank it, swam in it. And for fear of losing it didn't dare look inside. A sad story.

The crisis is temporarily resolved at the conclusion of the play. Kitty goes into the hospital for a week. Phil Ochsner and Edna Meyers, who appear together at the beginning and the end, have a promising future. As in real life, the forest fire, which blackened the skies of California and Nevada and knocked out the power in Reno, has subsided and is now under control. The emergency is over and the sky is clear and bright. Terry Case claims the fire "invigorates the seed buried in the soil" and "makes the seeds germinate." But the analogy between the natural and personal disaster, between putting out the fire and rescuing the actress, seems forced. Marilyn's mental illness was far more complicated than a forest fire. She managed to finish *The Misfits*, but it was followed by death, not rebirth.

Brian Dennehy, who acted in several of Miller's plays, said the subject of *Finishing the Picture* was Marilyn's "incredible stardom and how the actress became a commodity, consumed by everyone around her, including the writer. They used her to achieve success and she could not meet their oppressive demands. Miller didn't fully under-stand Marilyn's impossible situation, and suffered a terrible strain while trying to portray his own culpability."[20]

In his work Miller often returned to the most painful period of his life: his failure to unite the genius and the goddess, intelligence and beauty, fame and celebrity. His three major works on Marilyn amount to a dramatic trilogy – *The Misfits*, *After the Fall* and *Finishing the Picture*. They attempt to understand her character and explain why their marriage failed. They present an increasingly dark view of the actress and portray the high cost of creativity in an exploitative world. In the end, the miracle never happened. But she remained his tragic muse and her character, exalted and tormented, lived on in his work. Like a burnt-out star, her light, though extinct, continues to shine.

Appendix: Marilyn's Illnesses and Hospitalizations

1930s: tonsillectomy in childhood

Before 1946: 1st and 2nd suicide attempts by gas and by sleeping pills

June 1946: trench mouth after extraction of wisdom teeth, Las Vegas General Hospital

June 1946: measles, Las Vegas General Hospital

late 1940s–1950s: twelve abortions

December 1950: two plastic surgeries on nose and jaw

December 1950: 3rd suicide attempt, after Johnny Hyde's death

Spring 1951: abortion (with Elia Kazan)

April 28, 1952: appendicitis, Cedars of Lebanon Hospital, Los Angeles

1954: 1st bronchitis, Cedars of Lebanon, LA

November 6–12, 1954: 1st endometriosis, Cedars of Lebanon, LA

April 1956: 2nd bronchitis, during shooting of *Bus Stop*, St. Vincent's, LA

August 19, 1956: 1st miscarriage (with Miller)

August 1957: ectopic pregnancy (with Miller), Doctor's Hospital, New York. 4th suicide attempt

Fall 1958: 5th suicide attempt. Taken to hospital by Paula Strasberg

December 17, 1958: 2nd miscarriage (with Miller), Polyclinic Hospital, NY. 6th suicide attempt

June 22–26, 1959: surgery on Fallopian tubes, Lenox Hill Hospital, NY

August 28–September 4, 1960: drug addiction and nervous breakdown during *Misfits*, Westside Hospital, LA

February 7–10, 1961: 7th suicide attempt and nervous breakdown after divorce from Miller, Payne-Whitney, NY; and February 11–March 5, 1961: Neurological Institute, Columbia University Presbyterian Medical Center, NY

May 1961: 2nd chronic endometriosis, Cedars of Lebanon, LA

June 28–July 11, 1961: gallbladder removed, Polyclinic Hospital, NY —In hospital five times in the last ten months

July 20, 1962: 3rd chronic endometriosis, Cedars of Lebanon, LA

August 5, 1962: commits suicide by overdose of barbiturates

Notes

One: First Encounter

1. Arthur Miller, FBI file, February 19, 1951, p. 65; Arthur Miller, *Timebends* (New York, 1987), pp. 308; 303; Mel Gussow, *Conversations with Miller* (New York, 2002), p. 145.

2. Elia Kazan, *A Life* (New York, 1988), pp. 404; 409; Fred Guiles, *Legend: The Life and Death of Marilyn Monroe* (1984; Chelsea, Michigan, 1991), p. 173.

3. Christopher Bigsby, ed., *Remembering Arthur Miller* (London, 2005), p. 263; Joshua Logan, "Will Acting Spoil Marilyn Monroe?," *Movie Stars, Real People, and Me* (New York, 1978), p. 62; Kazan, *Life*, pp. 365, 367; 402.

4. Donald Spoto, *Marilyn Monroe* (New York, 1993), pp. 461–462; Guiles, *Legend*, p. 173; Kazan, *Life*, p. 413.

   A great deal of biographical material about Marilyn has disappeared. Her first husband, James Dougherty, destroyed the 200 letters she wrote to him when he was serving overseas in World War II. Miller's love letters to Marilyn – along with all her papers and her famous Red Diary – mysteriously vanished on the night of her death. Her psychiatrist destroyed all her confessional tapes, made at his request, before he died. There's no trace of Marilyn, despite her intimate relations with John and Robert Kennedy, in the Kennedy Library in Boston. Milton Greene's son (in a conversation with me on December 15, 2007) claimed that the vast archive of Monroe-Greene Productions had been stolen by a Monroe scholar. This loss of valuable evidence has left many unanswered questions about her life as well as many wild conspiracy theories about the cause of her death.

Two: Marilyn's Traumatic Childhood

1. Christopher Rand, *Los Angeles: The Ultimate City* (New York, 1967), p. 140; Marilyn Monroe, *My Story* (1974; New York, 1976), p. 10; See Maurice Zolotow, *Marilyn Monroe: The Uncensored Biography* (1960; New York, 1961), p. 5; Monroe, *My Story*, p. 11.

2. Natasha Lytess, as told to Jane Wilkie, "My Years with Marilyn," unpublished memoir, Harry Ransom Humanities Research Center, University of Texas, Austin, pp. 9–10; Sidney Skolsky, "Miss Caswell Calling," *Don't Get Me Wrong – I Love Hollywood* (New York, 1975), p. 221; Raymond Chandler, *Farewell, My Lovely* (1940; New York, 1992), pp. 25–26; Adam Victor, *The Marilyn Encyclopedia* (Woodstock, New York, 1999), p. 40.

3. Berniece Baker Miracle and Mona Rae Miracle, *My Sister Marilyn* (Chapel Hill, N.C., 1994), p. 7; James Dougherty, *The Secret Happiness of Marilyn Monroe* (Chicago, 1974), p. 88; André de Dienes, *Marilyn Mon Amour* (New York, 1985), p. 69; Guiles, *Legend*, p. 197.

4. Timothy Hacsi, *Second Home: Orphan Asylums and Poor Families in America* (Cambridge, Mass., 1997), pp. 213–214; Leroy Ashby, *Endangered Children: Dependence, Neglect, and Abuse in American History* (New York, 1997), pp. 104; 108, 119.

5. Oscar Wilde, *The Importance of Being Earnest* (1895), *Plays* (London, 1954), p. 267; Charles Dickens, "Autobiographical Fragment," in Edgar Johnson, *Charles Dickens: His Triumph and Tragedy* (New York, 1952), 1:34; Rudyard Kipling, "Baa Baa, Black Sheep" (1888), *Best Short Stories of Rudyard Kipling*, ed. Jeffrey Meyers (New York, 1987), p. 43.

6. Zolotow, *Marilyn Monroe*, p. 15; Monroe, *My Story*, p. 40; Charles Chaplin, *My Autobiography* (New York, 1964), p. 31.

7. Eileen Simpson, *Orphans: Real and Imaginary* (1987; New York, 1990), pp. 14, 165; 30, 25–26; 253.

8. Wolfson's "Notes on Marilyn Monroe," Margaret Herrick Library,

American Academy of Motion Picture Arts and Sciences, Beverly Hills, California; Monroe, *My Story*, p. 18; Ashby, *Endangered Children*, p. 118.

9. Monroe, *My Story*, pp. 20–21; Hans Lembourn, *Diary of a Lover of Marilyn Monroe*, trans. Hallberg Hallmundsson (1977; New York, 1979), p. 79; Monroe, *My Story*, p. 26.

10. Robert Mitchum, Introduction to Matthew Smith, *The Men Who Murdered Marilyn* (London, 1996), p. 1; Lena Pepitone and William Stadiem, *Marilyn Monroe Confidential* (1979; New York, 1980), p. 78; Shelley Winters, *Shelley II: The Middle of My Century* (New York, 1989), p. 32.

11. Dougherty, *Secret Happiness*, pp. 37, 45–46; 76; Monroe, *My Story*, p. 28; Guiles, *Legend*, p. 331; Spoto, *Marilyn Monroe*, pp. 78–79.

12. Letters in James Haspiel, *Marilyn: The Ultimate Look at the Legend* (New York, 1991), pp. 12, 13; 14; Victor, *Marilyn Encyclopedia*, p. 60.

13. Anthony Summers, *Goddess: The Secret Lives of Marilyn Monroe* (New York, 1985), p. 14; David Conover, *Finding Marilyn: A Romance* (New York, 1981), p. 38; Dougherty, *Secret Happiness*, p. 89.

Three: A Star is Born

1. Monroe, *My Story*, pp. 41, 42; Victor, *Marilyn Encyclopedia*, p. 279; Guiles, *Legend*, p. 96.

2. Michael Conway and Mark Ricci, *The Films of Marilyn Monroe* (Secaucus, N.J., 1964), p. 10; Edwin Hoyt, *Marilyn: The Tragic Venus* (New York, 1965), p. 179; Dennis Hale and Jonathan Eisen, *The California Dream* (New York, 1968), pp. 206; 223.

3. Peter Bogdanovich, "Marilyn Monroe," *Who the Hell's In It: Portraits and Conversations* (New York, 2004), p. 484; James Bacon, *Hollywood is a Four Letter Town* (Chicago, 1976), p. 134; Summers, *Goddess*, p. 93.

4. Lytess, "My Years with Marilyn," p. 20; Gloria Steinem, *Marilyn* (New York, 1986), p. 82; Lytess, "My Years with Marilyn," pp. 2, 5.

5. Charles Marowitz, *The Other Chekhov: A Biography of Michael Chekhov* (New York, 2004), pp. 214–215; Victor, *Marilyn Encyclopedia*, p. 53; Marowitz, *The Other Chekhov*, p. 211.

6. Monroe, *My Story*, pp. 77–78; Kazan, *Life*, pp. 405; 247; Monroe, *My Story*, pp. 92; 104; Gary Carey, with Joseph Mankiewicz, *More About "All About Eve"* (New York, 1972), p. 77.

7. W. R. Burnett, *The Asphalt Jungle* (New York, 1949), pp. 56–57; Letters from Joseph Breen to Louis Mayer, October 6 and September 26, 1949, John Huston papers, Herrick Library.

8. Letter from Sterling Hayden to John Huston, December 26, 1949; Letter from Howard Hawks to Huston, March 27, 1950; Letter from Budd Schulberg to Huston, August 30, 1950, Huston papers, Herrick Library.

9. Carey and Mankiewicz, *More About "All About Eve"*, p. 75; George Sanders, *Memoirs of a Professional Cad* (New York, 1960), pp. 70–71; Kenneth Geist, *Pictures Will Talk: The Life and Films of Joseph L. Mankiewicz* (New York, 1978), p. 170; Carey and Mankiewicz, *More About "All About Eve"*, pp. 79; 78.

10. Rainer Maria Rilke, *Letters to a Young Poet*, trans. M. D. Herter Norton (1903–08; New York, 1963), pp. 30; 38–39; 69; 61; Rainer Maria Rilke, "Archaic Torso of Apollo," *Translations from the Poetry*, trans. M. D. Herter Norton (New York, 1938), p. 181; Interview with Curtice Taylor, New York, December 10, 2007. Marilyn's topless photo appears in *Marilyn Monroe and the Camera*, with an interview by Georges Belmont (Boston, 1989), p. 47.

11. Douglas Miller and Marion Nowak, *The Fifties: The Way We Really Were* (Garden City, N.Y., 1977), pp. 320, 321, 314.

12. Robert Frost, "The Death of the Hired Man" (1914), *Poetry* (New York, 1975), p. 38; Ryan, in Zolotow, *Monroe*, p. 101; Lang, in Guiles, *Legend*, p. 193; Graham McCann, *Marilyn Monroe* (New Brunswick, N.J., 1988), p. 93.

13. William Wellman, Jr., "Howard Hawks: The Distance Runner," *Focus on Howard Hawks*, ed. Joseph McBride (Englewood Cliffs, N.J., 1972), p. 8; Niven Busch, in *Backstory: Interviews with Screenwriters of Hollywood's Golden Age*, ed. Pat McGilligan (Berkeley, 1986), p. 94; Victor, *Marilyn Encyclopedia*, p. 186; Todd McCarthy, *Howard Hawks: The Grey Fox of Hollywood* (New York, 1977), pp. 498; 499.

14. Bacon, *Hollywood is a Four Letter Town*, p. 145; Pete Martin, "Did Acting Spoil Marilyn Monroe?," *Pete Martin Calls On* (New York, 1962), p. 170; Carl Rollyson, *Marilyn Monroe: The Life of an Actress* (Ann Arbor, 1986), p. 59.

15. McCarthy, *Howard Hawks*, pp. 505, 506; Bacall, in Nora Johnson, *Flashback on Nunnally Johnson* (Garden City, N.Y., 1979), p. 210; Lauren Bacall, *By Myself* (New York, 1978), p. 229; Nunnally

Johnson, *Letters*, ed. Dorris Johnson and Ellen Leventhal (New York, 1981), p. 106; Johnson, in Norman Mailer, *Marilyn: A Biography* (New York, 1975), p. 34.

16. Summers, *Goddess*, p. 90; Guiles, *Legend*, p. 228; Zanuck, in Charles Feldman papers, American Film Institute, Los Angeles.
17. Nathanael West, *The Day of the Locust* (1939; New York, 1969), pp. 103, 68, 157, 158–159.

Four: Image and Identity

1. Daphne Merkin, "Platinum Pain," *New Yorker*, 74 (February 8, 1999), 72; Arnold Ludwig, "The Real Marilyn," *How Do We Know Who We Are?: A Biography of the Self* (New York, 1997), pp. 29–31; Summers, *Goddess*, p. 139.
2. Miller, *Timebends*, p. 436; Jack Cardiff, *The Magic Hour: The Life of a Cameraman* (London, 1996), p. 201; C. David Heymann, "Marilyn," *RFK: A Candid Biography of Robert F. Kennedy* (New York, 1998), p. 310; Cindy Adams, "Marilyn," *Lee Strasberg: The Imperfect Genius of the Actors Studio* (Garden City, N.Y., 1980), pp. 258–259.
3. Spoto, *Marilyn Monroe*, p. 174.
   Her agents, for example, were Harry Lipton at National Artists (1946–48), Johnny Hyde at William Morris (1949–50), Charles Feldman at Famous Artists (1951–55) and Lew Wasserman at Music Corporation of America (1955–62). Miller had the same agent, Kay Brown of MCA, for forty years.
4. Ezra Goodman, "The Girl with Three Blue Eyes," *The Fifty Year Decline and Fall of Hollywood* (New York, 1961), p. 233; Richard Meryman, "Fame Can Go By," *Life*, August 3, 1962, reprinted in Rollyson, *Marilyn Monroe*, p. 209; Mailer, *Marilyn*, pp. 204; 174; Guiles, *Legend*, pp. 283–284.
5. Winters, *Shelley II*, p. 108; George Masters and Norma Lee Browning, "To Killer George–Marilyn," *The Masters Way to Beauty* (New York, 1977), pp. 82–83; Joseph McBride, ed., *Hawks on Hawks* (Berkeley, 1982), p. 124; de Dienes, *Marilyn Mon Amour*, p. 129.
6. Strasberg, *Marilyn and Me*, p. 9; Spoto, *Marilyn Monroe*, p. 188; Strasberg, *Marilyn and Me*, p. 78.
7. Zolotow, *Marilyn Monroe*, p. 92. Christie's auction catalogue, *The Personal Property of Marilyn Monroe* (New York, October 28 and

29, 1999), pp. 346–347, lists books by Dostoyevsky, Flaubert, Lewis Carroll, Freud, Shaw, Conrad, Proust, Mann, Joyce, Lawrence, O'Neill, Fitzgerald, Hemingway, Greene, Odets, Camus, Tennessee Williams, Ellison, Kerouac, Styron and many others.

8. Miller, *Timebends*, p. 241; Sam Shaw and Norman Rosten, *Marilyn Among Friends* (New York, 1987), p. 191; Norman Rosten, *Marilyn: A Very Personal Story* (1974; London, 1980) p.55; Christie's, *Personal Property*, p. 345.

9. Masters, *Masters Way to Beauty*, p. 72; Wilder, in Hoyt, *Marilyn*, p. 156; Charlotte Chandler, *Nobody's Perfect. Billy Wilder: A Personal Biography* (New York, 2002), p. 182.

10. Roger Taylor, ed., *Marilyn Monroe in Her Own Words* (New York, 1983), p. 114; Neil Grant, ed., *Monroe: In Her Own Words* (New York, 1991), p. 33; Tina Brown, *The Diana Chronicles* (New York, 2007), p. 387; Eunice Murray, *Marilyn: The Last Months* (New York, 1975), p. 23; Brown, *Diana Chronicles*, p. 238.

11. Brown, *Diana Chronicles*, pp. 384; 6; 290; 200.

12. Rosten, *Marilyn*, p. 24; Meryman, "Fame Can Go By," in Rollyson, *Marilyn Monroe*, pp. 205–206; Brown, *Diana Chronicles*, p. 387.

13. Meryman, "Fame Can Go By," in Rollyson, *Marilyn Monroe*, p. 211; *The Ivan Moffat File*, ed. Gavin Lambert (New York, 2004), p. 260; Peter Manso, *Mailer: His Life and Times* (New York, 1985), p. 543.

Beginning with Jim Dougherty (1942), there were (in approximate order) lovers when she was a model: David Conover (1944) and André de Dienes (1946); breaking into movies: the actor John Carroll, Natasha Lytess, Fred Karger, Joseph Schenck, Harry Cohn, Johnny Hyde (all 1948); leading up to her second marriage: Tony Curtis (1949), Elia Kazan and Arthur Miller (both 1951), Nico Minardos and Joe DiMaggio (both 1952), Billy Travilla and Milton Greene (both 1953); after her second divorce: the voice coach Hal Schaefer and Frank Sinatra (both 1954); before marrying Miller: Marlon Brando, Yul Brynner and the wealthy New York businessman Henry Rosenfeld (all 1955); after Miller: Yves Montand (1960), Charles Feldman and the Mexican actor José Bolaños (both 1961), John Kennedy and Robert Kennedy (both 1962).

14. Halsman, in *Marilyn Monroe: A Composite View*, ed. Edward Wagenknecht (Philadelphia, 1969), p. 64; Strasberg, *Marilyn and Me*, p. 179; Mailer, *Marilyn*, p. 102; Strasberg, *Marilyn and Me*, p. 144; Steinem, *Marilyn*, p. 157.

15. Seymour Hersh, *The Dark Side of Camelot* (Boston, 1997), p. 104; Randall Riese and Neil Hitchens, *The Unabridged Marilyn: Her Life from A to Z* (New York, 1987), p. 476; de Dienes, in Goodman, *Fifty Year Decline*, p. 224; Masters, *Masters Way to Beauty*, p. 69.

16. Travilla, Minardos and Carmen, in Summers, *Goddess*, pp. 82–83; 69; 204.

Five: Joe DiMaggio

1. Monroe, *My Story*, pp. 125; 126; Gay Talese, "The Silent Season of a Hero," *Esquire*, 66 (July 1966), 43; Summers, *Goddess*, pp. 99–100; Mailer, *Marilyn*, p. 134.

2. Roger Kahn, *Joe and Marilyn* (1986; New York, 1988), p. 280; *The Indianhead*: 2nd U.S. Infantry Division (Korea), February 25, 1954, pp. 2–3; Photographer and Marilyn, in Spoto, *Marilyn Monroe*, pp. 265–266; 223; Pepitone, *Monroe Confidential*, pp. 32–33.

3. Victor, *Marilyn Encyclopedia*, p. 138; Letter from Ben Hecht to Gregson Bautzer, August 11, 1954; Letter from Rose Hecht to Marilyn's lawyer Loyd Wright, June 2, 1954; Jeffrey Meyers, *Somerset Maugham: A Life* (New York, 2004), p. 247; Letter from Rose Hecht to Ken McCormick, June 7, 1954; Letter from McCormick to Rose Hecht, July 30, 1954, Newberry Library, Chicago.

4. Barbara Leaming, *Marilyn Monroe* (New York, 1988), p. 87; George Barris, *Marilyn: Her Life in Her Own Words: Marilyn Monroe's Revealing Last Words and Photographs* (1995; New York, 2001), p. 106; Kahn, *Joe and Marilyn*, p. 284.

5. Compare George Axelrod's play, *The Seven Year Itch* (New York, 1953), p. 87, in which Ewell imagines a man covering his wife with kisses: "Inwardly, downwardly, pulsating, striving, now together, ending and unending, now, now, now!" and Hemingway's "Fathers and Sons" (1933), *Short Stories* (New York, 1953), p. 497, in which Nick Adams makes love to the Indian girl Trudy: "tightly, sweetly, moistly, lovely, tightly, achingly, fully, finally, unendingly, never-endingly, never-to-endingly, suddenly ended."

6. Censored lines, in Yona McDonough, *All the Available Light: A Marilyn Monroe Reader* (New York, 2002), p. 57. The first two photos are reproduced in this book; the third in *Playboy*, December 2005, p. 78.

7. Dougherty, in Spoto, *Marilyn Monroe*, p. 84; Wilder, in Earl Wilson, "Marilyn: Mad and Marvelous," *The Show Business That Nobody Knows* (Chicago, 1971), pp. 297–298; Wilder, in McCann, *Marilyn Monroe*, pp. 100-101.

8. *Pete Martin Calls On*, p. 184; Zolotow, *Marilyn Monroe*, p. 228; Talese, "Silent Season of a Hero," p. 45.

9. Richard Ben Cramer, *Joe DiMaggio: The Hero's Life* (New York, 2000), p. 373; Miracle, *My Sister Marilyn*, p. 161; Leaming, *Marilyn Monroe*, p. 379.

10. Gussow, *Conversations with Miller*, p. 146; *Pete Martin Calls On*, pp. 174; 157.

11. Lois Banner, *American Beauty* (New York, 1983), p. 284; Guiles, *Legend*, p. 218; Goodman, *Fifty Year Decline*, pp. 219–220.

12. Wagenknecht, ed., *Marilyn Monroe*, p. 156; *Pete Martin Calls On*, pp. 186; 160; Fyodor Dostoyevsky, *The Brothers Karamazov*, trans. Constance Garnett (New York, 1943), p. 443; Logan, *Movie Stars, Real People, and Me*, p.46.

13. Lytess, "My Years with Marilyn," p. 6; Robert Stack, *Straight Shooting* (New York, 1980), p. 184.

14. Letter from Ray Stark to Charles Feldman, December 1, 1953; Letters to Feldman, June 21 and 29, 1954; Letter from Jack Gordean to Feldman, July 1954; Samuel Shaw to Feldman, as recorded by Feldman's secretary Grace Dobish, April 2, 1955, Charles Feldman papers, American Film Institute.

15. Mailer, *Marilyn*, p. 172; Phone talk with Joshua Greene, December 15, 2007; Zolotow, *Marilyn Monroe*, pp. 242–243.

16. Joseph Persico, *Edward R. Murrow: An American Original* (1988; New York, 1990), p. 352; Letter from Darryl Zanuck to Charles Feldman, April 14, 1955, American Film Institute; Guiles, *Legend*, pp. 261; 309.

Six: Miller's Path to Fame

1. Matthew Roudané, ed., *Conversations with Arthur Miller* (Jackson, Miss., 1987) p. 185; Miller, *Timebends*, p. 4; Martin Gottfried, *Arthur Miller: His Life and Work* (New York, 2003) pp. 5; 8.

2. Miller, *Timebends*, p. 113; Roudané, *Conversations with Arthur Miller*, p. 311; Miller, *Timebends*, p. 213.

3. Roudané, *Conversations with Arthur Miller*, pp. 13–14; E.M. Halliday,

John Berryman and the Thirties: A Memoir (Amherst, Mass., 1987), pp. 132–133; Bigsby, *Remembering Arthur Miller*, p. 249.

4. Zolotow, *Marilyn Monroe*, p. 264; Richard Schickel, *Elia Kazan: A Biography* (New York, 2005), p. 228; Gottfried, *Arthur Miller*, p. 65.

5. Gottfried, *Arthur Miller*, pp. 114; 241–242; Miller, *Timebends*, p. 202.

6. Mary McCarthy, "The American Realist Playwrights" (1961), *Theatre Chronicles, 1937–1962* (New York, 1963), p. 225; Brater, *Arthur Miller*, p. 53; Joseph Conrad, "*Heart of Darkness*," *Three Great Tales* (New York, [1960]), p. 270; Arthur Miller, *Death of a Salesman* (New York, 1987), p. 48.

7. Interview with Curtice Taylor; Harold Clurman, *All People Are Famous* (New York, 1974), p. 247; Robert Lewis, *Slings and Arrows: Theater in My Life* (New York, 1984), p. 221.

8. Kazan and Nan Taylor, in Gottfried, *Arthur Miller*, pp. 150; 162; Miller, *Timebends*, pp. 194; 278–279.

Seven: Secret Courtship

1. Miller, *Timebends*, p. 356; Kazan, *Life*, p. 438; Interview with Joan Copeland, Amagansett, New York, November 12, 2007 and Copeland, in Gottfried, *Arthur Miller*, p. 246.

2. Ruth Miller, *Saul Bellow: A Biography of the Imagination* (New York, 1991), p. 87; Jeffrey Meyers, *Edmund Wilson: A Biography* (Boston, 1995), p. 289; Gottfried, *Arthur Miller*, p. 282; Miller, *Timebends*, p. 378; Letters from Sondra Bellow to Jeffrey Meyers, January 29 and February 3, 2008.

3. Saul Bellow, "Brothers' Keepers," *New Republic*, 114 (January 7, 1946), 30; Roudané, ed., *Conversations with Arthur Miller*, pp. 242, 287; Gottfried, *Arthur Miller*, p. 286; Letter from Miller to Bellow, June 2, 1956, University of Chicago Library.

4. Enoch Brater, *Arthur Miller: A Playwright's Life and Works* (London, 2005), p. 68; Conversation with Mary Slattery Miller, Brooklyn, New York, September 5, 1998.

5. Steinem, *Marilyn*, p. 102; Rosten, *Marilyn*, p. 33; Bigsby, *Remembering Miller*, p. 262.

6. Strasberg, *Marilyn and Me*, p. 73; Winters, *Shelley II*, p. 34; Kazan, *Life*, p. 407.

7. Simon Callow, *Orson Welles: Hello Americans*, Volume 2 (New York,

2006), p. 256; Jonathan Kobal, *People Will Talk* (New York, 1985), p. 613; Miller, *Timebends*, p. 379.

8. Kazan, *Life*, pp. 178, 415; Miller, *Timebends*, p. 536; Newman, in *Marilyn Monroe: Still Life*, American Masters video, 2006; Interview with Brian Dennehy, Woodstock, Conn., December 17, 2007.

9. Mailer, *Marilyn*, p. 85; Eli Wallach, *The Good, the Bad, and Me* (New York, 2005), p. 217 (Joshua Logan, Colin Clark and Wallach all favored the cute tripartite title ending with "and Me"); Winters, *Shelley II*, pp. 31; 34; Christie's, *Personal Property of Marilyn Monroe*, p. 69.

10. Truman Capote, "Marilyn Monroe," *The Dogs Bark: Public People and Private Places* (New York, 1973), pp. 378–379; Truman Capote, "A Beautiful Child," *Music for Chameleons* (1980; New York, 1981), pp. 229; 235, 241; 244; Virginia Spencer Carr, *The Lonely Hunter: A Biography of Carson McCullers* (Garden City, N.Y., 1976), p. 439.

11. F. R. Leavis, *New Bearings in English Poetry* (1932; London, 1963), p. 64; John Lehmann, *A Nest of Tigers: Edith, Osbert and Sacheverell Sitwell and Their Times* (London, 1968), pp. 247–248; John Pearson, *Façade: Edith, Osbert and Sacheverell Sitwell* (London, 1967), pp. 437–438.

12. Victoria Glendinning, *Edith Sitwell: A Unicorn Among Lions* (London, 1981), p. 322; Spoto, *Marilyn Monroe*, p. 376; Glendinning, *Edith Sitwell*, p. 305; Edith Sitwell, *Taken Care Of* (New York, 1965), pp. 221, 223; Weatherby, *Conversations with Marilyn*, p. 186.

Eight: New York and the Actors Studio

1. Margaret Brenman-Gibson, *Clifford Odets: American Playwright* (New York, 1981), p. 197; Susan Strasberg, *Marilyn and Me*, p. 31.

   In his autobiography, *Songs My Mother Taught Me* (New York, 1994), p. 85, Brando wrote: "After I had some success, Lee Strasberg tried to take credit for teaching me how to act. He never taught me anything."

   Strasberg made his late film debut in *Godfather II* (1974) and gave an excellent performance as the aging Jewish mobster, Hyman Roth.

2. Marowitz, *Michael Chekhov*, p. 216; Strasberg, in Conway and Ricci, *Films of Marilyn Monroe*, p. 7; Adams, *Lee Strasberg*, pp. 256–257.

3. Zolotow, *Marilyn Monroe*, p. 249; "Arthur Miller," *Writers at Work: The "Paris Review" Interviews*, Third Series, ed. George Plimpton (New York, 1967), pp. 211–212; Interview with Joan Copeland; Adams, *Lee Strasberg*, p. 255.

4. Eugene O'Neill, "*Anna Christie*," *Three Plays* (New York, 1949), p. 83; Kazan, *Life*, p. 713; Kobal, *People Will Talk*, pp. 140; 699.

5. Susan Strasberg, *Marilyn and Me*, pp. 79, 85; Lee Strasberg, in Chandler, *Nobody's Perfect*, p. 182; Tom Wood, *The Bright Side of Billy Wilder, Primarily* (Garden City, N.Y., 1970), p. 153.

6. Kazan, *Life*, pp. 539–540; Adams, *Lee Strasberg*, p. 278; Maugham, in Spoto, *Marilyn Monroe*, p. 453.

7. Guiles, *Legend*, p. 268; Gussow, *Conversations with Miller*, pp. 146–147, and Miller, *Timebends*, p. 420.

8. Colin Clark, *The Prince, the Showgirl and Me* (New York, 1996), p. 85; Paula, in Alice McIntyre, "Making *The Misfits* or Waiting for Monroe or Notes from Olympus," *Esquire*, 55 (March 1961), 75; Clark, *The Prince, the Showgirl and Me*, pp. 102, 103.

9. Adams, *Lee Strasberg*, p. 271; Susan Strasberg, *Bittersweet* (New York, 1980), p. 156; Guiles, *Legend*, pp. 284, 316.

10. Diana Trilling, *The Beginning of the Journey* (New York, 1993), p. 246.

11. Spoto, *Marilyn Monroe*, p. 355; Logan, *Movie Stars, Real People, and Me*, pp. 55–56; 65.

12. Interview with Don Murray, Santa Barbara, California, January 10, 2008.

13. Letter from Spyros Skouras to Buddy Adler, April 30, 1956, Skouras papers, Stanford University Library; Logan, *Movie Stars, Real People, and Me*, p. 66.

Nine: Betrayal and Guilt

1. Sylvia Plath, in the opening paragraph of her novel, *The Bell Jar* (1963), describes the execution of the Rosenbergs, which foreshadows her heroine's electro-shock treatments: "It was a queer, sultry summer, the summer they electrocuted the Rosenbergs. . . . The idea of being electrocuted makes me sick. . . . I couldn't help

wondering what it would be like, being burned alive all along your nerves."

2. William Chafe, *The Unfinished Journey: America Since World War II* (New York, 1986), pp. 98; 132; Arthur Miller, *Echoes Down the Corridor: Essays, 1944–2000*, ed. Steven Centola (New York, 2000), p. 190; Eric Goldman, *The Crucial Decade – and After: America, 1945–1960* (New York, 1960), p. 278; Eisenhower, in Samuel Eliot Morison, *The Oxford History of the American People* (New York, 1965), p. 1084.

3. David Caute, *The Great Fear: The Anti-Communist Purge Under Truman and Eisenhower* (New York, 1978), pp. 508–509; Kazan, *Life*, p. 461; Brater, *Arthur Miller*, p. 60.

4. Charles Williams, "Salem," *Witchcraft* (1941; New York, 1959), p. 288; Edmund Morgan, "Arthur Miller's *The Crucible* and the Salem Witch Trials: A Historian's View," *The Golden and the Brazen World: Papers in Literature and History, 1650-1800*, ed. John Wallace (Berkeley, 1985), pp. 175; 182; 184; Aldous Huxley, *The Devils of Loudon* (1952; New York, 1965), p. 122.

5. Miller, *Echoes Down the Corridor*, p. 291; Miller, *Timebends*, p. 337; Arthur Miller, *The Crucible* (New York, 1981), p. 54.

6. Odets, in Zolotow, *Marilyn Monroe*, p. 265; Kazan, *Life*, p. 367; Robert Warshow, "The Liberal Conscience in *The Crucible*," *The Immediate Experience* (1962; Cambridge, Mass., 2001), p. 167; Roudané, *Conversations with Arthur Miller*, p. 263.

7. Miller, *Echoes Down the Corridor*, p. 282; Miller, *The Hook*, p. 18, unpublished screenplay, 1949, Lilly Library, Indiana University; Schickel, *Elia Kazan*, pp. 225, 227.

   Leo Braudy, in an otherwise excellent study, *On the Waterfront* (London, 2005), p. 17, agrees with Schickel that *Waterfront* is not "a partial ripoff, if not an outright plagiarism, of the script for *The Hook*." But Barbara Leaming, *Marilyn Monroe*, p. 175, and Martin Gottfried, *Arthur Miller*, p. 231, point out some striking resemblances in the theme and atmosphere of both works.

8. Albert Wertheim, "*A View from the Bridge*," *The Cambridge Companion to Arthur Miller*, ed. Christopher Bigsby (Cambridge, England, 1997), pp. 107–108, and quoting *The Hook*, p. 173; Gottfried, *Arthur Miller*, p. 235; Christopher Bigsby, ed., *Arthur Miller and Company* (London, 1990), p. 126.

9. Budd Schulberg, *On the Waterfront: The Final Shooting Script*

(Hollywood, 1980), p. 132; Kazan, *Life*, p. 500; Brando, *Songs My Mother Taught Me*, p. 195.

Both Schulberg and Kazan spent their whole lives trying to exculpate themselves and justify their disgraceful behavior. Schulberg also tried to justify his earlier betrayal of Scott Fitzgerald in Hollywood. See Jeffrey Meyers, *Scott Fitzgerald: A Biography* (New York, 1994), pp. 313–315.

10. Miller, *Timebends*, pp. 152; 419; Miller, in Gottfried, *Arthur Miller*, p. 305; Eric Bentley, "Theatre," *New Republic*, 133 (December 19, 1955), 21.

Ten: Witch Hunt

1. Victor Navasky, *Naming Names* (1980; London, 1981), p. 212n; Miller, *Echoes Down the Corridor*, p. 290; Miller, *Timebends*, p. 406.
2. Letter from Arthur Miller to Lloyd Garrison, May 22, 1956, Library of Congress; Arthur Miller, FBI file.
3. Navasky, *Naming Names*, p. 202; Caute, *Great Fear*, p. 501.
4. Mary McCarthy, "Naming Names: The Arthur Miller Case," *On the Contrary: Articles of Belief, 1946–1961* (1961; New York, 1966), p. 148; Testimony of Miller, HUAC, FBI file, pp. 7, 10; 16; 26; 29.
5. Testimony of Miller, FBI file, pp. 38; 27; Kenneth Tynan, *Profiles* (1989; New York, 1990), p. 117; Testimony of Miller, FBI file, pp. 30, 31.
6. Lardner, in Jeffrey Meyers, *Bogart: A Life in Hollywood* (Boston, 1997), p. 207; Testimony of Miller, FBI file, pp. 33, 34, 36.

   When asked in 2000 if he'd ever been disappointed with the performance of his plays, Miller echoed his HUAC testimony and replied: "I don't want to mention names because some of these actors are still around and they've got enough trouble" (Enoch Brater, ed., *Arthur Miller's America: Theater & Culture in a Time of Change*, Ann Arbor, 2005, p. 252).
7. Miller, FBI file; Walter Goodman, *The Committee* (Baltimore, 1968), p. 392; Caute, *Great Fear*, p. 536; McCarthy, *On the Contrary*, pp. 149, 154.
8. Navasky, *Naming Names*, pp. 199, 200; 423; Lillian Hellman, "Lillian Hellman Wants a Little Respect for Her Agony," *Show*, 4 (May 1964), 12.

9. Navasky, *Naming Names*, p. 219; Letter from Arthur Miller to Saul Bellow, July 8, 1956, University of Chicago Library.

10. Bigsby, *Remembering Arthur Miller*, p. 63; "Arthur Miller," *"Paris Review" Interviews*, p. 228; Testimony of Miller, FBI file, p. 32; Rosten, *Marilyn*, p. 31.

11. Guiles, *Legend*, p. 302; Michiko Kakutani, "Arthur Miller," *The Poet at the Piano: Portraits of Writers* (New York, 1989), p. 163; Mailer, *Marilyn*, p. 93.

12. *Remembering Marilyn*, Vestron video, 1988; Meryman, in Rollyson, *Marilyn Monroe*, p. 212; Letter from Miller to Joseph Rauh, August 12, 1958, Library of Congress.

13. "Timon," in *Centinela Press* (Hawthorne, California), March 17, 1957, Miller, FBI file; Miller, *Timebends*, p. 403; Marilyn Monroe, FBI file.

14. Joseph Rauh, "Draft of statement to be issued by Arthur Miller in case of indictment," January 2, 1957; Rauh, "Basis of Appeal," p. 2, Library of Congress; "Arthur Miller," *"Paris Review" Interviews*, p. 228.

15. Letter from Rauh to Alan Howe, August 11, 1958; Miller, statement, August 7, 1958; Letter from Rauh to Allan Seager, January 10, 1959, Library of Congress.

16. Letter from Miller to Rauh, quoting Skouras, August 9, 1958; Letters from Miller to Rauh, November 13, 1957, June 12, 1959 and August 5, 1960, Library of Congress.

17. Bigsby, *Remembering Arthur Miller*, p. 268; Christopher Bigsby, *Arthur Miller: A Critical Study*, (Cambridge, England, 2005), p. 226.

Eleven: Marriage and England

1. Leaming, *Marilyn Monroe*, p. 275; Miller, *Timebends*, pp. 379; 522; Leaming, *Marilyn Monroe*, p. 245. For the photo, see Haspiel, *Marilyn*, p. 136.

2. Letter from Miller to Bellow, July 8, 1956, University of Chicago Library; Susan Strasberg, *Marilyn and Me*, p. 112; Guiles, *Legend*, pp. 306–307; Evelyn Waugh, *Brideshead Revisited* (1945; London, 1962), pp. 184–185; Christie's, *Personal Property*, p. 251.

3. Evan Zimroth, "Marilyn at the Mikvah," in McDonough, *All the Available Light*, p. 183; Telegram to Spyros Skouras, April 1961, Stanford University Library; Letter from Miller to Bellow, July 8,

1956, University of Chicago Library; Marilyn, in Clare Boothe Luce, in *All the Available Light*, p. 93.

4. Letter from Marilyn to Charles Feldman, April 18, 1955, American Film Institute; Telegram from Buddy Adler to Spyros Skouras, [1956], Stanford University Library; Rosten, *Marilyn*, p. 39; Sandra Shevey, *The Marilyn Scandal* (New York, 1987), p. 258.

5. Zolotow, *Marilyn Monroe*, p. 299; Clark, *The Prince, the Showgirl and Me*, p. 105; Hugo Vickers, *Vivien Leigh* (Boston, 1988), p. 239; Letter from Miller to Norman Rosten, October 13, 1956, courtesy of Patricia Rosten Filan.

6. Paula, in Mailer, *Marilyn*, p. 229; Anthony Holden, *Laurence Olivier* (New York, 1990), pp. 305; 306; Clark, *The Prince, the Showgirl and Me*, pp. 71; 73.

7. Olivier, in "N.B.," *Times Literary Supplement*, March 7, 2008, p. 36; Cardiff, *Magic Hour*, p. 207; Miller, in Guiles, *Legend*, p. 321.

8. Vickers, *Vivien Leigh*, p. 239; Donald Spoto, *Laurence Olivier: A Biography* (New York, 1992), p. 271; Olivier, in Clark, *The Prince, the Showgirl and Me*, p. 109; Pepitone, *Monroe Confidential*, p. 60.

9. Miller, *Timebends*, pp. 429; 418; Miller, in Guiles, *Legend*, pp. 314; 315; 320; 319.

10. Susan Strasberg, *Marilyn and Me*, p. 122; Miracle, *My Sister Marilyn*, p. 176; Gottfried, *Arthur Miller*, p. 303; Christie's, *Personal Property*, p. 345.

11. Letter from Miller to Norman Rosten, October 13, 1956, courtesy of Patricia Rosten Filan; Clark, *The Prince, the Showgirl and Me*, p. 210; Marilyn, in Spoto, *Marilyn Monroe*, p. 388; Winters, *Shelley II*, p. 216.

12. Miller, in Guiles, *Legend*, p. 276; Zolotow, *Marilyn Monroe*, p. 315; Interview with Arthur Miller, Roxbury, Conn., June 19, 1981; Phone talk with Joshua Greene, New York, October 22, 2007.

Twelve: Heading for Disaster

1. Mailer, *Marilyn*, p. 234; Miller, *Timebends*, pp. 468; 489; Norman Mailer, "Strawhead," *Vanity Fair*, 49 (April 1986), 63; Nora Johnson, *Flashback on Nunnally Johnson*, p. 277; Adams, *Lee Strasberg*, p. 268.

2. Interview with Curtice Taylor and Letter from Curtice Taylor to Jeffrey Meyers, February 12, 2008; Pepitone, *Monroe Confidential*, p. 14; Roudané, *Conversations with Arthur Miller*, p. 52.

3. Sylvia Plath, *Unabridged Journals*, ed. Karen Kukil (New York, 2000), pp. 513–514; Pepitone, *Monroe Confidential*, pp. 40; 30–31; Gottfried, *Arthur Miller*, p. 312.

4. Carson McCullers, *Illuminations and Night Glare: The Unfinished Autobiography* (Madison, Wisconsin, 1999), p. 61; Carr, *Lonely Hunter*, p. 480; Judith Thurman, *Isak Dinesen: The Life of a Storyteller* (New York, 1982), p. 424.

5. Carson McCullers, "Isak Dinesen: In Praise of Radiance," *Saturday Review*, March 16, 1963, p. 83; Thurman, *Isak Dinesen*, pp. 387n; 425.

6. James Atlas, *Saul Bellow: A Biography* (New York, 2000), pp. 276–277; *Conversations with Saul Bellow*, ed. Gloria Cronin and Ben Siegel (Jackson, Miss., 1994), p. 130; Jeffrey Meyers, *Robert Frost: A Biography* (Boston, 1996), p. 175.

7. Barris, *Marilyn in Her Own Words*, p. 132 and Meryman, in Rollyson, *Marilyn Monroe*, p. 206; Spoto, *Marilyn Monroe*, p. 408; Carl Sandburg, "Tribute to Marilyn Monroe from a Friend," *Look*, 26 (September 11, 1962), 91–92.

8. R.W.B. Lewis, ed., *A Century of Arts and Letters* (New York, 1998), p. 163; Interviews with the poet William Jay Smith, Cummington, Mass., October 31, 2007, and with Lydia Kaim, assistant to the director of the Academy, Kennet Square, Penna., December 9, 2007; Victor, *Marilyn Encyclopedia*, p. 299; Rosten, *Marilyn*, p. 68.

9. Meyers, *Robert Frost*, p. 339; Goldman, *Crucial Decade*, p. 331; Winters, *Shelley II*, pp. 271–272; Goldman, *Crucial Decade*, p. 331, and Gavin Lambert, "On Marilyn Monroe," *On Cukor* (New York, 1972), p. 177.

10. William Taubman, *Khrushchev: The Man and His Era* (New York, 2003), p. 431; Lambert, *On Cukor*, p. 177; Miller, *Timebends*, p. 405.

11. Winters, *Shelley II*, p. 273; Rosten, *Marilyn*, p. 20; Pepitone, *Monroe Confidential*, p. 144.

12. Stacy Schiff, *Véra (Mrs. Vladimir Nabokov)*, (1999; New York, 2000), p. 269n; Zolotow, *Marilyn Monroe*, p. 327; Vladimir Nabokov, *Pale Fire* (1962; New York, 1968), p. 35.

13. Marilyn, in David Shipman, *Movietalk* (New York, 1988), p. 78; Wagenknecht, ed., *Marilyn Monroe*, p. 21; Les Brown, *Variety*, August 15, 1962, p. 22.

14. Pepitone, *Monroe Confidential*, pp. 29, 38, 184; Ted Jordan, *Norma: My Secret Life with Marilyn Monroe* (New York, 1989), pp. 226–227.

15. Mailer, *Marilyn*, p. 243; W. J. Weatherby, *Conversations with Marilyn* (New York, 1976), p. 131; Guus Luitjers, ed., *Marilyn Monroe: A Never-Ending Dream* (New York, 1986), p. 81.

16. Pepitone, *Monroe Confidential*, p. 97; Kazan, *Life*, p. 668; Weatherby, *Conversations with Marilyn*, p. 144.

17. Stapleton, in Summers, *Goddess*, p. 181; Susan Strasberg, *Marilyn and Me*, p. 170; Pepitone, *Monroe Confidential*, p. 117.

    For the similar complaint of another dissatisfied woman, see Hemingway, "Cat in the Rain" (1925), *Short Stories*, p. 170: "I want to eat at a table with my own silver and I want candles. And I want it to be spring and I want to brush my hair out in front of a mirror and I want a kitty and I want some new clothes."

18. Letter from Marilyn to Norman and Hedda Rosten, [mid-1950s], courtesy of Patricia Rosten Filan; Jeffrey Meyers, "Miller's Outtakes," *American Drama*, 15 (Winter 2006), 87; *Conversations with Norman Mailer*, ed. Michael Lennon (Jackson, Miss., 1988), pp. 317; 203.

19. Rosten, in Manso, *Mailer*, pp. 538–539; Mailer, *Marilyn*, pp. 22, 23.

20. Susan Strasberg, *Bittersweet*, p. 156; Mailer, *Marilyn*, p. 170; Rosten, *Marilyn*, pp. 66–67.

21. Susan Strasberg, *Marilyn and Me*, p. 134; Miller, in Guiles, *Legend*, p. 333.

Thirteen: Billy Wilder and Yves Montand

1. The train going south stops in Washington, Charleston, Savannah, Jacksonville and Miami, as if it were traveling down the East Coast from New York instead of southeast from Chicago.

2. Tony Curtis and Barry Paris, *Tony Curtis: The Autobiography* (New York, 1993), pp. 169; 157; Interview with Walter Mirisch, Universal City, California, November 14, 2007; Maurice Zolotow, *Billy Wilder in Hollywood* (New York, 1977), p. 257.

3. Cameron Crowe, *Conversations with Wilder* (New York, 1999), pp. 159–160; Don Widener, *Lemmon: A Biography* (London, 1977), p. 170; Interview with Walter Mirisch; McCann, *Marilyn Monroe*, p. 105.

4. Wilder, who grew up during the waning years of the Austro-Hungarian Empire, was fond of Czech and Polish names that began and ended with "k." The janitor in *The Seven Year Itch* is

named Kruhulik; the heroine of *The Apartment*, played by Shirley MacLaine, is called Kubelik. Wilder named dubious characters in both *Sunset Boulevard* (1950) and *The Apartment* (1960) "Sheldrake," which also seemed comical, and may have reminded him of the German word *Dreck* ("filth" or "shit").

5. Little Bonaparte's speech to the convention quotes, ironically, both Alexander Pope's *Essay on Criticism* (1711): "To err is human, to forgive divine," and General Motors' president Charles Wilson's "What's good for the country is good for us."

   As the musicians approach the hotel, the script paraphrases Ira Gershwin's "Summertime" from *Porgy and Bess* (1935): "Wintertime and the livin' is easy, fish are jumpin' and the market is high." Billy Wilder and I. A. L. Diamond, "*Some Like It Hot*," *Best American Screenplays 2*, ed. Sam Thomas (New York, 1990), pp. 142, 141, 112.

6. Wilder and Diamond, *Some Like It Hot*, pp. 127–128; 107; 98; 108.

7. Wilder and Diamond, *Some Like It Hot*, pp. 108; 100; 108; 144; 145–146; 130.

8. Letter from Marilyn to Norman Rosten, October 27, 1958, courtesy of Patricia Rosten Filan; Gottfried, *Arthur Miller*, p. 319; Wilder, in Victor, *Marilyn Encyclopedia*, p. 194; Zolotow, *Billy Wilder in Hollywood*, pp. 260; 263–264.

9. Jay Leyda, *Voices of Film Experience: 1894 to the Present* (New York, 1977), pp. 507–508; *Billy Wilder: Interviews*, ed. Robert Horton (Jackson, Miss., 2001), p. 170.

10. Crowe, *Conversations with Wilder*, p. 37; Kevin Lally, *Wilder Times: The Life of Billy Wilder* (New York, 1996), p. 295; 293; Wood, *Bright Side of Billy Wilder*, p. 161.

11. Zolotow, *Billy Wilder in Hollywood*, pp. 265–267; Lally, *Wilder Times*, p. 294.

12. Laura Mulvey, in Jim Hillier and Peter Wollen, eds., *Howard Hawks: American Artist* (London, 1996), p. 216; Victor, *Marilyn Encyclopedia*, p. 204; Hervé Hamon and Patrick Rotman, *Yves Montand: You See, I Haven't Forgotten*, trans. Jeremy Leggatt (New York, 1992), pp. 317; 325; Mailer, *Marilyn*, p. 19.

13. Guiles, *Legend*, p. 377; Miller, *Timebends*, p. 466; Guiles, *Legend*, pp. 370–371; Simone Signoret, *Nostalgia Isn't What It Used to Be* (1976; New York, 1979), p. 339.

14. Montand, in Guiles, *Legend*, p. 371; Hamon, *Yves Montand*, pp. 320; 324; Luitjers, *Marilyn Monroe*, p. 81.

15. Pepitone, *Monroe Confidential*, p. 158; Christopher Isherwood, *Diaries: Volume One, 1939–1960*, ed. Katherine Bucknell (London, 1996), p. 899; Signoret, *Nostalgia*, pp. 336, 349.

16. Miller, in Leaming, *Marilyn Monroe*, p. 369; Hamon, *Yves Montand*, pp. 326; 328; George Cukor papers, Herrick Library, and Gottfried, *Arthur Miller*, p. 328.

Fourteen: Making *The Misfits*

1. Miller, *Timebends*, p. 457; Arthur Miller, "Please Don't Kill Anything," *I Don't Need You Any More* (New York, 1967), pp. 74, 75, 77; A. J. Liebling, "The Mustang Buzzers," *New Yorker*, April 3 and 10, 1954, partly reprinted in *Liebling at the "New Yorker": Uncollected Essays*, ed. James Barbour and Fred Warner (Albuquerque, 1994), pp. 134–135.

2. Miller, "The Misfits," *I Don't Need You Any More*, pp. 111; 93; 79; 94; 95, 96; 110; 112.

3. Arthur Miller and Serge Toubiana, *The Misfits: Story of a Shoot* (London, 2000), p. 60 and Letter from Arthur Miller to John Huston, July 14, 1958, Huston papers, Herrick Library; Lawrence Grobel, *The Hustons* (1989; New York, 1990), pp. 477–478; Letter from Miller to Huston, June 16, 1959, Huston papers, Herrick Library.

   At the end of *The Asphalt Jungle*, the Sterling Hayden character, who comes from the Kentucky bluegrass country, makes it back home at the end and dies of a bullet wound, surrounded and nuzzled by the horses on his old farm. Huston would also achieve a powerful climax at the end of *Under the Volcano* (1984), when gunfire frightens a horse that bolts and fatally injures the hero's wife.

4. "Arthur Miller Chez John Huston en Irlande," p. 36 (no author or source), Herrick Library, my translation; Interview with Angela Allen, London, November 22, 2007; James Goode, *The Making of "The Misfits"* (1963; New York, 1986), p. 100.

5. Goode, *Making "Misfits"*, p. 241; Eve Arnold, *Marilyn Monroe: An Appreciation* (New York, 1987), p. 92; Letter from John Huston to Mrs. J. J. O'Donahue, May 11, 1961, Huston papers, Herrick Library; J. M. Coetzee, "Arthur Miller, *The Misfits*," *Inner Workings: Literary Essays, 2000-2005* (New York, 2007), p. 225; Goode, *Making "Misfits"*, p. 90.

6. Arnold, *Marilyn Monroe*, p. 87; *Conversations with Capote*, ed. Lawrence Grobel (New York, 1985), p. 160; *John Huston: Interviews*, ed. Robert Emmet Long (Jackson, Miss., 2001), p. 173.

7. Interview with Curtice Taylor; Miller, *Timebends*, p. 461; *John Huston: Interviews*, pp. 172; 18.

8. McIntyre, *Making "The Misfits"*, p. 79; Letters from Arthur Miller to Saul Bellow, [Summer 1960], University of Chicago Library; Christie's *Personal Property*, pp. 69, 337, 68.

9. Interview with Angela Allen; Miller, *Timebends*, p. 479.

10. Allen, Huston and Nan Taylor in Guiles, *Legend*, pp. 385; 380; 387; Interview with Angela Allen.

11. Gussow, *Conversations with Miller*, p. 145; James Whitcomb, "Marilyn Monroe – The Sex Symbol Versus the Good Wife," *Cosmopolitan*, 149 (December 1960), 57.

12. Weatherby, *Conversations with Marilyn*, p. 70; Guiles, *Legend*, p. 397n; Gottfried, *Arthur Miller*, p. 326.

13. *John Huston: Interviews*, p. 110; John Huston, *An Open Book* (1980; New York, 1994), p. 288; Miller, in Guiles, *Legend*, p. 275.

14. Spoto, *Marilyn Monroe*, pp. 446; 434; Rosten, *Marilyn*, p. 77; Pepitone, *Monroe Confidential*, p. 150.

15. Wallach, *The Good, the Bad, and Me*, p. 226; Luitjers, *Marilyn Monroe*, p. 18; Miller, *Timebends*, pp. 470; 481.

16. Rosten, *Marilyn*, p. 75; Clift, in Weatherby, *Conversations with Marilyn*, p. 76; Miller, in Goode, *Making "Misfits"*, p. 300.

17. Miller and Toubiana, *The Misfits*, p. 37; James Salter, *Burning the Days* (New York, 1997), p. 272; Miller and Toubiana, *The Misfits*, pp. 44, 185.

Fifteen: *The Misfits*: Life into Art

1. Arthur Miller, *The Misfits* (New York: Dell, 1961), p. 53, and Miller, *Timebends*, p. 369; Miller, *Misfits* (Dell), pp. 169–170; 18; Bigsby, *Remembering Arthur Miller*, p. 264.

   In an early version of the script, which has a weaker ending, Gay speaks the last line to Perce, not Roslyn. This version was published in *Film Scripts Three*, ed. George Garrett, O.B. Hardison, Jr. and Jane Gelfman (1972; New York, 1989), pp. 204–382.

2. Coetzee, *Inner Workings*, p. 222; Leslie Fiedler, *Waiting for the End* (1964; London, 1967), p. 97.

3. Miller, *Misfits* (Dell), pp. 64; 58; Coetzee, *Inner Workings*, p. 224; Miller, *Echoes Down the Corridor*, p. 246.

4. Hollis Alpert, "Arthur Miller: Screenwriter," *Saturday Review of Literature*, 44 (February 4, 1961), 47; Miller, *Misfits* (Dell), pp. 135; 133, 185.

   The word "shit" is left out of the film.

5. Miller, *Misfits* (Dell), pp. 53, 60; 72–73, 33.

6. Miller, *Misfits* (Dell), p. 134; Goode, *Making "Misfits"*, p. 206; Wallace Stevens, "Stars at Tallapoosa," *Collected Poems* (1954; New York, 1982), p. 71.

   In *All My Sons* (1947; New York, 2000), p. 74, Miller wrote, "every man does have a star. The star of one's honesty. And you spend your life groping for it."

7. Marijane Meaker, "Marilyn and Norma Jeane," *Sudden Endings* (New York, 1964), p. 42n; Victor, *Marilyn Encyclopedia*, p. 115; *The Making of "The Misfits"*, unpublished script for twenty-minute featurette, Herrick Library; Conway, *Films of Marilyn Monroe*, p. 157.

8. Bigsby, *Remembering Arthur Miller*, pp. 91, 263; Brater, *Arthur Miller*, p. 87; Guiles, *Legend*, p. 376; Gottfried, *Arthur Miller*, p. 343; Letter from Arthur Miller to Jeffrey Meyers, January 17, 1981.

9. Miller, *Echoes Down the Corridor*, p. 190; Dr. Ralph Greenson, in Summers, *Goddess*, p. 189; Cardiff, *Magic Hour*, p. 212.

10. Weatherby, *Conversations with Marilyn*, p. 187; Jordan, *Norma*, p. 227.

11. Gussow, *Conversations with Miller*, p. 25; Bigsby, *Remembering Arthur Miller*, p. 271; Gussow, *Conversations with Miller*, p. 96.

12. *John Huston: Interviews*, pp. 109, 111; Huston, in Sarah Churchwell, *The Many Lives of Marilyn Monroe* (New York, 2004), p. 337.

13. Miracle, *My Sister Marilyn*, p. 183; Leaming, *Marilyn Monroe*, p. 380.

Sixteen: Something's Got to Give

1. Lambert, *On Cukor*, p. 174; Elisabeth Young-Bruehl, *Anna Freud: A Biography* (New York, 1988), p. 371; Greenson, in Spoto, *Marilyn Monroe*, p. 427; Letter from Ralph Greenson to Agnes Bene, December 9, 1969, Library of Congress.

2. Roberts, in Spoto, *Marilyn Monroe*, pp. 558; 429; Victor, *Marilyn Encylcopedia*, p. 209.

3. Greenson, in Summers, *Goddess*, p. 269; Miller, in Guiles, *Legend*, pp. 277, 276.

4. Susan Strasberg, *Marilyn and Me*, p. 227; Jane Russell, *Jane Russell: My Paths and My Detours* (New York, 1985), p. 280; Stephen Farber and Marc Green, "Romeo and Marilyn," *Hollywood on the Couch: A Candid Look at the Overheated Love Affair between Psychiatrists and Moviemakers* (New York, 1993), p. 94; Susan Strasberg, in *Remembering Marilyn*, Vestron video, 1988.

5. See Carol Brightman, *Writing Dangerously: Mary McCarthy and Her World* (New York, 1992), p. 176; David Roberts, *Jean Stafford: A Biography* (Boston, 1988), p. 254; Carr, *Lonely Hunter*, pp. 300–301.

6. Letter to Strasbergs, in Victor, *Marilyn Encylcopedia*, p. 190; Letter to Greenson, in Spoto, *Marilyn Monroe*, pp. 460; 462–463; 459.

7. Cardiff, *Magic Hour*, p. 213; Farber, *Hollywood on the Couch*, p. 94; Cramer, *Joe DiMaggio*, p. 391.

8. Miracle, *My Sister Marilyn*, p. 157; Cramer, *Joe DiMaggio*, p. 417; Victor, *Marilyn Encylcopedia*, p. 143.

9. Barris, *Marilyn: Her Own Words*, p. 143; Bogdanovich, *Who the Hell's In It*, pp. 417, 419.

10. Murray, *Marilyn: The Last Months*, p. 25; Kitty Kelley, *His Way: The Unauthorized Biography of Frank Sinatra* (1986; New York, 1987), p. 312; Monroe, FBI file, February 25, 1962.

   David Thomson's *In Nevada* (New York, 1999) provides a lurid account of this weekend. When I asked for his source, he did not provide it.

11. Pepitone, *Monroe Confidential*, p. 193; Ronald Brownstein, *The Power and the Glitter: The Hollywood-Washington Connection* (1990; New York, 1992), p. 317; Hersh, *Dark Side of Camelot*, p. 454.

12. Arthur Schlesinger, Jr., *Journals, 1952–2000* (New York, 2007), p. 162; Monroe, FBI file, July 18, 1962; Pepitone, *Monroe Confidential*, p. 211.

13. Summers, *Goddess*, p. 224; Heymann, *RFK*, p. 313; Summers, *Goddess*, paperback edition (New York, 1986), pp. 427–428; Heymann, *RFK*, p. 474.

14. Monroe, FBI file, January 26, 1965; Heymann, *RFK*, p. 319; Donald Wolfe, *The Last Days of Marilyn Monroe* (New York, 1998), p. 93.

15. Jean Negulesco, "Marilyn Monroe: A Vulnerable Phenomenon," *Things I Did . . . and Things I Think I Did* (New York, 1984), p.

224; Guiles, *Legend*, p. 422; Walter Bernstein, "Marilyn Monroe's Last Picture Show," *Esquire*, 80 (July 1973), 106; 108; Interview with Walter Bernstein, New York, December 2, 2007.

16. Bernstein, in *Marilyn: The Final Days*, Prometheus video, 2001, which includes about thirty rough minutes of the movie; Interview with Walter Bernstein.

17. Kennedy, in Rollyson, *Marilyn Monroe*, p. 194; Arthur Schlesinger, Jr., *Robert Kennedy and His Times* (1978; New York, 1979), p. 636; Interview with Billy Wilder, Beverly Hills, California, September 12, 1995; Tynan, *Profiles*, p. 144.

18. Patrick McGilligan, *George Cukor: A Double Life* (New York, 1997), pp. 272–273; Emanuel Levy, *George Cukor: Master of Elegance* (New York, 1994), p. 272.

19. Interview with Walter Mirisch; *Marilyn: The Final Days*, Prometheus video, 2001.

Something's Got to Give was never completed. In 1963 the remake was remade as *Move Over Darling*, with Doris Day as a feeble stand-in for Marilyn.

Seventeen: Suicide

1. Letter from Richard Meryman to Jeffrey Meyers, February 10, 2008; Monroe, FBI file, February 21, 1962; Frost, "Provide, Provide" (1934), *Poetry*, p. 307.

2. Lawford, in Leaming, *Marilyn Monroe*, p. 425; Patricia Seaton Lawford and Ted Schwarz, *The Peter Lawford Story* (New York, 1988), p. 176; Shaw and Rosten, *Marilyn Among Friends*, p. 190; Rosten, in Wagenknecht, ed., *Marilyn Monroe*, p. 102.

3. Conrad, *Heart of Darkness*, p. 246; Monroe, *My Story*, p. 66.

4. Greenson, in Summers, *Goddess*, pp. 190, 243; Heymann, *RFK*, p. 312; Greenson, in Spoto, *Marilyn Monroe*, p. 515.

5. Thomas Noguchi, with Joseph DiMona, "Marilyn Monroe," *Coroner* (New York, 1983), pp. 72; 74; Engelberg, in *Marilyn: The Final Days*, Prometheus video, 2001; Huston, in Wagenknecht, ed., *Marilyn Monroe*, p. 168.

6. Noguchi, *Coroner*, pp. 72; 70, 80; 56; 79–80; 85.

7. For the conspiracy theories, see Farber, *Hollywood on the Couch*, p. 105; Heymann, *RFK*, p. 325; Noguchi, *Coroner*, p. 83.

Ted Jordan claimed that he owned the Red Diary, which

contained Marilyn's secret thoughts but did not have any secret information. He was never able to produce that diary.

8. Monroe, FBI file, July 9, 1963; Hersh, *Dark Side of Camelot*, p. 104; Frank Saunders, with James Southwood, *The Torn Lace Curtain* (New York, 1982), pp. 141–142.

9. Letter from Ralph Greenson to Anna Freud, June 22, 1962; Letter from Anna Freud to Ralph Greenson, July 2, 1962, Library of Congress; Letter from Greenson to Norman Rosten, August 15, 1962, courtesy of Patricia Rosten Filan.

10. Greenson, in Victor, *Marilyn Encyclopedia*, p. 132; Letters from Ralph Greenson to Anna Freud, August 20, 1962, January 13, 1963 and May 27, 1963, Library of Congress.

11. Ralph Greenson, "On Transitional Objects and Transference," *Explorations in Psychoanalysis* (New York, 1978), pp. 493–494.

12. Cramer, *Joe DiMaggio*, p. 418; Gladys Baker, in Barris, *Marilyn: Her Own Words*, p. 157; Strasberg, in Conway, *Films of Marilyn Monroe*, p. 7.

13. Riese and Hitchens, *Unabridged Marilyn*, p. 553; Adams, *Lee Strasberg*, p. 27; Samuel Johnson, "The Vanity of Human Wishes" (1749), *Complete English Poems*, ed. J. D. Fleeman (New York, 1971), p. 85.

    In the Monroe file, no date, the FBI reported that a " 'French-type' movie depicted Marilyn Monroe, deceased actress, in unnatural acts with unknown male. . . . DiMaggio had attempted to purchase this film from ★★★ and had offered him $25,000 . . . but he would not part with it."

14. Miller, in Brater, *Arthur Miller*, p. 102; Miller, *Timebends*, p. 531; Weatherby, *Conversations with Marilyn*, p. 219; Miller, in Summers, *Goddess*, p. 314.

15. Miller, in Guiles, *Legend*, p. 441; Bigsby, *Remembering Arthur Miller*, p. 60; Miller, *Timebends*, pp. 528; 242.

Eighteen: Miller's Tragic Muse

1. Charles Baudelaire, *Selected Letters*, trans. and ed. Rosemary Lloyd (Chicago, 1986), p. 49; Henry Popkin, "Arthur Miller: The Strange Encounter," *Sewanee Review*, 68 (1960), 56; Miller, *Timebends*, p. 326.

2. Richard and Nancy Meyer, "*After the Fall*: A View from the Director's Notebook," *Theatre*, 2 (1965), 57, 68; Arthur Miller,

After the Fall: Final Stage Version (New York, 1964), p. 1, and Miller, *Timebends*, p. 536.

3. Gottfried, *Arthur Miller*, p. 365; Miller, *After the Fall*, pp. 40; 39; 28; 29–30.

4. Rebecca Buselle, "In Remembrance: Inge Morath," *Aperture*, 171 (2003), 76; Miller, *After the Fall*, p. 22; Gottfried, *Arthur Miller*, p. 346.

5. Albert Camus, *The Fall*, trans. Justin O'Brien (1956; New York, 1957), p. 70; Roudané, *Conversations with Arthur Miller*, p. 336; Miller, *After the Fall*, pp. 67 and 111.

6. Miller, *After the Fall*, pp. 44, 47, 71, 72, 80 ("whereas"); 24, 77.

7. Miller, *After the Fall*, p. 108; Roudané, *Conversations with Arthur Miller*, pp. 354, 357.

8. Miller, *After the Fall*, pp. 44; 47; 82; 72.

   See Mailer, *Marilyn*, p. 93, quoting her on the Communists: "They're for the people, aren't they?"

9. David Savran, *Communists, Cowboys and Queers: The Politics of Masculinity in the Work of Arthur Miller and Tennessee Williams* (Minneapolis, 1992), p. 56; Roudané, *Conversations with Arthur Miller*, p. 79; Gottfried, *Arthur Miller*, p. 363; Arthur Miller, "With Respect for Her Agony – But with Love," *Life*, February 7, 1964, p. 66.

10. Meyer, "Director's Notebook," pp. 63, 65, 70; Kazan, *Life*, p. 630.

11. Miller, *After the Fall*, pp. 96; 107; 83; 97.

12. Robert Brustein, "Arthur Miller: Mea Culpa," *New Republic*, 150 (February 8, 1964), 26, 28; Russell, in Jeffrey Meyers, *D. H. Lawrence and the Experience of Italy* (Philadelphia, 1982), p. 82; Richard Gilman, "The Stage: Still Falling," *Commonweal*, 79 (February 17, 1964), 601; Noël Coward, *Diaries*, ed. Graham Payn and Sheridan Morley (Boston, 1982), pp. 557–558.

13. Gussow, *Conversations with Miller*, p. 182; Miller, *Timebends*, p. 229; Oriana Fallaci, "A Propos of *After the Fall*," *World Theatre*, 14 (January 1965), 79.

14. Miller, *"Paris Review" Interviews*, p. 224; Letter from Heather Kenney, Roxbury Probate Court, to Jeffrey Meyers, October 11, 2007.

15. Arthur Miller, *Broken Glass* (New York, 1994), pp. 7, 107; 63; 68; 69; 70.

   Impotence is also a major theme in *A View From the Bridge*.

16. Miller, *Broken Glass*, pp. 26; 83; 131; 137.

17. Arthur Miller, *Mr. Peters' Connections* (New York, 1999), pp. 4; 53; 13; 22; 24; 54.

18. Arthur Miller, "The Bare Manuscript," *Presence* (New York, 2007), pp. 70; 90.

19. Arthur Miller, *Finishing the Picture*, unpublished last play (2004), pp. 8; 42; Miller, *Timebends*, p. 385; Miller, *Finishing the Picture*, pp. 29; 21; 21; 24.

20. Miller, *Finishing the Picture*, pp. 42; 92; 32, 94; Interview with Brian Dennehy.

Bibliography

I. Arthur Miller

Bigsby, Christopher. *Arthur Miller: A Critical Study*. Cambridge, England: Cambridge University Press, 2005.

———, ed. *The Cambridge Companion to Arthur Miller*. Cambridge: Cambridge University Press, 1997.

———, ed. *Remembering Arthur Miller*. London: Methuen, 2005.

Bloom, Harold, ed. *Arthur Miller: Modern Critical Views*. New Edition. New York: Chelsea House, 2007.

Brater, Enoch. *Arthur Miller: A Playwright's Life and Works*. London: Thames & Hudson, 2005.

Caute, David. *The Great Fear: The Anti-Communist Purge Under Truman and Eisenhower*. New York: Simon and Schuster, 1978.

Corrigan, Robert, ed. *Arthur Miller: A Collection of Critical Essays*. Englewood Cliffs, N.J.: Prentice-Hall, 1969.

Goldstein, Laurence, "The Fiction of Arthur Miller," *Michigan Quarterly Review*, 37 (Fall 1998), 725–745.

Gottfried, Martin. *Arthur Miller: His Life and Work*. New York: Da Capo, 2003.

Gussow, Mel. *Conversations with Arthur Miller*. New York: Applause, 2002.

Hellman, Lillian, "Lillian Hellman Wants a Little Respect for Her Agony," *Show*, 4 (May 1964), 12–13.

Kazan, Elia. *A Life*. New York: Knopf, 1988.

Koorey, Stefani. *Arthur Miller's Life and Literature: An Annotated Comprehensive Guide.* Lanham, Maryland: Scarecrow Press, 2000.

Levin, David, "Salem Witchcraft in Recent Fiction and Drama," *New England Quarterly,* 28 (December 1955), 538–542.

Liebling, A.J. "The Mustang Buzzers" (1954). *Liebling at the "New Yorker": Uncollected Essays.* Ed. James Barbour and Fred Warner. Albuquerque: University of New Mexico Press, 1994. Pp. 131–147.

Mandelstam, Nadezhda, "Letters to Arthur Miller and Inge Morath," ed. Michael Wachtel, *Russian Review,* 61 (October 2002), 505–516.

McCarthy, Mary. "Naming Names: The Arthur Miller Case." *On the Contrary: Articles of Belief, 1946–1961.* New York: Farrar, Straus and Giroux, 1966. Pp. 147–154.

——. "The American Realist Playwrights." *Theatre Chronicles, 1937–1962.* New York: Farrar, Straus and Giroux, 1963. Pp. 225–227.

Meyers, Jeffrey. "Review of Arthur Miller's *Timebends,*" *National Review,* 40 (January 22, 1988), 58–60.

——. "Arthur Miller." *Privileged Moments: Encounters with Writers.* Madison: University of Wisconsin Press, 2000. Pp. 30–50.

——. "Miller's Outtakes," *American Drama,* 15 (Winter 2006), 85–88.

——. "Review of Arthur Miller's *Presence,*" Toronto *Globe and Mail,* August 4, 2007, pp. D4–D5.

——. "Marilyn and the Literati," *Michigan Quarterly Review,* 47 (Winter 2008), 18–27.

——. "Miller's Tragic Muse," *Yale Review,* 96 (April 2008), 1–26.

——. "Marilyn's Houses," *Architectural Digest,* 65 (November 2008), 60, 66, 70.

Miller, Arthur. *After the Fall.* Final Stage Version. New York: Viking, 1964.

——. *Broken Glass.* New York: Penguin, 1994.

——. *Conversations with Arthur Miller.* Ed. Matthew Roudané. Jackson: University Press of Mississippi, 1987.

——. *"The Crucible": Text and Criticism.* Ed. Gerald Weales. New York: Penguin, 1977.

——. *Echoes Down the Corridor: Collected Essays, 1944–2000.* Ed. Steven Centola. New York: Viking, 2000.

——. *Finishing the Picture.* Unpublished last play. Produced at the Goodman Theatre, Chicago, October 2004.

——. *The Hook.* Unpublished screenplay, 1949.

——. "Please Don't Kill Anything" (1960) and "The Misfits" (1957). *I Don't Need You Any More*. New York: Viking, 1967. Pp. 71–77, 78–113.

——. "*The Misfits*" (1960). *Film Scripts Three*. Ed. George Garrett, O.B. Hardison, Jr. and Jane Gelfman. 1972; New York: Irvington, 1989. Pp. 202–382.

——. *The Misfits*. New York: Dell, 1961.

——. *Mr Peters' Connections*. New York: Penguin, 1999.

——. "My Wife Marilyn," *Life*, December 22, 1958, pp. 146–147.

——. *Presence*. New York: Viking, 2007.

——. *Theater Essays*. Ed. Robert Martin. London: Penguin, 1978.

——. *Timebends*. New York: Grove, 1987.

——. *A View from the Bridge*. New York: Viking, 1955.

——. "With Respect for Her Agony – But with Love," *Life*, February 7, 1964, p. 66.

—— and Serge Toubiana. *The Misfits: Story of a Shoot*. London: Phaidon, 2000.

Morgan, Edmund. "Arthur Miller's *The Crucible* and the Salem Witch Trials: A Historian's View." *The Golden and the Brazen World: Papers in Literature and History, 1650–1800*. Ed. John Wallace. Berkeley: University of California Press, 1985. Pp. 171–186.

Moss, Leonard. *Arthur Miller*. New York: Twayne, 1967.

Navasky, Victor. *Naming Names*. 1980; London: Penguin, 1981.

Popkin, Henry, "Arthur Miller: The Strange Encounter," *Sewanee Review*, 68 (1960), 34–60.

Rahv, Philip. "Arthur Miller and the Fallacy of Profundity." *The Myth and the Powerhouse*. New York: Farrar, Straus and Giroux, 1965. Pp. 225–233.

Schleuter, June and James Flanagan. *Arthur Miller*. New York: Ungar, 1987.

Warshow, Robert. "The Liberal Conscience in *The Crucible*" (1953). *The Immediate Experience*. Garden City, New York: Doubleday, 1962. Pp. 189–203.

II. Marilyn Monroe

Bernstein, Walter, "Marilyn Monroe's Last Picture Show," *Esquire*, 80 (July 1973), 105–108, 178.

Berryman, Eileen. *Orphans: Real and Imaginary*. 1987; New York: Signet, 1990.

Bogdanovich, Peter. "Marilyn Monroe." *Who the Hell's in It: Portraits and Conversations*. New York: Knopf, 2004. Pp. 482–492.

Cardiff, Jack. "Marilyn." *Magic Hour: The Life of a Cameraman*. London: Faber, 1996. Pp. 195–214.

Carey, Gary, with Joseph Mankiewicz. *More About "All About Eve"*. New York: Random House, 1972. Pp. 75–79.

Christie's. *The Personal Property of Marilyn Monroe*. Auction catalogue, New York, October 28 and 29, 1999.

Churchwell, Sarah. *The Many Lives of Marilyn Monroe*. New York: Holt, 2004.

Clark, Colin. *The Prince, the Showgirl and Me*. New York: St. Martin's, 1996.

Cramer, Richard Ben. *Joe DiMaggio: The Hero's Life*. New York: Simon and Schuster, 2000.

Crowe, Cameron. *Conversations with Billy Wilder*. New York: Knopf, 1999.

Dougherty, James. *The Secret Happiness of Marilyn Monroe*. Chicago: Playboy, 1976.

Goode, James. *The Making of "The Misfits"*. 1963; New York: Limelight, 1986.

Goodman, Ezra. "The Girl with Three Blue Eyes." *The Fifty Year Decline and Fall of Hollywood*. New York: Simon and Schuster, 1961. Pp. 213–236.

Greenson, Ralph. "On Transitional Objects and Transference." *Explorations in Psychoanalysis*. New York: International Universities Press, 1978. Pp. 493–494.

Grobel, Lawrence. *The Hustons*. 1989; New York: Avon, 1990.

Guiles, Fred. *Legend: The Life and Death of Marilyn Monroe*. 1984; Chelsea, Michigan: Scarborough House, 1991.

Halberstam, David. "Marilyn Monroe." *The Fifties*. New York: Villard, 1993. Pp. 564–571.

Hersh, Seymour. *The Dark Side of Camelot*. Boston: Little, Brown, 1997. Pp. 102–106.

Heymann, C. David. "Marilyn." *RFK: A Candid Biography of Robert F. Kennedy*. New York: Penguin Putnam, 1998. Pp. 304–325, 539–541.

Holden, Anthony. *Laurence Olivier*. New York: Collier, 1990. Pp. 301–313.

Hoyt, Edwin. *Marilyn: The Tragic Venus*. New York: Duell, Sloan and Pearce, 1965.

Huston, John. *An Open Book*. 1980; New York: Da Capo, 1994.

Karasek, Hellmuth. *Billy Wilder: Eine Nahaufnahme*. Hamburg: Hoffmann und Campe, 1992. Pp. 387–402.

Lawford, Patricia Seaton and Ted Schwarz. *The Peter Lawford Story*. New York: Carroll & Graf, 1988.

Leaming, Barbara. *Marilyn Monroe*. New York: Three Rivers, 1988.

Lesser, Wendy. "The Disembodied Body of Marilyn Monroe." *His Other Half: Looking at Women Through Art*. Cambridge, Mass.: Harvard University Press, 1991. Pp. 193–224.

Ludwig, Arnold. "The Real Marilyn." *How Do We Know Who We Are?: A Biography of the Self*. New York: Oxford University Press, 1997. Pp. 13–34, 267–269.

Mailer, Norman. *Marilyn: A Biography*. New York: Warner, 1975.

——. *Of Women and Their Elegance*. 1980; Tor Books, 1981.

——. "Strawhead," *Vanity Fair*, 49 (April 1989), 58–67.

Martin, Pete. "Did Acting Spoil Marilyn Monroe?" *Pete Martin Calls On*. New York: Simon and Schuster, 1962. Pp. 157–191.

Masters, George and Lee Browning. "To Killer George – Marilyn." *The Masters Way to Beauty*. New York: Dutton, 1977. Pp. 60–83.

McCann, Graham. *Marilyn Monroe*. 1987; New Brunswick, N.J.: Rutgers University Press, 1988.

McDonough, Yona, ed. *All the Available Light: A Marilyn Monroe Reader*. New York: Simon and Schuster, 2002.

McIntyre, Alice, "Making *The Misfits* or Waiting for Monroe or Notes from Olympus," *Esquire*, 55 (March 1961), 74–81.

Merkin, Daphne, "Platinum Pain," *New Yorker*, 74 (February 8, 1999), 72–79.

Meryman, Richard. "Fame Can Go By," *Life*, August 3, 1962, pp. 32–38.

Monroe, Marilyn. *My Story*. 1974; New York: Stein and Day, 1976.

Murray, Eunice, with Rose Shade. *Marilyn: The Last Months*. New York: Pyramid, 1975.

Noguchi, Thomas, with Joseph DiMona. "Marilyn Monroe." *Coroner*. New York: Simon and Schuster, 1983. Pp. 54–86.

Odets, Clifford, "Marilyn Monroe," *Show*, 2 (October 1962), 67, 136.

Otash, Fred. "Frank Sinatra and the Wrong-Door Raid." *Investigation Hollywood!* Chicago: Regnery, 1976. Pp. 73–84.

Pepitone, Lena and William Stadiem. *Marilyn Monroe Confidential*. 1979; New York: Pocket Books, 1980.

Rollyson, Carl, "*Marilyn*: Mailer's Novel Biography," *Biography*, 1 (1978), 49–67.

——. *Marilyn Monroe: The Life of the Actress*. Ann Arbor: UMI Research Press, 1986.

Rosten, Norman. *Marilyn: A Very Personal Story*. 1974; London: Millington, 1980.

Schwartz, Delmore. "Marilyn Monroe and *The Seven Year Itch*" (1955). *Selected Essays*. Ed. Donald Dike and David Zucker. Chicago: University of Chicago Press, 1970. Pp. 458–461.

Spada, James. *Peter Lawford: The Man Who Kept the Secrets*. New York: Bantam, 1991. Pp. 317–331.

Spoto, Donald. *Marilyn Monroe: The Biography*. New York: HarperCollins, 1993.

Steinem, Gloria. Photos by George Barris. *Marilyn*. New York: MJF Books, 1986.

Strasberg, Susan. *Marilyn and Me: Sisters, Rivals, Friends*. New York: Warner, 1992.

Summers, Anthony. *Goddess: The Secret Lives of Marilyn Monroe*. New York: Macmillan, 1985.

Talese, Gay, "The Silent Season of a Hero," *Esquire*, 66 (July 1966), 41–45, 112, 114 (on DiMaggio).

Theroux, Paul. *Two Stars*. New York: Penguin, 2005.

Trilling, Diana. "The Death of Marilyn Monroe." *Claremont Essays*. 1964; London: Secker & Warburg, 1965. Pp. 229–243.

Victor, Adam. *The Marilyn Encyclopedia*. Woodstock, New York: Overlook, 1999.

Wagenknecht, Edward, ed. *Marilyn Monroe: A Composite View*. Philadelphia: Chilton, 1969.

Wallach, Eli. "*The Misfits*." *The Good, the Bad, and Me*. New York: Harcourt, 2005. Pp. 207–229.

Weatherby, W.J. *Conversations with Marilyn*. New York: Mason-Charter, 1976.

Winters, Shelley. *Shelley II: The Middle of My Century*. New York: Simon and Schuster, 1989.

Zolotow, Maurice. *Marilyn Monroe: The Uncensored Biography*. 1960; New York: Bantam, 1961.

Index

–compiled by Valerie Meyers